ISRAELI IDENTITY

CASS SERIES: ISRAELI HISTORY, POLITICS AND SOCIETY
Series Editor: Efraim Karsh
ISSN: 1368–4795

This series provides a multidisciplinary examination of all aspects of Israeli history, politics and society and serves as a means of communication between the various communities interested in Israel: academics. policy-makers, practitioners, journalists and the informed public.

1. *Peace in the Middle East: The Challenge for Israel*, edited by Efraim Karsh.
2. *The Shaping of Israeli Identity: Myth, Memory and Trauma*, edited by Robert Wistrich and David Ohana.
3. *Between War and Peace: Dilemmas of Israeli Security*, edited by Efraim Karsh.
4. *US–Israeli Relations at the Crossroads*, edited by Gabriel Sheffer.
5. *Revisiting the Yom Kippur War*, edited by P. R. Kumaraswamy.
6. *Israel: The Dynamics of Change and Continuity*, edited by David Levi-Faur, Gabriel Sheffer and David Vogel.
7. *In Search of Identity: Jewish Aspects in Israeli Culture*, edited by Dan Urian and Efraim Karsh.
8. *Israel at the Polls, 1996*, edited by Daniel J. Elazar and Shmuel Sandler.
9. *From Rabin to Netanyahu: Israel's Troubled Agenda*, edited by Efraim Karsh.
10. *Fabricating Israeli History: The 'New Historians'*, second revised edition, by Efraim Karsh.
11. *Divided Against Zion: Anti-Zionist Opposition in Britain to a Jewish State in Palestine, 1945–1948*, by Rory Miller.
12. *Peacemaking in a Divided Society: Israel After Rabin*, edited by Sasson Sofer.
13. *Israeli–Egyptian Relations: 1980–2000*, by Ephraim Dowek.
14. *Global Politics: Essays in Honour of David Vital*, edited by Abraham Ben-Zvi and Aharon Klieman.
15. *Parties, Elections and Cleavages; Israel in Comparative and Theoretical Perspective*, edited by Reuven Y. Hazan and Moshe Maor.
16. *Israel and the Polls 1999*, edited by Daniel J. Elazar and M. Ben Mollov.
17. *Public Policy in Israel*, edited by David Nachmias and Gila Menahem.

Israel: The First Hundred Years (Mini Series), edited by Efraim Karsh.
1. *Israel's Transition from Community to State*, edited by Efraim Karsh.
2. *From War to Peace?* edited by Efraim Karsh.
3. *Politics and Society Since 1948*, edited by Efraim Karsh.
4. *Israel in the International Arena*, edited by Efraim Karsh.
5. *Israel in the Next Century*, edited by Efraim Karsh.

Israeli Identity

*In Search of a Successor
to the
Pioneer, Tsabar and Settler*

By

LILLY WEISSBROD

FRANK CASS
LONDON • PORTLAND, OR

First published in 2002 in Great Britain by
FRANK CASS PUBLISHERS
Crown House, 47 Chase Side, Southgate
London N14 5BP

and in the United States of America by
FRANK CASS PUBLISHERS
c/o ISBS, 5824 N.E. Hassalo Street
Portland, Oregon, 97213-3644

Website: www.frankcass.com

British Library Cataloguing in Publication Data

ISBN 0-7146-5376-4 (cloth)
ISSN 1368-4795

Library of Congress Cataloging-in-Publication Data

A catalog record for this book is available
from the Library of Congress

Typeset by FiSH Books, London WC1
Printed in Great Britain by
MPG Books Ltd, Victoria Square, Bodmin, Cornwall.

*To my best friends
Lior, Omer and Michal*

Contents

Introduction

Two papers,[1] eventually led to the writing of this book. In these, I examined the impact of the DOP (Declaration of Principles signed between Israel and the PLO) on Gush Emunim and on the Israeli public in general. At the time, few observers agreed with my assessment that the Oslo process was eroding Israeli identity, beginning with the settler population in the occupied territories, particularly the hard-core believers in Gush Emunim doctrine, and spreading to the public at large. But when Prime Minister Rabin was assassinated, Israeli soul-searching came out into the open and has since developed into a full-scale identity crisis.

On 13 September 1993, Israel and the PLO signed the DOP at an official ceremony on the lawn of the White House in Washington DC. According to a poll published on that day, the DOP enjoyed the support of 62 per cent of respondents.[2] Ostensibly, this indicated genuine relief at the prospect of a peaceful, normal existence for a state which had experienced five major wars since its foundation in 1948, as well as almost constant clashes and acts of terrorism in the interim. Furthermore, a peace treaty with another Arab adversary was known to be achievable after peace with Egypt had been signed. Since the convening of the Madrid Conference in late 1991, peace was becoming ever more viable.

The DOP, though, was not just another peace process with a former Arab enemy. It was a total turnabout in Israeli policy. The DOP constituted a peace process with the PLO, an organization which until then had been regarded by Israel as an outcast. At the Madrid Conference and at the bilateral talks which followed it, both the hawkish Likud government and the more dovish Labour government of Israel, elected in June 1992, refused to hold separate talks with the Palestinian delegation because it was acting for the PLO as representative of the Palestinian population of the West Bank and Gaza Strip. Israel regarded the PLO as a terrorist organization, a totally unfit partner for negotiations. While hopes for peace were being dashed by the ongoing stalemate in the official negotiations, a secret unofficial tract of talks between PLO representatives and Israeli academics, initiated and guided by the director of the Israeli Foreign Ministry, Yossi Beilin, resulted in the DOP, confirmed by the Israeli government on 30 August 1992 and officially signed a fortnight later.

The DOP constituted a watershed in Israeli policy. It legitimized what had until then been condemned as a terrorist organization, whose covenant proclaimed that its purpose was the annihilation of Israel by armed conflict. The DOP also recognized the Palestinians as a people with equal rights to the territory of Mandatory Palestine, the area of the Holy Land or the Land of Israel, which was now to be shared by the two peoples. Thus, while a majority of the Israeli public initially endorsed the DOP as the fulfilment of its hope for peace, the implications of this document gradually became clear.

The crisis among adherents of Gush Emunim doctrine preceded that of the general public and was evident very soon after the signing of the DOP. The settlers were the most fully representative of the prevalent Israeli self-image, which justified Israeli proprietorship of the entire Holy Land because it was the legacy of the Jewish people, as repeatedly stated in the Bible. They were the most committed to the values underlying Israeli identity, the ones who were putting its norms into daily practice. If Israel relinquished some part of the Holy Land, the Gush Emunim faithful could not continue settling the entire land in order to hasten redemption, as their doctrine prescribed. They had lost their *raison d'être*. What did they stand for, then, and who were they? Their identity crisis was inevitable.

The general public reacted more slowly, as the implications of the peace process gradually sank in. Israel was relinquishing part of its religious–historical territorial heritage voluntarily and that reawakened a dormant ambivalence regarding Israeli identity. Social identity forms a boundary between that society and others by means of core values specific to the society.[3] I use the term 'social identity' rather than the more common one 'national identity' principally because Jewish Israelis are not a nation by any of the many definitions of that term. They regard themselves as part of the Jewish nation, at least half of whose members live in countries other than Israel. Therefore, social identity seems a more fitting term in the Israeli case. It is also more appropriate because this book confines itself to the study of the identity problems of the Jewish majority in Israel which, for better or worse, is a society apart from that of the Arab minority. The identity dilemma of the Arab minority is of an altogether different nature, namely the tension between citizenship in Israel and membership in the Arab nation which is hostile to Israel. Their case requires a separate treatment which is beyond the scope of this book.

I wish to point out that I use the terms 'Israelis' and 'Israeli identity' merely as a short form for 'Jewish Israelis' and 'Jewish Israeli identity'. This does not imply in any way that I do not regard members of the Arab minority as full citizens of the State of Israel. Israeli Arabs will be discussed, but only insofar as their affairs and claims impinge on the identity discourse of Jewish Israelis.

For Israelis, identity articulation has been a particularly difficult task. In addition to differentiating themselves from other societies in general, and from world Jewry in particular, the Israeli definition of who they are must also contain an assertion of their moral right to be where they are. That is so because Palestinian Arabs have been claiming a right to the same territory since the arrival of the first Jewish settlers. Israeli identity had always been somewhat equivocal because it never contained a wholly satisfactory solution to this problem. Yet, until the signature of the DOP, the leadership had always been able to allay any apprehensions on this score and provide an identity articulation which justified the Israeli presence within its current territorial frontiers. The justification prior to the signature of the DOP had been the inalienable right of Jews to their ancient homeland, as testified in the Bible. This assertion had been bolstered by security arguments to make it more acceptable to secular Israelis. However, relinquishing its claim to part of the land implied a denial of this inalienable right and undermined the Israeli self-image; it even raised doubts regarding the Israeli right to the remainder of the land.

The leadership was apparently unaware of the dilemma which its reversal of policy was creating, for it did not convey a single and clear message justifying this step. However, recognition of it, initially confined mainly to intellectuals, spread as the peace process proceeded. With the assassination of Prime Minister Yitzhak Rabin on 4 November 1995, it became a malaise of the public at large. It would seem that the elaborate rituals of mourning over a Prime Minister who had not been overly popular[4] expressed more than grief and shock over the loss of a statesman. Nor could they be interpreted solely as mourning over the demise of the peace process, which was not seriously jeopardized by the assassination. In addition, they appear to have also revealed the realization that social consensus had been disrupted and that this could no longer be ignored. For, surely, political assassination is the ultimate disregard for the most basic ground rules regulating the means to resolve social conflict without disrupting the fabric altogether.

In order to understand why the peace process with the Palestinians produced such doubts about what constituted the Israeli self-image, it became necessary to analyse previous adjustments to Israeli identity, why they had occurred and how one articulation of identity had changed into the next. This monograph is the result of an investigation of 100 years of

Israeli identity articulation, yet it makes no claim to be a historical study. It is not a full account of events during that period, but merely of those which are relevant to the subject of the book. Nor have I attempted to uncover any new evidence, but rather to shed a different light on well-known and well-documented events related to the subject at hand.

Shifts in Israeli identity formulation were found to be linked primarily to changes in Israel's frontiers, accompanied by morally convincing justifications given by the leadership for Jewish residence within these. The Oslo process was not preceded or followed by any clear message justifying the intended territorial contraction of Israel, nor did it delineate the future borders. Therefore, no smooth transition was possible to a new identity articulation adapted to the new territorial reality; the latter remained unclear and no proper guidance from the leadership was forthcoming. This is postulated to be one reason for the ensuing breakdown of consensus, which has meanwhile developed into a full-scale crisis of identity.

Israel, like most modern societies, is pluralistic. It consists of numerous groups, each with its own agenda. That, in itself, does not preclude a common agenda, that is, core values recognized by all to regulate the relations between the groups and to distinguish them, as one entity, from other societies. When the various groups no longer acknowledge a common agenda, the identity of the society as a whole disintegrates, creating a crisis. This can lead to either a total breakup of the social fabric, and in the extreme case to secession, or to a search for a redefined glue, a reinterpretation of core values adapted to reality and to which all, or most groups can agree. The latter is the process now underway in Israel. It is a clear symptom of the identity crisis which I postulated.

After the Wye Memorandum had been signed, the Likud government resigned, an election campaign was set in motion and the Labour candidate won the premiership back from Likud. During the 1999 election campaign, the full scale of the Israeli identity crisis became evident. Parties broke up, a multitude of new, completely sectorial ones entered the race and special interests seemed to be overriding any common ones. Israeli society was not yet completely torn apart, though. Rather, each fragment, aware of the danger of dissolution, was trying to reunite the society by advocating its own version of what is most common to all and would serve as a new glue.

The elections revealed a fierce debate regarding the desired nature of Israeli society, that is, its future self-image. All groups seemed to agree that Jewishness of some sort was their only common denominator and they vied with each other over a definition of what the nature of that Jewishness should be. Should Israel be a society governed by Jewish religious law, or by one prevalent in secular democracies? If the latter, then how Jewish–ethnic may this democracy be without violating democratic values of equality, particularly as these pertain to the Arab minority? How much cultural pluralism can an ethnic democracy support? Furthermore, should Israel be Western religious, Western secular, Oriental religious or Oriental secular? These struggles were going on while Israel was attempting to bring the conflict with the Palestinians and with Syria to a peaceful solution and redelineate its physical boundaries. Meanwhile, these attempts have failed. Instead, new violence has broken out, putting to naught all understandings of the Oslo Accords, or so most Israelis believe. In consequence, a new consensus has developed, overriding the previous rifts, but since the Israeli boundaries remain as blurred as ever, so does Israeli identity. Its final nature is not yet in sight, but will certainly affect not just Israel, but the politics and economy of the entire region.

NOTES

1. L. Weissbrod, 'Gush Emunim and the Israeli–Palestinian Peace Process', *Israel Affairs*, Vol. 3, No. 1, 1996, pp.86–103; 'Israeli Identity in Transition', *Israel Affairs*, Vol. 3, Nos. 3 & 4, 1997, pp.47–65. Large sections of these papers are included in Chapter 5.
2. Guttman Institute of Applied Social Research, *Jerusalem Post*, 13 September 1993.
3. D. Conversi, 'Reassessing Current Theories of Nationalism as Boundary Maintenance and Creation', *Nationalism and Ethnic Politics*, Vol. 1, No. 1, 1995. pp.73–85
4. According to surveys, his rating as prime minister had been consistently lower than that of the Likud leader, Netanyahu. In one poll, it reached a low of 32% against 45% for Netanyahu (Gallup, *Jerusalem Post*, 28 April 1995) and never rose above 42% against 46% for Netanyahu (Dahaf, *Jerusalem Post*, 23 October 1993.

1. The Pioneer:
An Ambivalent Identity

CONDITIONS FOR THE RISE OF ZIONISM

Early Zionists rejected the two Jewish self-identifications prevalent at the turn of the century, namely that of assimilated Jewry, who constituted the majority in Western Europe, and that of orthodox Jewry, the majority in Eastern Europe. They formulated a third self-identification within the larger community of Jews. Early Zionists drew upon some Jewish values and norms in common with assimilated and orthodox Jews, but broke away from most of the ideas held by these two sections of the Jewish people. In order to understand their revolutionary premises, early Zionists need to be juxtaposed with assimilated and orthodox Jews. A short summary of the basic premises of the latter two, both of whom justified the status quo of life in the diaspora, is therefore in order.

Once Jews had been granted legal rights in Western Europe, starting in the early nineteenth century, many believed they could divorce their religious identity from their ethnic one and become nationals of their countries of residence of the Mosaic faith. (They preferred the term 'Mosaic' over 'Jewish' because it was devoid of an ethnic connotation). In doing so they ignored two problems. Firstly, Judaism is a communal, mono-ethnic religion and cannot be separated from the identification with the community of Jews except by a far-reaching reinterpretation. Assimilated Jews tried to solve this dilemma variously. Some held fast to their faith and secularized it only in the sense of confining its practices to the private sphere, hoping that the ethnic loyalty which Judaism entailed would either be disregarded or accepted by gentile society (at a time when pluralism was not a politically correct value). At the other extreme, there were those willing to jettison their faith altogether and retain merely some vestige of their ethnic minority membership. Most assimilated Jews occupied a position somewhere along this continuum. At the same time, all of them distanced themselves from orthodox Jewry by denying the inherent link in Judaism between the social and the religious community. Secondly, assimilated Jews did not take account of their social rejection by gentile society, which continued despite the political rights granted to Jews.[1] In contrast, early Zionists asserted that assimilation would always remain unilateral: the hostile gentile society would never accept Jews as equals, irrespective of their degree of acculturation and assimilation.

Assimilation was much less widespread in Eastern Europe. The Russian Empire eased restrictions somewhat for a small minority of Jews only. A select few were permitted to acquire a general education and move out of the Jewish Pale to which the majority were confined and where orthodoxy was the norm. Thus, Eastern European Zionists, who were the majority in the Zionist movement, rebelled against the orthodox, whose interpretation of the Messianic message was a major obstacle to Zionist aims.

Messianism is a core value in Judaism, put forward in the Book of Isaiah: an offspring of the royal House of David will bring back to Zion Jews from all their countries of exile and institute in Zion a social order of perfect justice (11), as well as a state of perfect peace in the world (2:1–4), both governed by the law of God. The people of Israel are also rebuked for their sinful ways and exhorted to purify themselves and practice righteousness (1:16). This combined Messianic message contains two elements. Firstly, it promises social and political redemption in an order of perfect justice following the ingathering of the exiles, to which liberation from foreign rule was later added. Secondly, it promises individual salvation by self-purification. The numerous Messianic movements which arose throughout 2,000 years of Jewish exile bear witness to the focal importance of this idea in Judaism, as do the prayers for His Coming and for the return to Zion.

The Messianic message is twofold and its two elements, of political and of individual salvation, have been vying with each other for predominance. The numerous self-proclaimed Messiahs who called on Jews to return to Zion as a precondition for establishing the aspired Kingdom of God regarded political redemption as the key to social and individual salvation. The religious establishment was of the opposite view. It proclaimed the Messiahs 'false' and heretics and asserted that ethical purification had to come first. This also held true when orthodoxy split into two competing schools in the eighteenth century, namely the mystical Hassidim and the scholarly Mitnagdim. Both taught that man must not interfere with God's will, or compete with Him. Most Hassidic rabbis would not emigrate to Palestine for fear of precipitating salvation, while the Mitnagdim went even further and considered the Hassidim sinful for indulging in over-zealous prayer for the coming of the Messiah. Furthermore, God was in exile, together with the Jewish people, so that a return to Palestine would be useless unless God also returned to the Holy Land. Since that would occur only with the coming of the Messiah, a return of the people to Palestine would not bring them nearer to God and would not hasten salvation. Finally, suffering in the diaspora was a duty imposed by God on the Jewish people and was a means to purification and perfection. Thus, spiritual preparation was obligatory and an early return to Zion was a sinful presumption.[2]

The desire to return to the land, called Palestine by the Romans and by its biblical names Zion, the Land of Israel, or the Holy Land by Jews, was a continuous and inherent constituent of Judaism, a core value associated with deliverance by the Messiah from persecution and suffering. Whenever conditions deteriorated, the longing for His coming became more acute, at times culminating in one of the numerous 'false' Messianic movements. Zionism was no exception, though it was not a Messianic movement in the accepted sense, but rather a substitute for it. Here again, a distinction must be made between conditions in Eastern and Western Europe at the end of the nineteenth century.

In the Russian Empire, Jews enjoyed even fewer civil rights than the other subjects of the absolute monarch. The vast majority were confined geographically to urban residence in the Jewish Pale, with the exception of some larger cities in this region, and were legally excluded from numerous professions and trades. That situation deteriorated further with the onset of industrialization, which impoverished Russian Jews who were principally craftsmen and small tradesmen. Their products could not compete with cheap, mass-produced goods, nor could they compete with the abundant and more accommodating liberated serfs. The latter moved to urban centres and created an excessive supply of labour, which reduced wages. Furthermore, Jews were still orthodox and could not work in factories operating on Saturday. Therefore, they could not join the industrial labour force. Their plight was exacerbated by the pogroms of 1881, resulting in the emigration of about 1 million Jews during 1880–97.[3]

The mass Jewish immigration from the Russian Empire, begun in the middle of the nineteenth century and gathering momentum towards the end, fed the anxieties of Western European assimilated Jews. Mounting anti-Semitism disabused them somewhat of the panacea of assimilation. Now they feared that a mass influx of orthodox Eastern European Jews might augment anti-Semitism even further. One way of warding off this danger was to divert the flow to a Jewish state in Palestine: one resolution at the First Zionist Congress called for the settling in Palestine of farmers, craftsmen and artisans,[4] typically the trades of Russian Jews. No mention was made of the wealthy, or of professionals.

These were necessary conditions for the rise of Zionism, but not sufficient ones, since only a minority of Jews became Zionists. Of the estimated 10 million Jews at the time, by 1901 only about 1 per cent had become members of the Zionist Organization by paying the Shekel, a nominal membership fee,[5] and of the estimated 1 million Jewish emigrants during 1880–97, only about 7,000 were practising Zionists who went to Palestine.[6] The majority of the assimilated persisted in their belief that anti-Semitism was a temporary phenomenon, a vestige of the past which would soon subside. Moreover, viewed as a national movement aiming at political independence, Zionism was regarded as an obstacle to their demand for fully equal rights in their countries of residence.[7] The majority of orthodox Jews remained within the mainstream and opposed a hastening of the Messiah by emigration to Zion. Furthermore, viewed as a secular movement, they regarded Zionism as a threat to Judaism.

The harsh economic and political conditions in Palestine at the time, an underdeveloped country under arbitrary Ottoman rule, certainly served as a major deterrent to Jewish emigration there, especially since the USA and Canada imposed few restrictions on immigrants and were by far more alluring. The few who disregarded these disadvantages must needs have been motivated by the ancient Jewish longing for Zion. The debate over Uganda as an ostensibly immediately available alternative to Palestine, held at the sixth Zionist Congress in 1903, bears witness to their overriding preference for Palestine, despite the fact that Zionists were aware of its disadvantages. One delegate stated that, even if offered the most sumptuous countries, flowing with milk and honey, Jews still preferred the bare rocks of Palestine because they were in Palestine. Another one declared that Zion was the country loved, the country of Jewish aspiration. Because of that, only Palestine could command sufficient self-sacrifice to make possible the building of a country.[8] Indeed, Uganda and any other alternative destinations were rejected over-whelmingly at the following seventh Zionist Congress in 1905.

SCHOOLS OF EARLY ZIONISM

Clearly, Zionists held in common with orthodox Jews the longing to return to Zion. However, paradoxically, Jews who deliberately chose to return to Palestine had to contend with the religious interdiction against it and did so in two ways. A minority of religious Jews chose the arduous way of contesting the religious dictum by contrary religious arguments. The majority chose the more obvious and easier solution of rejecting the religious establishment and its interdiction altogether and opted for a secular worldview. It must be noted that a secular worldview is not synonymous with atheism. Instead, a secular worldview differs from the religious one by putting human fate into human hands rather than into those of God. One can then practise one's religion out of respect for tradition, or out of the belief in God as the Prime Mover, Who has endowed humans with free choice and the responsibility to determine their own history. As will be seen below, some of the secular Zionists belonged to this category, while others were complete freethinkers. This applies equally to those who did not emigrate to Palestine themselves, but supported this course of action.

Post-Zionist[9] claims to the contrary, early Zionism was neither a purely national liberation movement, nor a colonialist one, though both nationalism and colonialism were very widespread at the time and undoubtedly influenced and legitimized the Zionist enterprise. Its prime motive was not to attain political independence, but to establish an ideal Jewish society for which political independence was the means: the various schools of Zionism argued about the type of idealized model they wished to create rather than about military or diplomatic tactics necessary for its attainment. Also, though they were European Jews settling in the Middle East, they were not expanding from some mother country in order to enhance its trade, to find additional Lebensraum, or to 'carry the white man's burden'. Moreover, early Zionism was not a monolithic ideational structure. Various groups interpreted their wish to return to Zion each according to its own light. The determination to emigrate to Palestine provided them with their distinct identity *vis-à-vis* other Jews, while their various readings of the Messianic message competed for dominance within the Zionist Organization, and still do so within Israeli society.

Religious Zionism

Religious Zionists, who subsequently formed the Mizrahi party within the Zionist Organization, were a minority at the time. They retained the religious worldview according to which human history is determined by God, but they viewed the reinstatement of political independence as a tool for safeguarding Jewish religion. Though of marginal influence in early Zionism, they were among its precursors, while their successors became focal in the reformulation of Israeli identity after the 1967 war.

By the mid-nineteenth century, some religious scholars were already reasoning against the interpretation given to the Messianic idea by the orthodox establishment. In a book published in 1862, Rabbi Kalisher urged Jews to settle in Palestine because that was the meaning of miraculous redemption. Rabbi Alkalai and Rabbi Jaffe claimed that a few individuals might emigrate to Palestine and 'prepare the way', or even build the Temple. Rabbi Jaffe maintained that even without a Temple, more commandments could be fulfilled in Palestine than in the diaspora, so that emigration to it could not possibly be sinful. Rabbi Reines brought evidence that living in Palestine was a religious commandment like any other and should not be ignored.[10] These teachings could not attract much following. They were coached in religious terminology and intended to set up a society in Palestine to be a replica of the ancient biblical one, including an almost exclusively agricultural economy. At a time of modernization and secularization, when assimilation was already perceived by many Jews as an alternative means of liberation, they ignored the scientific and technological knowledge accrued since biblical times. Such ideas could hardly appeal to assimilated Jews, nor could an open challenge to the orthodox prohibition against hastening salvation appeal to most Jews.

For all their innovation, the above teachings merely raised doubts concerning the absolute temporal priority which the orthodox establishment was giving to self-purification over social and political redemption, both of which are contained in the Messianic message. The ultimate challenge to orthodoxy as an altogether damaging method of preserving Judaism was made subsequently in the early twentieth century by Rabbi Kuk, who put his teachings into practice and settled in Palestine. He maintained that the orthodox injunction to return to Palestine had become a danger to the existence of Jews as a people, whose faith had been their bond, and to Judaism as a creed. Both were seriously threatened by assimilation in the diaspora and only Zionism could abate this process.

A return to Zion and its rebuilding served two complementary purposes: a spiritual–religious revival and a renewed unity of the Jewish people. Nationhood was an integral part of the Jewish religion, a divine principle reinforcing the covenant between God and the Jewish people, which might otherwise be forgotten. Jewish nationhood did not contradict the Messianic vision of international peace and union among all peoples. On the contrary, it enhanced it because international peace could come about only if and when the Jewish people set an example of perfection to the world. Moreover, Jews could embody holiness only when united because Judaism was a collective faith; salvation pertained to the entire community and to the individual only as a part of it. Therefore, the unity of Israel superseded all religious scruples. Rabbi Kuk argued further that Jewish national unity could be achieved only through Zionism, which was its ultimate manifestation. For Jews, the belief in any ideals would necessarily re-establish the belief in God, due to the mystical union between the Jewish people and the Bible. Zionism was the modern form of Jewish idealism and would, therefore, create faith and national unity.

Furthermore, the fundamental quality of the Jewish soul was the capacity for prophecy. This was why the people of Israel had been given their mission of redemption and salvation. Palestine was the land appointed by God for the flow of His grace, and prophecy was possible only there. Rabbi Kuk advocated tolerance towards secular, or even atheistic pioneers, who were partaking in the holy task of building Palestine, for they would be redeemed eventually. In Palestine, a new synthesis would take place between the barren precepts of orthodox Judaism and the secularity of the pioneers, tantamount to a religious revival. The new Judaism would be a recurrence of the prophetic quality. Therefore, the building of Palestine was as focal a commandment as any other: there, the people would once more become an instrument of Divine inspiration to all mankind.[11]

The teachings of Rabbi Kuk were modernizing. They allowed for a measure of pluralism (tolerance towards freethinkers) and incorporated nationalism, one of the chief secular ideologies at the time, as a means towards realization of the Messianic idea. Therefore, they had a greater impact than the teachings of his predecessors. His adherents became modern observant Jews, integrated into the economic and political life of the community in Palestine and Israel and distinct from the traditional orthodox, who shut themselves off increasingly in their own ultra-orthodox enclaves. A reinterpretation of these teachings by his son after the 1967 war became focal to Israeli identity and will be discussed in a later chapter.

As noted earlier, both religious and secular Zionists delineated themselves *vis-à-vis* other Jews as promoters of emigration to Palestine and/or potential and actual emigrants. Yet, the longing for Zion among the secular majority of Zionists, demonstrated in the Uganda debate at the Sixth Congress and in the resolutions of the Seventh, was not shared by all spokesmen and formulators of the ideas which comprised early Zionism. Ironically, several leaders of schools of Zionism, including the political Zionism of Theodor Herzl, the founder of the movement and its organization, opted for Palestine for pragmatic reasons, rather than in principle. Expediency dictated the choice of Palestine if they wished to mobilize a following and influence the decisions of the Zionist Organization, because the bulk of members were driven to support and/or join it by the longing for Zion basic to diaspora Jews. The formulators of political, normalizing, syndicalist and Marxist Zionism belonging to the category of those who wished to reshape the Jewish people, realized that a sovereign territory was a necessary condition for this process and concluded that Palestine was the only feasible destination which could mobilize recruits or supporters. All of these schools had their adherents and exerted considerable influence on Zionist praxis and thought. These schools of thought were all Messianic in being utopian, that is, they wished to set up ideal societies, but their only link with Judaism was the choice of Palestine and the choice of Jews to populate their future societies. None of them drew expressly on Judaic core values.

Political Zionism

Political Zionism was formulated by Theodor Herzl, the founder of the Zionist movement and the convener of its first congress. His was the body of ideas which set the entire process in motion. Yet despite using Zion as the name of the movement (Zion was the Jebusite fortress in Jerusalem within which King David founded his capital; it became synonymous with Jerusalem and the symbol of Jewish longing to return to their homeland), Herzl defined Zionism as a movement to obtain an autonomous state for the Jewish people by diplomatic negotiations. In his very first act toward the realization of this aim, his meeting with the Jewish philanthropist Baron Hirsch on 2 June 1895, he insisted that establishment of a political centre for the Jews was his focal concern. However, neither at this meeting, nor in a letter sent to Baron Hirsch on the following day, was Palestine mentioned as the location of the future state.[12] Palestine did not become his proposed solution until he published his principal Zionist manifesto 'Judenstaat' in 1896, and even then he was hesitant. After weighing the pros and cons of Palestine and Argentina he decided in favour of the former because of its historic meaning for Jews.[13]

Though pronouncing at the First Congress that Zionism was first and foremost the return to Judaism and only then the return to the Jewish land, the choice of Palestine over some other country was the limit of Herzl's Judaism. The principal resolution of the First Congress, where Herzl held complete sway, stated that Zionism sought to obtain for the Jewish people a publicly recognized, legally secured home in Palestine.[14] There was no mention of national revival, of being truly Jewish in this future homeland, nor any mention of the Jewish religion, laws, customs or culture. Instead, in his novel *Altneuland*, Herzl depicted the future Jewish state as the model of a nineteenth-century liberal democracy, based on modern technology, with welfare state institutions, such as a seven-hour working day, housing for workers and public works for the unemployed.

How much of an afterthought Palestine really was for Herzl and the other supporters of political Zionism is evident from their readiness to settle for a substitute, as long as it was guaranteed by international law, or at least by a major power. In 1902, Herzl negotiated with the British Colonial Office over settlement of Jews in Cyprus, El-Arish or the Sinai

Peninsula. Later, Uganda was tentatively offered as a Jewish national homeland and Herzl accepted the proposal and put it to the vote at the Sixth Congress. The importance of international guarantees, or the 'charter', as it was named, was such that political Zionists discouraged settlement in Palestine unless so secured. Extremists even proposed to stop all emigration there until colonization was granted public–legal security.[15] The entire Uganda affair revolved around this concept of legal recognition.

For political Zionists, Zionism was the solution to an immediate problem, rather than the realization of an ancient, ever-present idea. (The support for the Uganda plan was explained by the immediate need created by the pogrom in Kishinev in 1903.) The basic idea of political Zionism was the emigration of oppressed and persecuted Jews to an internationally recognized autonomous state. Palestine as a destination was only incidental to this aim. Due to Herzl's exclusive leadership, this school of thought was decisive at first: the Uganda proposal was accepted with a clear majority of 295:178 at the Sixth Congress, but was rejected by the following Seventh Congress held after Herzl's death, when the influence of political Zionism waned.

The idea of the charter was not discredited when political Zionism lost its dominant influence. International guarantees continued to be sought and were eventually obtained in 1917 with the Balfour Declaration and reiterated by the UN Partition Plan of 1947. Diplomatic negotiations as the primary tactics of achieving Zionist aims were also taken up again in the early 1920s by the Revisionist movement. But this later brand of political Zionism could not mobilize sufficient support either in Palestine, or in the Zionist Organization. By the time the successors of the Revisionists, the Likud party, came to power in Israel, they were discarding political Zionism altogether.

Normalizing Zionism

This school of Zionism did not play a significant role in the political struggles of the Zionist Organization, yet the ideas of its proponents had considerable influence on other brands of Zionism. Their aim was to turn Jews into a normal people like any other they knew, namely European, while Palestine was merely the viable venue. The chief formulators of normalizing Zionism were Berdichewsky, Pinsker and Brenner. Berdichewsky rejected everything associated with Jewishness, and Jewish religion in particular. He thought that Jews were incapable of integrating in the modern world as long as they were stultified by the restraints of an archaic, collective religion, which hindered the free development of a modern individualistic human being. The Jewish individual could find fulfilment and become psychologically normal, like any other national, by life in a free society of his own. Palestine was the place best-suited to this purpose.[16]

Pinsker diagnosed the Jewish psyche as sick due to the way of life imposed on Jews; their religion was merely one of the pathogens. Jews had to emancipate themselves from their pathological psychological traits, which were the outcome of living as strangers in a hostile environment, by adopting the values and norms of Western culture. Normalization, the cure, could only be effected when the environment was changed.[17] However, Palestine was not mentioned in his manifesto *Autoemanzipation* (first published in 1882). Pinsker adopted Palestine as the national destination later, under the influence of more traditional Jewish thinkers, yet made no mention even then of Jewish culture, or the link between its revival and Zion.

Brenner, of a later generation, used more modern psychoanalytical terms, but his diagnosis of the Jewish people was essentially the same. The Jewish personality was neurotic, as were the social relations among Jews, and between Jews and gentiles, due to the debilitating influence of Jewish religion and clericalism. The only cure for this was productive work, since it created productive relations, the only ones guaranteeing a healthy social structure and a healthy personality. No Messiah would save the Jews; they could redeem themselves only by their own effort in their own country, Palestine, where they could set up a normal constructive society, comprising all trades (unlike the skewed Jewish society in the diaspora, where Jews were excluded from most productive professions). Neither Jewish religion nor Jewish culture served as foci of identity, but rather a life of labour in a country of their own.[18]

Besides influencing most other schools of Zionism, normalizing Zionism has had two offshoots. One was the Canaanite movement, which advocated a complete divorce of Jews in Palestine from the Jewish people living elsewhere. It promulgated identification and unification of the former with the indigenous population of Canaan, or Greater Syria. It failed to mobilize any political support in Palestine, but its ideas infiltrated Israeli thought and later influenced Tsabar identity to an appreciable degree. The second offshoot are the Post-zionists, who want to normalize the state rather than the people of Israel. Though adopted by a small minority of Israeli society, Post-zionist ideas have prompted and guided the initiation of the Oslo Accords and the conduct of negotiations with the Palestinian Authority.

Marxist and Syndicalist Zionism

These two socialist versions of Zionism were based on ideologies which negate any state at all, so that they are alien to the very essence of Zionism, the re-establishment of a sovereign Jewish state in Zion. Marxism and anarchist syndicalism also negate religion and ethnic specificity and hold in common with Jewish Messianism only the utopian aspect of setting up a perfectly just society. To make their ideas compatible with Zionism, the proponents of Marxist and syndicalist Zionism emphasized the latter aspect and the constraints put on Jews in the diaspora to put the socialist dream into practice. Zionism was the default option, so to speak.

The chief ideologue of Marxist Zionism was Borochov, who created a synthesis between Marxism and Jewish nationalism, two contradictory sets of ideas. Class conflict and the ultimate victory of the proletariat would redeem Jews, as they would any other people. Since Jews had been left at the wayside and had not been allowed to become part of the labour force, a national solidarity of proletarian Jews had to be created, nationality being the feeling of closeness based on a common historical past, rooted in common conditions of production. Borochov maintained that the most important condition of production was territory and chose Palestine because Jews were at a disadvantage anywhere else. The classless society would be established in Palestine after a class conflict between the Jewish proletariat and Jewish capitalists, the latter to be encouraged to come there for just that purpose. The class conflict would serve to establish the desired social order and to create an independent Jewish state in Palestine, for the Ottoman government would undoubtedly side with the Jewish capitalists and be defeated with the latter in the unavoidable conflict and victory.[19]

As a movement, Marxist Zionism was very short-lived, yet it had a lasting impact quite disproportionate to the number of its followers. It propelled some of its adherents to emigrate to Palestine in the early twentieth century and provided them with the political mindset to become the leaders of the entire Zionist enterprise in Palestine, after they had abandoned Marxism in favour of Labour Zionism.

Similar to Borochov, Syrkin, the chief spokesman of syndicalist Zionism, realized that the predominantly *petit-bourgeois* Jews of the diaspora would never be accepted by the socialist movement. They had to create their own classless society, apart from gentiles, according to the syndicalist model: without a class struggle and without a state. Syrkin considered Palestine the preferred destination because of its historical significance for Jews. Ideological considerations aside, syndicalism was the most viable social structure under the conditions prevailing in Palestine at the time. Syrkin argued that building up a new society required large numbers of immigrants. Most of them would necessarily come from the low income level, since the rich were always a minority in any society. However, poor people could not survive in an underdeveloped country, such as Palestine, under free market conditions. They would have to compete with cheap Arab labour, because Arab living standards were lower than those of the poorest Europeans. Syrkin therefore advocated settlement on national land of large industrial–agricultural communes on a syndicalist basis, without any political framework.[20]

Syndicalist Zionism as such never took on – an anarchistic society was too much at odds with the spirit of the time, in which nationalism and the nation state predominated – but the cooperative idea became a major component of Zionism as practised in Jewish Palestine, as was the egalitarian principle underlying both socialist brands of Zionism. In addition to their obvious economic advantages in an underdeveloped country which had no labour market to speak of, cooperatives prevented the formation of income gaps and provided for solidarity and the mutual support needed to sustain the hardships of Palestinian reality at the time. The cooperative idea gave rise to the first communal agricultural settlements, Kvutsot, to the He-haluts movement which recruited young people during the second and third waves of immigration (1904–18 and 1919–24 respectively), to the Kibbutz movements and to the movement of cooperative settlements and cooperative organizations and enterprises so unique to Jewish Palestine and Israel.

The three remaining schools of secular Zionism, namely cultural–historical, mystical and Labour Zionism, were secular in placing human fate in human hands, yet they were emphatically Jewish. They wished diaspora Jews to become more Jewish, rather than less so; returning to the Jewish natural habitat, the Land of Israel, was an integral part of this desired process. For these brands of Zionism, no other destination was at all relevant. They differed, though, in what they conceived to be enhanced Jewishness.

Cultural and Historical Zionism

These can be differentiated analytically, but in practice the ideas and proponents of the two overlap and distinctions are difficult. Unlike the largely assimilated proponents of the above-mentioned secular schools, cultural–historical Zionists wanted to retain the Judaism they had been reared on, though in a new guise. The initiator was Smolenskin (born 1842), who feared that growing assimilation might cause the disappearance of Jews as a people. He believed that Jews had a historic mission to fulfil, commanded by God. Their extinction would be a breach of this covenant with God. At first, he chiefly advocated intensified Jewish traditional–religious education and the teaching of Hebrew, to revive self-identity and Jewish self-respect. However, by 1878 he had realized that this could not be achieved in the diaspora and supported mass emigration in order to create a legal–cultural centre in Palestine.[21]

The most prominent proponent of cultural–historical Zionism was Ahad Haam (his pen name, his given name was Asher Zvi Ginzberg). Basing his ideas on the historic ethical mission of the Jewish people, which is prophesied in the Bible to occur in the Messianic era when the Jews return to Zion, he emphasized the importance of establishing a cultural (not necessarily political) centre there. The aim of the return to Zion was not to alleviate the suffering of Jews, nor to normalize them psychologically, but to encourage their renewed cultural activity. It was imperative to emigrate to the Land of Israel, and nowhere else, because this was the country where Jewish culture had once flourished and the only country where it was likely to do so again. There were unbreakable historical ties between the Jewish people and their homeland, the severance of which had rendered the Jews culturally impotent. They would be productive only in their ancient language, Hebrew, which they had used during their creative period. Consequently, Ahad Haam was opposed to the use of Yiddish, the vernacular spoken by Eastern European Jews, which was just as Jewishly distinctive and had the advantage of being known to all. It would have been a much more expedient choice. By simple secularization Ahad Haam transformed the Jewish people's Messianic mission of being a light unto the nations to meaning unique cultural creativity. Their great contribution to world culture, the Bible, had been in their own language made when they were living in their own land and there they must return if they were to produce anything of equal value.[22]

History and culture were intimately linked in this school of thought. The school had its greatest impact on the revival of the Hebrew language, a feat greatly assisted by the lifework of Eliezer Ben Yehuda, who emigrated to Palestine and was instrumental in this revival; he compiled the first Hebrew dictionary. The school also served as guideline to the Yishuv (the Jewish community in Mandatory Palestine) in setting up an independent Hebrew educational system (Hebrew schools, a university and a technical college) and encouraged the early flourishing of Hebrew letters and art. However, the majority of Zionists rejected the assumption that cultural revival was their primary aim, or that a Jewish cultural centre in Palestine without political independence sufficed as a Zionist goal.

Mystical Zionism

Mystical Zionism was not really a school with followers, but rather the thesis of one philosopher, Martin Buber. It combined elements of religious with historical–cultural Zionism and gave a coherent expression to the intrinsic longing of Jews for their homeland, to which even assimilated Zionists referred. In his book *Israel und Palaestina* Buber claimed that the use of the term Zion was not accidental. The movement for political independence and national revival was named after a country, Zion, and not after a nation, because the continued desire of Jews to return to Palestine was due to the holy union created by God between a people and its country. Yet the holiness of this union was not purely religious, since Jews aspired to a social life in a concrete geographical location and not to some future existence in Heaven. The holy union between people and country was mystical, as it was future-oriented and included the idea of a new social order.[23] Buber secularized the Messianic message merely by purging it of its strict association with an established ritual framework. The union between the Jewish God, the Jewish people and the Jewish land was mystical, rather than purely religious, and Zionism was its realization.

Labour Zionism

This school of Zionism is described last because it incorporated elements of most other schools of Zionism and, principally, because it was the ideology which became dominant in the Yishuv and contributed most to the identity which eventually distinguished Yishuv members from other Zionist and non-Zionist Jews in the diaspora.

A.D. Gordon, the formulator of Labour Zionism, was religious until he became a Zionist in his late thirties and decided to put his convictions into practice in his forties; he settled in Palestine with the first of the second wave of immigrants who began arriving in 1904. Having been religious, his brand of Zionism was firmly rooted in Judaism, whose core values it retained, though stripped of traditional ritual or obedience to the authority of the orthodox establishment. Gordon's Zionism was pantheistic and forged all three components of the Messianic message into one complete whole.

Gordon maintained that communion with God was achieved by communion with nature, which meant actual physical contact with it through physical labour. The ultimate communion of a Jew with his God was by contact with Palestinian soil, where the essence of the infinite, of truth, holiness, beauty and courage were conceived in a manner different from all other countries. The return to Palestine was the realization of the Jewish people's dream, but the soil would only belong to them if they tilled it, if they took physical possession of it. Thus, Jewish resurrection would be complete when Jews tilled the soil of Palestine. They would then attain the ultimate union with God and, each individually, raise their humanity to a higher plane. Another necessary condition for redemption was a revolutionary social change, a restratification induced by this praxis (in the early Marxist sense). It was necessary to abandon the life that was created by others as completely as their land and create a new life in Palestine, a life of physical agricultural labour. Because of his emphasis on individual salvation, he rejected the concept of the proletariat: wage labourers would never experience the creativity of work. To do that, it was necessary to become self-employed farmers in collective settlements.[24]

Gordon included most points raised by the various brands of Zionism in a single line of thought. Labour Zionism explained and justified the Jewish need of political independence (political Zionism), for productive labour (normalizing Zionism), for restratification and egalitarianism on a cooperative basis (Marxist and syndicalist Zionism), as well as the Jewish need to return to Palestine for the sake of a cultural renaissance (cultural Zionism) and the inherent link between Jews and their homeland (mystical Zionism). The reunion of God with His people was secularized by Labour Zionism into a pantheistic union of man with the soil through labour. The latter formed the basis for a complete social revolution, egalitarianism, and for a complete transformation of the individual who attained grace, as it were, by this praxis.

LABOUR ZIONISM AND THE PIONEER

Labour Zionism became the dominant ideology in the Yishuv, and Labour the dominant party, not least because the leaders promulgating it, former Marxist Zionists, were highly skilful politicians who set up a well-organized party machinery and institutions on which many penniless settlers depended economically, principally the Histadrut. Established by Labour in 1920 and controlled by it, it served as both a country-wide labour union and as the employer of an extensive administrative staff and of a relatively large labour force in its numerous industrial enterprises. In addition, it controlled the communal and cooperative settlements, whose produce it marketed through Tnuva, and whom it provided with supplies by Ha-mashbir. It also controlled a bank, Bank Ha-po'alim, which was the chief credit source for its various enterprises and agricultural settlements. In addition, the Histadrut also supplied its members with labour exchange and health services. In order to finance these enterprises, the Labour-controlled Histadrut required funds beyond anything the underdeveloped economy of Palestine could provide. To obtain these, Labour succeeded in setting itself up as the channel through which funds flowed from the Zionist Organization to settlers in Palestine.[25] Since the non-socialist parties outnumbered Labour in seats in the Zionist

Organization until 1935, the persuasiveness of Labour Zionism must have played some part in the ability of Labour to obtain those funds and wield its economic power in Palestine.

To be a successful mobilizing tool, an ideology has to have the broadest possible appeal by drawing on values common to most, that is, core values.[26] Labour Zionism was the best candidate. Unlike the other schools of Zionism, it reinterpreted all three components of the Messianic message. Furthermore, by incorporating components of most branches of Zionism, it could appeal to adherents of those as well, at least to some extent. Also, though this mystical, pantheistic doctrine may seem a far cry from a practical programme of social action, it was not a utopia. It claimed to solve the pressing Jewish problem of immediate rescue from persecution by emigration to Palestine: Gordon himself did just that and most of his writing stems from that period of his life. It also provided answers for the immediate economic problems facing the immigrants in Palestine by advocating small cooperative settlements. Combined with the asceticism advocated by He-haluts, the movement which was most successful in inducing young people to settle in Palestine, and with the revival of the Hebrew language and culture, this ideology helped form the self-image of the Jewish settlers, that is, their identity.

Ideology is intimately linked with social identity. An ideology consists of a blueprint for the ideal structure of a given society, present (a legitimizing ideology) or future (a revolutionary ideology). In order to be accepted by a majority, it must justify the desired social order by core values of the society which it addresses, for these are the most common to all. Communism illustrates this point. Marxism purports to base the inevitability of historical processes on economic forces and the universal values of justice, equity and egalitarianism. Yet, in order to attain sufficient acquiescence to maintain their totalitarian regimes, communist states each had to imbue this universal ideology with core values of their own societies – Stalinism was as emphatically Russian as Maoism was Chinese and East German communism was German. Ideology also includes a programme of political action intended to bring about the ideal social structure it promulgates (in the case of a revolutionary ideology), or to maintain the status quo presented as the best of all possible worlds (a legitimizing ideology). Identity, on the other hand, is not action-oriented. It is an assertion of belonging to a society whose structure, norms and values are in congruence with the core values of that society. When asserting to be a member of a society, one naturally also identifies at least partially with its dominant ideology unless, or until one perceives this ideology to have diverted appreciably from the core values. A pre-eminent ideology and the preoccupation with social identity play a less prominent role in long-established societies, yet they are not absent there either, despite the assertions of modernists and postmodernists. New societies have to articulate the values which consolidate them, while those are already taken for granted in old ones and are largely removed from the public agenda. In periods of crisis, however, they are frequently evoked by political leaders in any society, pluralistic or otherwise, in order to rally support and create solidarity. Prime Minister Thatcher called on the British spirit of fair-play competitiveness and mercantile enterprise and the innovative spirit of the islander in order to overcome resistance to her economic programme, just as President Bush invoked the American role of disseminating democracy and protection of the underdog (Kuwait) in order to rally domestic support for the Gulf War.

The link between Labour Zionism and Yishuv identity is easily established. Eisenstadt, the dean of Israeli sociologists, described the institutionalization of the 'Haluts image', the ideal Pioneer, whose characteristics were self-sacrifice and relinquishment of any material rewards, a collective orientation and an emphasis on physical agricultural labour. All these were aimed at bringing about a new society of perfect justice and equality, a revival of Jewish culture and the Hebrew language and a transcendental orientation. This image was certainly never fully realized by the majority, but it constituted the ideal to be emulated, at least to some degree. Very few members of any society actually personify all the traits, norms and values projected by its identity, yet its principles serve as guidelines in concrete situations and as beacons of mutual recognition.

Ostensibly, Yishuv identity was more than adequate. The Pioneer distinguished the Yishuv from diaspora Zionists by portraying the Yishuv as the vanguard, the actual implementers as distinct from mere supporters of Zionism. Yet it did not alienate the Yishuv from diaspora Zionists, since it regarded the latter as the pool from which additional Yishuv members would be drawn. It also distinguished the Yishuv from Jews in general, but again without alienation. By separating the ethnic from the religious definition of Jewishness, Yishuv members could regard themselves as part of the Jewish people despite Orthodox claims to the contrary. Indeed, the Pioneer remained emphatically Jewish, which also served to delineate the Yishuv from the rest of the world. Moreover, this identity tapped a core value of Judaism, making it consistent with Jewishness in the past, yet innovative and adapted to the present. Best of all, by seeing themselves as fulfillers of the Messianic idea in an updated guise, Yishuv members could regard themselves as ethically immaculate. However, this very Jewishness and emphasis on high ethical standards made Yishuv identity problematic on several counts.

THE INHERENT AMBIVALENCE OF YISHUV IDENTITY

Firstly, history and culture replaced religion as the contemporary Jews' link with their ancient homeland, yet the Bible was the only document which could, and did, serve as a title deed to the Land of Israel and it was the only remaining expression of Jewish culture created in that homeland when it was still a sovereign Jewish state. Katzenelson, of the top Labour Zionist leadership and decidedly secular, underlined the role of the Bible as the connecting link between the Jewish people and their homeland.[27] Moreover, the Bible has been a major subject in all secular Yishuv and Israeli schools, elementary and secondary, but is an undeniably religious text. To overcome this contradiction, it was reinterpreted to be a purely historical document, which it certainly is not. Subsequently, extensive archaeological excavations were encouraged in order to substantiate the historicity of the Bible and, thus, the Jewish historical claim to the territory of the Land of Israel. Neither solution has been completely satisfactory.

Two other problems follow from the first. If the Jewish claim to the Land of Israel derives solely from their possession of it in the distant past, how could it counter the similar historical claim by local Arabs to 1,000 years of settlement in the same territory, surely a valid tenure. Worse still, the Pioneer, as a secularized version of the Messianic returnee to Zion, professed to represent a perfectly just society, to be a model to the world. This was difficult to reconcile with the protests of local Arabs that they were being forcibly driven from their land and jobs, hardly commensurate with absolute justice.

Early Zionists did not ignore the Arab presence in Palestine, as has been frequently claimed. In 1905, during the Seventh Zionist Congress, Epstein, a teacher from Palestine, already warned of the Arab determination to hold fast to their land. He delivered his lecture, which was published two years later,[28] at the Ivria Cultural Association, but delegates to the congress heard of it and it triggered counter-arguments at the congress. Zionist leaders and intellectuals in general, and Yishuv ones in particular, did try to come to terms with the Arab presence in Palestine, provided the solutions offered did not detract from the validity of their own right to the land. The subject has been investigated thoroughly, so that a brief summary suffices. The two dilemmas were recognized equally throughout the pre-state period, but emphasis on one or the other shifted according to external events.

Roughly until the Young Turk Revolt in 1908, local Arabs could be viewed as no more than residents of Palestine, indistinguishable from other subjects of the Ottoman Empire, with no separate identity of their own. This was so because, at the time, the Ottoman Empire based its legitimacy on Islam and tried to obliterate any ethnic distinctiveness of its subjects. The question then boiled down to convincing the Palestinian Arabs that their fears of economic competition were unfounded. The nature of Arab protests at the time seemed to justify such a view: in 1891, Jerusalem notables petitioned the authorities in Constantinople to put a stop to Jewish immigration to Palestine because Jews posed an economic threat to Arabs there. In line with this, Zionist leaders tried to allay such fears. Ahad Haam warned against exploitation of Arab labourers by Jewish farmers; Herzl promised that the enlightened modernizing Jewish settlers would raise the living standards of the entire population and would never discriminate against other religionists; Borochov predicted that any possible future confrontation would be class-based rather than a national conflict, with Jewish and Arab labourers siding against Arab landowners.[29] Articles in the Yishuv press were of a similar nature, though some already addressed the second dilemma of historical rights to the land, which became more prominent after 1908.

The Young Turk Revolt turned the Islamic Ottoman Empire into a secular Turkish state in which Arabs, particularly in Syria and Palestine, began to demand autonomy or even independence. This fostered the gradual delineation of a separate Palestinian-Arab self-image. Their intellectuals, at least, began to regard the conflict as one over national rights to the land. Zionist emphasis, and that of the Yishuv in particular, therefore shifted to addressing this question. In the Hebrew press in Palestine, there were calls for Semitic solidarity against the Turks to supersede opposing Arab and Jewish claims, as well as proposals to share the country. At the same time, other articles insisted on the inalienable historic right of Jews to the land which would be realized either by violent conflict – might is right – or by the democratic principle of majority rule, once Jews became the majority by mass immigration.[30]

The Balfour Declaration of 1917 seemed to obviate any further argument. The greatest empire of the time and, subsequently, the League of Nations recognized the Jewish historic right to the land. Therefore, emphasis could again shift to the ethical question of justice to the Arabs who, though stripped of their political right to the land, should not be expropriated by a society with a utopian vision of ethical perfection. Nevertheless, Labour Zionism, which became increasingly dominant at the time, addressed the ethical aspect of both dilemmas. Historical rights were a claim which had yet to be validated. Where purely juridical considerations could not decide a case, ethical criteria had to be employed. Gordon argued that, though undersigned by international approbation, Jews had to stake their claim by tilling the land. Reclamation of the soil, turned into desert by long Arab neglect, would be proof of the Jewish stronger link to it. Those who loved the land best and were willing to make the greatest sacrifice had the firmer right to it. However, Arabs must not be dispossessed and tenants must be fairly recompensed when land was bought from absentee owners. Proprietorship over the empty stretches was to be decided by the willingness to turn them into arable by hard labour.[31] The same view was taken up by Ben-Gurion, then already among the Labour leadership.[32]

This view had a major flaw, however. In order to prove their greater love of the land, Jews first had to acquire it. The very act of changing ownership tipped the scales in favour of the new owner. Greater devotion was merely additional evidence, not an initial decisive proof. No matter how the solution to the dilemma was formulated, it remained self-contradictory. Perfect justice cannot be reconciled with settlement of a country already occupied by others: in order to settle, one has to deny the others' rights of tenure. Nor could perfect justice be maintained in the economic sphere, given the harsh conditions of survival in Palestine at the time. Labour Zionist leaders, who had to deal with reality, were hard-pushed to find practical guidelines consonant with such lofty ideals. Thus, Arab protests against Jewish immigration, voiced during and after the 1920 and 1921 riots, were claimed to be totally unjustified. Yishuv leaders maintained that Jewish rights of tenure in Palestine were at least equal to those of the Arabs: Jews were *ipso facto* residents returning to their internationally recognized homeland, in which Arabs could claim only social and economic rights. These latter could and would be guaranteed by fair compensation to expropriated tenant farmers and by improving the lot of Arab labourers: an eventual agrarian reform in those parts of the land not purchased by Jews would turn tenants into freeholders; Arab labourers were invited to join the newly established Jewish labour union. At the same time, Jews insisted on exclusively Jewish labour on Jewish land, ostensibly in order to stake their claim to their heritage. In reality, pressure was exerted to dismiss Arabs working on Jewish farms under the slogan 'Conquest of Labour'. The policy of safeguarding workplaces for the penniless new immigrants, despite their higher cost to the employers and the doubtful ethics underlying this protectionist practice, was also justified on the grounds of preventing exploitation of Arab proletarians by Jewish capitalists.[33]

The ongoing debate on these topics at various meetings of the Labour movement shows, though, that the leaders, and probably many members, were aware of the inconsistency of their arguments and needed self-persuasion to reconcile their emotional certainty regarding their right to their homeland with their ethical convictions, once these two no longer derived from Divine Will. The latter need not be questioned, while secular human decisions require scrutiny if high moral ground is to be maintained. Viewed from the perspective of the present, these and later self-contradictory excuses and justifications seem cynical or self-deceptive, though they were not because, at the time, Palestinian Arab words and actions gave rise to these arguments, or at least confirmed them. Until the middle of the 1920s, the Yishuv leadership seemed justified in concentrating on the purely economic issue of the Arab presence in Palestine. Oddly enough, this was so not despite, but because of nascent Arab nationalism.

In return for taking a small part in the British fight against the Turks during the First World War, McMahon, the British Commissioner in Egypt, on 25 October 1915 informed Husayn, Sharif of Mecca, that Britain would support the independence of the Arabs. The boundaries of the future Arab state were not accurately defined. Subsequently, a dispute arose about the inclusion of the eastern Mediterranean littoral and in the following bargaining exchange Palestine was not mentioned at all. This vague formulation later led to contradictory interpretations. The Sykes–Picot agreement of May 1916 between Britain and France provided for two new Arab states between Damascus and Aqaba, and for complete British, French and international control of the coastal plane up to the River Jordan. This plan contradicted the single Arab state promised to Sharif Husayn. The final political structure in the Fertile Crescent broke up the area into a multiplicity of states, all of them then under the mandatory government or control of either Britain or France, but all of them with nominal Arab rule, with the exception of Palestine. In Palestine, the Balfour Declaration of 1917 promised the Jews a homeland.

The Balfour Declaration, and the failure to establish any Arab rule there, singled out Palestine among the states in the Fertile Crescent. The surrounding states became a reference group for Palestinian Arabs and that fostered their grievances, yet did not produce cohesive action, except for short outbreaks of violence in 1920 and in 1921. Various associations were set up during the 1920s, but were again dissolved due to fierce competition among them which rendered them ineffectual. Moreover, when Arab grievances were investigated by the Haycraft Commission following the 1921 disturbances, the report lists Arab objections that

> there was an undue number of Jews in government service in Palestine; part of the Zionist programme was to flood Palestine with people other than the Arabs...Jewish immigrants were an economic danger, were more competitive, were arrogant and contemptuous towards the Arabs, and the laxness of government supervision of immigration had permitted the entry into the country of 'Bolshevik' Jews.[34]

In view of the fact that it was principally economic grievances that were put forward by Arabs, Yishuv leaders were able to disregard the political dilemma and consider it resolved. Pan-Islamic and pan-Arab assertions provided further evidence that Arabs were no more than residents in Palestine, without any claims to it on a national basis.

When the British promised Sharif Husayn of Mecca a single Arab state in the Fertile Crescent, he intended to head it as Caliph because he was of the Bani Hashim clan of the Quraishi tribe, the tribe of the Prophet. This was to revive the original Muslim state in its ancient heartland, unadulterated by the corruption of the Ottoman Turks. He declared himself King of the Hijaz in 1916, when McMahon's promises were made on behalf of Great Britain, and sent his troops to fight alongside the British in order to liberate the territory which was to become his Arab–Muslim kingdom. The boundaries of this state, though ill-defined by McMahon, approximated those of the Arab Muslim heartland at the very beginning of the Arab Empire. His son Faisal was indeed installed as King in Damascus, the fitting capital of the renewed Arab–Muslim polity. However, Faisal's reign as head of the Arab–Muslim state was short-lived, as was that of his father. Husayn officially made claim to the Caliphate when this office was abolished in Turkey in 1924, but his claim was not recognized. He was then forced to abdicate as King of the Hijaz. Due to the Anglo-French agreement of 1916, Syria subsequently came under French mandatory rule and Faisal was removed to become King of Iraq instead, while his brother Abdallah was installed as Amir of Transjordan. Despite the fact that the Hashemite Islamic–Arab state had been curtailed and split, the ideas of Muslim and/or Arab political unity which it fostered have persisted in various guises to the present.[35]

Arab leaders in Palestine made use of these ideas in order to rally support for their cause against the Jewish incursion. They thus supplied the Yishuv leaders with an argument in favour of their exclusive title to Palestine. In 1921, Haj Amin al-Husayni was appointed Mufti of Jerusalem. A Mufti holds a religious–legal function of giving rulings on interpretations of the law. In Islam, as in Judaism, the legal code is part of religious doctrine and derives from the Holy Scriptures, in the case of Islam the Quran. Mufti is thus a very highly respected position, which can be turned into legal–social–political power sanctioned by religion, which is precisely what Haj Amin al-Husayni did.

In place of the economic and national grievances put forward in 1921, al-Husayni presented Jewish immigration as a threat to the Islamic identity of Palestinian Arabs. The Supreme Muslim Council, of which he was a leading member, and which initiated the 1929 riots,[36] focused Palestinian Arab resentment on the alleged Jewish assault on places in Jerusalem holy to both Jews and Muslims. Yet the 1929 riots failed to tip the scales and eliminate the Zionist threat. Therefore, the Mufti, who was by then the leader of Arab opposition to Zionism and the British Mandate in Palestine, tried to turn the Palestinian problem into the cause of all Muslims in order to receive material and diplomatic support from the neighbouring countries. For this purpose, the injustice done to the Palestinian Arabs was presented as an affront to Muslims as one *umma* (the Muslim religious community which is a political unit at the same time). In line with this aim, the Mufti convened the General Islamic Conference in Jerusalem on 6 December 1931. The Conference was organized with the aid of the Caliphate Society of India and, therefore, its declared objectives constituted a compromise between the Palestinian aims of the Mufti and the purely Islamic ones of Shawkat Ali, President of the Caliphate Society. Besides supporting the nomination of a new Caliph, the Conference also promoted turning Jerusalem into the new Islamic centre, in competition with Cairo, by establishing an Islamic university there.[37] The Palestinian Arab turn to pan-Islam was augmented by their turn to pan-Arabism. The 'Arab Conference' was held on 16 December 1931, ten days after the Islamic Conference. It was a private reception held at the home of a Jerusalem lawyer, which called for Arab unity and a struggle against imperialism. As its title suggests, it invoked pan-Arab values rather than Islamic ones.

The appeal by Palestinian Arabs to neighbouring Arabs for help in the name of Muslim or Arab unity corroborated the Hashemite protestations that Arabs were one nation, so that Palestinian Arabs were not a separate entity. Zionists no longer had to rely on historical evidence showing that Palestine had never been an independent polity since the conquest of the Jewish state by the Romans. The Arabs themselves implied that such was the case and Zionists could not agree more. Once an Arab state had been set up under King Faisal of the Hashemite clan, Palestinian Arabs vacillated between separateness and their membership in the Arab or Muslim nation. In 1919 Palestinian Arab leaders preferred joining Greater Syria, then ruled by King Faisal, to remaining a separate political entity under Christian British rule which encouraged Jewish immigration. The unclear conception of Palestine as a territorial entity is demonstrated by the declaration of the Syrian Congress held in Damascus in July 1919, which delegates from Palestine attended: 'We reject Zionist claims to establish a Jewish commonwealth in that part of southern Syria which is known by the name of Palestine.'[38] Zionist leaders were naturally encouraged by this and held friendly negotiations with King Faisal while he still reigned in Damascus and the single Arab state still seemed viable.[39] After the breakup of the latter in 1920, the option of regarding Palestinian Arabs as part of that state, or of the Arab nation, became increasingly unrealistic until it was revived by the two above conferences and the subsequent growing involvement of the neighbouring Arab states in the Palestinian Arab cause.

In 1930, Beilinson, of the Labour Zionist leadership, was among the first to justify the Jewish presence in Palestine by pointing out that Arabs had a sufficiently large homeland in the neighbouring countries.[40] Subsequently, Ben-Gurion reformulated this idea. The problem of the local Arabs would be resolved on a civic basis once Jews became a majority in Palestine, for democratic majority rule would then prevail. The real adversary was the Arab nation. Acceptance and peace had to be sought with it in a federation with the neighbouring Arab states, since the latter constituted the Arab nation.[41] This line of reasoning was reiterated by Haim Weizmann, President of the Zionist Organization, at his testimony before the UN Palestine Committee on 18 October 1947.

Arab statements and actions could indeed be taken as evidence of Arab unity as a nation, in which case Palestinian Arabs were part of it without separate claims. This held true despite the Arab Revolt of 1936–39. The 1936 disturbances started as a general strike, declared on 15 April 1936 by the secular-nationalist Istiqlal (independence) party. It was an act of civil disobedience against the mandatory government, that is an anti-imperialist rebellion, because the British parliament had failed to pass a bill setting up a representative government in Palestine, while nominal sovereignty had been granted to Syria, Lebanon and Egypt. A more immediate reason was probably the massive immigration of Jews from Germany after the Nazi regime had come to power, since a stop to Jewish immigration was the chief demand made by the Arab Higher Committee, a body controlled by the Muslim camp and headed from 1936 onwards by Mufti Amin al-Husayni. Its other demands were a halt to Jewish land purchases and a one-man-one-vote government which would automatically guarantee the Arabs a decisive majority. It must be noted that, although the general strike was initiated by the secular Istiqlal, the cry was immediately taken up by the religiously dominated Arab Higher Committee. The latter then changed the nature of the rebellion from an economic boycott against the British into widespread riots against Jews. The 1936–39 Arab campaign received active official support from Egypt and Iraq, which had become semi-autonomous and could extend actual help to the Palestinian Arabs, as did the Muslim Brothers in Egypt,[42] an activist pan-Islamic group. Syria and Lebanon, the cradle of pan-Arabism, could give only ideological support to the Arab Revolt because they remained under French Mandate.

Indeed, conceiving the Arabs as a single bloc was not just wishful thinking on the part of Yishuv leaders. Britain too consulted the Arab states with regard to the Palestinian problem, regarding them as relevant parties to the conflict. The well-known Round Table Conference, held in London in 1939, is a case in point. Furthermore, Arab reunification was again raised as a possibility. In 1942, Nuri al-Said, Premier of Iraq, proposed the 'Fertile Crescent Plan', a merger of Iraq, Syria, Lebanon, Palestine and Transjordan under the Hashemite rule of King Faisal. This was the first official expression of pan-Arab aspirations, after the Arab state promised to Sharif Husayn of Mecca had come to nothing, and it was followed in 1947 by a counter-proposal made by King Abdallah, also of the Hashemite dynasty of Jordan, calling for a 'Greater Syria' under his rule. In response to such centripetal forces, Britain helped to found the Arab League in 1944 in Alexandria. Its members were Egypt, Saudi Arabia, Iraq, Syria, Lebanon, Transjordan (Yemen joined later) and Palestine.

At first, however, Britain regarded the Arab Revolt as a local uprising and proceeded to deal with it accordingly. The Peel Commission of 1937 proposed the partition of Palestine into two separate states, the Jewish one to be allotted a fraction of the area of Mandatory Palestine. The Arabs rejected the proposal outright, demanding sovereignty over the entire territory of Palestine, while the Yishuv and diaspora Zionist leaders accepted the proposal in principle, but contested the demarcated borders. Even so, Jewish agreement on partition was reached after prolonged and fierce debate, as well as with great reluctance. By proposing partition, the British had implicitly recognized Palestinian Arabs as a separate national entity with rights to Palestine equal to those of Jews; by complying with this proposal, so did Zionists. This was incompatible with the argument that Palestinian Arabs were simply part of the Arab nation. Worse still, it constituted a betrayal of the one aspect of Labour Zionism common to all sectors of the Yishuv, and of Zionism in general, namely of the inalienable historical/religious right of Jews to their entire homeland, the Land of Israel. The dilemma would recur when the UN Partition Plan was accepted by the Yishuv leadership, but by then an acceptable way out had been found. Meanwhile, torn between pragmatic considerations and ideological commitment, Ben-Gurion excused acceptance of partition as an interim stage in the eventual realization of Zionism.[43]

Such tactics appeared unseemly to those who insisted on their Zionist faith. Beilinson, Katzenelson, Kaplansky, Golda Meyerson, Bar Yehuda and Tabenkin were among the fiercest opponents. The debate at the Twentieth Zionist Congress in 1937 lasted for eight days and ended in no more than a conditional agreement to the partition proposal.[44] Katzenelson stated that the right of Jewish refugees (from Nazi Germany) was weightier than the Arab right to a sovereign state. Palestinian Arabs could move to other Arab countries if they did not wish to live in a Jewish state encompassing all of Palestine; Ben-Gurion argued similarly.[45]

The need to repeat such excuses and justifications at the Zionist Congress, at various party meetings and at meetings with young and old throughout the country[46] indicates that the various audiences might have had some scruples regarding the justice of their cause. In the specific circumstances of Palestine at the time, national redemption and ethical perfection were as self-contradictory as is the secular version of national redemption whose title deed is the Bible. Pioneer identity was ambiguous, based as it was on an ideology whose components were mutually exclusive. Yet, no direct evidence indicates that people were aware of this ambiguity at the time. Arab intransigence, the rise of Nazism and, later, knowledge of the Holocaust and the indifference of the 'enlightened' world to the Jewish catastrophe are some of the explanations for this self-defensive and even self-righteous stance. Under such universal siege, it is easy to disregard the less serious plight of one's adversary. Moreover, Labour Zionist leaders strengthened the resolve of the Yishuv and allayed any possible compunctions by a tireless effort of speeches, articles in the press and in party organs, as well as by films. Far from imposing their views, they persuaded an ever-growing following. Thus, they ensured their dominant position and the acceptance of an identity which, by its very nature, should have been unsatisfactory.

The lack of success of the two main opposition groups to Labour Zionism also testifies to the entrenched identity of most Yishuv members. Both addressed the very dilemma of the Pioneer discussed above because both acknowledged that Palestinian Arabs were a nation. The solutions offered by the two groups to the problem raised by this recognition were as different as the assumptions on which they were based. Yet, though less ambivalent and grounded in a more realistic assessment of the situation then prevalent in Palestine, neither group could mobilize a majority support, or indent Yishuv identity as it had coalesced.

Brit Shalom

The first main opposition group, Brit Shalom (Covenant of Peace) was founded in 1925. Its members were mainly central European intellectuals who proposed a bi-national state in Palestine. This would prevent Arab rights from being curtailed, and preclude Jewish domination of another unwilling people. Bi-nationalism would ensure Jewish high ethical standards and would also prevent a violent confrontation.[47] The group remained a marginal debating society until 1930, when its views came under serious attack. When local Arab actions began to imply that they saw themselves as part of the Arab/Muslim nation, recognition of them as a separate nation despite their own claims seemed foolish, and even damaging; consequently, Brit Shalom dissolved itself in 1933.

In 1939, veterans of Brit Shalom reorganized into a League promoting a bi-national state. The idea again became viable because the Arab Revolt, though aided by surrounding Arab states, made the argument less convincing that local Arabs could not have separate national aspirations. Moreover, the Messianic dictum of universal peace was being increasingly violated by Jewish militant retaliation for Arab attacks. The League was then joined by more newly arrived intellectuals, notably Martin Buber, the formulator of mystical Zionism, by the two Marxist parties Ha-shomer Ha-tsair and Poalei Tsion Smol and by the Aliya Hadasha party of German immigrants. It was renamed Ihud in 1942. According to Buber, means had to be as ethical as the aims they served, otherwise they would contaminate the latter. The return to Zion was a supremely ethical act which must not be sullied by violence or domination of another people. Only by mutual agreement of the two peoples with equal rights to the same land could a just solution be reached and that must needs be a bi-national one.[48] Faithful to the ethics of perfect justice, Ihud would not have the Arab population outnumbered by Jews in the future. It advocated further Jewish immigration of war refugees, but only until numerical parity had been reached.

Bi-nationalism was a non-starter: the Arabs rejected it for the same reason as did the Yishuv, namely because it denied the exclusive right of either people to the land. Even as a utopian solution it was inferior to Labour Zionism because it gave precedence to social redemption over the national one, while Labour Zionism managed to preserve both components of Zionism/Messianism, even though the combination was equivocal. In 1942, the Zionist Organization adopted the Biltmore Programme, which insisted on a Jewish state in Palestine. As the first news of the Holocaust spread shortly afterwards, underlining the need for unlimited refugee immigration after the war, the Ihud proposals became even less acceptable and the group gradually lost all influence.

The Revisionists

The second major opposition group were the Revisionists. They failed to become a viable alternative to Labour Zionism for several reasons, some of which were discussed elsewhere.[49] One reason, however, is pertinent to the present analysis, namely the precedence which their ideology gave to national redemption over the social one. If adopted, Yishuv members would have had to forego any claim to being the chosen people in the ethical sense, while Labour Zionism provided an identity of revivers of the national heritage who were also ethically immaculate.

The Revisionist party was founded by Vladimir (Zeev) Jabotinsky in 1923, after he had resigned from the Zionist Executive in protest against its inadequate policies: Jewish immigration was faltering because it had failed to recruit the necessary funds and had failed to counter mandatory limitations on immigration; it had also failed to prevent Arab violence against Jews in the 1920–21 riots. Once established, Jabotinsky formulated a more explicit platform for the Revisionist party. Its ideology claimed to be an updated version of Herzl's political Zionism. Its principal themes were the establishment of a Jewish majority in Palestine, and the reintroduction of political Zionist tactics aimed at inducing the mandatory government to facilitate Jewish mass immigration by administrative and fiscal measures. Information, persuasion, and the pressure of Jewish public opinion were proposed as supplementary tactics. Two additional themes were not derived directly from political Zionism, but did not contradict its premises either. They were an emphasis on self-defence in Palestine and social neutrality, that is non-identification with either side of the class conflict.[50]

Revisionist ideology remained basically unchanged in the following ten years except for its economic neutrality, which became a cautious partisanship of a capitalist economy. The change was presumably due to the 1924–27 influx of Jewish immigrants who came to Palestine due to economic discrimination in Poland. Few alternative destinations were available to them since the United States had by then restricted immigration. Indifferent, or even hostile, to Labour Zionist ideals of egalitarian agricultural labour, this new population settled mainly in towns and wished to hold on to its previous occupations, principally trade, crafts and the professions. The new bourgeois immigrants were potential recruits to the Revisionist movement, since they were in no way affiliated to the Labour party in Palestine and did not share its socialist ideology. The Revisionist appeal to them became outspoken by 1930, when the movement demanded that Zionist funds be allocated to their absorption. By 1935, Jabotinsky declared class conflict both absurd and detrimental to Jewish solidarity[51] and another Revisionist publication openly advocated a private enterprise economy in Palestine.

The initial avoidance of addressing the social salvation component of the Messianic idea was not remedied by advocating capitalism, hardly ethically superior to the egalitarian socialism of Labour Zionism, though realistically more operable. Furthermore, Revisionism stressed national independence much more than its redemption. Jabotinsky spoke of the Jewish mission to the world, once statehood had been achieved, but did not specify the nature of this mission, hinting at pacifism as a possible one. That clearly contradicted the Revisionist stress on militarism. Reintroducing the practice of the biblical jubilee – an economic redistribution every 50 years – as well as some welfare-state measures and attention to women's rights as mothers and educators of the future generation were the extent of Revisionist social salvation.[53]

The Revisionists acknowledged that local Arabs were a separate nation with claims to Palestine and failed to present a convincing argument for Jewish superior claims, except for international approbation and greater Jewish military and numerical strength – hence the stress on self-defence and on the creation of a Jewish majority. This was no match for Labour Zionism, which could justify Jewish resettlement of its ancient homeland by an updated version of Messianism, even if it was to some extent self-contradictory. Indeed, when the Revisionists seemed to become a real threat to Labour dominance with the onset of German bourgeois immigration to Palestine in 1933, Labour was even able to ostracize the Revisionists and make this outcast image stick for many years to come. The assassination in 1933 of Haim Arlosorof, a leading Labour politician, of which Labour rightly or wrongly accused the Revisionists (the crime was never solved) set off a campaign of Revisionist delegitimation. Allegations against the Revisionists were based on the extremist minority views of Abba Ahimeir, a member of the Palestine Revisionist Central Committee. They were thus not fabricated, but the views of a minority group were exploited to discredit the entire party. The Revisionists were portrayed as assassins, saboteurs of Zionist institutions, negotiators with renowned anti-Semites, Fascists, a party definitely beyond the pale. Revisionist tactics of secession from most Yishuv organizations undoubtedly helped to reinforce this outsider image.[54]

Neither the allegations themselves, based on feeble and biased evidence, nor the politically incompetent counter-measures taken by the Revisionists, can fully account for the immense success of the delegitimation campaign, whose effects lasted well into the 1970s. This is particularly evident when compared with similar accusations levelled at the entire Right after the assassination of Prime Minister Rabin in 1995. In the latter case, the evidence was unequivocal: the assassin was apprehended on the spot and admitted to be of the extreme religious Right; furthermore, prior to the assassination, demonstrations by the Right against the Oslo Accords and statements by Rightist rabbis had demonized the prime minister. Yet, no delegitimation of the Likud followed, instead, its leader Benjamin Netanyahu was elected prime minister. It would seem that Labour legitimacy in the Yishuv period, and the partial loss of it at present, account for the different outcomes. The delegitimation campaign of 1933 could stick when made by a party enjoying full legitimacy: Labour articulated and implemented the core value of Messianism most fully and this provided Yishuv members with an identity which ethically justified the status quo. Any real challenge to the basic premises of Labour were tantamount to sacrilege and the challengers were political outcasts. Thus, despite a preponderance of bourgeois parties in the Zionist congresses and of bourgeois sectors in the Yishuv, especially after the immigration of

German Jews as of 1933, the Revisionists failed to mobilize a majority following in either, or to have an impact on Yishuv identity. The latter remained basically intact until the establishment of the State of Israel in 1948, despite its ambiguity and despite the decreasing fit between reality and the ideal self-image of the Pioneer.

NOTES

1. For example, W. Laquer, *A History of Zionism* (Tel Aviv: Schocken, 1974), pp.13–40.
2. M. Buber, *Israel und Palaestina: zur Geschichte einer Idee* (Zurich: Artemis, 1950), pp.85–119, 132; Letters by rabbis in M.H.A. Bloch (ed.), *A Book to Make the Sleeping Speak: Opinions of Torah Scholars opposed to Zionism* (New York: Tiferet, 1959).
3. *Protokoll des I. Zionisten-Kongresses in Basel vom 29 bis 31 August 1897* (Prague: Barissa, 1911), p.124.
4. *Protokoll des I. Zionisten-Kongresses in Basel*, p.131.
5. Computed from the balance sheet of the Fifth Zionist Congress, *Stenographisches Protokoll der Verhandlungen des V. Zionisten-Kongresses in Basel, 26, 27, 28, 29 und 30 Dezember 1901*, (Vienna: Verlag des Vereines Erez Israel, 1901), p.21. Even if the number of sympathizers was twice, or even three times that amount, they still constituted a mere 2%–3% of Jews at the time.
6. *Protokoll des I. Zionisten-Kongresses in Basel*, p.124.
7. J. Frankel, 'Assimilation and Survival Among European Jews in the 19th Century: Towards a New Historiography?', in J. Reinharz *et al.* (eds), *Jewish Nationalism and Politics: New Perspectives* (Jerusalem: Zalman Shazar Centre, 1996), pp.23–56.
8. *Stenographisches Protokoll der Verhandlungen des VI. Zionisten-Kongresses in Basel, 23, 24, 26, 27 und 28 August 1903*, (Vienna: Verlag des Vereines Erez Israel, 1903), pp. 157, 162, 168–9.
9. Postzionism is a school of historians and sociologists which is highly critical of the interpretation given to Israeli events by what it calls Zionist historiography. The claims Post-zionists have made and the impact of these on the Israeli public debate will be discussed in later chapters.
10. Rabbi Ts.H., Kalisher, *The Call of Zion* (Jerusalem, 1925); Y. Werfel, *Writings of Rabbi Yehuda Alkalai* (Jerusalem: Rav Kuk Institute, 1960) p.181; J. Jaffe, *Love of Zion and Jerusalem* (Jerusalem: Wallenstein, 1947), pp.26, 65–6; Y.Y. Reines, *New Light on Zion* (Vylna: Rom, 1901), pp.26–7.
11. Rabbi Y.A.H. Kuk, *Orot Ha-kodesh* (Jerusalem: Rabbi Y.A.H. Kuk Publications, 1938), p.135; *Orot* (Jerusalem: Rabbi Y.A.H. Kuk Institute, 1950), pp.48–9, 119–72; *Adar Ha-yakar Ve-'ikvey Ha-tson* (Jerusalem: Rabbi Y.A.H. Kuk Publications, 1967), pp. 107–56; *Epistles of R.Y.A.H.* (Jerusalem: Jerusalem Publications, 1923), p.284; Rabbi Y.L.H. Fishmann, *Azkara: A Religious–Scientific Collection* (Jerusalem: Rav Kuk Institute, 1937/38), pp.61, 66, 74, 90.
12. T. Herzl, 'Tagebuecher Vol. I', *Gesammelte zionistische Schriften*, Vol. II (Berlin: Juedischer Verlag, 1905), pp.21–36.
13. T. Herzl, 'Judenstaat', *Gesammelte zionistische Schriften*, Vol. I (Berlin: Juedischer Verlag, 1905), pp.42–45
14. *Protokoll des I. Zionisten-Kongresses in Basel*, pp.16, 137.
15. Ibid., pp.143–56
16. M.J. Berdichewsky, *Collected Essays* (Tel Aviv: Am Oved, 1952), pp.38–40, 382.
17. L. Pinsker, *Autoemanzipation* (Berlin: Yuedischer Verlag, 1919), pp.18–19. 28–9.
18. Y.H. Brenner, *Collected Writings* Vol. 7 (Tel Aviv: Am Oved, 1976), p.185; 'In the Press and In Literature', *Ha-po'el Ha-tsa'ir*, No. 3, 1910; 'In Memoriam of Yalag', *Ha-po'el Ha-tsa'ir*, Nos. 25–6, 1913.
19. B. Borochov, 'Class Conflict and the National Question', *Collected Essays* (Tel Aviv: Marx-Engels Publications, 1934), pp.13–48; 'Bases of Proletarian Zionism (Our Platform), ibid., pp. 51–199; *Collected Writings* (Tel Aviv: Ha-kibbuts Ha-meuhadd & Sifriyat Ha-po'alim, 1955), pp.311–14.
20. N. Syrkin, *Essays* (Tel Aviv: Davar, 1939), pp. 34–59.
21. P. Smolenskin, 'The People's Covenant', *Ha-sha'ar*, No. 4, 1864; G. Winer, *The Founding Fathers of Israel* (New York: Bloch, 1971), p.70.
22. Ahad Haam, 'Flesh and Spirit', in Ahad Haam *At the Crossroads* (Berlin: Jeudischer Verlag, 1921), pp.222–32; 'The Time Has Come', in L. Simon (ed.), *Essays on Zionism and Judaism* (London: Routledge, 1922), pp.91–113; 'A Spiritual Centre', in Simon (ed.) *Essays on Zionism*, pp.120–9.

23. M. Buber, *Israel und Palaestina*, esp. pp.7–12.
24. A.D. Gordon, *Selected Essays* (New York: League for Labour Palestine, 1938), pp.2, 60, 250–1; *Nation and Labour* (Jerusalem: Zionist Federation, 1952), p.497. 'Letters from the Galilee', in A. Yaari (ed.), *Letters from Palestine* (Tel Aviv: Zionist Federation & Gazit, 1943), pp.508–18.
25. The process is discussed in detail in Y. Shapiro, *The Formative Years of the Israeli Labour Party* (London: Sage, 1976), pp.71–82.
26. J.A. Goldstone, 'Ideology, Cultural Frameworks and the Process of Revolution', *Theory and Society* Vol. 20, No. 4, 1991, pp.405–53.
27. B. Katzenelson, *Essays*, Vol. 11 (Tel Aviv: Mapai Publications, 1948), pp.32–3.
28. Y. Epstein, 'An Unasked Question', *Ha-shiloah*, No. 17, 1907/8.
29. Y. Gorni, *The Arab Question and the Jewish Problem* (Tel Aviv: Am Oved, 1985), pp.32–40; *Selected Essays From the Period of the Second Wave of Immigrants* (Tel Aviv: Tel Aviv University, 1966), pp.35–45.
30. Y. Gorni, 'The Roots of Acknowledging Jewish–Arab Confrontation and its Reflection in the Hebrew Press During 1900–1918' *Ha-tsionut* Vol. 4, 1975, pp.72–113.
31. A.D. Gordon, 'Our Work from Now On' (1918), *Nation and Labour*, pp.243–6.
32. D. Ben-Gurion, 'Rights of Jews and Others in Palestine', *Der Yidisher Kempfer*, No. 4, 1918, pp.68–73.
33. Y. Gorni, *The Arab Question and the Jewish Problem* (Tel Aviv: Am Oved, 1985), pp.128–67.
34. *Great Britain Foreign Office, Palestine Commission on the Jaffa Riots, 1921*, Parliamentary Papers, Cmd 1540, London 1921, p.51.
35. For a detailed discussion of pan-Islam and pan-Arabism, see L. Weissbrod, *Arab Relations With Jewish Immigrants and Israel 1891–1991: The Hundred Years Conflict* (Lewiston: Edwin Mellen, 1992), pp.125–71.
36. M. al-Tawil, *The Recent Disturbances in Erets Yisrael* (Jerusalem: Abiksos, 1930), p.48.
37. T. Mayer, 'Egypt and the General Islamic Conference of Jerusalem in 1931', *Middle Eastern Studies*, Vol. 18, No.3, 1982, pp. 311–22.
38. Quoted in A. Shapira, 'The Balfour Declaration – A Backward Look', in S. Stempler (ed.), *The History of the Yishuv: Landmarks Before Statehood* (Jerusalem: Ministry of Defence, 1983), pp. 217–30.
39. See the Faisal–Frankfurter correspondence of 1919 and the testimony of Haim Weizmann before the UN Palestine Committee in 1947, both quoted in M.S. Chertoff (ed.), *Zionism* (New York: Herzl Press, 1975), pp.11–14.
40. Y. Gorni, Y, *The Arab Question*, p.282.
41. Y. Gorni, *The Arab Question*, pp.282–97; Ben-Gurion address contained in the protocol of the Mapai Centre meeting held on 19 March 1941, Labour Party Archives.
42. P. Mansfield, *The Middle East: A Political and Economic Survey* (London: Oxford University Press, 1973), p. 74.
43. In his letter to Moshe Shertok of 3 July 1937 (Ben-Gurion Archives); in his letter to his son Amos of 5 October 1937 in *Letters to Paula and the Children* (Tel Aviv: Am Oved, 1968), pp.211–13; in his address at the 20th Zionist Congress in 1937.
44. M. Bar-Zohar, *Ben Gurion*, Vol. 1 (Tel Aviv: Am Oved, 1978), p.367.
45. B. Katzenelson, *Address at the Zionist Executive on 10.11.42*, 25/294: D. Ben-Gurion, *Address at the Jewish Agency Directorate in Jerusalem on 7.5.44*.
46. For example, H. Weizmann, 'Letter to Felix Frankfurter of July 1939'; Katzenelson addressing young people in Mikve Yisrael on 30 July 1944 and at a lecture in Ashdod Ya'acov on 7 July 1944, all quoted in Y. Gorni, *The Arab Question*, pp.378–82.
47. *Our Aims* (Jerusalem: Brit Shalom Publications, 1927/28).
48. M. Buber, 'Policy and Ethics', *Ba'ayot*, April 1945, pp.110–13.
49. L. Weissbrod, 'Economic Factors and Political Strategies: The Defeat of the Revisionists in Mandatory Palestine', *Middle Eastern Studies*, Vol. 19, No. 3, 1983, pp.326–44; 'The Rise and Fall of the Revisionist Party, 1928–1935', *The Jerusalem Quarterly*, No. 30, 1948, pp.80–93.
50. V. Jabotinsky, *Was wollen die Zionisten–Revisionisten* (Paris: Imprimerie polyglotte, 1926), pp.4–24.
51. V. Jabotinsky, *Die Idee des Betar* (Lyck: Kaulbars, 1935), pp.10–14.
52. *Blue-White Papers* (London: The World Union of Zionist Revisionists, 1935), p.13.
53. V. Jabotinsky, *Die Idee des Betar*, pp.8–10, 22–30.
54. For a detailed account of these events, see L. Weissbrod, 'Economic Factors and Political Strategies'.

2. The Tsabar: A Self-Defensive Identity

The establishment of the State of Israel was a watershed in the articulation of Israeli identity. It turned the ambivalent Yishuv identity into an assertive, yet self-defensive one. The change was not sudden and was perceived only gradually. Like all later watersheds in Israeli identity, it revolved around the basic dilemma of the Zionist enterprise, namely the right to settle in a land already occupied by others. Zionism translated into secular terms the Messianic hope of returning to Zion in order to institute a perfectly just society, to be a model to the world. Therefore, injustice to the present residents of Zion could not be brushed off easily. As Zionists, the Yishuv leaders could not renounce the Jewish claim to the biblical Land of Israel, which corresponded roughly to Mandatory Palestine (since the establishment of Transjordan, all but the Revisionists had relinquished the Jewish right to those parts of Transjordan incorporated in the Holy Land at some time in history). The logical conclusion was an outright rejection of Palestinian Arab claims to the same territory, but that would have disregarded justice, the ultimate purpose of the original Messianic idea. Moreover, external circumstances also ruled out such an option. The international community in general, and the British mandatory government in particular, rejected any Jewish exclusive right to the land; the Yishuv was ill equipped to defy Palestinian Arabs without outside aid in light of the threatening intervention of surrounding Arab states. Ideological constraints and pragmatic considerations were at loggerheads, resulting in a compromise of sorts.

Zionist leaders first suggested[1] and later agreed to a partition of the land into two separate states, a Jewish and an Arab one. A concession to Palestinian Arab rights is implicit in the agreement to partition. Once this is admitted, it is impossible to draw the line, especially when partition of a possession claimed equally by two owners is not effected by mutual agreement: Palestinian Arabs absolutely rejected any Jewish claim to part of the land. The case then remains unsettled and ones' own rights seem more dubious. On the other hand, a concession to Palestinian Arabs can also be seen to clinch one's claim to the remaining part of the land, proving that one is more ethical, because the more generous side. Indeed, the implementors of Messianic national redemption did not admit Palestinian Arab rights and could, therefore, insist on Jewish ethical superiority in forgoing part of their own ones. Consequently, the agreement to partition was presented as given under duress and not as a relinquishment of Jewish rights to any part, or to the whole of the Land of Israel. At the same time, agreement to partition was also interpreted as a supreme ethical act, a gesture of magnanimity in line with the Messianic principle of perfect justice. Thereupon, it absolved the State of Israel of any further moral obligations towards Palestinian Arabs. These two justifications of partition were a compromise within the framework of the Messianic message: neither perfect justice nor national redemption were wholly satisfied. It also reversed the order of priority within the Messianic message so that national redemption became the ultimate aim. Justice remained important, but to be exercised only insofar as it did not obstruct the main target. The subsequent reformulation of Zionism ostensibly resolved the predicament for Israelis until the latter regained salience when the territory of the Holy Land became a major issue once more.

CONTRACTION OF LABOUR ZIONISM

As already stated, ideology is closely linked to collective identity as an articulator of unique core values. A common acceptance of these makes people recognizable to each other as members of the same society. Therefore, the discussion of a change in collective identity must be preceded by an analysis of transitions in the ideology to which it is linked. By the late 1950s, Labour Zionism had been eroded almost completely and replaced by étatisme, but this was not done by a sudden reformulation of the Messianic idea. Rather, it was a gradual shift in emphasis from one component of the ideology to another, culminating in a reversal of priorities. Labour Zionism had transformed the elements of the Messianic idea to mean national redemption by a return to Palestine, social salvation by instituting an egalitarian socio-economic system of perfect justice, and personal salvation as a merging with God by tilling the Holy Soil. The latter was of prime importance at first: the true implementers of Labour Zionism saw themselves and were seen as the

Pioneers, those who not merely settled in Palestine and renounced a career of economic advancement, but those who also farmed the land cooperatively. Despite the influx of largely bourgeois immigrants from Poland during 1924–27 and from Germany during 1933–39, Labour Zionist leaders could and did present the small number of actual pioneers[2] as the vanguard whom everybody should emulate. Representing this vanguard legitimized the dominant position of Labour in the Yishuv. This vanguard was regarded as the elite by the entire Yishuv, including supporters of parties other than Labour.

De-emphasis of Individual Salvation

In the early 1940s, after two Kibbutz movements had seceded from the Labour party, the claim of representing the pioneers was no longer tenable. A shift in emphasis became necessary, whereby the Pioneer was gradually replaced by the entire working class as the focus of Labour Zionism. Pioneering was not discarded at once, or altogether, if Labour preeminence was to be maintained. Rather, it was mentioned less frequently, while an egalitarian working class, or the labour movement, were gradually introduced into speeches and articles, at first alongside pioneering and finally in its place. The change was thus performed slowly, almost imperceptibly, and noted only much later. The following serves to illustrate this shift. In the 1930s, pioneering was presented as the ultimate realization of Zionism, or as Ben-Gurion put it, 'the first line of Zionism'.[3] The Labour weekly went even further, insisting that it was the only legitimate realization of Zionism. It admonished the Zionist Organization for its unselective immigration policy, which allowed non-pioneering elements to change the unsullied character of the Yishuv.[4] By 1938, another article in the same weekly already described the Hebrew Labour movement as the carrier of Zionism.[5] In 1942, Ben-Gurion described the pioneers as the implementers of Zionism on one occasion, while not mentioning them at all at the Fifth Labour Party Conference, where he ascribed this role to the entire working class.[6] By 1944, the ideological shift had become explicit when Ben-Gurion stated that a Jewish state could not be achieved by the sole effort of Hebrew workers, but decidedly not without their effort.[7] Due to the time lag between ideological change and its perception, the Pioneer remained the quintessence of Yishuv identity. When the prestige of Kibbutz and Moshav members declined after the establishment of Israel, the young among them tried to retain it by excelling in the armed forces, and thus becoming the embodiment of the new Israeli identity.[8]

The shift from pioneering to the working class gave Zionism a narrower definition. It depleted original Labour Zionism of individual salvation by eliminating physical contact with the soil as a means to immersion in the Divine. The working-class redefinition of Zionism implied national and social redemption only. Yet soon after, ideological depletion was carried further when ingathering of the exiles, the national redemption component of the Messianic idea, gained predominance, shifting social justice (the working class) to a secondary position of importance in the definition of Zionism. It remained an important component, but ceased to be the ultimate aim. This made it easier to relegate to a similarly secondary position considerations of justice toward Palestinian Arabs. The shift was precipitated by world events.

De-emphasizing Perfect Justice

The Nazi occupation of Europe during the Second World War put all of European Jewry in peril. Despite their plight, the White Paper issued by the British in 1939 restricted the number of Jewish immigrants to Palestine to a trickle. Many illegal immigrant boats organized by the Hagana, the underground defence organization of the Yishuv, capsized, or were seized by the British and their passengers deported. Even before the extent of the Holocaust became known (in the autumn of 1942), Ben-Gurion realized that unrestricted immigration of the Jewish refugees would become an imperative after the war.[9] Under these circumstances, insistence on a working-class elite and selective immigration became totally irrelevant.

Furthermore, with European Jews cut off, American Jews became the major potential supporters of Zionism, for its community now amounted to about 50 per cent of remaining Jews. Its support was needed both financially and to lobby the US administration to intervene with the mandatory government on behalf of the Yishuv. An appeal to this community required an altogether different approach. Up to the Second World War, the majority of American Jews had not been actively engaged in Zionist affairs. Since they had preferred America to Palestine as their destination during the big Jewish exodus from Eastern Europe at the turn of the century, it was more difficult for them to identify with Zionism as an aim. Consequently, a large part of this community was non-Zionist, or even anti-Zionist. They were anxious to identify with the United States politically, as well as culturally, for they wished to become fully-fledged citizens of their country of choice. Identification with Palestine as a homeland might be interpreted as disloyalty to the United States. Therefore, their support of the Jewish cause had been mainly material: financial aid to Jewish victims of persecution and towards the development of Palestine.[10]

When an energetic political mobilization of American Jews became necessary, emphasis on the working class as the carrier of socialism was likely to alienate most potential recruits. Having adopted the American value system, they were less likely to be socialist. It was clearly advantageous to put forward a version of Zionism which demoted socialism to secondary importance, while emphasizing refugees and a Jewish state to take them in. This strategy was indeed successful. American delegates to the Zionist Congress increased from 18 per cent in 1937 to 32.3 per cent in 1946. Labour could not expect to gain directly from the recruitment of American Jews, and it did not. It went down to 20.6 per cent of the seats in 1946, from 43.1 per cent in 1937, while the General Zionists, a liberal democratic party which garnered most of the American Jewish votes, went up from 23 per cent in 1937 to 28.3 per cent in 1946 (the balance was due to the re-entry of the Revisionists into the Zionist Organization and to the separate list of the Ha-shomer Ha-tsa'ir Kibbutz movement).[11] Though Labour did not retain its dominance in the Zionist Organization, it had at least become a respectable coalition partner for the liberal General Zionists, partly because socialism was being played down in its definition of Zionism. Indeed, a coalition was immediately formed when Ben-Gurion and Abba Hillel Silver, leader of American General Zionists, managed to oust President Haim Weizmann at the Twenty-second Congress by carrying a decision not to elect a president. They then shared power as chairmen of the Zionist Directorates in Jerusalem and New York respectively.[12]

According predominance to mass immigration was a gradual process, in which the previous components of Zionism were still being mentioned, but less frequently. In October 1941, Ben-Gurion already stressed the primary importance of mass immigration, yet described it as applied Zionism in contrast to the ultimate aim of social and national salvation. However, by 1942, Ben-Gurion was instrumental in making immigration the official definition of Zionism. He went on a prolonged information campaign among American Zionists in order to overcome their misgivings regarding the programme he had formulated. Even so, when advocating this programme at the Biltmore Hotel Conference, he still upheld the implementers of social salvation (the working class) as the mainstay of refugee transportation and absorption.[13] The resolutions adopted unanimously by American Zionists at the Conference comprised three major points. These were (in that order) the demand for unrestricted immigration, commissioning the Jewish Agency with handling all transport and absorption of refugee immigrants and the demand to set up a Jewish commonwealth in Palestine.[14]

The shift to immigration and a Jewish state depleted Zionism of egalitarian socialism. The principle of perfect justice was not jettisoned altogether, though egalitarian socialism was no longer its supreme expression. Absolute economic egalitarianism had never existed even in the Histadrut sector of the Yishuv. An official Histadrut publication of 1929 and a study of Histadrut urban wage policy in the pre-state period found considerable differentials between wages of skilled and unskilled labour, despite the declared principle of equal wages for all, with increments allowed only for dependents and for seniority on the job.[15] However, after 1948 any pretence to egalitarianism was abandoned in favour of equity socialism. In Israel, wage differentials increased nominally to a ratio of 3:1 between the top and bottom income groups. This ratio, low by Western standards, was artificially retained in order to tally with the principle of equity.[16]

Shortly after 1948, some already noted the contraction of Zionism into national redemption, narrowly defined as the State of Israel and its defence. It was criticized and lamented principally by those who had been the carriers of original Labour Zionism or its disseminators, namely Kibbutz members and educators. Here follow a few examples. In the early 1950s, it was noted regretfully that Zionism no longer incorporated pioneering and absolute social justice, that there had been a total change of values among young Israelis and in Israeli society in general, and that egalitarianism was being replaced by a capitalist economy.[17] To remedy this, it was necessary to reimbue pupils with pioneering values which had been lost.[18] By 1968, educational researchers already regarded the phenomenon as irreversible, noting that the only value taught at school was patriotism.[19]

Similarly, the second aspect of justice, namely that towards Palestinian Arabs, was retained, but subjected to national redemption to a greater extent than previously. The demand for unlimited Jewish immigration and a Jewish state accorded national redemption supremacy over absolute justice. The resolutions of the Biltmore programme show the 'ingathering of exiles' to be the target and the Jewish commonwealth (a vague term meaning anything from a measure of autonomy to an independent state) to be the means. This order of priorities was a logical outcome of events up to the establishment of Israel.

The common cause against Nazism and the dearth of potential immigrants during the Second World War ruled out any active opposition to the White Paper policy, but with the end of the war, when Holocaust survivors were kept in camps in Europe and the White Paper was not rescinded, an open rebellion broke out in Palestine. From early 1946 onward, the Yishuv organized a series of illegal immigrant boats, few of which managed to evade British naval capture. In response, the Hebrew Rebellion Movement carried out acts of sabotage against British installations, which grew in violence as British retaliatory measures became harsher. In May 1946, the Anglo-American Committee of Inquiry, initiated by Britain, recommended that 100,000 Jewish refugees be immediately admitted into Palestine. When the British refused to honour the recommendations of the Committee, an end of the Mandate and a Jewish state became the official aim: in December 1946, the Zionist Congress voted in favour of partition and the establishment of an independent Jewish state (the term commonwealth was no longer used since it would have implied continued dependence on Britain). Only the more militant and the more timid opposed the resolution, namely those who insisted that the Jewish state encompass all of Palestine and those who feared international and Arab reactions to such a demand. Ben-Gurion, who supported the resolution, countered both objections in his speech at the Congress: the express needs of the Holocaust survivors necessitated an independent homeland which would take them in, and the compromise of partition would ensure American support against Palestinian Arab objections and possible hostile actions.[20] In articles in the Labour weekly, Ben-Gurion and other authors reiterated this concept of the Jewish state as a tool for immigration.[21]

Primacy of the State

The order of priorities then changed, though, immigration becoming the tool for obtaining an independent state. Events and documents do not bear out the claim by Zartal that the Holocaust and illegal immigration had been used cynically from the start as a propaganda tool to arouse international sympathy for a Jewish state. The compassion felt for the Holocaust survivors was superficial and patronizing, of the 'I told you so' variety, probably because no outsider could as yet comprehend the horror experienced by the victims, nor the emotional damage sustained by the survivors. With hindsight it seems callous to have subjected the illegal immigrants to the hardships of the journey. Yet it would seem that the genuine wish to be a haven for refugees and to increase the Jewish population of Palestine, namely the ingathering of exiles, was the initial guiding principle of the illegal immigration operation, and was met by success at first, as Zartal herself admits. During August–December 1945, 1,036 refugees were brought to Palestine on eight boats without detection. However, all nine boats arriving during January–July 1946 were intercepted and their passengers interned in Atlit, in Palestine. When the Atlit camp was filled to capacity in August 1946, the incoming illegal immigrants were deported and interned in Cyprus.[22]

This is when ulterior motives may be imputed to the Yishuv leaders, because from then on, immigration as such became fairly pointless. The refugees were merely transported from one internment camp in Europe to another one in Cyprus, and at peril, at that, because the boats were hardly seaworthy. The refugee transports then became a tool; it was probably no coincidence that the *Exodus* arrived at the beginning of July 1947, just while the UN Commission of Inquiry was in Palestine, for the boat never tried to evade British detection. With the *Exodus* tragedy still fresh in mind (three refugees were killed and the remainder sent back to Germany), Ben-Gurion could appeal to the conscience of the Commission members when pleading for a Jewish state.[23]

When immigrants became a security asset during the 1948 War and after, priority clearly shifted from immigration to the state. Many young immigrants were immediately drafted to join the fighting; subsequently, immigrants were settled along the borders and in outlying areas in order to stake a claim to territorial proprietorship. Over 100,000 immigrants arrived during 1948. Newspapers and cautious Labour leaders suggested a selective immigration policy in order to ease the absorption of such numbers in a population totalling only 700,000 and an economy devastated by the war. However, Ben-Gurion was adamant, insisting that large numbers of immigrants were imperative to secure tiny Israel against the multitude of its Arab enemies.[24]

The establishment of Israel and, especially, the 1948 war, which turned the UN resolution and the Yishuv Proclamation of Independence into a political reality, put the final seal on the previous ideological shifts. The State and its security became the overriding consideration, while the other lofty ethical targets of the Messianic idea should and would be pursued only if they did not interfere with it. In tandem with the ideological change, Israeli self-perception was redefined, the Pioneer turning into the Tsabar. The changes were triggered by external events – the Jewish refugees, British denial of their entry into Palestine, the Palestinian Arab rejection of the UN Partition Plan and the invasion by Arab armies of the territory designated for the Palestinian Arabs and their attempt to conquer the rest of Palestine, in which initially they succeeded in part. However, the direction these changes took was largely guided by the original Zionist dilemma and the need to resolve it. The Proclamation of Independence and Israeli actions during and after the war bear witness to the self-defeating desire to satisfy the dictum of perfect justice without impairing the Jewish rightful claim to Palestine.

THE 1948 WAR – NATIONAL REDEMPTION VERSUS PERFECT JUSTICE

Although the Zionist Congress had itself proposed partition, and though the Yishuv had accepted the UN Partition Plan of 29 November 1947, which implied recognition of Palestinian Arab rights to the land, this step was presented as a temporary concession made under duress.[25] Consistent with this view, Ben-Gurion refused to delineate the borders of Israel in its Proclamation of Independence.[26] At the same time, the continuing claim to all of Palestine was contradicted by the assertion of Yishuv magnanimity in agreeing to part with some of its rightful possession.[27] However, the Yishuv/Israel could not possibly be both magnanimous, which implies volition guided by ethical considerations, and acting under duress, which implies expediency.

The alternating use of the two justifications for agreeing to partition and for subsequent Israeli government actions should not be viewed as cynical manipulations to excuse wrongdoing. Israeli leaders were indeed torn between the imperatives of absolute justice and national redemption. The dilemma resulted in equivocal acts, such as granting full social and political equality to all citizens (including the Arab minority) in the Proclamation of Independence, read on 14 May 1948, then granting immediate entry and citizenship to Jewish immigrants, and only to them, in the Law of Return passed on 5 July 1950. The ambivalent treatment and attitude towards Palestinian Arabs during the war provides further evidence for the impossible attempt to mete out justice to the party whose rights one denies. Even Dr. Morris, a harsh critic of Israeli actions at the time, conceded the absence of any clear policy to expel Arabs from Israeli territory.[28] In a later paper, he retracted on this point, claiming that he had been misled by the deliberate falsification of official Israeli documents, but this later assertion has been decisively refuted by Professor Karsh.[29] In some cases, fleeing Arabs were even asked to stay, or return. This would seem uncalled for in an existential war, when the entire enemy population may be regarded as belligerents, a common practice during the Second World War. Such acts must be largely attributed to the attempt to honour the principle of justice. That of national redemption, translated into security of the State in as large a part of Palestine as it was possible to achieve, was satisfied simultaneously and in contradiction to the former: the flight of Arabs was mostly welcomed and acts of expulsion were not censored.[30]

As the war wore on, and especially after it had been won, the State as national redemption won over all other aspects of Zionism. The principle of justice was seen to have been satisfied conclusively by the agreement to partition, absolving Israel of any further obligation towards its adversaries, both as regards its final extended territory[31] and as regards the Palestinian Arab refugees. The argument presented to the Palestine Reconciliation Commission reflected the two main reasons used in order to reconcile the principle of justice with that of national redemption. Under UN pressure, Israel agreed to readmit 100,000 Arab refugees.

However, it stressed that it did not do so because it felt any responsibility for the refugee status of Palestinians, but merely as a humanitarian gesture which was conditional on a peace treaty with the neighbouring Arab states.[32]

Tying the Palestinian refugee problem to peace with the Arab states rather than with the Palestinians proper shows clearly that Israel no longer regarded Palestinian Arabs as a party to the conflict which was to be settled. Critics have frequently accused the Israeli leadership of the time of fabricating the absence of a Palestinian national entity. It would seem that this assertion is guided, at least in part, by hindsight. By their actions and statements, Palestinian Arabs and the Arab states corroborated the argument already voiced in the 1930s that Palestinian Arabs were not a separate ethnic or political entity; therefore, no injustice had been done to them by depriving them of a state of their own. Firstly, the Arab Higher Committee, which claimed to be the representative body of Palestinian Arabs, let the Arab League negotiate with the UN on its behalf, thus implying that Palestinians were not an independent side in the conflict with the Jews.[33] Subsequently, six Arab armies invaded Palestine, but made no move to set up a Palestinian state in territories they conquered and retained: the short-lived Palestinian government in the Gaza Strip was dissolved at the end of 1948 and replaced by an Egyptian governorship, while Transjordan never even considered establishing a Palestinian state in the West Bank. Instead, it annexed the territory and became the Kingdom of Jordan (East and West Banks). Furthermore, the UN obviously drew the same conclusions from these Arab acts. Once the Arab Higher Committee had refused to meet UNSCOP, the UN no longer regarded the Palestinians as a party to the conflict: the Count Bernadotte Plan proposed a Greater Transjordan, ignoring the Palestinians completely, as did the Lausanne Conference of 1949, at which armistice agreements were drawn up between Israel and its Arab neighbours. The Palestinians were not a party to the negotiations.

The argument that there was no Palestinian people and, therefore, no rights had been violated by Jewish immigrants and later by Israel, was subsequently bolstered by Israeli academic studies publicized as information material. It was shown that under Moslem rule, Palestine had never been a separate political entity or a cultural centre; that in the nineteenth century, the sparse population of about 300,000 had been a motley group of settlers from all over the Middle East; that Palestinian identity developed only after 1948.[34]

Israeli insistence that it would only readmit Palestinian refugees on humanitarian grounds reflected the second main reason why justice had not been violated. Palestinian Arabs had begun attacks against Jews on the day following the UN resolution on partition. These attacks had then been supplanted by severe fighting with six regular Arab armies. Israel therefore asserted that the Arabs were the aggressor and Israel had merely been defending itself. The refugees were the outcome of the Palestinian refusal to agree to partition and of Arab aggression. They were not Israel's responsibility. Palestinians had fled because their leaders had done so first and had probably been encouraged by their own leaders and the Arab armies to do so as a temporary measure, as some Arab sources indicate.[35] Israel admitted that some expulsions had occurred, but these accounted for only 10,000–30,000 of the 726,000–800,000 Palestinian refugees[36] and were depicted as exceptions, unavoidable due to the exigencies of war. In some cases, Israeli commanders deliberately spread panic among the Arab population in order to induce them to flee. Once again this was not an official policy, though such actions were not condemned either. In fact, they were possibly helped along by Arab actions in at least one instance. New research by Palestinian scholars indicates that in the most notorious case, that of the Dir Yassin massacre, the ensuing panic was due to exaggerations of the casualty numbers spread by both Israeli and Arab authorities.[37] In the main, opportunities were exploited whenever available to encourage Arab departure, in line with the target of national redemption, defined as a Jewish state, while perfect justice precluded wanton expulsions of civilians on any large scale. National redemption was gaining precedence and justice was taking second place. Justice could be exercised only if it did not imperil the State.

Subsequently, the large influx into Israel of refugees from Moslem countries, which had become very hostile to their Jewish minorities, or had expelled them outright, was claimed to absolve Israel from any further accountability: Palestinian refugees and Israeli citizens who had fled Arab states constituted a *de facto* population exchange, which closed the entire issue, including that of compensation for property lost by the Palestinian refugees.[38]

THE TSABAR

The Upright Warrior

Ever since conscripts replaced mercenaries, the distinction between civilians and soldiers has become blurred. In war, the entire population of the adversary is regarded as the enemy, because any one of its members could be a concealed fighter in civilian guise. The process of stereotyping the entire adversary population as the enemy was particularly pertinent during the events leading up to the 1948 war and throughout it. During the clashes immediately following the UN partition resolution,

Palestinian Arab fighters were not a regular army easily distinguishable from non-combatant civilians. Furthermore, the war was existential for Jews. Initially, the Jewish forces were inferior in material and troops and faced a real danger of physical annihilation (with the massacres of Jews in Jaffa in 1921 and in Hebron in 1929 still vividly remembered). At the least, Jews saw their enterprise in jeopardy, which is no less traumatic for people who have made personal sacrifices in order to realize an ideal, as evidenced by the present plight of Gush Emunim, to be discussed below (see pp.152–61). In such a situation, everyone who is not for you is against you and is regarded as your enemy.

Stereotypes of Palestinian Arabs had developed early on, due to wishful thinking, the scarcity of close contacts, prejudice, and so on. They comprised the admiring image of the tolerant Moslem and romantic oriental, the derisive image of the primitive native, and the patronizingly compassionate one of the ignorant underdog to be liberated.[39] However, a clear distinction was made between Palestinian Arabs in general and those who actually carried out attacks against Jews. The latter were labelled bandits, that is outlaws, the exception to the rule. The war changed that, and all these stereotypes were combined into one. According to an analysis of Hebrew newspaper articles published during the 1948 war, all Arabs were perceived as primitive and cruel orientals in contrast to the enlightened ethical Western Israelis. No reference was made to individual Arabs as innocent bystanders; rather, a generalized image of the cruel enemy predominated.[40]

The enlightened Israeli was the other side of the coin, so to speak. His was an eminently just war. Firstly, the war was inevitable, imposed by the aggressor. Secondly, as a corollary to the argument that Palestinian Arabs were part of the Arab nation, Israelis were fighting against that entire multitudinous nation. Therefore, it was a war in which the few (Israelis) defended themselves against the many. This conception of the 1948 war (and of all subsequent ones up to the Lebanon war of 1982) was articulated by Ben-Gurion,[41] and is documented by the above-mentioned research on newspaper articles as well as by historians.[42] The image of 'the few against the many', frequently invoked, may actually have frightened many; yet, paradoxically, rather than creating an identity of the eternal victim, the projected Israeli self-image was that of the invincible hero who had overcome overwhelming odds. The hardened fighter became the essence of Israeli identity, to which all newcomers were expected to adapt. In letters of condolence to bereaved parents,[43] Ben-Gurion articulated what subsequently became normative in Israeli society. It was improper to mourn the fallen who, 'by their death have given us life'; their death was not in vain and the steadfastness of the bereaved also contributed to the struggle. The present public debate on the appropriateness of showing on television soldiers weeping at the graveside of their comrades indicates how persistent this norm has been. Moreover, until the Lebanon war, the public never openly questioned the need for, or the justice of, the wars waged against Arabs, nor the justification for the continuing human sacrifices.[44]

The IDF (Israel Defence Forces) replaced the Pioneer as the carrier and defender of the State, the symbol of national resurrection. The extraneous tasks which it fulfilled initially made it a natural successor to the Pioneer. In an address to senior officers in 1950, Ben-Gurion spelled out his vision of the IDF as the Israeli pioneers. The IDF was to serve as pioneers, educators, nation builders and reclaimers of the desert; general conscription was to serve as the crucible in which new immigrants were to be forged into a revived nation, cleansed of impurities accumulated in the diaspora.[45] In the first decade of the State, the IDF indeed carried out all of these tasks. Immigrant soldiers were taught Hebrew, women soldiers were assigned as teachers to outlying immigrant settlements, Nahal (a corps which combined combat duties with agricultural labour) set up agricultural outposts in the Negev and Arava deserts, IDF boarding schools trained technicians and the IDF established military industrial plants employing thousands. Some of these roles continue to this day, notably the military industry, technical boarding schools and young immigrant integration.

The IDF has also served as a venue of mobility, underscoring the democratic openness on which Israeli society prides itself and which was beginning to supplant socialism as the hallmark of Israeliness. Democracy, in the sense of representing the entire population, is inherent in the structure of the IDF. It is a relatively small standing army which reaches full strength only with the call-up of reserves. It is thus a citizens' army, despite an overrepresentation in its officer corps of some sectors of society (Kibbutz members, as already noted, and, more recently, young members of the national religious camp). Until quite recently, there had been general consensus that the IDF represented Israeli core values more fully than any other organization of Israeli society. It stands for defence of the fatherland, service to the State and excellence, the latter linked to the emerging definition of democracy to be discussed below (see pp. 57–61). Even at present, when its prestige has declined, service in the IDF still constitutes an entry ticket to society, being a condition of employment in many workplaces.

Despite all the above, militarism never became a constituent of Israeli identity, firstly because most adult men combine short stints of military service as reservists with long periods of civilian life and, secondly because the principle of perfect justice has been retained, though subsidiary to national redemption. War as such has never been exalted.

The wars which Israel fought were all defined as defensive wars and its armed forces designated defence forces. Peace with its neighbours has been underscored as its principal target, frustrated by the intransigence of its adversaries.[46] Many Israeli military actions which could have been and are now interpreted as provocations, or as clearly offensive operations, especially the 1956 Sinai war, did not raise undue doubts regarding their justification because, by their actions and statements, Arab leaders and states lent ample support to it: Israel faced continuous hostile infiltrations, violent border incidents, a refusal to recognize its existence and rabid statements of intent to obliterate it. All these are too well known to require a detailed account.

Furthermore, the Israeli warrior is also conceived to fight justly by maintaining purity of arms, the guiding principle which distinguishes the ethically motivated fighter from the savage warrior. Purity of arms means fighting in self-defence and only against belligerents, excluding innocent civilians.[47] In practice, the principle was violated on numerous occasions, notably during the retaliatory operations of 1949–56. When all Arabs are indiscriminately regarded as the enemy, purity of arms becomes meaningless. Yet, the latter was upheld too, probably on as many occasions as it was disregarded. Retaliatory operations were carried out in response to severe or numerous provocations. Infiltrations across the border began immediately after the 1948 war, some politically motivated, but most economically. However, even the latter caused considerable damage to property and often ended in violence. In all, Israel suffered 286 killed and 477 wounded between 1949 and 1956, as well as a continuous sense of insecurity. Initially, during 1949–50, it responded by shoot-to-kill and by punitive expulsions. These were followed, during 1951–53, by collective punishment of civilian targets, namely villages which had harboured infiltrators. After the raid on Qibiya in October 1953, retaliatory attacks were confined to military targets.[48] They ended with the Sinai Campaign of 1956, when their futility was recognized. Ben-Gurion realized that, even in collaboration with Britain and France, he could not refashion the Middle East and impose peace on unwilling neighbours.

The above pattern of retaliatory operations bears witness to the paradox inherent in the concept 'purity of arms'. Weapons are always lethal. Shoot-to-kill targets the actual infiltrator, but without first establishing whether any violence is intended (some infiltrators merely wished to collect belongings left behind, or to graze their flocks on land they still considered their own). Compunctions about killing innocent people, in contravention to purity of arms, put a stop to this policy within a short time. However, the need to retaliate persisted for 'security and immigration (in that order) have priority above all else'.[49] Initially, the collective punishment did not seem unethical, since all Arabs were the enemy. Evidence for this view is provided by one columnist who recollects his own attitude as a soldier at the time.[50] The immoral aspect of stereotyping Arabs in that way was realized only when it culminated in the Qibiya raid. There, houses were demolished without first ensuring that they had been vacated, resulting in 69 dead. This brought home the incompatibility of the stereotyped Arab enemy with purity of arms, the latter meaning an ethically immaculate IDF. At the government meeting held on 18 October 1953, three days after the raid, it was decided to clear the IDF of responsibility for the operation so that it might retain its pure image. Instead, vigilante new immigrant border settlers were blamed for the incident. The only cabinet minister who criticized the operation on moral grounds, quoting transgression against Jewish values, was Moshe Shapira of the religious Mizrahi Worker party.[51] His view seems subsequently to have been adopted and military targets became the sole objective of retaliation.

The Patriot vis-à-vis *Zionists and the Diaspora*

The fact that only one cabinet minister expressed ethical outrage at the operation on the grounds of Jewish values, is indicative of a further shift in Zionist ideology which was taking place at the time. The concept of Zionism, already reduced to political renaissance of the Jewish people, was undergoing a gradual depletion of content until it became a derogatory term in Israel. The process was triggered by the reformulation of relations between the Zionist Organization and the newly established State of Israel. Throughout the pre-state period, the Yishuv was dependent on the Zionist Organization, which represented Zionists among world Jewry. The Zionist Organization supplied the funds needed to build up a new society in an underdeveloped country. It also provided diplomatic and political aid, namely negotiations and lobbying with the British government and, later, with the United States government against hostile mandatory policies. When the State was established, Israel needed funds more than ever, in light of the costly 1948 war and the influx of masses of destitute refugees from Europe and Arab countries (Israel doubled its population between 1947 and 1950). Yet, as a newly sovereign state, it refused to submit to any external authority.

As a first step in shaking off dependency, Ben-Gurion, the Israeli premier, diverted the funds collected by and from non-Zionists directly to the Zionist Organization instead of the former practice of channelling them via the New York Executive. Since the non-Zionists were the richer and more powerful sector of American Jewry, this diminished the clout of American Zionists, as witnessed by the protests of the latter and the heated debate over this issue.[52] As a next step, attempts were made to divest the Jewish Agency of its control over the allocation of funds collected by the Zionist Organization from non-Zionists,[53] in contradiction to the mandate it had received in the Biltmore Programme, where no such distinction had been made. Once the Jewish Agency was restricted to the distribution of Zionist funds, it had little money to allocate and, therefore, little influence on Israeli affairs.

The right of an external body to determine the distribution of funds in Israel was not merely an abstract issue of sovereignty and prestige. At the time, the money served mainly for the absorption of immigrants, namely their housing, clothing and creation of workplaces for them by public works, setting up labour-intensive industries and collective agricultural settlements. Many of these immigrants lacked the economic skills to strike out on their own and depended on public aid for their initial survival. At the same time, they were mostly religious and *petit-bourgeois*, with no socialist leanings and therefore unlikely to vote for Labour. On the other hand, they were politically naive, coming mostly from non-democratic countries, and could easily be manipulated. Since Jewish immigrants are granted immediate citizenship in Israel, it was important that the Zionist Organization did not influence their voting behaviour, seeing that General Zionists were the largest single party in that body during 1946–51. Indeed the power distribution did not change significantly after the establishment of Israel because the government could allocate funds for immigrant settlement according to a party key, ensuring the electoral support of each group for the party which took care of it.[54] In light of this, Ben-Gurion, in an address to the Zionist General Council in May 1949, insisted on a division of authority between the State, to be in charge of Israeli citizens, and the Zionist Organization, to be in charge of world Jewry.[55]

Since no organization is likely to give up any sphere of its authority willingly, Ben-Gurion had to use strong arguments to back up his demand. He contended that if the Zionist Organization insisted on its prerogative of controlling the allocation of funds in Israel, it would also have to abide by the other article of the Biltmore Programme, which insisted on mass immigration. This could mean every Zionist having an obligation to emigrate to Israel. Interpreted this way, it left American Zionists in an awkward position. If they could emigrate to Israel, but did not, could they still claim to be Zionists? A negative answer was the logical conclusion drawn by some. The bulk of American Zionists argued differently. The aim of Zionism was not merely the establishment of Israel and support of it, but also the ethical–religious mission of the Jewish people to create the good society on earth, and this still needed to be accomplished. Dispersion of the Jewish people was conducive to this. Jews could not possibly have an effective moral influence on the world if they all lived in a small country on the fringe of Western civilization. To spread the ethical gospel, most Jews would do better to stay abroad and merely draw moral succour from the cultural centre in Israel. Moreover, Israel was too small to contain the entire Jewish people and could only serve as a cultural centre.[56] Other American Zionist leaders reiterated this view at the Conference of European Jews, held in Paris in September 1949.[57]

Henceforth, the ultimate aim of Zionism became the bone of contention. Ben-Gurion insisted that 'From now on the principal agent of its (Zionist) realization is the state.'[58] Zionism had acquired a new definition and had become synonymous with the State of Israel, requiring every Zionist to live there. American Zionists conceded that Israel was the pivot of Jewish destiny, but was only one of several Jewish centres, though unlike any other; it served to intensify the Jewishness of the Jewish people.[59] They did not object to emigration to Israel, but disputed the right of Israel to put pressure on American Zionists to do so. Instead, they coined the distinction between *galut* – involuntary exile – and *tfutsa* – voluntary life in the diaspora. Rose Halperin, President of Hadassa, stated that some Israeli leaders had recently started to identify a Zionist with the pioneering movement, so that Zionism was no longer 'the ingathering of exiles', but 'the ingathering of all the exiles'.[60] The conclusion was clear: as long as a Jew aided Israel by contributing money to it, and performed his part in a rather unspecified historical mission of the Jewish people, he was entitled to call himself a Zionist.

Israeli leaders thought otherwise. The less prominent Labour politicians were forthright, insisting that any Jew unwilling to come and live in Israel was no longer a Zionist, but, at best, a friend of Israel; that a good Zionist in America could not content himself with contributions and hope that pioneers would come from Morocco, Algiers and Iran; and that American Jews were perceived in Israel as sitting in the dock.[61] The top leadership was more cautious at first, unwilling to antagonize American Zionists unduly because of the need for their aid. Yet their change of attitude became perceptible. While at the Twenty-second Congress, in 1946, Ben-Gurion had still defined the Jewish state as the place where Jews could come, not where they were morally obliged to come, at the General Zionist Council in May 1949 he already said that 'Zionism is pointless nowadays without a certain measure of pioneering.'[62] This did not yet preclude Jews in the diaspora from being Zionists, if they engaged in 'pioneering'. Subsequently, Berl Locker, Ben-Gurion's successor on the Zionist Executive, was more outspoken. He maintained that there was no distinction between *galut* and *tfutsa*; Zionism was no longer philanthropy, but the duty of every adherent to pay for immigration as if he were a citizen of Israel. Put another way, 'A Zionist is not only one who emigrates to Israel. That is the highest level of Zionism. A Zionist is one who supports the efforts of the State of Israel unconditionally... But a Zionist is above all one who contributes... not only his money, but principally the thing dearest to him: his sons.'[63]

The manoeuvre intended to prevent the interference of the Zionist Organization in Israeli affairs turned into an additional accelerator in the ideological shift to national redemption, achieved by the establishment of the State of Israel. Diaspora Zionists contested this interpretation of Zionism and an impasse ensued. At an ideological seminar held on 17 May 1962 for members of the Zionist Executive and the Zionist Directorate, speakers argued with the Israeli definition, according to which only Israelis could be Zionists.[64] A large part of the debates at the Twenty-sixth Zionist Congress, held at the turn of 1964/1965, focused on the demand by Israeli delegates that all Zionists immigrate to Israel, while diaspora delegates argued that financial aid was a legitimate substitute. Goldmann agreed that the proportion of the Jewish people living in Israel should be doubled, from 15 per cent to 30 per cent. However, he by no means meant to encourage large-scale immigration to Israel from the United States, he merely wished to engage in diplomatic activity in order to liberate Soviet Jewry, so that they could emigrate to Israel.[65]

The refusal of diaspora Zionists to concede defeat in this contest over the definition of Zionism posed a challenge to the emergent Israeli identity. If Zionists could also live abroad, there was no moral justification for waging wars in order to establish and defend Israel. Israel had to be the ultimate aim of Zionism. In order to substantiate this claim, the incompatibility of Zionism with life in the diaspora was extended to everything associated with the diaspora. Negation of the diaspora had always been part of Labour ideology, but in earlier periods it had meant negation of a way of life and of attitudes to life; it had never been an attack on actually living abroad. Even if some Israeli youngsters had already concluded that Jews in the diaspora were inferior and undignified, as compared to themselves,[66] this had never before been voiced by the leadership.

A simplistic conclusion drawn by children now became a widespread one when it reinforced the new self-image developed in the wake of the war and when it received official sanction. Ben-Gurion advocated the study of archaeology as a substitute for more recent Jewish history, since the latter was concerned mainly with the diaspora. Jewish history had its importance 'but in the State of Israel we aspire to some other Israeli wisdom'.[67] On another occasion he wrote that 'It is difficult to reconcile the glorification of life in exile with the ideology which was given the name Zionism 70 years ago and which rejects exile.'[68] In speeches, letters, articles and books, Ben-Gurion restricted Jewish history to biblical times, especially to the period of complete sovereignty up to the destruction of the First Temple. He quoted extensively from the Bible and hardly from the Mishna and Talmud, which smacked of diaspora.[69] The secular schooling system (Israeli state-funded schools are divided into secular and religious ones) conformed to this line of thought in its selection of historical and literary material. The result soon became evident.

Israeli-born authors were noted for expressing disdain for diaspora Jews and a feeling of their own superiority. The indifference of Israeli-born youngsters to diaspora Jewry was pointed out, as well as their rejection of the past because it connoted life in exile. A paper analysing the recorded conversations of kibbutz-born soldiers who fought in the 1967 war came to similar conclusions: all expressed negative feelings towards the diaspora.[70] This attitude was carried to its logical conclusion by the Canaanites, who declared themselves part of the indigenous Middle Eastern people of Canaan and ridiculed diaspora Jews. The Canaanite identity of Israeli youngsters was pointed out as sufficiently widespread to undermine absorption of immigrants in Israel. Immigrants were regarded as diaspora Jews, and therefore inferior outsiders not to be accepted easily into Israeli society.[71]

The final step in this process was the derogation of the term Zionism. If diaspora Jews refused to accept the synonymity of Zionism and Israel, then Zionism had become a term depicting Jews living in the diaspora and extending aid to Israel. Consequently, Jews in Israel could not be Zionists by definition, as even Zur, the Chairman of the Zionist Executive, admitted.[72] Labour organs and publications affiliated with Labour started dissipating this view among the Israeli public by a gradual purge of the term 'Zionism'. *Ba-ma'ale*, the organ of the Working Youth movement affiliated to Labour, serves as a pertinent early example of this practice, because of its didactic nature. In 1949, an article discussing the Jewish National Fund, an institution of the Zionist Organization, did not once mention the word Zionism; when discussing the transfer of the remains of Herzl, the founder of Zionism, to Israel, a two-page article mentioned the word Zionism just once, as did a manifesto of the Working Youth Centre, commemorating Tel Hai; in the syllabus of the movement, Zionism was not mentioned at all.[73] This contrasts sharply with articles published earlier in the same periodical. Then, the Working Youth movement had been described as teaching its members Zionism, socialism and a life of fulfilment (in that order); the literature for instructors had included material on Zionist writers.[74] By 1952, the effect of this practice was already noticeable in kibbutz publications. One writer commented that the so-called Zionism of diaspora youth movements aroused no response in Israeli youngsters, being imbued with the spirit of the diaspora, a wholly negative attribute; educational problems were discussed without a single mention of the term Zionism. Articles whose subject matter would lead one to expect some use of the term 'Zionism' never mentioned it. When describing the heroic period of the first waves of immigration to Palestine, Zionism was replaced by immigration and social revolution as the ideals then sought, by national and social dictates, or by the fatherland and pioneering. Moreover, a booklet published by the Zionist Organization itself did not mention Zionism either. A research on values taught to Israeli children did not list Zionism as one of them.[75]

Avoiding the use of the term Zionism as applicable to Israelis culminated in its derogation. If it applied only to diaspora Jews, and the diaspora was viewed as a distasteful, even despicable, state of existence for Jews, then Zionism had to become a derogatory term, which it did. Zionism was held in low esteem in Israel. This applied equally to the term Zionism, to the Zionist Organization and to persons calling themselves Zionists. Authors remarked that 'The word "Zionist", a word which aroused associations of noble-mindedness, has become a derogatory term in many circles in Israel', or that 'Zionism, the ideology of transition (from the diaspora to Israel) has been put into quotation marks'. In a humorous dictionary of spoken Hebrew, edited by D. Ben Amotz and N. Ben Yehuda, Zionism was defined as (1) nonsense, bombastic or meaningless sayings, admonitions; (2) a synonym for rhetoric, bringing up ideals in a debate, use of empty phraseology. According to another author, after the establishment of Israel, Zionism entered a long period of stagnation, wrapping itself in a layer of empty rhetoric. Zionist talk gradually stopped and Zionist teaching at schools degenerated until it became a deterrent scarecrow.[76]

The Native-Born

Disdain of Zionism was logically extended even to Jewishness, the ethnic identity of diaspora Jews. This produced a rupture between Israeliness and Jewishness, a peculiar phenomenon for people who consider themselves the founders of the Jewish state for the Jewish people. A study conducted in 1964/65 questioned Israeli youngsters on the relative importance they attached to Jewishness versus Israeliness in their lives. Only 68 per cent regarded being Jewish as important, as against 90 per cent who regarded being Israeli as important. Their parents did not make a similar distinction, regarding both as equally focal.[77] Another study of Israeli university students led to similar results. In 1966, only 56 per cent felt Jewish identity to be central to their lives, while 90 per cent felt thus about Israeli identity. When the same sample was interviewed once more in 1969, percentages had changed to 66 per cent and 96 per cent respectively.[78] By the 1960s, American Jewish intellectuals also became aware of the growing detachment of Israeli from Jewish identity.[79]

This begs the question of what people understood by Israeliness, or, put another way, how they defined themselves as Israelis. Numerous studies have reached similar conclusions on this subject,[80] so that a brief summary will suffice. The Israeli was the Tsabar, the native-born, courageous, physically strong and aggressive individual, informal, self-assured, the upright warrior who loved his/her country patriotically and was willing to defend it because it was his/hers by birthright, rather than because of having historical–religious claims on it as a Jew.

IMPLICATIONS OF TSABAR IDENTITY

Israeli identity thus defined has several implications. Firstly, regarding Israel as a birthright and the consequent aggressiveness and self-assurance of the Tsabar indicate the absence of any need to justify the Israeli presence in Israel. The agreement to partition in 1947 was seen as justice done, as having satisfied the principle of perfect justice regarding the Palestinian Arabs. Israelis could now feel legitimate proprietorship over their part of the land, bounded by the armistice lines of 1949. They had been fighting in self-defence and as morally as possible, therefore legitimately.

Secondly, when attachment to the physical country in its post-1948 boundaries supplanted the devotion to the land of one's forefathers, the link with Zionism and Jewishness was broken, as noted earlier. The result was a growing detachment from the interpretation given to the Messianic idea by Labour Zionism. As the Tsabar saw it, national redemption meant self-determination as understood by the international community, that is, obtaining a sovereign state. That had been achieved by the establishment of the State of Israel. By taking in all Jews wishing to come and granting them immediate citizenship, Israel was repaying any debt still due to Zionism. That is why immigration has remained a goal of primary importance in Israel, irrespective of subsequent resentment of the newcomers by veteran Israelis as competitors in the workplace and as recipients of other scarce resources. Perfect justice was acknowledged to be a utopian concept. Now that Israel was a state like any other, it needed to do no better than emulate the enlightened West and be a welfare democracy. Since Arab countries surrounding Israel were not, democracy could distinguish Israel from its neighbours and serve as a core constituent of its identity.

Thirdly, the most radical transformation occurred to individual salvation, the first component of Labour Zionism to have been de-emphasized.

In line with the detachment from Judaism and Jewishness, and with the turning to enlightened Western values, salvation was translated into self-realization, understood to be careerism. This was not a completely new phenomenon. In 1937, a study conducted of the urban population in the Yishuv compared the career choices of young men with those of their fathers. It showed a clear trend of the young to take up higher-income occupations in preference to occupations serving the community.[81] After 1948 however, individual advancement and material rewards became widespread and openly admitted goals. Evidence is provided by the numerous industrial actions in the public sector, comprising clerical and administrative occupations, and by professional groups, all aimed at better pay and higher status.[82] Such an open admission of non-egalitarian aims occurred only after the goal of truncated Zionism was perceived to have been achieved. Once an Israeli had served in the army and had defended his State, he had done his duty and could go on with his own life.

Ben-Gurion, who was very astute, soon realized the possible repercussions of the change in Israeli identity which he had been so instrumental in producing. Original Labour Zionism had aimed at fashioning a new Jewish person in a new Jewish society, both shedding the distortions created by life in exile. This happened indeed after 1948, though not quite in the direction envisioned. When Ben-Gurion unexpectedly stepped down from his public office in 1953 and retired to Sde Boker in the Negev, second thoughts about the undesired effects of the Zionist endeavour may have played a part in his decision – he never fully explained his temporary retirement. In 1954, he appealed to Moshav members and secondary school pupils to abandon careerism and to revert to pioneering and to helping new immigrants. He also appealed to school teachers to imbue their pupils with the values of settlement and defence rather than self-realization. He even tried to change the Israeli electoral system so that a stronger Labour camp could resuscitate the spirit of service to the community which was giving way to individualism.[83] All these attempts at turning back the clock failed, except for the initiative of some 200 second-generation Moshav members to volunteer as instructors in new immigrant Moshavim.

Furthermore, realizing that democracy had replaced other Zionist interpretations of justice, Ben-Gurion attempted to give democracy an Israeli content in order to distinguish Israel from the West. The concept of the 'chosen people' in the sense of 'a light upon the nations' (rather than a people chosen to suffer for its sins) was to set Israel off. Interpreting the 'light upon the nations' as scientific and artistic excellence and innovation was a secularized Jewish core value dissociated from the diaspora and in line with the self-realization inherent in the concept of democracy. If individual achievement had replaced salvation in Israel, then this must be intellectual rather than material. Only then could Israel revive its ancient greatness.[84] The cultural Zionism of Ahad Haam and the Declaration of Independence had already foreshadowed this idea: Jews had once before enriched the world with the ethics of the Bible when living in their native land and they would do so again in Israel. A similar intellectual greatness would be their hallmark and make Israel unique among democracies.

Some of the self-assurance and brashness of the Tsabar may possibly derive from a simplistic understanding of the 'chosen people' concept. For example, Israelis boasted of their invincible army, playing down any of its fiascoes; they were also inordinately proud of their excellent and competitive agricultural products, disregarding the resultant depletion of their water resources. The upright warrior image corresponded to the moral aspect of the 'chosen people' idea, as did Israeli insistence on the rectitude of its political system. That is one reason why the corruption scandals, which came to light in the 1970s, created such public uproar and were one of the factors causing Labour to lose the 1977 elections.

INCONSISTENCIES IN TSABAR IDENTITY

There was an element of bravado and self-defensiveness in Israeli identity defined in this way, for the latter again comprised mutually exclusive elements. Firstly, the chosen people had been the entire Jewish people chosen by God to fulfil a religious-ethical mission. The secularized version, on the other hand, applied to Israelis alone, exacerbating their alienation from the rest of Jewry. Furthermore, no matter how upright the warrior, he was a warrior all the same, hardly an ethical model for the world. Both these points have already been discussed. Secondly, the collective of 'chosen people', which was obviously Jewish, excluded Arab Israelis and this clashed with the democratic values included in Tsabar identity. Thirdly, the Tsabar was the native-born Israeli, excluding new immigrants and, particularly, adult ones from Moslem countries who were unable to emulate the 'virtues' of the Tsabar.

The Arab Minority

The clash between democracy and the exclusion of Arab Israelis from Israeli identity is encoded in the Declaration of Independence, which often serves in lieu of the constitution never written in Israel. In it, Israel declared itself a Jewish state, yet undertook to 'uphold the full social and political equality of all its citizens, without distinction of race, creed or sex'. In line with its Jewish, that is, ethnic character, the equality of all citizens was almost immediately violated by passing the Law of Return, which grants preferential rights to Jewish immigrants: automatic entry and immediate citizenship. Worse still, Israel also curtailed the rights of its Arab minority when it imposed military rule on the Arabs living in border areas, restricting their free movement and evicting some from their border villages. Restrictions were eased in 1957 and lifted in 1966, after prolonged public pressure and parliamentary debate. The Law of Return is still in force.

It may seem strange that it took almost ten years, from 1948 until 1957 and beyond, for Israelis to perceive this contradiction in their avowed self-definition and act in order to resolve it. The continuing hostilities with its Arab neighbours were used as extenuating circumstances. The military rule was seen as a precaution serving to prevent any possible hostile actions by a population likely to harbour persons in sympathy with Israel's enemies. This was a poor excuse because Israeli Arabs did not engage in any subversive acts, except for isolated cases. It would therefore seem that the stereotyping of all Arabs as the enemy, rather than facts on the ground, guided the reluctance to lift the military rule. The stereotyping which took place during the 1948 war, as mentioned above, was probably a major reason for the prolonged 'blindness' of Israelis to the incompatibility of their democratic self-image and the curtailment of civic rights of the Arab minority.

The uncritical acceptance of minority discrimination was also facilitated by the nature of democracy as conceived in Israel. Democracy is a generic term, interpreted by each society in line with its own value system. In Israel, democracy was seen as the rule by the majority elected by democratic procedures. The rights of minorities and of individuals were subordinated to that of the majority. Israeli law reflects this preference for the rights of the State, which represents the majority, as do rulings of the High Court of Justice. During the first 25 years of its existence, there were only two exceptional cases in 1948/49 in which the High Court ruled in favour of Israeli Arabs because their legal rights had been violated during interrogation. Altogether, the judiciary preferred the good of the community, as it saw it.[85] Viewed in this light, inequality of the minority did not clash too strongly with the value of democracy. (Since the 1970s, the conception of democracy has been changing gradually, as will be discussed in later chapters.)

Israelis finally became aware of the incompatibility between democracy and the restrictions put on civic rights of part of the population. However, they remained ignorant of a more basic paradox in their self-image, namely that between their growing rejection of Jewishness and their insistence on the ethnic nature of their State, which is religiously defined.

Judaism is a mono-ethnic faith. Consequently, religion and ethnicity could not be fully separated in Israel. The Law of Return illustrates this point. Initially, in order to qualify for immigration and automatic citizenship, an immigrant merely had to declare him/herself to be a *bona fide* Jew and not to be of any other religion. Subsequently, the legal definition of a Jew for purposes of citizenship became strictly religious, defined by the orthodox version of Jewish oral law. Israel is ethnic in the cultural–symbolic sense as well. Almost all its official holidays are religiously or historically Jewish, as are its official symbols. Being Moslem or Christian, Israeli Arabs cannot identify with these. The 'blindness' to this inherent exclusion of Israeli Arabs from Israeli society, because of their non-Jewishness and despite the Israeli scorn of Jewishness, is difficult to explain. There was no public debate on the subject at the time, so that no arguments for or against the Jewish character of Israel can be used to understand how Israelis coped with this paradox. One can only conjecture that they simply did not conceive this as a paradox at the time, the way it has been in the 1990s. One possible reason is the fact that, at the time, the rejection of Jewishness was not explicitly formulated, as was the rejection of the diaspora and of Zionism, it simply followed from these – something that Israelis felt but did not express in so many words. The Canaanites were the only group which articulated the non-Jewish character of Israeli society as they wished it to be. They remained a fringe group with a tiny following. Their ideas became widely accepted due to their influence on intellectuals,[86] although they were not expressly stated, a possible reason why the non-Jewishness of the Tsabar was not challenged by any significant sector of society at the time, did not become a subject of public debate and was simply taken for granted.

New Immigrants

The attitude of Israeli institutions and of the public towards new immigrants revealed an even more blatant inconsistency in Tsabar identity than did that towards the Arab minority. Jewish refugees were let into the country unconditionally, including the old and the sick. Moreover, ingathering of the exiles was such an express target that emissaries were sent to Jewish communities not under threat of imminent persecution in order to encourage them to emigrate to Israel. The ingathering of exiles is as much a constituent of national redemption as is the establishment of a Jewish state in the Land of Israel. This goal was pursued vigorously by the Tsabar, underlining the ethnic loyalty from which, paradoxically, he distanced himself. As a result, though welcomed and even enticed to come, once in Israel the new immigrants were treated with disdain as outsiders unless and until they had assimilated beyond recognition. They represented the diaspora and Jewishness, both of which were largely excluded from Israeliness.

This applied as much to immigrants from Europe as it did to those from Moslem countries. The former, Holocaust survivors, were regarded as the typical diaspora Jews who, unlike Israelis, had not stood up to their adversaries and had died 'like sheep led to their slaughter', a phrase frequently used with derision. In one episode of the TV series *Tkuma*, screened for the jubilee of Israel (in 1997/98), former Holocaust survivors bore vivid witness to the ambivalent reception they had got upon their arrival: great efforts at bringing them to Israel, followed by an exhibition of Israeli superiority, little empathy with the ordeal they had experienced and expectations that they adapt and become Tsabars almost overnight. European immigrants could do so with relative speed because of their cultural similarity to veteran Israelis, because they were mostly young and parentless (few older people had survived the Holocaust) and were, therefore, more amenable to adaptation. Furthermore, they had the basic economic skills necessary to function in the Israeli economy and, eventually, to compete successfully in the marketplace. In the longer run, their absorption did not create a social problem, which is probably why no social research was conducted on them at the time. Evidence regarding their absorption must necessarily be impressionistic, relying on subjective accounts. Because they did not become an apparent problem, Israelis could remain unaware of the inconsistency in Tsabar identity created by a simultaneous embrace and recoil from Holocaust survivors. The latter played their part in this self-deception by trying, and mostly succeeding, in becoming, at least outwardly, indistinguishable from the Tsabar. However, recent memoirs, as well as books and interviews of them and their children have revealed their consternation at having been welcomed in Israel as fellow Jews, yet at the same time at having been scorned because they were Jews and not Israelis. Some of this ambivalence continues to this day, as witnessed by the extraordinary efforts of Israel to bring Jews from the Soviet Union and from Ethiopia to Israel and the stigma attached to these immigrants after their arrival.

The integration of European immigrants did not produce a social problem, but that of immigrants from Moslem countries did. Indeed, the problem haunts Israeli society to this day. Many immigrants from Moslem countries came from pre-modern or modernizing societies. They lacked the formal education and skills required to function efficiently in the Israeli economy. To make matters worse, many were settled in outlying areas, far from the veteran population, leaving them largely to their own poor devices. Cultural differences with Israeli society were also enormous: they were practising Jews and had adopted norms from the

Moslem milieu in which they had lived for centuries. Besides, whole families arrived, parental influence persisted and the young were exposed to clashing norms, which made adaptation more difficult. Studies of 'Oriental' immigrants, as they have been labelled, were numerous at the time, many of them reflecting the patronizing Israeli view. One collection of studies[87] is particularly revealing. Absorption was considered problematic because the authors claimed that the immigrants were primitive, lacked psychic maturity, were ritualistic and apathetic, as well as overly traditional. One researcher suggested that immigrant children be placed with foster parents so as to remove them from the harmful influence of their families. This set the tone for later studies.[88]

The immigrants from Moslem countries perceived the condescending and scornful attitude of the Tsabar as ethnic discrimination, which it soon became. The ethnic stratification of Israeli society is well documented. Moreover, the stereotype of primitive, uneducated and bigoted people, lacking any modern economic and political skills, was applied to all immigrants from Moslem countries, including those with a Western education who had not come from pre-modern societies (for example from urban centres in Iraq or Egypt). Stereotyping was widespread, exercised by the veteran public as well as by the establishment. For example, all official statistics and most researches classified (and most still do) the Jewish population of Israel into just two groups of European–American and of Asian–African origin respectively. No distinctions are made between individual countries of origin. In 1959, Moroccan young men, who had completed military service yet were unemployed and felt underprivileged and scorned, rioted in Wadi Salib, a slum district in Haifa. In response, a few veteran Israelis originating from Moslem countries were coopted into the government. The latter were neither Moroccan, nor new immigrants, and did not represent the interests of the rioters in any way, yet this gesture of cooptation was expected to calm down the rising frustration and feelings of discrimination which were directed against the Ashkenazi (European-origin) Labour establishment. One eventual consequence of the disregard for the grievances of orientals was a gradual shift of their electoral support to the Herut opposition party (successor to the Revisionists), which undoubtedly helped the Likud party (the product of several mergers, in which Herut was the nucleus and retained the top leadership) to power in 1977.

Since then, second-generation Orientals, many of Moroccan origin, have entered the political elite and, subsequently, other elites in increasing numbers; Shas, a religious party headed exclusively by Orientals, has had growing electoral success. The resentment continues, though, now voiced more poignantly by the intellectuals among Orientals, as well as by Shas.

The rancour is no longer ignored, but is still understood by both sides to have been caused by ethnic discrimination practised by the Labour establishment at the time. In 1977, Ehud Barak, the Labour leader, apologized officially to Orientals for the sins committed by Labour in the past. Even now, neither side comprehends the implications for Israeli identity of the embrace–recoil attitude to Jewish newcomers. Stigmatization of new immigrants continues in Israel. But due to a novel religious interpretation of the Messianic message by part of the Israeli public, the latter now denigrate new immigrants for not being Jewish enough, in contrast to the past when they were regarded as being too Jewish. The secular part of the public, which has no reservations on that score, still retains the old attitude and expects the newcomers to become instant Israelis. The subject will be taken up in a later chapter.

A FIRM IDENTITY NEVERTHELESS

The above inconsistencies notwithstanding, Israelis did not question their self-image. This may seem surprising in light of the fact that some of the ambivalence was blatant. The severe restrictions imposed on the Arab minority were pointed out to be incompatible with civic rights in a democracy, and this was done compellingly enough to bring about the lifting of most limitations. Similarly, the riots and protests of some Moroccan immigrants were loud and clear. They should have sensitized Israelis to the fact that they were undoing by discrimination the ingathering of exiles, of which they prided themselves. Yet neither exhortation penetrated the armour of Tsabar identity. Instead, the lifting of restrictions on the Arab minority was seen as yet another magnanimous act by the upright warrior towards the enemy, rather than the restoration of civic rights due to all Israeli citizens. The protest of immigrants from Moslem countries was seen as a distortion of reality: Israelis simply saw the immigrants for what they were; Israel was the Messianic message come true; Israelis were the superior beings prophesied in that message and newcomers were inferior by definition until moulded in the new image. If Israeli efforts at re-education and absorption failed, this was at least as much the fault of the immigrants as of the absorbing society: they lacked motivation, they clung to their traditional norms with unreasonable tenacity and, at best, they were just impatient.[89]

So far, I have described the mechanisms by which Israelis protected their identity conception from disruptive forces. It now remains to understand why they did so in the first place. For surely, self-images change with circumstances, as even the Israeli case demonstrates: the Tsabar was nothing like the Pioneer. One may postulate from this example that a dramatic change in circumstances is a necessary condition for a redefinition of identity. In Israel, changes in the territorial boundaries seem to play a key role in this process because the boundaries of Israel are so intricately linked to the need of justifying the Israeli presence in the ancient homeland. Once an identity has been articulated and adopted which justifies Israeli presence in a given section of the land, Israelis are likely to hold fast to it and ignore those few who point out the contradictions inherent in the ongoing identity formulation which is, in all its transformations, based on the Messianic message.

Herut

The feebleness of the opposition during the period discussed exemplifies this point. The challenge to Tsabar identity came principally from two directions, namely the extreme right and the extreme left of the political spectrum. Herut, founded in 1948, was a radical offspring of the Revisionist party. It rejected the partition of Palestine agreed upon in 1947, as stated in its first platform paper, 'The Herut Movement'. Herut accused Labour of betraying the Jewish heritage, but it justified its stand on étatiste grounds only. As Menahem Begin, the leader of Herut, stated in 1966, 'One cannot play with the right on a land: either you have it or not...one cannot divide the land either. Any partition is temporary.'[90] Neither he, nor his predecessor Jabotinsky addressed the issue of perfect justice which had induced Labour to agree to partition, because they saw themselves as followers of Herzl's political Zionism. In Revisionism, as in Herut ideology, the Messianic idea was no more than an addendum to nationalism which focuses on ethnic self-determination in a sovereign territory.

As already discussed in the previous chapter, Revisionism failed to garner any substantial support because it could not match the Labour Zionist interpretation of Messianism which provided ethical as well as historical justification for the return to the homeland. Likud did not improve on that ideologically or electorally: as long as it ran its own list, it never won more than 13.8 per cent of the votes. Labour justification for partition and for the right to the State of Israel were somewhat self-contradictory, but they were more convincing than the statement that might is right. Tsabar identity, articulated by the Labour leadership, was wholly satisfactory because it justified the situation on the ground, obeying both imperatives of national redemption and perfect justice to the extent that these could be accomplished at the time. The delegitimation of the Revisionists, which spilled over to the Herut party, was another reason why Herut could not unseat Labour and redefine

Israeli identity. However, Labour was able to delegitimize a challenge to its interpretation of the Messianic message just because it enjoyed such consensus regarding its own legitimacy.

The Peace Council

The second challenge came from the opposite end of the political spectrum, namely the extreme left. The Israeli Peace Council was established in 1950 as a branch of the World Peace Council. The latter campaigned against nuclear armament and was supported by the USSR and by European communist parties. The Israeli branch consisted primarily of members of Maki, the communist party, and Mapam, a party left of Labour which favoured bi-nationalism and an alliance with the USSR rather than with the West. As its name indicates, the Israeli Peace Council focused on peace with Israel's Arab neighbours and on an accommodation with Palestinian Arabs. It disintegrated in mid-1955, having failed to have any impact on Israeli public opinion or policies. Unlike Brit Shalom of the Yishuv period, it did not even attempt to base its programme on Zionism. Instead, it used Marxism as its guideline and thus put itself outside what was considered a legitimate public debate. Its support of the USSR, despite the Soviet anti-Zionist and anti-Israel stand, made the Council a pariah similar to Herut. Ben-Gurion frequently proclaimed that he was willing to enter a coalition with any party save Herut or Maki.

The other parties did not challenge Labour hegemony at all and willingly formed coalitions with Labour when invited to do so. All Israeli governments were coalitions with Labour. The latter never had an absolute majority, but was consistently the single largest party and was entrusted with forming the government. The other parties merely fought for the specific interests of their respective constituencies. They accepted the legitimacy of Labour, that is, its merit to govern, as did the majority of the public. Since Tsabar identity was a product of Labour words and deeds, any assault on it was doomed to failure, sanctioned as it was by the leadership which had provided Israelis with a sovereign state, as promised in the Bible, and within borders in which they felt justified to live. As in the Yishuv period, Labour was seen as the only party which articulated and implemented the core values of Messianism, even though in a version far removed from the original, but nevertheless providing Israelis with an identity which justified the *status quo* ethically. Short of a change in the latter, any challenge to the basic premises on which Israeli identity rested was regarded as impermissible and unworthy of public debate.

NOTES

1. The Zionist Executive resolved to propose partition to the mandatory government in 1946. Its chairman Ben-Gurion reluctantly condoned the decision by abstaining from the vote and endorsed it only subsequently because it was expedient. See M. Bar-Zohar, *Ben-Gurion*, Vol.1 (Tel-Aviv: Am Oved, 1978), pp.550–3.
2. Kibbutz and Moshav (cooperative settlement) members constituted 7.2% of the Yishuv population in 1936, the year in which they reached the highest proportion. Computed from H. Darin-Drabkin, *The Other Society – Kibbutz in the Test of Economy and Society* (Tel-Aviv: Hakibuts Ha-artsi, 1961), p.81 and H. Viteles, *A History of the Cooperative Movement in Israel* (London: Vallentine Mitchell, 1968), pp.247–50.
3. *Stenographisches Protokoll der Verhandlungen des XVII. Zionisten-Kongresses und der zweiten Tagung des Council der Jewish Agency für Palaestina, Basel, 30. Juni bis 17 Julin 1931 (London: Zentralbüro der zionistischen Organisation, 1931)* p.153.
4. B. Vost, 'The Problem of Immigration at the 19th Congress', *Ha-po'el Ha-tsa'ir*, 11 October 1935.
5. Y. Lofban, 'Our Fourth Conference', *Ha-po'el Ha-tsa'ir*, 27 May 1938.
6. D. Ben-Gurion, 'Test and Implementation, 1942', *In Battle*, Vol. 4 (Tel-Aviv: Am Oved, 1957), pp.30–42; 'Mission and Way, 1942', *In Battle*, Vol. 4, pp.57–102.
7. D. Ben-Gurion, 'Towards a Decision, 1944', *In Battle*, Vol.5, pp. 178–83.
8. Y. Talmon-Garber, 'The Position of the Communal Settlement Movement in Israeli Society', in S. Shor (ed.), *The Kibbutz and Israeli Society* (Tel-Aviv: Ha-Kibuts Ha-artsi, 1972), pp.49–52; B. Kimmerling, 'Status Conceptions of Security Roles in Israel', *Medina U-mimshal*, Vol.1, No.1, 1971/72, pp.141–9.
9. For example Ben-Gurion at a press conference on 26 February 1941, quoted in *In Battle*, Vol. 3, pp.50–51.
10. Y. Shapiro, *Leadership of the American Zionist Organization* (Urbana: University of Illinois Press, 1971), pp.251–7; *The 22nd Zionist Congress, Basle 9–24 December 1946* (Jerusalem: Executive of the Zionist Organization, 1946), pp.45–54.
11. Computed from *20th Zionist Congress & 5th Session of the Jewish Agency Council, Zurich 3–21 August 1937* (Jerusalem: Zionist Federation and Jewish Agency, n.d.), pp.XIV–XVIII, and *22nd Zionist Congress*, pp.XXI–XXII.
12. J. Gorni, *Collaboration and Strife: Haim Weizmann and the Palestine Workers' Movement* (Tel-Aviv: Ha-kibuts Ha-menhad, 1976), pp. 161, 196.
13. D. Ben-Gurion, 'Targets of Zionism at this Hour, 1941', *In Battle*, Vol.4, pp.9–29; 'Test and Implementation, 1942', ibid., pp.30–42.
14. M. Bar-Zohar, *Ben-Gurion*, Vol. 1 (Tel-Aviv: Am Oved), pp.440–3.
15. *Summaries*, No. 1 (Histadrut Statistics and Information Department, 1929), p.23; Z. Sussmann, *Differentials and Egalitarianism in the Histadrut* (Ramat Gan: Massada, 1974), pp.9–12.
16. See R. Klinov and N. Halevi, *The Economic Development of Israel* (Jerusalem: Academic Press, 1968), pp.39–100.
17. The following articles in *Niv Ha-kvutsa*: A. Aderet, 'Trends and Struggles Within Israeli Youth', Vol. 4, No. 4, 1955, pp.714–29; A. Barzel, 'Ways of the Youth Movement in Israel', Vol. 1, No. 4, 1952, pp.91–4; K. Luz, 'The Union and its Task', Vol. 1, No. 1, 1952, pp.20–6; Z. Shefer, 'Values and Ways', Vol. 1, No 3, 1952, pp.9–15.
18. Ben-Yehuda, B., *Foundations and Ways* (Jerusalem: Jewish National Fund, 1952), pp.8–27.
19. A. Adar and H. Adler, 'Teaching Values at Immigrant Children Schools', in S.N. Eisenstadt et al. (eds.), *Education and Society in Israel* (Jerusalem: Akademon, 1968), pp.57–86.
20. *22nd Zionist Congress*, pp.331–8.
21. For example D. Ben-Gurion, 'For Establishment of the State', *Ha-po'el Ha-tsa'ir*, 16 December 1947; Y. Lofban, 'Hard Times', *Ha-po'el Ha-tsa'ir*, 5 March 1947.
22. E. Zartal, 'Anonymous Souls: The Illegal Immigrants and the Aliya Bet Institution in the Struggle to Set up the State and After', *Ha-tsionut*, Vol. 14, 1989, pp.107–26.
23. D. Ben-Gurion, 'Testimony Before UN Commission, 4.7.47', *In Battle*, Vol. 5, p.208.
24. D. Ben-Gurion, 'Address at Mapai Council, 12.1.49', *When Israel Fought* (Tel-Aviv: Am Oved, 1957).
25. D. Ben-Gurion, 'Address at Reception for 1st Zionist Congress Participants, 17.8.47', *In Battle*, p.215.
26. M. Bar-Zohar, *Ben-Gurion*, Vol. 2, pp.744–5.
27. Ben-Gurion testimony to the Anglo-American Committee of Inquiry, quoted in S. Chertoff

(ed.), *Zionism* (New York: Herzl Press, 1975), pp.38–40

28. B. Morris, *The Birth of the Palestinian Refugee Problem, 1947–1949* (New York: Cambridge University Press, 1987), pp.132–55.
29. B. Morris, 'Falsifying the Record: A Fresh Look at Zionist Documentation of 1948', *Journal of Palestine Studies*, Vol. 24. No. 3, 1995, pp.44–62; E. Karsh, 'Benny Morris and the Reign of Error', *Middle East Quarterly*, Vol. 6, No. 1, 1999, pp.15–28.
30. G. Meir, *My Life* (Tel-Aviv: Ma'ariv, 1975) pp.203–4.
31. For example Ben-Gurion address to his colleagues, *Protocol of the People's Administration Meeting*, 12 May 1948, *When Israel Fought*.
32. V. Shifter, 'The 1949 Israeli Offer to Repatriate 100,000 Palestinian Refugees', *Middle East Focus*, Vol. 9, No. 2, 1986, pp.13–18.
33. I. Pappe, *The Making of the Arab–Israeli Conflict 1947–1951* (London: Tauris, 1992), pp.26, 102. Whenever possible, I refer to authors outspokenly critical of Israeli policy towards the Palestinians, such as I. Pappe, B. Morris and E. Zartal. It makes my own more evenly balanced arguments less assailable.
34. *Aspects of the Palestinian Problem*, Information Briefing 29 (Jerusalem: Israel Information Centre, 1974); S. Katz, *The Jewish Presence in Palestine* (Jerusalem: Israel Academic Committee on the Middle East, n.d.); R.J.Z. Werblowsky, *Zionism, Israel and the Palestinians* (Jerusalem: Israel University Study Group for Middle Eastern Affairs, 1975).
35. I.Pappe, *The Making of the Arab–Israeli Conflict*, pp.98–9; articles in *Falastin*, 19 February 1949, *Akhbar al-Yom*, 12 October 1969, *Ad-Difa'a*, 6 September 1954.
36. B. Morris, *The Birth of the Palestinian Refugee Problem*, pp.253, 297.
37. D. Rubinstein, 'The Question Is Not How Many, But Why', *Ha-arets*, 28 January 1998.
38. *Myths and Facts: A Concise Record of the Arab–Israeli Conflict* (Washington: Near East Report, 1976), pp.2–3.
39. Y. Gorni, 'The Roots of Acknowledging the Jewish–Arab Confrontation and its Reflection in the Hebrew Press During 1900–1918', *Ha-tsionut*, Vol. 4, 1975, pp.72–113.
40. N. Gertz, 'The War of Liberation', *Ha-tsionut*, Vol. 14, 1989, pp.9–50.
41. For example D. Ben-Gurion, *War Diary*, 21 November 1948, Vol. 3 (Tel-Aviv: Ministry of Defence, 1982), p.835.
42. Y. Reinhartz, 'The Transition From Yishuv to Sovereign State – Social and Ideological Changes', *Ha-tsionut*, Vol. 14, 1989, pp.253–62; A. Shapira, *Land and Power* (Tel-Aviv: Am Oved, 1992) pp.485–8.
43. For example *Letter of Ben-Gurion to Yitshak Rosenthal, 25.11.48*, Ben-Gurion Archives.
44. For a discussion of this point, see L. Weissbrod, 'Protest and Dissidence in Israel', *Political Anthropology*, Vol. 4, 1984, pp.51–68.
45. D. Ben-Gurion, 'Address to Senior IDF Officers, 6.4.50', *Uniqueness and Vocation* (Tel-Aviv: Ma'arahot, 1971), pp.130–1.
46. This is the principal thesis of A. Shapira, *Land and Power*.
47. A. Shapira, *Land and Power*, p.485; M. Bar-Zohar, *Ben-Gurion*, Vol.2, p.873.
48. B. Morris, *Israel's Border Wars 1949–1956* (Oxford: Clarendon Press, 1993), pp.34–66, 97–158.
49. D. Ben-Gurion, 'Address At a Meeting With Industrialists, 4.2.51', *Vision and Way* (Tel-Aviv: Mapai Publications, 1951–57), Vol. 3, p.56.
50. D. Rubinstein, '40 Years Later', *Ha-arets*, 4 October 1996.
51. Y. Melmann, 'The White Lie About Qibiya', *Ha-arets*, 18 April 1997, based on recently released government protocols.
52. A. Avi-Hai, *Ben-Gurion: State Builder* (Jerusalem: Academic Press, 1974), pp.226–39; *Session of the Zionist Executive Committee in Jerusalem 5–15 May 1949* (Jerusalem: 1949), pp.233–5, 259–65.
53. *Session of the Zionist Executive Committee 19–28 April 1950* (Jerusalem: 1950), pp.13-22; *Knesset Reports*, 15 May 1950 (Jerusalem: The Knesset Press, 1950), p.1367.
54. M. Lissak and D. Horowitz, *From Yishuv to State* (Jerusalem: Hebrew University, 1972), pp.1–30.
55. *Problems of the Zionist Organization Upon the Establishment of the State*, Vol. 1 (Jerusalem: Zionist Executive, 1950), pp.18–20.
56. A.H. Silver,'The Case of Zionism', *The Reader's Digest*, 1949, pp.28–32.
57. A. Ross, 'The Zionist Meeting in Paris', *Ha-po'el Ha-tsa'ir*, No. 4, 1949.
58. *Problems of the Zionist Organization*, Vol. 1, p.3.
59. E. Shmueli, 'On Two Jewish Thinkers in America', *Ha-po'el Ha-tsa'ir*, No. 20, 1957.
60. *Problems of the Zionist Organization*, Vol. 1, p.49, Vol. 2, pp.53–6; *Session of the Zionist Executive 1950*, pp.86–7.
61. B.H., 'Zionism is Alive', *Ba-ma'ale*, Nos. 6–7, 1949, p.122; *Session of the Zionist Executive 1950*,

p.117; *The 23rd Zionist Congress Jerusalem, 13–30 August 1951* (Jerusalem: Executive of the Zionist Organization, 1951), pp.52, 72–3.

62. *The 22nd Zionist Congress, Basle, 9–24 December 1946*, (Jerusalem: Executive of the Zionist Organization, 1946), pp.59–74; *Problems of the Zionist Organization*, Vol. 1, p.39.

63. B. Locker, *In the Throes of Survival and Revival* (Jerusalem: Bialik Institute, 1963), pp.230–7.

64. *Zionist Thought At Present* (Jerusalem: Executive of the World Zionist Organization, 1962).

65. *The 26th Zionist Congress, Jerusalem 30.12.64–10.1.65* (Jerusalem: World Zionist Organization, 1966), pp.215–42, 317–21.

66. A. Riger, *Hebrew Education in Palestine*, Vol. 1 (Tel-Aviv: Dvir, 1940), pp.243–52.

67. *Israel Government Yearbook*, 1952 (Tel-Aviv: The Government Press, 1952), pp.VII–XXXI.

68. D. Ben-Gurion, 'Answer to the Disputants', *Davar*, 9 October 1957.

69. E. Don-Yihya, 'Etatism and Judaism in Ben-Gurion's Discourse and Policy', *Ha-tsionut*, Vol. 14, 1989, Vol. 14, pp.51–88.

70. A. Rubinstein, *To Be a Free People* (Tel-Aviv: Schocken, 1977), pp.133–9; H.M. Sachar, *A History of Israel From the Rise of Zionism to Our Time*, (Jerusalem: Steinmatzky, 1976), pp.593–5; H. Keikh, 'The Six Day War and Jewish Identity', *Shdemot*, No. 32, 1969, pp.18–26.

71. A. Eban, 'Top Priority', *Petah*, January 1968, pp.61–79.

72. *Zionist Thought at Present*, p.7.

73. The following articles in *Ba-ma'ale*, 1949: T. Hatagli, 'The Jewish National Fund is 47 Years Old', No. 1, pp.4–5; 'Tel Hai Commemoration Day', No. 5; Shalom, 'With the Return of Herzl', No. 15, pp.306–7; M. Stanover, 'Following the 30th Council', No. 10, p.202.

74. The following articles in *Ba-ma'ale*, 1943: 'When Our Federation Was Founded', No. 19; M. Yoske, 'Organization of Educational Action', Nos 17–18.

75. The following articles in *Niv Ha-kvutsa*, Vol. 1, 1952, No. 4: A. Barzel, 'Ways of the Israeli Youth Movement'; M. Mandel, 'Gnawing at the Roots'; the following articles in *Niv Ha-kvutsa*, Vol. 4, 1954, pp.45–59; A. Haft, 'Abundant Harvest', No. 6, pp.25–8; Tanhum, 'From the First Days', No. 1, pp.5–9; A. Ofir, 'The Anvil', No. 1, pp.3–4. The other sources are: *A Handbook of Youth Leaders: The Month of Elul* (Jerusalem: Youth & Hehalutz Department of the Zionist Organization, 1955); B. Shalom, 'Wither Jewish Youth', *Focus*, Vol. 2, No. 1, 1958, pp.79–88; O. Adar and H. Adler, 'Teaching Values'.

76. H.M. Amishai, 'Talk of Oldsters', *Shdemot*, No. 38, 1970, pp.5–11; R. Gurdis, 'Israel and the Diaspora', *Gesher*, Vol. 22, No. 3, 1976, pp.37–52; Y. Ilam, 'Crisis of Zionism – Crisis of Judaism', *Be-tfutsot Ha-gola*, Vol. 17, No. 75/76, 1975, pp.52–8.

77. S.N. Herman, *Israelis and Jews: The Continuity of an Identity* (New York: Random House, 1970), pp.49, 51.

78. E. Etzioni-Halevi, with R. Shapira, *Political Culture in Israel: Cleavage and Integration Among Israeli Jews* (New York: Praeger, 1977), p.165.

79. Dialogues between American and Israeli intellectuals published in *Congress Bi-Weekly*, September 1962, September 1963, September 1964, October 1965, April 1967.

80. M. Lissak, 'Society and Class Images in the Yishuv and in Israeli Society', in S.N. Eisenstadt *et al.* (eds) *Integration and Development in Israel* (Jerusalem: Israel University Press, 1970), pp.141–61; Y. Ben David, 'Membership in Youth Movements and Social Status', in S.N. Eisenstadt *et al.* (eds), *The Social Structure of Israel* (Jerusalem: Akademon, 1966), pp.457–81; B. Kimmerling, 'Status Perception of Security Occupations in Israel', *Medina U-mimshal*, Vol. 1, No. 1, pp.141–9; A. Shapira, *Land and Power* (Tel-Aviv:Am Oved, 1992), pp.485–96; A. Rubinstein, *From Herzl to Rabin: 100 Years of Zionism* (Tel Aviv: Schocken, 1997), pp.56–115.

81. D. Weinrieb, 'The Second Generation in Palestine and Its Occupational Choice', *Metsuda*, Vol. 7, 1954, pp.245–330.

82. It was noted as a new phenomenon in Israel by sociologists, for example S.N. Eisenstadt, *Israeli Society* (Jerusalem: Magnes Press, 1976), pp.143–9; M. Derber, 'Israel's Wage Differentials: A Persisting Problem', in S.N. Eisenstadt *et al. Integration and Development in Israel*, pp.185–201.

83. D. Ben-Gurion, *Vision and Way*, pp.206–91.

84. D. Ben-Gurion, *Address at Mapai Centre Meeting, 26.11.52*, Labour Party Archives; 'Affinity to the Glory of Israel', *Vision and Way*, Vol. 5, p.63; 'Investigating an Issue', *Hazut*, Vol. 3, 1957, p.29.

85. A. Rubinstein, 'Four Verdicts', *Ha-arets*, 21 September 1973; *The Constitutional Law of Israel* (Jerusalem: Schocken, 1969), pp.117–33; Y. Shapiro, *Democracy in Israel* (Ramat Gan: Massada, 1977), pp.25–46; P. Lahav, 'Power and Office: the Supreme Court in its First Decade', *Iyunei Mishpat*, Vol. 14, No. 3, 1989, pp.470–501.

86. See A. Rubinstein, *From Herzl to Rabin*, pp.48–55, 181–95.

87. C. Frankenstein, *Between Past and Future* (Jerusalem: Henrietta Szold Foundation, 1953).

88. E. Cohen, *et al, Summary Report: Research on Immigrant Absorption in a Development Town* (Jerusalem: Hebrew University, 1962); S. Deshen, 'Images of a Village', *Ha-uma*, Vol. 9, No. 4, 1972, pp.442–7; O. Shapira (ed.), *Immigrant Moshavim in Israel* (Jerusalem: Jewish Agency, 1972); D. Giladi (ed.), *Immigrant Moshavim* (Tel-Aviv: Tnu'at Ha-moshavim, 1972); M. Lissak, 'Stratification Patterns and Mobility Aspirations: Sources of Mobility Motivation', *Megamot*, Vol. 15, No. 1, 1967, pp.66–82.

89. S.N. Eisenstadt, *Immigrant Absorption* (Jerusalem: Jewish Agency and Hebrew University, 1952), pp.64–110; M. Hen, 'Class Composition and Oriental Pupil Attitudes Towards Israeli Society', *Megamot*, Vol. 19, No. 2, 1973, pp.117–26; M. Lissak, 'Stratification Patterns and Mobility Aspirations'; H. Adler, 'Secondary School As a Socially and Educationally Selective Factor', in S.N. Eisenstadt *et al. Education and Society in Israel* (Jerusalem: Akademon, 1968), pp.215–25.

90. M. Begin, 'Concepts and Problems in Foreign Policy', *Ha-uma*, Vol. 16, 1966, pp.461–87.

3. The Erosion of the Tsabar Identity

The 1948 war and the establishment of the State of Israel constituted a watershed in the identity perception of the Jewish citizens of Israel. The 1967 war, on the other hand, produced a complete sea change in their self-image. By the early 1950s, the Pioneer had gradually evolved into the Tsabar, but the latter was consistent with the former, both being based on the same Zionist translation of the Messianic idea into secular terms. Tsabar identity had merely shed a large part of the Pioneer value system and reinterpreted another part of it into pragmatic, non-utopian norms. After 1967, the entire self-image of some Israelis began to be transformed altogether by interpreting the Messianic idea in a novel religious way. When gradually adopted by part of the secular majority, this became the quasi-religious identity of the Settler. The change from Tsabar to Settler was no gradual erosion of some traits or constituents of Zionist ideology. Instead, it was a completely new definition of Zionism as the literal Messianic message coming true. As in the past, the reformulation of Israeli identity was linked to the borders of the State of Israel. Collective identity always delineates the boundaries of the collective. In the case of Israel, these boundaries depend to a larger extent than usual on the territorial borders of the area for whose possession an ethical justification is required.

Tsabar identity had succeeded in vindicating Israeli sovereignty within the 1949 armistice lines, which became accepted by Israelis as permanent borders. These lines were suddenly obliterated in 1967 by the conquest of the entire West Bank, the Gaza Strip, the Sinai Peninsula and the Golan Heights. Israelis very soon realized that they needed some new justification for their proprietorship of this added territory, a proprietorship they felt very keenly. The reasoning behind Tsabar identity would no longer suffice. The latter could exonerate the feeling of pride in the military victory over the armies of three Arab states. The upright warrior had not just defended his state, he had turned the impending disaster, as the situation leading up to the 1967 war had been perceived by Israelis, into a resounding victory. However, Tsabar identity could provide no justification for the euphoria that gripped Israelis after the war. There was a widespread feeling of long-lost possessions being retrieved, of finally coming home and therefore, a general reluctance to withdraw. The ethical magnanimity of accepting partition had made the warrior upright; holding on to the occupied territories due to a sense of proprietorship invalidated any assertion of perfect justice having been done. The dilemma was acute and eroded Tsabar identity. It was then solved in two ways which subsequently converged to some extent, creating the new identity formulation of the Settler.

THE 1967 WAR

The euphoria which gripped Israelis after the 1967 war was due as much to the feeling of homecoming as to the enormous relief over the war's outcome. With hindsight, the anxiety preceding the war seems unwarranted, seeing how superior to their enemies the Israeli armed forces turned out to be. However, at the time, Israel could not be sure that the Soviet weaponry of Egypt and Syria was no match for their Western one, that the Arab armies would not act in unison, or that Egypt did not really intend to go to war, as some analysts now claim. Though described in detail by numerous authors, a brief summary of events leading to the war is in order nevertheless, if one is to understand the feeling of doom and the subsequent relief and elation.

The 1967 war revolved around two issues. One was the Israeli–Syrian conflict over water resources. It began in the 1950s, when Israel started to build a water carrier from Lake Kineret (the Sea of Galilee) to the arid Negev. Lake Kineret is fed by the River Jordan which, in turn, is fed by tributaries, most of which originate in Syria. Syria tried to foil the project by attacking the construction sites and, subsequently, by shelling Israeli settlements at the foot of the Golan Heights. Israel retaliated in kind and completed the carrier in 1964. Since diversion of water from Lake Kineret, all of which lies within Israeli territory, did not deprive Syria of any water, this conflict must be viewed to have been subsidiary to the second, primary issue of inter-Arab rivalry. Gun battles with Israel served to demonstrate Syrian steadfastness in implementing the destruction of Israel, the only pan-Arab target on which there was continuing consensus in the Arab camp. One must bear in mind that pan-Arabism guided both Egyptian Nasserism and Syrian Ba'athism, creating rivalry between the two states because each interpreted pan-Arabism as Arab unity under its own hegemony.[1]

The leadership of Egyptian President, Gamal Abd al-Nasser, and Egyptian pre-eminence in the Arab camp were challenged by the Ba'ath, becoming more pronounced once the Ba'ath came into power in Syria in 1963 and especially when a radical faction of it took over in 1966. Syria tried to draw Egypt and other Arab regimes into the struggle against Israel, hopefully under its own aegis, knowing full well that Nasser could not lag behind if he wanted to maintain his position in the Arab camp. Thus, Nasser was induced to convene the First Arab Summit Conference in Cairo in January 1964, before completion of the Israeli water carrier, and a meeting of Arab Heads of State in Cairo in May 1965, after its completion. The resolutions of both seemed ominous to Israel: to plan to divert water from the River Jordan north of Lake Kineret and to establish a unified Arab command. When Syria began work on the Yarmouk project (to divert the Jordan water), mutual military attacks escalated, accompanied by an increasingly hostile Syrian rhetoric and its hosting of Palestinian al-Fatah terrorist attacks. Matters came to a head on 7 April 1967, when Israel shot down six Syrian Migs following a Syrian artillery attack on Israeli tractors on the shores of Lake Kineret. Syria realized that it needed the help of another front to weaken Israeli military power. Egypt, however, embroiled since 1962 in a civil war in the Yemen, which was not going too well, was loth to become engaged on another front. To overcome Egyptian reluctance to engage in another war, a Soviet delegation went to Cairo and reported that Israel was concentrating large forces on the Syrian frontier. This was a gross exaggeration, but Egypt could not know that, nor could it afford to refuse the Syrian appeal without losing credibility in the Arab camp. A state of emergency proclaimed in Egypt on 15 May 1967 was followed by the entry of seven Egyptian divisions into the Sinai on 20 May 1967, after the UN observer force had been withdrawn on 18 May 1967 upon Egyptian request. The next steps towards the confrontation with Israel followed in quick succession: Egypt closed the Tiran Straits to Israeli shipping on 22 May 1967 and a defence pact was signed with Jordan and Iraq on 30 May 1967.

Each of these steps heightened the tension and apprehension in Israel. Hostile bickering in the north (Syria) had suddenly been overshadowed by actions in the south (Egypt) ostensibly intended to provoke a full-scale war, since closing the Tiran Straits was known to be regarded by Israel as a *casus belli*. To this front was added a possible second one in the east (Jordan) and almost certainly a third one in the north, where it had all begun. The situation was seemingly as perilous as that faced by Israel in 1948. The hesitations of the Israeli government to go to war, due to international pressure and because Chief-of-Staff Yitzhak Rabin doubted the readiness of the armed forces,[2] the fear of Soviet intervention, intelligence reports that Egyptian forces in the Sinai were equipped with chemical weapons (which brought the Holocaust to mind) and the prolonged mobilization of reserves created an atmosphere of impending doom. To make matters worse, Levy Eshkol, premier and defence minister, was perceived as weak and incompetent to lead the country in this crisis situation. For the first time in its history, public protest erupted in Israel, on 29 May 1967. On 1 June 1967, the cabinet was forced to form a wall-to-wall government, including Gahal, and to appoint Moshe Dayan, chief-of-staff during the Sinai Campaign, to the post of minister of defence. Israel attacked on 5 May 1967. The war lasted for six days and ended in a resounding victory for Israel on all three fronts.

THE TSABAR IN EXTENDED ISRAEL – A DISCREPANCY

Perception of the Discrepancy

The great relief felt after the pent-up apprehensions preceding the 1967 war explains the pride felt by Israelis over the victory. The Tsabar had proved his mettle indeed. Within a single week, Israel had defeated three well-equipped Arab armies. Moreover, it had occupied an extensive area, namely the Sinai Peninsula and the Gaza Strip previously held by Egypt, the West Bank previously held by Jordan and the Golan Heights previously held by Syria. The occupation of these, and especially that of the West Bank, triggered the spontaneous euphoria which took hold of the Israeli public. The newspaper photographs of soldiers crying at the Western Wall, the frantic, pilgrimage-like visits paid by Israelis to all sites with a religious–historical significance, and the declaration of united Jerusalem as the eternal capital of Israel are just some of the manifestations of that euphoria, which has been abundantly documented. The elation was heightened by the totally unexpected turn of events. Neither the political nor the military leadership had foreseen any of these events, as evidenced by the lack of any strategic, or even tactical plans for the eventuality of fighting and winning on three fronts. Naturally, the public was even less prepared for the outcome of the war and the shock contributed to the general elation.

Some of the fighters themselves reacted differently, however. The loss of human life, both Israeli and Arab, raised questions as to the morality of any war, even one of self-defence, but above all, some began to doubt the justice of the euphoria following the war. *Talks of Warriors,*[3] published in 1967 immediately after the war, and *Talks In the Kibbutz Among Young People,*[4] published in 1969, were two collections of recorded interviews with soldiers who had fought in the war and who were native Israeli Kibbutz members. The two books, and especially the first one, became very widely publicized in Israel. Significantly, Kibbutz members were the first to perceive the lack of fit between Tsabar identity and the euphoria over occupying territory beyond the borders of Israel. As mentioned earlier, Kibbutz members were seeing themselves as the epitome of the Tsabar, just as they had previously been the embodiment of the Pioneer. Being the carriers of that identity, they were more fully aware of all its aspects. Tsabar identity applied to the State of Israel only, not to the Sinai, the West Bank or the Golan Heights. The Tsabar was morally immaculate because he had magnanimously relinquished his claim to these territories. By what right could he now rejoice in holding them?

Original Labour Zionism could have justified the joy of returning to the ancient heritage, but the Tsabar had jettisoned Jewishness, the diaspora and even the term Zionism. The interviewed soldiers realized that Zionism had become nothing more than patriotism, the obligation to go to war and protect the security of Israel.[5] By doing so, 'Zionism has reached a dead end because it has realized itself, according to the restricted criteria it has adopted.'[6] Winning the war was a patriotic act compatible with Tsabar identity, but holding on to territorial conquests was unjustified ethically. Having relinquished Jewishness, the Tsabar could no longer lay claim to land which was part of the Jewish heritage, but outside Israeli borders.

Occupying territory was unethical in itself; killing people to achieve this was even worse. The ambivalence in a statement, such as 'I had no compunctions when I fired, but I was glad he [the enemy] got away'[7] can best be explained by another dilemma raised by the 1967 war. Tsabar morality also depended on confining the fighting to defensive actions against armed forces, excluding civilians, but occupation of densely populated areas, notably the Gaza Strip and the West Bank, had victimized large numbers of civilians. The link between the war, the Jewish heritage and Zionism was a recurrent theme in *Talks of Warriors*. According to one soldier, the fighting 'has made us think more about Zionism and our right to Erets Yisrael'. Another stated that Zionism, the ideology of immigrating to Erets Yisrael, was intricately linked to the conflict with the Arabs: the entire conflict was unethical, as was the settlement of Palestine in the past and in the future, unless it was effected by Jews reclaiming their heritage.[8] This was the dilemma in a nutshell. The two statements expressed the realization that Tsabar identity was inadequate under the new circumstances and they evoked Pioneer Zionism (note the renewed use of the term Zionism) as a possible remedy. As will be shown, this attempt to turn the clock back ideationally was made repeatedly by the various peace movements, but to little avail, principally because some of the values composing Labour Zionism (notably egalitarianism and the glory of agricultural labour) were totally anachronistic in 1970s Israel.

The dilemma was discussed in a symposium held in 1967 (published in 1968)[9] by some of the young people interviewed in *Talks of Warriors* and by students at Yeshivat Merkaz Ha-rav, the Yeshiva (Talmudic college) headed by Rabbi Kuk Junior. All the religious participants in the symposium had been soldiers in the 1967 war. Unlike highly orthodox Yeshiva students, who are exempt from military service in Israel, the ones taking part in the symposium belonged to the Religious Zionist camp of Rabbi Kuk. Most young men in this camp serve in the military. Being religious, and yet doing their national service makes these youngsters an integral part of Israel and prevents their seclusion within orthodoxy. They thus demonstrate their recognition of the State of Israel. (The latter is still a subject of controversy in orthodox circles in Israel, since some deny the identity between Israel and Zion and refuse to regard Israel as the restoration of the Holy Land.)

The debate was highly illuminating. The Kibbutz members taking part felt guilty about the vanquished enemy and saw a conflict between patriotism, which means avoiding future wars by fighting the enemy now, and pacifism, which regards the sanctity of human life above all else. Such a conflict is possible only when doubts arise about the moral justification of the war. The religious students were not callous – killing enemy soldiers had raised similar ethical questions for them – but Jewish identity provided their answer to the dilemma. It was not normal to feel such guilt. 'I am convinced that our struggle is just and that justifies killing any man who comes to kill us...I know my heart ached.'[10] It was as Jews that they regarded the struggle as just. Being religious, they had never relinquished Jewishness, which is a faith and ethnic identity in one.

The proceedings of the symposium were published in *Shdemot*, the Kibbutz periodical, and secular Kibbutz youngsters soon drew the conclusion that Jewishness was the answer to their dilemma. The impact of the symposium discussions can be traced in subsequent articles in that periodical, as well as in *Talks in the Kibbutz Among Young People*, published in 1969. Secularity was frequently blamed for the crisis, defined as a crisis of identity. Young Kibbutz members, who realized most completely how inadequate Tsabar identity had become, were also the first to seek a renewed identity through Jewish values and history. Thus, Israeli identity was equated with Jewish identity and the remedy proposed for the crisis was the reintroduction into Kibbutz life of traditional Jewish holidays and symbols; since original Zionism had lost most of its contents, a new Zionism was needed, linked with Judaism and with the identification with world Jewry; the 1967 war had brought the diaspora nearer and had initiated a search for Jewish identity over and above Israeliness.[11] In several articles, the new hankering after Jewish tradition was connected with the Holocaust.[12] The possibility of total annihilation in the war had reminded Israelis of the Holocaust. The Tsabar had relegated the Holocaust, together with the rest of recent Jewish history, to near oblivion and had replaced them with the cult of archaeology. Ancient relics stressed the link with the ancient past, when Jews had lived in their own land before the exile. A closure of this historical gap, epitomized by a sympathetic interest in the Holocaust, became one means of redefining Israeli identity.

The link between religiosity and Jewishness was not confined to the Yeshiva students mentioned above. Rather, it applied to religious Israeli youngsters in general and was merely underscored by the statements of the students. A study of Israeli pupils, conducted in 1964, confirms the link retained by young religious Israelis with their Jewish identification, in contrast to secular Israeli youngsters.[13] Sixty-eight per cent of the respondent pupils of Israeli schools identified themselves as Jews. But when broken down by orthodoxy, 98 per cent of the religious pupils, 78 per cent of the traditional ones and only 46 per cent of secular ones did so.[14]

The religious participants in the 1967 symposium held in common with most young religious Israelis the lack of alienation from Jewishness typical of the Tsabar. However, they differed from the rest of young religious Israelis in being the first to project their Jewishness onto the perception of the occupied territories. This was so because they had had what they perceived to have been a mystical experience. At a reunion of some participants of the symposium, Yoel Ben Nun, one of the former Yeshiva students, related that this had happened at the Yeshiva one day before Egypt had moved its troops into the Sinai Desert. Rabbi Kuk Junior, their mentor, suddenly loudly bewailed the 1948 partition of the Holy Land, which meant to him the abandonment of the most holy sites of Judaism. He had never expressed such sentiments before and his disciples were stunned. When Israel conquered all these holy sites a month later, the students interpreted his outburst as an inspired prophecy, heralding the liberation of the Holy Land and the Coming of the Messiah.[15]

At the symposium, the religious participants were already inspired by these ideas of Rabbi Kuk, still vague at the time. Shortly after the war, Hanan Porat organized a group of fellow students from Yeshivat Merkaz Ha-rav to resettle his native Gush Etsion, a cluster of settlements occupied by Jordan between 1948 and 1967. As Jews, they had no compunctions about retrieving their ancient Jewish heritage, that is, occupying the heartland of the ancient Kingdoms of Judea and Israel and holding on to it. Thus, action on the ground helped to formulate the originally vague ideas expressed by Rabbi Kuk and these, in turn, motivated additional religious youngsters to act. The interaction between word and deed eventually crystallized into the fully-fledged Gush Emunim doctrine and settlement movement, of which the above Yeshiva students comprised the nucleus. The doctrine, its mystical–religious elements played down in order to be palatable to secular Israelis, became the basis for the Settler identity, which replaced the Tsabar and of which Gush Emunim members became the carriers.

Official Policy in the Territories and Its Justification

Ironically, the policies of the Arab states, notably the resolutions of the Khartoum Conference, facilitated the process of legitimizing the retention of the occupied territories, as they had in the past apparently confirmed the non-existence of a separate Palestinian entity. There is general consensus that the Israeli authorities had not gone to war in 1967 with any targets in sight, except for the immediate one of pushing the Egyptian troops back to a safe distance. Israel had not anticipated any such war.[16] Official Israeli documents of the period are still classified, so that one must rely on personal and, sometimes, contradictory accounts of events. At first, the government seems to have remained true to the values underlying Tsabar identity. Some border adjustments notwithstanding, it wished to retreat to the original Israeli borders and to translate the military victory into peace with the defeated Arab states, or possibly only with Egypt and Syria. It is almost certain that one week after the end of the war, using the United States as an intermediary, Israel informed Syria and Egypt of its willingness to withdraw entirely, or almost entirely from the Sinai Peninsula and from the Golan Heights in return for a peace treaty. It is not clear whether a similar offer was made to Jordan, but it is certain that Israel considered East Jerusalem and the Gaza Strip non-negotiable. According to one source, Defence Minister Dayan was considering an independent Palestinian state in the West Bank.[17]

At this point, Arab policy inadvertently favoured the Israeli sentiments underlying its euphoria. The Arab rejection of its peace offer, embodied in the three 'No's (No Negotiations, No Recognition, No Peace) of the Khartoum Conference held in September 1967, ostensibly absolved Israel from any further need to see perfect justice done. It had again been magnanimous and had again been rejected. The ball was now in the Arab court, or, as Dayan reportedly said, 'I am waiting for their call.' Consequently, the cabinet withdrew the peace proposal and official spokesmen became less clear on the subject of the territories. For instance, Foreign Minister Abba Eban, in a speech to the United Nations on 8 October 1968, did not mention the subject of troop withdrawals. Prime Minister Golda Meir, speaking to the Knesset on 5 May 1969, likewise ignored the issue. At a later Knesset address, on 16 March 1971, she mentioned the possibility of border adjustments in return for a peace treaty, but neither she nor other Israeli public figures were explicit with regard to the specifics.[18]

At the same time, the government immediately incorporated East Jerusalem into the municipality of Jerusalem and began encouraging Jewish settlement along the Jordan Rift Valley, on the Golan Heights and in the Rafah Salient. This policy was guided by the original Labour Zionist principle of staking out your claim by tilling the soil, restrained by strategic security considerations, chiefly as laid out in the Allon Plan. As Allon explained in retrospect,[19] the principal restraint on claim-staking (Jewish settlement in all of Mandatory Palestine) was the more basic Labour Zionist value of the Jewishness of Israel. His plan of retaining under Israeli sovereignty and, therefore, settling only sparsely populated areas of strategic importance was guided by demographic considerations. At the end of 1967, the population of the occupied territories amounted to approximately 1,060,000, while that of Israel consisted of 2,383,600 Jews and 392,700 Arabs. The total Arab population (in Israel and the occupied territories) thus amounted to 1,452,700. The annual growth rate of Israeli Jews was 1.6 per cent and that of Israeli Arabs 3.7 per cent. Assuming that the natural growth rate of a population is a function of its stage of modernization, it followed that the growth rate of the population in the territories would be at least as high as that of Israeli Arabs, or higher. With a growth rate over twice as high as that of Jews, the Arab population could be expected to reach parity with the Jews at the end of the century. On the implicit assumption that once a stake had been claimed it could not be relinquished, Allon reasoned that it was essential to refrain from settling any densely populated areas so as to prevent the eventual formation of a bi-national state. On the other hand, those areas settled by Jews would remain security guardians of Israel. Though the Allon Plan never became official policy, settlements were indeed put up wherever Israel intended to retain sovereignty. According to their own statements, Premier Meir and Defence Minister Dayan, who, together with Allon were the leading spokesmen on policy in the territories, shared this overall view.[20]

The Allon Plan and Israeli policy in the territories demonstrate the inappropriateness of Tsabar identity in the new situation of extended borders. Labour did not even try to justify its actions by the values underlying Tsabar identity. Instead, it invoked Pioneer values of claim-staking. Since it was constrained by inevitable international censure and demographic considerations from annexing the territories and implementing this value fully, it had to compromise, using security as a further, superimposed justification for its actions. The latter, though, was based on Tsabar identity which had placed security at the top of its priorities. The renewed emphasis on the Jewishness of the State (the demographic misgivings) again reverted to Pioneer values, since the Tsabar had shed Jewishness to a large extent. This mix of values evoked, none of which could be fully implemented, would probably have sufficed to undermine Labour legitimacy. The process would possibly have been slower, though, had Labour policy not offended so blatantly against the principle of justice underlying both identity formulations which it called upon to justify its actions. Israel set up a civil administration in the occupied territories, headed by retired or active military officers. It thus ruled coercively over a hostile foreign population or, at least, an unwilling one.

Perfect Justice versus *Coercive Rule and Palestinian Self-Determination*

The rule over an alien population would not have seemed so offensive had it not coincided with the impact of New Left ideology on Western thought and action. The New Left ideas most relevant to Israel were and still are those of individual self-determination and self-realization denied by the social, economic and political power of the State.[21] From that follows the right to national self-determination denied by capitalist imperialism.[22] These ideas were brought home to the general public by the student unrest of 1968 and the protest against the Vietnam War until they became widespread staple values of progressive circles in the West. They were quickly taken up by national liberation movements, of which the PLO (Palestinian Liberation Organization) was no exception.

The Arab states bordering on Israel ostensibly fought all the wars (1948, 1956, 1967) on behalf of the Palestinians, but the latter were justifiably wary of their hosts' true intentions. Palestinians were given neither independence in any territory, nor citizenship rights, except in Jordan. To a large extent, they were confined to refugee camps and their employment opportunities curbed. This unsympathetic treatment enhanced their sense of being a separate entity, despite the prevalence of pan-Arabism at the time. Almost from the start, not all Palestinians sat idly by, awaiting their deliverance by their Arab brethren. Egypt set up squads of Fidayin (Palestinian guerilla groups) in 1951, who carried out border raids in Israel. The Fidayin were the antecedents of al-Fatah, established in Kuwait and Qatar in 1958. The Fidayin operated under the auspices of the Arab governments and were under the command of their armies. Al-Fatah, on the other hand, was an independent Palestinian organization, operating under its own command. Its propaganda reinforced Palestinian nationalist sentiments and finally pressured the Arab states to convene the first Arab Summit Conference in January 1964. The latter recommended formation of a Palestinian entity under Arab auspices, in order to counter this independent trend. In response, a Palestinian conference was convened in Jerusalem in May 1964. It established the PLO as the executive and the PNC (Palestinian National Council) as the political agency of the Palestinian entity. The PLO was still oriented largely to military formations fighting as units in armies of the various Arab states, notably Egypt. In contrast, al-Fatah and other groups competing with it espoused the strategy of independent Palestinian guerilla warfare against Israel. Al-Fatah strategy made indubitable sense after the 1967 war. The latter showed up the inability of Arab armies to defeat Israel in open battle for the time being, so that the guerilla tactics of the small radical Palestinian groups proved to be a superior way. Consequently, these groups, and specifically al-Fatah, joined the PLO in a bid to take over power from the moderates. After the war and up to the end of 1967, al-Fatah competed with Israel over the compliance of the West Bank population, but failed to organize a widespread uprising there against the Israeli occupation forces.

To carry out raids across the border from Jordan, in line with its tactics, al-Fatah established bases near the border in Jordan. Israeli retaliatory strikes, notably one against the base in Karama on 21 March 1968, induced Jordan to close them down. Al-Fatah had meanwhile also established training bases in southern Lebanon. In February 1969, the radical wing gained the upper hand within the PLO and Yassir Arafat, the leader of al-Fatah, became chairman of the PLO. Obviously strengthened by this success, al-Fatah, in the name of all Palestinian organizations, demanded a free rein in Jordan and representation in the Jordanian government. All Palestinians had been granted the right of Jordanian citizenship, but not of proportional or group representation in government. The ensuing tension and challenge to his authority finally induced King Hussein of Jordan to expel the PLO from Jordan in September 1970 after heavy fighting and a near-intervention by Syria in favour of the Palestinians. The badly beaten PLO forces now moved to South Lebanon, but their freedom of action had also been curtailed there, because the Lebanese government feared Israeli retaliation.

The expulsion of the PLO from Jordan, the more efficient Israeli control of a confrontation line now confined to the Lebanese border, and some curtailment of al-Fatah actions by the Lebanese government precluded the type of warfare recommended in the Palestinian National Covenant. Consequently, al-Fatah compensated by turning its attacks to Israeli targets outside Israel, especially in Europe. Tactics which could previously be called guerilla raids in enemy territory, even though conducted against the civilian population, now became terrorist operations on neutral territory. Once this step had been taken by al-Fatah, using the cover name 'Black September', other more Leftist groups within the PLO radicalized the issue further by extending the range of targets from Israelis to all Jews, as well as to the USA as a supporter of Israel.

PLO ideology is an uneasy truce between the various doctrines of the groups constituting it, ranging from al-Fatah Palestinian nationalism to PFLP (Popular Front for the Liberation of Palestine) pan-Arab Leninism. It would be cumbersome to elaborate the various ideologies in depth, since the popular image of the movement and its influence on Israeli thought are the only ones relevant to the subject of this book. That image was predominantly New Left, summarized by the 'secular democratic state' proposed for liberated Palestine. Furthermore, New Leftism was the aspect most emphasized in PLO propaganda because it was the dominant revolutionary ideology in the West at the time and could mobilize the most sympathy from Westerners. Israelis, too, saw the PLO in this light, which also guided much of PLO action against Israel.

PLO doctrine, as articulated in its covenant,[23] incorporated those aspects of New Leftism which pertained to underdeveloped countries and their national liberation movements. Palestinians had the right of control over their political fate (article 3), which legitimized both the total war declared against Israel and the demand for recognition by the Arab states as an independent entity (articles 1, 2, 13). The inherent contradiction between pan-Arabism and Palestinian separateness was resolved by declaring the Palestinians to be the vanguard in the overall Arab struggle against Israel (article 14). The struggle was directed against the 'Zionist' state, which was allied with imperialism (article 22) and not against the Jews in Israel as such. Israelis might even be recruited to join the Arab resistance movement.[24] Guerilla warfare and urban terrorism were the tactics proposed by the New Left. The PLO at first insisted on employing the former, rather than fighting in regular units of the Arab armed forces (articles 26–30), but it subsequently switched to terrorism, when it could no longer operate effectively across the border.

TSABAR IDENTITY UNDER SIEGE

The short discussion of the PLO helps to put into context official Israeli policy regarding the territories inhabited by Palestinians (the Golan Heights have a largely Druze population and the Sinai desert a Bedouin one), as well as the opposition which gradually built up against this policy along the entire range of the political spectrum. The final result was a delegitimation of Labour, which had been in power since the 1930s. The initial opposition came from the Left.

The Peace Movement

This was in fact composed of several movements, which came together, or divided, in a series of changing coalitions. All of them advocated peace and the withdrawal of Israel from the occupied territories. Since the territories were, and still are, a major issue with respect to the subject at hand, groups agreeing on this point may be treated as one movement. Siah, one of the main groups of the peace movement, was established in 1968 by young members of Ha-kibuts Ha-artsi (affiliated to the leftist Mapam party) and ex-members of Maki (the Israeli Zionist communist party). Leftist students joined Siah subsequently. The name 'Siah' is the Hebrew acronym of 'Israeli New Left' and Siah was indeed influenced by New Leftism: Zionism was the national liberation movement of the Jewish people and, as such, had to recognize the equal right of Palestinian national independence. Therefore, Israel should withdraw from the territories occupied in 1967. The social programme of Siah was also New Leftist in regarding capitalism as a system which must be overthrown. Siah activities followed from its ideology. Its members demonstrated against Jewish settlements in the occupied territories, against the continued banishment of some Israeli Arabs from their original villages and against the banning of Bedouins from certain areas in the Sinai; they participated in Black Panther demonstrations (see pp.85–6) and distributed milk to underprivileged families.

This New Left nucleus was also joined by people who had no socialist convictions, but who believed that peace could only be achieved if some territories were returned to the Arabs. The extended leadership of the peace movement included former members of the Canaanites, some academics, former members of IZL (the pre-state military underground of the Revisionists) and Lehi (a splinter group of IZL), and even some religious members.[25]

There was no consensus on the extent of territories to be returned, nor on who they should be returned to. Some favoured an independent Palestinian state on the West Bank, others simply insisted on withdrawal in stages or on withdrawal in return for peace.[26] The important thing was the intent to withdraw. The reasons for withdrawal were principally moral, and were both secular and religious. Though the establishment of a Jewish state in Israel was the fulfilment of the Messianic dream, it was unethical to disregard the equal rights of the Palestinians and to occupy foreign territories. Furthermore, the demographic problem discussed above was also invoked as a reason for withdrawal. Israel would eventually turn into an Arab state if democratic principles prevailed, or into a state with apartheid policies if they did not. Neither alternative was compatible with Zionism.[27] Religious arguments stressed Jewish survival as the supreme value of Judaism. If survival was threatened by the occupation of territories, they must be relinquished. Furthermore, peace was a major element of the Messianic idea and must be pursued at all cost.[28] There was a fair measure of consensus on the practical reasons for withdrawal, such as external political pressure and the need for a gesture of goodwill to make Israel more acceptable to its Arab neighbours.[29]

The peace movement contained a small radical faction of former Matspen members. Matspen was formed in 1962 and can be described as an anti-Zionist New Left group. Even before the 1967 war, the group had supported a federal socialist supra-national state in Palestine, to be a stage in the socialist union of the Middle East. After the 1967 war, their arguments became more emphatic since Israel was now viewed as a properly imperialist state.[30] The radical faction of the peace movement accepted these premises, but did not reject the Zionist aim of a Jewish state. Consequently, they proposed a bi-national state, in which each ethnic group retained its identity.[31]

To summarize, the peace movement wanted to restore things to the *status quo ante* in order to preserve Tsabar identity, though with a New Leftist substratum. Tsabar identity had been tailored to Israel in its pre-1967 borders and was, therefore, inconsistent with post-1967 reality. The peace movement wished to change reality in order to make it consistent with the values it espoused. That in itself does not explain its failure to affect Israeli policy: revolutionary movements have been known to succeed against greater odds. In the present case, though, the similarity between its values and those of the official PLO doctrine greatly reduced its chances of garnering a substantial following. The PLO was the self-declared enemy. To concede the justice of its cause was tantamount to treason. The prospects of the peace movement declined further when the PLO began resorting to terror. Terrorism is the use of violence against unsuspecting and indiscriminately selected targets in order to gain political ends by a group using undercover tactics in order to avoid retaliation. Terrorists are thus persons using criminal means to gain political ends. Raids inside Israel might be admitted as legitimate guerilla tactics even if carried out against civilians; but the murder of Israeli civilians abroad, and later of non-Israeli civilians abroad, is clearly criminal in deed, even if not in intent, and is morally inadmissible. A withdrawal which might leave the field to the PLO had no hope of mobilizing support in Israel. The Israeli policy of holding on to the occupied territories was therefore not seriously challenged, especially during the War of Attrition along the Suez Canal, which lasted from April 1969 to August 1970 and which diverted attention to pressing security affairs.

It seems that Tsabar identity, and Labour legitimacy which rested on it, had to be undermined further before the strategy was challenged by which the government justified the continued occupation of the territories. The War of Attrition along the Suez Canal should have refuted the claim that extended borders provided greater security; the war merely showed that the new borders moved the conflict to a new territory. If settlements were established along the new borders, as they were in the Jordan Rift Valley and on the Golan Heights, no added security was really gained. Yet the public largely ignored this warning signal and continued to do so even after the October 1973 war, when settlements on the Golan Heights indeed had to be evacuated. Claim-staking and defence of the territory thus obtained were values appropriate to pioneering days, but could hardly be applied to territory conquered in war unless fortified by an ethical justification. As will be shown, this was already being done, but a fully formulated doctrine defining a new Israeli identity had not yet filtered through to the public at large. Until this occurred, Tsabar identity, though badly eroded, was not entirely rejected.

Discord and Ethnic Unrest

The erosion of Labour legitimacy came from several directions, not all of them related to the issue of the territories. Public opinion surveys conducted prior to 1973 showed Israelis to be dissatisfied with the conduct of internal affairs in their country. There was a feeling of political powerlessness and disgust with rampant corruption in public life, caused by several unsavoury political scandals.[32]

At the same time, the Black Panthers revived the issue of discrimination against Orientals, dormant since 1957. They were a group of under-privileged youths of Moroccan origin who demanded improvement of their lot by means of violent demonstrations. The emphasis they put on the ethnic aspect of their grievances was highly unsettling, for it challenged a major aspect of Tsabar identity at a time when it was already under the assault of political reality. The actual underprivileged condition of any one group of immigrants laid bare the inability, or unwillingness, of the Tsabar to turn all Jewish immigrants into Israelis. Open violent demonstrations revealed hidden disunity within Israeli society. The economic circumstances of the Moroccan community had not deteriorated in absolute terms. Yet, during the economic boom which followed the 1967 war, their sense of relative deprivation was the more acute; with Tsabar identity under siege anyway, they felt free to express grievances, where before they had been under an ideological constraint to keep silent.

Labour must have been keenly aware of the assault on its legitimacy by the Black Panthers, as evidenced by its reaction to their demonstrations in comparison to steps taken after the Wadi Salib riots of 1957, as well as by the social research conclusions following the events. While a cooptation of unrelated Orientals and public censure of the 'uncivilized' rioters had been the principal outcome in 1957, Panther leaders themselves were coopted, resources were allocated for slum rehabilitation and affirmative action programmes were introduced in schools. Furthermore, researchers now admitted the existence of ethnic stratification in Israel.[33]

THE OCTOBER 1973 WAR

The October 1973 War was not a turning point in the self-image of Israelis, nor the beginning of the end of Labour hegemony, as has frequently been claimed. As already noted, Labour legitimacy was already in decline at the time, yet the process was gradual and Labour still won the 1973 elections which followed the war. However, the war provided the *coup de grâce* to Tsabar identity. By further undermining Labour legitimacy, it paved the way for the success of the opposition from the other end of the political spectrum, which advocated a new articulation of Israeli identity to fit the new political reality of expanded borders.

In contrast to 1967, when Syria lured Egypt into a confrontation with Israel, it was Egypt which drew Syria into the 1973 war. The economic cost to Egypt of the 1967 defeat was very high, exacerbating an already severely strained economy. The best chance of recovery was the reopening of the Suez Canal for shipping, as its closure had cost Egypt about 36 per cent of its export revenues. The War of Attrition had failed to achieve this aim and had depleted Egyptian economic resources even further. President Sadat, well aware of Egyptian economic and military constraints, settled for the limited objective of crossing the Suez Canal and occupying as much territory on its eastern bank as possible. This is implied in the strategic directives issued to the Egyptian commanders-in-chief on 5 October 1973. Besides, a successful entrenchment across the Suez Canal would restore Egyptian self-confidence and the respect of the Arab world[34] and would force Israel to resume negotiations for a political settlement with Egypt by both exploding the myth of Israeli invincibility and by inducing the USA to intervene and start the process of negotiation.[35] To ensure success, Sadat, according to his own account, induced a reluctant Syria to join forces with Egypt. Preparations for the campaign were made as secretly as possible and their limited objective was masked by very belligerent rhetoric directed against Israel.[36]

Israel was complacent enough to swallow the bait. Correctly assessing Syrian and Egyptian incapability of launching and winning a full-scale war, its political leaders and intelligence service ignored or disbelieved the obvious indices of an impending attack, never considering the possibility of one with limited objectives.[37] As a result, Israel was unprepared, was overrun on 6 October 1973, could turn the tide in its favour only gradually from the third day onwards and consequently suffered heavy casualties. A final cease-fire was reached on 26 October 1973, but the reserves remained mobilized, most of them until after the disengagement agreement with Egypt had come into effect in February 1974, and some of them even longer until the disengagement agreement with Syria at the end of May 1974.

PROTEST AND DISSIDENCE AFTER THE 1973 WAR

Initially, the Israeli public was too stunned by the 1973 debacle to respond at all. Furthermore, protest was put in abeyance by the setting up of an enquiry commission, charged with fixing the blame for the fiasco. In the December 1973 elections, Labour lost some support, declining in strength by about 7 per cent, but still remained the largest single party and formed the new government. Protest got under way only after the enquiry commission had submitted its interim report on 2 April 1974. On the face of it, this seems surprising. The IDF had been unprepared, had rallied belatedly, had suffered excessive losses and had barely restored the *status quo ante*. As a result, the Tsabar image was irrevocably tarnished, since he had failed to perform his primary task – defence of the state – to perfection. What is more, the commission put all the blame on the military, disqualifying itself from dealing with the responsibility of the government. Yet it was not Tsabar identity which came under attack, except for those same perceptive and sensitized young Kibbutz members who had already recognized his demise in 1967. As one participant in the 1967 symposium later put it, it became clear after the 1973 war that Labour Zionism and Tsabar identity could no longer provide the answer to the most fundamental question of the right by which Israelis were in Israel and of what the purpose of their fighting was.[38] For most, though, that was too intractable a dilemma to tackle on their own. Only when Gush Emunim later provided a convincing solution to this existential Israeli question did the question itself surface and many of those early protesters joined Gush Emunim.[39] Rather than face a total loss of identity, protesters targeted the Labour government for refusing to share responsibility. This was seen to be in line with the general ossification and decline in moral fibre of Labour. The protest was voiced by several groups, all but one of them very short-lived. All the transient groups were fairly similar in their aims and actions, so that one may serve as an example. The availability of research material was the major factor in choosing Our Israel.

Our Israel

Our Israel protested against the betrayal of Pioneer values, primarily against the egoism which had replaced the former ideal of public service in Israeli society. The group criticized the Labour party system because it based its power on economic dependence on the party, and objected to the party structure, which had become oligarchic due to central control of appointments. It demanded a change in the electoral system to one based on constituencies, the introduction of ministerial responsibility, an independent economic and security control system and depolitization of the armed forces. In addition to advocating these measures, which were intended to increase direct influence of the citizen on the government, it also objected to economic inequality, corruption and the deterioration of human relations in Israeli society.[40] The movement, which had formed in February 1974, disintegrated in the autumn of that year because of dwindling public support.

Shinui (Change)

The only long-lived protest group was the one which eventually became Dash (Hebrew acronym for Democratic Movement for Change), the party which was instrumental in defeating Labour at the 1977 elections. Shinui began as a protest rally in January 1974, not directed against the military fiasco as much as against the infringement of the liberal democratic principle of ministerial responsibility, so blatantly flouted by the government. (Demonstrators believed the government should have stepped down immediately, irrespective of the eventual findings of the commission.) The government did resign in May 1974 due to ongoing public pressure, but this step was regarded by Shinui as purely cosmetic, for Labour remained in power under Premier Yitzhak Rabin. The movement thus continued, promulgating the targets spelled out in the platform it had published in July 1974.

The Shinui platform[41] underlined the Jewish character of Israel and mentioned a necessary, though unspecified link with world Jewry. Withdrawal from most occupied territories, notably Judea and Samaria (the West Bank) and the Gaza Strip was imperative in order to obtain peace and international support. Withdrawal would also safeguard the Jewishness of Israel. Furthermore, the equal rights of Palestinian self-determination were recognized, although the PLO was ruled out as the representative of the Palestinians. In the economic sphere, restricted government intervention was demanded, as well as abolition of economic dependence on the government. These measures were assumed to result in greater economic equality, without explaining the logical or factual link between proposed measures and expected outcomes. Similarly, the educational underachievement of Orientals was to be remedied by sports and cultural activities, rather than by improved longer hours of instruction. Demands for a constitution and incorporation of constituencies in the present proportional election system were intended to secure a greater measure of direct democracy and individual rights.

Neither Our Israel nor Shinui tackled the problem of identity. Our Israel disregarded the issue altogether, while Shinui proposed a withdrawal in order to fit reality to Tsabar identity. Similar to the Peace Movement, it did not suggest any concrete steps towards this end. Nor did it take account of the growing reluctance of both the public and the government to relinquish the territories occupied in 1967. The reluctance of the Israeli government to withdraw has been too well documented to need further elaboration. That of the public is indicated by a research conducted in 1975, which compared pupil and adult attitudes regarding the occupied territories. Sixty-five per cent of young respondents opposed any withdrawal at all, as against 47 per cent of adults (which was still nearly half of the adult respondents). Seventy per cent of young respondents opposed a withdrawal from the West Bank, as against 56 per cent of adults. Support for settlements on the Golan Heights was 88 per cent among pupils and 82 per cent among adults, for those in the Jordan Rift Valley it was 82 per cent among pupils and 75 per cent among adults and for those in Judea it was 80 per cent among pupils and 65 per cent among adults.[42] A public holding such views was clearly rejecting the framework within which Tsabar identity was valid and seeking, or having found already, a new identity formulation which justified such views. Parties and movements advocating withdrawal were unlikely to mobilize broad support from this public, especially from the young. The difference in hawkishness between young and older voters are significant and will be discussed below. Nevertheless, Shinui drew some support, especially after it merged with the Democratic Movement shortly before the 1977 elections. The combined Dash party won 11.6 per cent of the votes.

NASCENT NEW ZIONISM

The Peace Movement and the above protest groups proposed a return to a previous political reality which could be defended ethically by the values held dear at the time. They implied that the present Labour leadership was betraying these Tsabar values and should therefore be replaced by true implementers of Tsabar values. In contrast, two other groups, which eventually merged, glorified the new political reality and proposed a new set of values in order to justify it morally. As already reported, the first to realize the lack of fit between Tsabar identity and Israel in its extended borders were Kibbutz youngsters and students at Yeshivat Merkaz Ha-rav. From these two groups, disaffection quickly spread to broader circles in both camps, namely in Labour on the one hand and in the NRP (National Religious Party) on the other hand. Each circle formulated a justification for the new status quo, the combination of which finally crystallized into Settler identity, based on a novel interpretation of the Messianic idea. It was eventually adopted by at least half of the Israeli public.

The Land of Israel Movement

This movement was established immediately after the 1967 war, on 20 August 1967, by members of Labour and Labour-affiliated parties, such as Rafi (which had split off and rejoined Labour) and Mapam (left of Labour), as well as members of the cooperative settlement movement. Its aim was to prevent the withdrawal of Israeli forces from occupied territories. Its reasons were military as well as political: Israel needed a strategic depth to prevent surprise attacks on its populated areas. Since the Arabs would recognize neither the old nor the new borders, the new ones were politically no more damaging than the old ones had been, but had this military advantage. Soon after the establishment of the movement, some of the above-mentioned Yeshivat Merkaz Ha-rav students and their followers asked for its aid in establishing a settlement in Gush Etsion, in Judea. The idea of settlements in the occupied territories was taken up by the Land of Israel Movement, though this made its strategic argument null and void: the occupied territories could not serve as a buffer zone if they were settled by Jews. Consequently, strategic considerations were replaced by the ingathering of the exiles, a chief component of the Messianic message. To accommodate the millions of future immigrants, the State had to remain as large as possible.[43] Mapam members added a further aspect to this doctrine: they reinterpreted the original Labour Zionist emphasis on physical contact with the soil as a means to salvation: in 1970s Israel, it was Erets Yisrael – the Land of Israel (meaning Israel and the occupied territories) – which had an intrinsic wholeness, a mystical geography, which must not be violated.[44] The switch from soil to Land was significant. Instead of physical labour on the soil, it was now the shock of recognition, when a person begins to know himself in Erets Yisrael, when it allows him to redeem and know himself.[45]

Regarding social salvation, the Leftist members of the Movement leadership, largely Kibbutz members, were soon overruled by the concepts formulated by the leading ideologue Livne, a former Labourite.[46] Livne envisioned a completely novel social order, based on Judaic values, but incorporating solutions to some of the issues raised by the New Left. Livne's main criticism was levelled against the materialism, excessive consumption and inflated living standard of Israeli society. These increased Israel's economic dependence on the United States, forcing it to give in to pressures in matters of security. They also undermined the human qualities of social relations. Inner life could be enriched once the rush for stimuli gratification subsided. Furthermore, quality of life in Israel had deteriorated because of its ecological problems as much as due to its economic corruption. The majority of the population lived concentrated along the coastal strip. The purely ecological problem of congestion had become an ethical one. Physical pollution bred emotional tension, crowding caused alienation, continuous stimuli drove people to mutual provocation, noise stifled attention and forced proximity blunted kindness.

Under the favourable conditions created in the West Bank settlements, a new Israeli could evolve whose values were derived from Judaism rather than socialism. Marxism was as alien to Judaism as was capitalism, whose materialism and over-consumption had corrupted Israeli society. The imitation of Western values was idolatry, un-Jewish behaviour, which would destroy Israel. Instead of agricultural collectives, hardly a feasible economic desideratum in a country which suffers from an acute water shortage, Livne proposed a new type of industrial community to be set up on the West Bank, where the Judaic values of mutual responsibility and mutual aid were to replace egalitarianism. The cohesion of small communities would counteract the alienation in Israeli society induced by its imitation of Western values. Since Judaism was a communal religion, the individual could achieve salvation only as a member of the community. In the settlements, service to the group would replace egoism and lead to self-fulfilment and a closer approach to personal perfection.

Jewishness is the focus of this new doctrine. Israel was established for the ingathering of the entire Jewish people, not for the welfare of its present citizens. Judaic values would provide Israelis with a distinctiveness *vis-à-vis* the rest of the world, would reestablish the link with world Jewry and would justify the Israeli presence in the occupied territories, which were the heart of historical Erets Yisrael. Israelis were simply returning to their origins. This was the new Zionist ethos which the Land of Israel Movement underscored. From late 1973 onwards, Livne reintroduced the term Zionism, which still had a derogatory connotation in Israel, and which was completely absent from the statements of the Peace Movement and the protest movements. (The term became generally popular in Israel only after the condemnation of Zionism by the United Nations on 10 November 1975. Outraged, the Zionist Council in Israel organized demonstrations under the slogan 'I am a Zionist'. Buttons bearing this slogan were distributed and one suddenly saw many Israelis wearing them.)

As it stood, this doctrine had the serious flaw of inconsistency. Firstly, Livne insisted that the Arabs would regard the territories as worthy of exchange for peace only if they were settled: they viewed areas empty of Jews as Arab anyway, unworthy of barter. That argument implied a willingness to evacuate the settlements and withdraw in return for peace, which contradicted the historical argument underlying the principal idea of the Land of Israel Movement, namely an absolute refusal to relinquish any part of the homeland. This, in turn, left unresolved the dilemma which had haunted Zionism since its inception: a secular–historical justification of the Jewish presence in Palestine was an inadequate rational defence against the equally valid historical claim of the Palestinians. The doctrine became viable as the basis for Settler identity only after religious justifications supplanted secular ones.

Gush Emunim (the Block of the Faithful)

As already related, immediately after the 1967 war, Hanan Porat organized a group of young men born in Kfar Etsion to return and settle there. Kfar Etsion had been a religious settlement in Judea (Gush Etsion) taken by Jordan during the 1948 war. Porat asked the Land of Israel Movement to intercede on their behalf with the government for permission to settle there. This initiated the idea of settling in the occupied territories. In 1968, Kfar Etsion was established, as was a religious quarter in Hebron, named Kiryat Arba. The leader of the latter, Rabbi Levinger, together with Porat and his comrades, formed the nucleus of what was to become Gush Emunim. Most of these young men had been members of Bnei 'Akiva, the youth movement of the religious Kibbutz movement. Many of them had studied at Yeshivat Merkaz Ha-rav and were greatly influenced by the ideas expressed by Rabbi Kuk Junior, head of that Yeshiva.

Gush Emunim was founded in February 1974 in protest against the return of territories demanded by the peace initiative of Dr Kissinger. They also opposed the campaigns of the other protest groups. In their view, the latter were crying over spilt milk (the military fiasco and undemocratic governance), while an immediate danger needed to be averted. Moreover, the other groups were merely protesting verbally, while Gush Emunim intended to counter government policies by the positive action of settling the territories. In line with this, Gush Emunim organized demonstrative settlement at three locations on the West Bank in October 1974. Several days later they were forcibly evacuated by troops and consequently held a rally under the slogan 'Judea and Samaria are ours'. In November 1974, they applied for permission to set up on the West Bank a collective centre of educational services and science-based industry, a settlement based on agriculture and industry, an industrial and tourist village, another agricultural settlement and three cities. The request was turned down. In December 1974, they obtained permission to revive an ancient religious custom and light torches in Judea and Samaria to commemorate the victory of the Maccabees. In January 1975, three groups of settlers formed, one to establish a town. In March 1975, a second attempt to settle Sebastia, the ancient capital of the Kingdom of Israel, again ended in evacuation, whereupon they organized the Samaria march in order to emphasize that this was Jewish territory.

The attempted settlements, rallies and the march were carried out on a mass scale. Gush Emunim succeeded in mobilizing considerable numbers of sympathizers who had no intention of living on the West Bank themselves, but were willing to assist others in doing so. The government was adamant in its refusal to permit these settlements, because they were of no strategic importance, in contrast to the government-sponsored ones in the Jordan Valley and the Gaza Strip. Gush Emunim settlers were removed by troops and, since they offered passive resistance, these operations usually turned into a fracas, amply covered by the mass media. Gush Emunim leaders were usually arrested and then released without charge. As negotiations over the interim agreement with Egypt progressed, Gush Emunim concentrated its efforts on preventing a withdrawal from the Sinai. Together with Likud they staged a demonstration at the Western Wall in Jerusalem in January 1975, then held a massive demonstration in Jerusalem in August 1975.

The above are only some of the campaigns launched by Gush Emunim during 1974–75, all of which conformed to the pattern of attempted settlements, usually thwarted, and protests against an Israeli withdrawal from occupied territories. By 1976, government opposition to Gush Emunim settlements was crumbling. In April 1976, they organized a march under the slogan 'Erets Yisrael', claiming that they had been promised participation by American Jews and lobbying in the American Senate. They appealed to members of workers' committees of the Histadrut, to the underprivileged inhabitants of development towns and to Kibbutz members. Indeed, Kibbutz and cooperative settlement members published an appeal in the daily press, calling on their colleagues to join the march of Gush Emunim in order to 'express our love and devotion to Erets Yisrael'.[49] The march was a great success, mobilizing 30,000 sympathizers. These included not just obvious supporters, such as the hawkish Likud leaders, but also Kibbutz members and members of the young faction of the NRP (National Religious Party).

The NRP had been expressly dovish, despite its name. It called itself 'national' in order to stress its recognition of the State of Israel as the divinely promised homeland of the Jewish people, in contrast to other orthodox circles, which denied that link. From the beginning of 1975, though, the young generation of NRP leaders was getting increasingly involved with Gush Emunim, in opposition to the dovish stand of the older leadership. The young NRP leaders joined the above march, joined a demonstration of Gush Emunim and Likud against the withdrawal from Sinai and even held a sit-down strike at the home of the minister of the interior, who was the leader of the NRP. The purpose of the latter was to induce the NRP, a partner in the government coalition, to vote against the interim agreement with Egypt. By September 1975, the young NRP leaders stated publicly that they regarded themselves as the political representatives of Gush Emunim,[48] though the latter refused to be affiliated with any party.

Support also came from diaspora Jewry. The press reported that Rabbi Miller, an American Jewish leader, regarded the Gush as the true representative of the Jewish People and that the Chief Rabbi of South Africa had stated his support of them.[49] At the end of 1976, American Wizo (the Zionist Women's Organization) leaders invited Gush Emunim leaders to present their views. In July 1976, Gush leaders addressed the Jewish Agency Settlement Committee and won them over. In view of such massive support, the government felt unable to act decisively against the Gush. They had been forcibly evacuated during 1974–75, but when they made fresh attempts at settlement in 1976, they were tacitly allowed to remain in Kadum and in Elon More.

Gush Emunim Doctrine

The question which immediately comes to mind is: what was the reason for such massive support from such unlikely quarters? Both the Pioneer and the Tsabar had been outspokenly secular; Jewish religion had not played a part in Israeli identity, especially in that of the Tsabar, who had gone further than the Pioneer and removed himself from Jewish tradition and the Jewish people. Moreover, self-declared religious persons had never exceeded 30 per cent of the Jewish Israeli population, nor had the religious parties ever gained more than 15.4 per cent of the votes.[50] (Since they confined their activity principally to safeguarding the narrow religious interests of their constituents, many observant people with broader social–political interests voted for secular parties.) Gush

Emunim, with their crocheted skullcaps, were identified by all and sundry as a group of religious youths. The NRP, with which Gush Emunim members and their families had previously been associated, had always been non-militant and the Tsabar was anti-religious rather than non-religious. Yet a small group of religious youths managed to defy government decisions without producing a public outcry and were finally instrumental in forcing the government to resign. They accomplished the latter with the aid of the young minority faction in the NRP. The explanation for this mobilization of sympathy and active support would seem to lie chiefly in the ability of their ideology to provide a new articulation of Israeli identity consistent with the new political situation of extended borders. In analysing this ideology, only slight mention will be made of its more profound theological aspects, as these do not seem pertinent to the purpose at hand. The religious mysticism of the doctrine certainly motivated the actual members of the Gush, a small group of devotees, but its political appeal must be attributed mainly to those components mentioned in the daily press. These were most likely to be generally understood and were the ones to which the general public had easy access.

Gush Emunim was inspired by the teachings of Rabbi Abraham Yitzhak Hacohen Kuk (Senior) already outlined in Chapter 2. To recapitulate, he regarded nationalism as the establishment of a spiritual-religious nationhood. The means to this end were immigration to Palestine and its rebuilding, since the Jewish genius, prophecy, could thrive only there. Going to Palestine and living there was a commandment in its own right, and not merely a derivative of those commandments which could only be obeyed in Palestine, as the orthodox establishment asserted.[51] Furthermore, the building of Palestine, the First World War and the Balfour Declaration were signs of the beginning of redemption, heralding the coming of the Messiah.[52] Rabbi Kuk was tolerant of the atheistic pioneers, because they were instrumental in the process of redemption and, therefore, subconsciously repentant of their rejection of religion.[53] Observant Jews who did not strive for a revolution to bring about perfect justice, and whom he called 'souls in search of perfection', were lower in the mystical hierarchy than 'souls of chaos', the atheistic revolutionaries. The 'souls of chaos' sinned against biblical commandments because of the frustration inherent in the Messianic idea: the delay in the coming of the Messiah prevented the approach of the era of perfect justice which they envisioned. This sin was minute compared to the acceptance of an imperfect world.[54]

At the time, the teachings of Rabbi Kuk Senior mobilized only a small number of followers who would not abandon their religious faith, yet wished to take part in the ongoing national revival. The orthodox establishment branded Rabbi Kuk a heretic: his distinction between ethical and religious transgressions and his insistence that nationalism would not replace religion, but enhance it, were revolutionary innovations unacceptable in his time. The atheistic Pioneers, on the other hand, had no need of a religious doctrine, since they believed themselves to have a perfectly consistent justification for their actions, which provided them with a wholly satisfactory identity. The teachings of Rabbi Kuk Senior became influential, however, when the secular ideology underlying Tsabar identity could no longer justify political reality, whereas a transformation of his teachings into a proper ideology could.

As already noted, an ideology is a blueprint for the ideal structure of a given society. In order to have a broad appeal, this ideal structure must rest on core values of that society, because the latter are common to all members. In addition, the ideology must lay out a programme of political action which will bring about the desired structure. Consequently, it must be firmly grounded in political reality and provide practical answers to pressing social and/or political issues unresolved by the prevalent ideology. Thus, timing was crucial for the success of Gush Emunim ideology. The retention of the occupied territories without a convincing justification for this policy created an identity dilemma; the translation by Rabbi Zvi Yehuda Hacohen Kuk (Junior) of the original mystical religious doctrine into an ideology coincided with the creation of this dilemma. As the perception of the identity dilemma spread gradually, so did the sympathy and support for Gush Emunim, carriers of a new ideology which could be the bedrock for the articulation of a new Israeli identity.

Rabbi Kuk Junior reinterpreted his father's advocacy of immigration and the building of Palestine to mean settlement of the entire land liberated in the 1967 war. The land was promised to the Jews by God and was, therefore, non-transferable.[55] Rabbi Kuk and his disciples viewed the return to what they regarded as the liberated parts of the land as 'one of the six strokes of the process of redemption'.[56] Rabbi Kuk Senior had regarded the return to Palestine as heralding the coming of the Messiah; Gush Emunim shifted the timing to the immediate present, believing that if they could prove proprietorship of the Holy Land, of the parts already liberated, this would hasten redemption.[57] Because of its sacred significance, settlement of the land required total devotion, even to the point of martyrdom.[58] The Ashkenazy Chief Rabbi of Israel went even further and claimed that the settlement of liberated Erets Yisrael was a commandment overriding all others.[59]

Since the return to the liberated land is a sacred mission, no opposition to it may be tolerated. Rabbi Kuk Junior asserted that the government was not legitimate if it did not represent the people's interest, which was redemption by settlement. Those who demanded Israel's withdrawal from Judea and Samaria, and those who submitted to this request (the government), would be cursed by God.[60] 'We are commanded by the Bible, not by the government. The Bible overrides the government, it is eternal and this government is temporary and invalid.'[61] Therefore, said the spokesman of Gush Emunim, settlement was above the law.[62] Gush leaders conceded that they recognized the State of Israel, but Erets Yisrael was a much broader concept.[63] The moderate Gush members wanted to push for the resignation of the government, while the more radical faction, including Rabbi Kuk Junior, actually incited its followers to civil rebellion.[64]

The tolerance of Rabbi Kuk Senior had been confined to the pioneers who built Palestine. The disciples of his son extended tolerance to the entire Jewish people. 'I do not accept these concepts of religious/non-religious...the Jewish people is one unit and there are thousands of degrees of Jewishness.'[65] This statement of principle was put into actual practice. Gush Emunim appealed to secular bodies to join it in its campaigns; the disciples of Rabbi Kuk held symposia with Kibbutz members; Gush Emunim later merged with the secular Land of Israel Movement and with the Vered Circle, the latter a group of Kibbutz and Moshav members. All this was done without any overt religious coercion and no attempt was made to bring pressure of any kind on the non-observant, which was unique in Israeli relationships between orthodox and non-religious groups. Their tolerance was shown most of all by their inclusion of non-observant members in their settlements, while maintaining harmonious relations among all. Rabbi Kuk Senior had believed that the pioneers would eventually shed their atheism as a result of their sacred work in the Holy Land. Gush Emunim translated this into more practical terms. According to Porat, the settlement of the land was an integral part of the Jewish worldview, which was based on religion. Judaism included 'putting the world aright in the Kingdom of God, social reformation, the sanctity of man, love between men'.[66] This initial Gush tolerance was missionary work, in line with the teachings of Rabbi Kuk Senior: acceptance of the non-observant would bring them back into the fold by example, not by dispute.

The experiment succeeded only as long as the secular settlers remained unaware of this covert aim, however. Eventually, most mixed settlements became homogenous by voluntary migration. Yet initially, the pronounced tolerance of the Gush contributed greatly to their general appeal, as well as making religious observance respectable in formerly atheist Israel. 'Repenters', or converts to orthodoxy, became a growing phenomenon in Israel. Gush Emunim assumed that this conversion was a new Judaism which was markedly Zionist, or, conversely, that Zionism was being imbued with religion, but their hopes were largely dashed, at least until recently. Most converts became strictly orthodox. At the time, this implied indifference to the entire issue of the occupied territories and their settlement.

Early New Zionism

Gush Emunim, the Land of Israel Movement and the Vered Circle merged at the end of September 1977. The leading article in their joint organ stated that 'In Gush Emunim, the Land of Israel Movement has found its vanguard and its army of implementers.'[67] The political merger was the culmination of ideological fusion. Gush statements gave religious meaning to the national, social and individual salvation advocated by Livne. Settlement attained religious significance as a stage in the coming of the Messiah; Livne's ecological and moral reasons for the need of social and individual reformation received a religious connotation by being put into terms of conversion to Jewish values and norms, though not necessarily the strictly orthodox ones.

The merger provided an apparent continuity between Pioneer and Settler identities, skipping over the Tsabar. The Tsabar, who had compromised on a reduced territory, as well as on the social and individual salvation aspects of Messianism, was not even condemned. He was largely ignored as an aberration of Zionism, for he had betrayed its values and rejected the term itself. Gush Emunim reintroduced the term Zionism and stressed that they were its only true contemporary implementers and the successors to the original pioneers. They were not innovators, but continued the true way of the Zionist movement, which was immigration and settlement. According to Livne, they were the only ones to bring about concrete Zionist progress, as had been the second wave of immigrants in the past. Even those who did not fully agree with their political views and considered them extremists would have to concede that it had been extremists like them who had created and realized Zionism.[68]

The emphasis on continuity with the secular Pioneer was decidedly an asset in drawing sympathy and support from the largely secular Israeli population. Firstly, evoking core values as interpreted by the heroic founding fathers has great emotional appeal. Secondly, stressing continuity with the Pioneer obscured the profound difference between his secular worldview and the religious one of Gush Emunim, a difference which, if properly noted, might have alienated secular supporters. Contrary to the secular worldview, according to which everything material and abstract derives from human endeavour, God's Will is the source of everything according to the religious worldview. The latter places human history and fate in God's care, with humans the mere instruments of His Will. Human responsibility lies in interpreting the Divine Will correctly, rather than judging the situation objectively and acting upon that. Once Gush Emunim claimed to know that settlement of the Holy Land was the ultimate commandment by God, rational considerations could play a tactical role in their course of action at best, but could not divert them from the overall strategy ordained by God. In consequence, the Gush was largely indifferent to world opinion and the actual political and military dangers incurred by their actions.[69] The Land of Israel Movement had justified such actions in strategic terms. As the ideological fusion with Gush Emunim progressed, the combined reasoning became increasingly mystical, in line with arguments of Rabbi Kuk Junior. Settlement was a commandment to bring about redemption, which must be preceded by apocalyptic events; yet Jewry would overcome and survive them if it had sufficient faith.[70]

The practical drawbacks to such indifference to the world, due to its religious worldview, were overshadowed by decided advantages to identity formation. Principally, by distancing itself from the rest of the world, Gush Emunim doctrine sharply delineated Israelis in comparison to all others by emphasizing the cultural–national uniqueness of Judaism–Jewishness–Israeliness. Livne had already pointed to the distortions in Israeli society which resulted from the imitation of Western values. For religious Jews, cultural and national seclusion are taken for granted, since both nationhood and national culture originate in the Jewish religion, which sets Jews apart from the rest of the world. As the influence of Gush Emunim spread, rejection of Westernization and reemphasis of Jewish uniqueness became increasingly accepted in Israel. One writer, himself with a Western education, concluded that Jewish nationhood was based on the covenant between God and His people. 'We have to take a great stride towards dissimilation... [since] Zionism is the conclusion of Jewish history, of Jewish thought.'[71]

Uniqueness, as articulated by the Gush, spelled more than just seclusion; it also rescinded the alienation of the Tsabar from world Jewry. It revived the Pioneer stance of the Israeli as the vanguard of the Jewish people. When invited to talk to American Zionist ladies, a Gush leader said,

> We reject the principle of the Zionist establishment, which claims that the function of diaspora Jews is to collect funds and recruit political aid for Israel. We believe that you are full and equal partners in our entire struggle and in everything that occurs here.[72]

New Zionism, the combined ideology, transformed the statehood of the Tsabar into nationhood. By doing this, it bridged the chasm between

Israel and the diaspora: statehood excluded the diaspora, while nationhood included it. It made Jewishness, Zionism and Israeliness three levels in a single unity.

The historical rationale for settling in an already inhabited land, which had been so problematic for the atheists who had used the Bible as their title deed, was completely consistent with religious New Zionism, so that religion and history could be used interchangeably. Thus Livne described the attempted settlement of Elon More as a renewed covenant between the people of Israel and Samaria, while he regarded the new borders as the original frontiers of the ancient fatherland.[73] Furthermore, New Zionism transformed the original Messianic idea in a novel way. Return to Zion was translated into settlement of the land. Social salvation became a new type of communality, which fused private initiative with group solidarity as a typical Jewish value. Individual salvation was reinterpreted in Jewish terms to mean perfect neighbourly relations, mutual aid and mutual responsibility, which constituted the perfect ethical state of the individual.[74] The dilemma posed by the Messianic idea was resolved heretically, by denying the orthodox interpretation and insisting that the return to the Holy Land was the ultimate command- ment. At the same time, New Zionism also invalidated the Pioneer and Tsabar interpretations of the Messianic message. Egalitarianism was replaced by equity, individual mystical salvation was replaced by salvation of the individual as a member of the Jewish community; love of the soil was replaced by love of the Holy Land, agriculture by industry and rural collective settlements by urban ones. Collectivity was redefined in Jewish terms of communality and Israeli statism by pan-Jewishness. By doing so, Gush Emunim challenged the very legitimacy of Labour, which stood for the previous value system and the identity resting on it.

GENERATIONAL CHANGE IN IDENTITY ARTICULATION

The 1967 war was a sea change in the self-image of Israelis in more ways than one, for it also spearheaded a generational rift in ideological and political allegiance. Paradoxically, this was due in large part to the successful socialization to which the young had been subjected. It has been noted that the young had been surprisingly conformist in the Yishuv era and during the early years of Israel.[75] The young of the 1970s had been exposed to the truncated version of Labour Zionism which underlay Tsabar identity. As noted earlier, by far fewer young people than their elders incorporated Jewishness or Zionism in their self-image. Therefore, they could not fall back on previous values when faced with the moral dilemma posed by the retention of 'foreign' territory conquered in war.

Talk of Warriors and *Talks in the Kibbutz Among Young People*, the two books mentioned earlier, showed that the first to voice their doubts about the war and its outcome were young Kibbutz members, the sons of those pioneers who had been the truest implementors of Labour Zionism. To retain their elite position, Kibbutz natives had internalized Tsabar identity more vigorously than most and had implemented its norms as faithfully as possible – by volunteering for elite military units, by competing successfully for top military command positions and by seeking self-realization in the intellectually more demanding jobs which Kibbutz industry was offering. Just because they had been such enthusiastic Tsabars, they were more acutely aware of the inadequacy of their self-image in the face of the new political reality.

Other young people were somewhat slower in perceiving the dilemma, but did not remain far behind. The wave of protest in Israel, starting in 1967 and coming to a head after the 1973 war, was initiated partly by the young. Siah, the nucleus of the peace movement, was founded by students, as was Our Israel (one of the reform movements)[76] and Gush Emunim. More significantly, survey data show some interesting age differences in political allegiance. At the 1969 elections, age differences in party support began to appear. Among Labour voters, only 38 per cent belonged to the 18–24 age group, as against 61 per cent of the 50+ age group.[77] By 1973, a survey of intended voting held shortly before the elections showed that among the 18–35 age group, 43 per cent favoured the Likud party and only 30 per cent favoured Labour, while the corresponding percentages for the 36+ age group were 18 per cent in favour of Likud and 48 per cent in favour of Labour. In the 1973 elections, actual voting of the young male population could be directly observed. The elections were held shortly after the war and none of the reserves had been discharged yet. Army polls were delayed and were counted separately. The results were in line with the intended voting behaviour quoted above.[78]

The more militant stance of the young, expressed in their preference for Likud, which had always been associated with militancy in foreign policy, indicated their protest and frustration. Labour practised a militant policy, yet was unable to justify it by the value system it espoused. The Tsabar had become immoral and many of the young rejected that image. They preferred to identify with a party which was honestly combative and nationalistic, without the subterfuge used by Labour. When New Zionism provided them with an alternative identity which resolved their predicament, the young were more apt to accept it, as the following data show. In 1975, opposition to an interim agreement with Egypt which would require a withdrawal from Sinai (against which Gush Emunim held numerous demonstrations) rose with decreasing age; in 1977, reported opposition to withdrawal from the occupied territories rose with decreasing age; in 1975, 65 per cent of pupils opposed withdrawal, as against 47 per cent of adults; 80 per cent of pupils supported settlements on the West Bank, while only 65 per cent of adults did so. Moreover, Zionist identification of pupils rose from 66 per cent in 1973 (prior to the formation of Gush Emunim) to 75 per cent in 1975 (after the latter's founding and prior to the condemnation of Zionism at the UN).[79]

The year 1977 also saw the electoral defeat of Labour after 50 years of dominance (including 20 years in the Yishuv period). By 1977, New Zionism had not spread widely yet, nor had the Settler become the image with which over half the Israeli population later identified. But three years after its foundation, Gush Emunim already precipitated a general trend towards hawkish attitudes among the young and a rebellion within the NRP. At the end of 1976, the young faction of the NRP, which openly associated itself with Gush Emunim, rebelled against the older party leadership and its pacifist stance. It convinced the latter that the party might lose half its constituency, due to a growing loss of orthodox support, unless it disassociated itself from the increasingly unpopular Labour party.[80] The young NRP faction induced its party to break coalition discipline, ostensibly because some secular cabinet ministers had desecrated the Sabbath. In consequence, Labour was forced to end its coalition with the NRP and to call for early elections.

The results of the 1977 elections demonstrated that the Settler had not yet replaced the Tsabar, but that Labour, which represented the Tsabar, was no longer considered worthy of ruling: it had lost its legitimacy. In 1973 Labour support decreased from 39.6 per cent in 1973 to 24.6 per cent. Dash, the reform movement which ran for the elections for the first time, gained 11.6 per cent of the votes, while Likud increased in 1973 from 30.2 per cent to 33.4 per cent. Likud thus became the largest single party and was commissioned to form the next government, not because it gained a substantial increase in support, but because Labour had lost so much support, mainly to Dash. Likud had thus won by default.

The NRP and Likud, the two parties which could be associated with New Zionism, together gained 4 per cent more votes than in 1973, while Dash gained 11.6 per cent. Obviously, the prevalent dissatisfaction and protest in Israel were channelled mainly into support of the reform movement. The Israeli public was not yet ready for a radical change: while 63 per cent of Likud voters had wanted a change of regime and 20 per cent had wanted to punish Labour, 33 per cent of Dash voters had wanted to give the new party a chance, 33 per cent had been attracted by the new candidates and only 33 per cent had regarded its platform as a promise of real change.[81] Plainly, most people voting for Dash wanted reform only, while those in favour of a complete change were still a minority. They became a majority within a relatively short time once the now ruling Likud party adopted New Zionism and pronounced Gush Emunim as its vanguard.

NOTES

1. For a discussion of this point, see L. Weissbrod, *Arab Relations with Jewish Immigrants and Israel, 1891–1991; The Hundred Years Conflict* (Lewiston: Edwin Mellen, 1992), especially pp.140–54.
2. According to then Israeli Foreign Minister Abba Eban, quoted in M. Brecher, 'Eban and Israeli Foreign Policy: Diplomacy, War and Disengagement', in B. Frankel (ed.), *A Restless Mind: Essays in Honour of Amos Perlmutter* (London: Frank Cass, 1996), pp.104–43.
3. *Talks of Warriors*, (Tel-Aviv: Group of Young Kibbutz Members Publication, 1967).
4. *Talks In the Kibbutz Among Young People*, (Tel-Aviv: Am Oved, 1969).
5. *Talks of Warriors*, pp.31–2, 50–5.
6. *Talks In the Kibbutz*, p.12.
7. *Talks of Warriors*, p.13
8. *Talks of Warriors*, p.13, *Talks In the Kibbutz*, pp.49–62.
9. 'Talks of Warriors at Yeshivat Ha-rav Kuk', *Shdemot*, No. 29, 1968, pp.15–27.
10. Ibid., p.22.
11. *Talks in The Kibbutz*, pp.10–33; M.H. Amishai, 'Talks of Oldsters' *Shdemot*, No. 38, 1978, pp. 5–11; the following Hebrew articles in *Shdemot*: M. Ayali, 'Where Is Sincerity, Whence Wholeness?', No. 32, 1969, pp.128–9; 'Cast Anchor in Life Once More', No. 32, 1969, pp.70–2.
12. 'Cast Anchor In Life Once More'; *Talks of Warriors*, pp.62–75; M. Zur, 'Secular Messianism', *Shdemot*, No. 27, 1968, pp.14–15.
13. As mentioned earlier, Tsabar identity had been adopted more readily by the young than by the older generation, so that a study of the young provides a clearer measure of differences in Jewish identification in Israel at the time.
14. S.N. Herman, *Israelis and Jews: The Continuity of an Identity* (New York: Random House, 1970), pp.49, 51.
15. 'After the Shofar at the Western Wall', *Ha-arets*, 6 June 1997.
16. This point is conceded by severely critical historians and political sociologists, such as B. Morris in his review of two books on the war entitled 'The Transfer Atmosphere of the Six Day War', *Ha-arets*, 6 August 1997, or Z. Sternhell in 'The Big Madness', *Ha-arets*, 6 June 1997, as well as by those considered mainline scholars, such as S. Avineri in his paper 'The Eshkol Government: Strength and Weakness', delivered at the conference 'Six Days – Thirty Years', held at Tel-Aviv University on 26–28 May 1997.
17. M. Bar-On, *Personal Signature: Moshe Dayan in the Six Day War and After* (Tel-Aviv: Yedi'ot Ahronot, 1997), p.113.
18. Y. Nedava, *The Israel–Arab Conflict* (Ramat-Gan: Revivim, 1983), pp.48–51, 86–8.
19. Y. Allon, 'The West Bank and Gaza Within the Framework of a Middle East Peace Settlement', *Middle East Review*, Vol. 12, No. 2, 1979/80, pp.15–18.
20. See Y. Nedava, *The Israel–Arab Conflict*, p.398, quoting Dayan's speech in the Knesset during the debate on the Camp David Accord, and M.S. Chertoff, *Zionism* (New York: Herzl Press, 1975), pp.61–75, reprint of an article by Golda Meir published in *Foreign Affairs* in 1973.
21. See, for example, H. Marcuse, *One-Dimensional Man* (London: Routledge & Kegan Paul, 1964), pp.1–15, 225–51.
22. See, for example, C.W. Mills, *The Marxists* (Harmondsworth: Penguin, 1963), pp.437–49; E.J. Bacciocco, *The New Left in America: Reform and Revolution 1956 to 1970* (Stamford: Hoover Institution, 1974), p.161.
23. *The Palestinian National Covenant 1968*.
24. 'The Democratic State', *Al-Anwar*, 8 March 1970.
25. R.J. Isaac, 'The Land of Israel Movement: A Study in Political Deinstitutionalisation', Ph.D. Thesis, City University of New York, 1971, pp.262–71.
26. Ibid., p.383; J. Arieli, 'Drift or Mastery', *New Outlook*, October 1969, pp.14–16; R. Cohen, 'The Security of Israel and Her Borders', *Siah*, November 1969, pp.15–18.
27. A.L. Eliav, *Glory in the Land of the Living* (Tel-Aviv: Am Oved, 1972), pp.68–9, 142–3, 158–61.
28. R.J. Isaac, 'The Land of Israel Movement', pp.262–71.

29. Ibid., pp.260–1, 295–6.
30. A. Sprinzak, *Budding Politics of De-Legitimacy in Israel 1967–1972* (Jerusalem: Levi Eshkol Institute, 1973) pp.42–51.
31. R.J. Isaac, 'The Land of Israel Movement', pp.288–91.
32. M. Livne, 'Our Israel – The Rise and Fall of a Protest Movement', M.A. Thesis, Tel-Aviv University, 1977, pp.26–31.
33. See, for example, S. Smooha and Y. Peres, 'Ethnic Disparity in Israel', *Megamot*, Vol. 20, No. 1, 1974, pp.5–28; M. Smilansky, 'Coping of the Educational System With Problems of Special-Care Pupils', in H. Ormian (ed.), *Education in Israel* (Jerusalem: Ministry of Education, 1973), pp.121–40.
34. A. El-Sadat, *In Search of Identity: An Autobiography* (Glasgow: Collins, 1978), pp.298, 389–90.
35. H. Kissinger, *Years of Upheaval* (London: Weidenfeld & Nicholson and Michael Joseph, 1982), pp.637–8, 481–3.
36. For a fuller discussion, see L. Weissbrod, *The Hundred Years Conflict*, pp.52–9.
37. H. Kissinger, *Years of Upheaval*, pp.462–5; interview with Abba Eban, then Israeli Foreign Minister, quoted in M. Brecher, 'Eban and Israeli Foreign Policy'.
38. M. Tsur, M., *Doing It the Hard Way* (Tel-Aviv: Am Oved, 1976), pp.9–13.
39. M. Bar-On, 'The Winter Years 74–77', *Politika*, No. 51, 1993, pp.38–41.
40. M. Livne, *Our Israel*, pp.36–47, 83–4.
41. *Shinui Platform Proposal*, 16 July 1974.
42. Y. Levy and E.L. Guttman, *Values and Attitudes of Pupils in Israel* (Jerusalem: Institute of Applied Social Research, 1976), p.50.
43. H. Canaan, 'Pact of the Faithful', *Ha-arets*, 11 November 1977; A. Teicher, 'We Swore by the Flag of Zion and Our Holy Land', *Ha-arets*, 11 November 1977; R.J. Isaac, *The Land of Israel Movement*, pp.182–8.
44. R.J. Isaac, 'The Land of Israel Movement', pp.188–90.
45. H. Fisch, 'The Great Jewish Revolution', *Zot Ha-arets*, 21 November 1969.
46. Livne's conceptual framework enumerated below is taken from a collection of his essays published by Gush Emunim: E. Livne, *On the Road to Alon More – Zionism Through 'Emunim'* (Jerusalem: Gush Emunim Publications, 1976).
47. *Ma'ariv*, 13 April 1976.
48. *Ma'ariv*, 11 September 1975.
49. *Ma'ariv*, 1 January 1975, 23 May 1976.
50. E. Etzioni-Halevi, with R. Shapira, *Political Culture in Israel: Cleavage and Integration Among Israeli Jews* (New York: Praeger, 1977), pp.46, 173.
51. Z. Yaron, *The Philosophy of Rabbi Kuk* (Jerusalem: World Zionist Organisation, 1974), pp.237–96.
52. Rabbi A.Y.H. Kuk, *Epistles of R.A.Y.H.* (Jerusalem: Rav Kuk Institute, 1963/65), Vol. 3, pp.133, 173; M. Friedman, *Society and Religion: the Non-Zionist Orthodoxy in Erets Yisrael 1918–1936* (Jerusalem: Yad Ben Zvi, 1978), p.99.
53. M. Friedman, *Society and Religion*, pp.92–6.
54. Rabbi A.Y.H. Kuk, *Orot* (Jerusalem: Rabbi Y.A.H. Kuk Publication, 1950), pp.119–37; *Adar Ha-yakar Ve-'Ikvey Ha-tson* (Jerusalem: Rav Kuk Institute, 1967), pp.107–56.
55. *Ma'ariv*, 6 May 1974; *Jerusalem Post*, 4 January 1974; 'Manifesto of Rabbi Kuk', *Gush Emunim*, 1 September 1977.
56. 'Talks of Warriors at Yeshivat Ha-rav Kuk'.
57. M. Michelson, 'Gush Emunim Plans Fourth Settlement', *Ma'ariv*, 24 January 1975.
58. *Ptahim*, March 1975; *Ma'ariv*, 6 May 1975.
59. *The 28th Zionist Congress, Jerusalem, 18–27 January 1972* (Jerusalem: World Zionist Organization, 1974) , 1972, pp.90–3.
60. J. O'Dea, 'Gush Emunim: Roots and Ambiguities: the Perspective of the Sociology of Religion', *Forum*, Vol. 2, No. 25, 1976, pp.39–50.
61. 'Proclamation of Rabbi Y.Z.H. Kuk', published in the Hebrew press on 2 August 1974.
62. Z. Kessler, 'We Are the Majority of the People and In the Knesset', *Ma'ariv*, 11 October 1974.
63. 'Dialogue With Gush Emunim', *Yedi'ot Ahronot*, 3 October 1976.
64. J. O'Dea, 'Gush Emunim'.
65. 'Talks of Warriors at Yeshivat Ha-rav Kuk'.
66. 'Shdemot Meets Gush Emunim', *Shdemot*, No. 58, 1976, pp.31–48.
67. *Zot Ha-arets*, 30 September 1977.
68. E. Livne, 'The Atrocity', *Ma'ariv*, 10 October 1974.
69. The following Hebrew articles in *Be-tfutsot Ha-gola*: A. Goldmann, 'Simplified Messianism', Vol. 18, Nos 79–80, 1977, pp.112–13; Z. Lamm, 'Traditional Patterns and Processes of

Modernization in Judaism', Vol. 17, Nos 73–74, 1974, pp.62–72.

70. E. Livne, *On the Road to Alon More*, Introduction, written before the final merger but when ideational fusion had already progressed.
71. S. Levin, 'Address', *The Zionist Council: In Preparation for the Zionist General Council Meeting* (Jerusalem, 1975), pp.15–21.
72. M. Roy, 'Gush Emunim Tries to Get Round Diaspora Jewry', *Yedi'ot Ahronot*, 10 December 1976.
73. E. Livne, 'The Big Day of Alon More', *Ma'ariv*, 2 September 1974; *On the Road to Alon More*, pp.69–72.
74. 'From the Desk of the Gush Emunim Secretariat', *Zot Ha-arets*, 25 November 1977.
75. Y. Shapiro, *Democracy in Israel* (Ramat Gan: Massada, 1977), pp.171–5.
76. M. Livne, *Our Israel*, pp.36–41, 83–4.
77. A. Arian, *The Choosing People: Voting Behaviour in Israel* (Cleveland: Case Western Reserve University Press, 1973), p.42.
78. Y. Peres, *et al.* 'Predicting and Explaining Voters' Behavior', in A. Arian (ed.), *The Elections in Israel 1973* (Jerusalem: Academic Press, 1975), pp.189–202.
79. Z. Peled, *Attitudes of the Israeli Public to the Interim Agreement* (Jerusalem: Institute of Applied Social Research, 1975), p.17; Pori Public Opinion Poll, *Ha-arets*, 7 November 1977; Y. Levy and E.L. Guttman, *Values and Attitudes of Pupils in Israel*, pp.34, 50.
80. Indeed, the NRP gained 0.9% in the ensuing 1977 elections, compared to its strength in 1973. Some of its new support came from the secular Kibbutzim of the Ein Vered Circle, as an election analysis of Kibbutzim showed.
81. A. Tirosh, 'The People of Israel Do Not Regret Their Vote', *Ma'ariv*, 21 June 1977.

4. The Settler: A Quasi-Religious Identity

As it stood, New Zionism could not become widely accepted. To be that, tapping core values and proposing practical ways to solve ongoing pressing issues are not enough. The tenets of an ideology must be phrased so as to be acceptable to the majority of the society. In addition, the ideology must convince persons of another persuasion that it is a viable political blueprint, and not just an abstract body of ideas. Therefore, an ideology needs the sponsorship of skilful politicians, who the public is willing to recognize as its representatives and who are seen to be able to put the precepts of the ideology into practice. Initially, New Zionism was found wanting on both counts. Firstly, although Gush Emunim doctrine had been overlaid by a secular stratum when fused with the ideas of the Land of Israel Movement, the religious aspects were still too prominent for New Zionism to appeal to most secular Israelis and too heretic to appeal to most orthodox ones. Secondly, the young faction of the NRP were the only politicians claiming to represent Gush Emunim. They were still vying for leadership positions within a religious minority party, hardly a powerful sponsor for a new religious ideology in a largely secular society. But the results of the 1977 elections changed all that.

LIKUD ADOPTION OF NEW ZIONISM

The Need for Legitimation

The 1977 election results were unforeseen and unintended, causing general consternation in Israel. During the subsequent weeks, the press reported a general atmosphere of fear and uncertainty. Leading articles warned against the expected aggressiveness of the prime minister designate, Menahem Begin; since Likud had won by default, the electorate had not given Begin its mandate to pursue his declared policies;

unless he realized this, the outcome would be a disaster. The elections were also called a political earthquake whose damage could only be controlled by the formation of a wall-to-wall coalition to avert Likud foreign policy intentions. Dash leaders were reported to be stunned and terrified, since they felt responsible for having brought Likud into power.[1]

More significantly still, Likud itself was confounded by its own victory. In fact, a large Likud notice appeared in the press five days after the elections to assuage fears by declaring 'We shall protect the State of Israel to the utmost.' Likud immediately sent an ambassador of goodwill to the United States to point out that Begin was no longer a terrorist (Begin had headed the IZL, the underground organization affiliated with the Revisionists). Likud was also mobilizing popular outsiders, notably General Moshe Dayan, to make itself more respectable. The general fear that had seized Israel when Likud came into power must be put down to the illegitimate image of it which Labour had created and perpetuated over the years, as noted earlier. The Revisionists, of whom Herut (the hawkish nucleus of Likud) was the successor, had been called Fascists in the 1930s and terrorists and anti-Zionists in the 1940s. For many years, Ben-Gurion never addressed Begin directly and spoke of him in the most derogatory terms. The image of Herut, as rabidly nationalist, anti-socialist and reckless had been so successfully imprinted on the Jewish public at large, and on Israelis in particular, that it remained practically unchanged until 1977; but then, neither had Revisionist ideology changed much over the years. As noted earlier in Chapter 2, Revisionist doctrine had stressed national redemption to the exclusion of the other two aspects of Messianism and had completely ignored the principle of perfect justice so essential to resolving the dilemma of claiming proprietorship of a country inhabited by others. This blatant lack of an ethical underpinning had facilitated the delegitimation of the Revisionists by Labour: it stood to reason that people who asserted that might was the main right to a land also claimed by others were altogether immoral and unfit to lead and to govern. Begin and his party, Likud, were well aware of this. To counteract the challenge to its newly acquired power position, Likud sought legitimacy by adopting and revising New Zionism, an ideology which did not contradict its own, yet added those dimensions required for a broad public appeal. This was made convincing and effective by turning Gush Emunim into the vanguard, the true implementers of New Zionism, with Likud its representative.

Legitimacy-Building Measures

Begin's first act after the elections was to go to Elon More, the Gush Emunim settlement on the West Bank, and make a public promise that many more such settlements would now be established. Having been charged with forming the new government, Begin went from the president's residence straight to Rabbi Kuk Junior to receive his blessing; he then proceeded to the Western Wall to say a prayer. Begin had been moderately observant, but this sudden demonstrative religiosity was surprising enough to elicit comment in the press. Moreover, his religiosity was pointedly associated with Gush Emunim: Begin visited Rabbi Kuk, and not the Chief Rabbi of Israel, as might have been expected.

In September 1977, newspapers carried a picture of Begin and General Ariel Sharon holding a Torah scroll in Kadum, a Gush Emunim settlement. On another occasion, Begin was shown kissing Rabbi Kuk's hand, a gesture of reverence most unusual in 'egalitarian' Israel. By September 1977, three Gush Emunim settlements had been declared legal by the government and an announcement was made that three more would follow. This happened after the United States had specifically demanded a three-month moratorium on settlements in the West Bank. Nevertheless, Gush Emunim was reported to have been promised the authorization of numerous settlements. Porat, the Gush leader, was reported as saying that a close friendship had developed between Begin and Gush Emunim leaders; the government secretary was consulting Gush leaders on how to explain to the world the spiritual significance of settlement in Erets Yisrael.[2]

Words and gestures were supplemented by the inclusion of General Sharon, the avowed patron of Gush Emunim, in the Likud inner circle. Sharon had run on a separate list for the 1977 elections and had won only 1.9 per cent of the votes. A simple merger with Likud would not have qualified him for any cabinet post. Instead, his list was incorporated in Herut, the major faction of Likud, and he was appointed Minister of Agriculture and chairman of the Ministerial Committee for Settlement. That newly created committee was unique in having the authority of a government plenum, so that its decisions were final and required no further ratification.

The above steps would have indicated a wholesale adoption of New Zionism, which might easily have proved to be counterproductive. For a party to be considered fit to rule, it must stand for principles regarding which there is wide consensus. In its search for legitimacy, Likud secularized and popularized New Zionism in order to turn it into a basis for a new Israeli identity, to replace the compromised Tsabar. Likud leaders presumably realized that an Israeli identity rooted in a literal reading of biblical texts was incompatible with the secular worldview of the majority of Israelis. Early New Zionism had sought continuity with the Pioneer, skipping over the Tsabar altogether. Revised New Zionism, formulated by a party seeking legitimacy, rather than by a group of religiously motivated rebels, was more expedient. A complete break with Tsabar identity might have alienated too great a part of the public which still clung to the virtues of the Tsabar. Likud therefore revised New Zionism by stressing the secular aspect of Messianism, namely national redemption, though in Greater Israel rather than in Israel within the Green Line, and by augmenting this claim with security arguments of the Tsabar, the upright warrior. This could be done because Judaism is a mono-national religion, so that nation and religion are interchangeable: Jewish Messianism carries a clearly political message of national independence, as well as the religious one of salvation. Revised New Zionism could therefore create a new consensus by largely disregarding the strictly religious aspect of Jewishness and concentrating instead on its national aspect. The Tsabar virtues of survival and defence could then supplement national historical rights to Erets Yisrael; military strength, defiance of the world and tenacity could augment the Judaic values of mutual responsibility and service to the nation as demarcation lines of Israeli identity.[3]

At the same time, settlement proper of Greater Israel was presented as a continuation of Pioneer virtues,[4] while the concept of perfect justice was introduced into revised New Zionism to create continuity with both the Pioneer and the Tsabar. The assertion that the Jewish people had an eternal, inalienable right to the entire Land of Israel, reiterated in all Likud platform papers, invalidated any Palestinian claim to sovereignty in this country, or in parts thereof. In order to justify this ethically, Likud linked that right to Jewish moral virtues: Jews had practised and disseminated ethics and morality since ancient times;[5] Israel aimed at setting up a morally exemplary society.[6] Therefore, Israel would not evict any Palestinian inhabitants. Justice dictated respect for their tenurial rights. Furthermore, Likud offered Palestinians the option of becoming Israeli citizens or foreign residents enjoying cultural autonomy. Ostensibly, the principle of justice was being put into practice and absolved Israelis from any further need to justify their sovereignty in the Land of Israel.

LIKUD ENTRENCHMENT

All these measures seem to have attained their purpose. The creation of facts on the ground (settlements) in order to make the retention of the occupied territories irreversible emphasized the practical political aspect of New Zionism. In doing so, Likud helped to obscure its religious implications and to make it increasingly acceptable to a large sector of Israeli society. This, in turn, legitimized the formerly ostracized Likud party. The changes in attitude were pronounced. Fluctuations occurred in support of Likud and of the precepts of New Zionism, but Likud remained in power until 1992 and regained it in 1996, while New Zionism and Settler identity were seriously challenged only by the Oslo Accords signed in 1993. The first ostensible obstacle to the legitimation process of Likud presented itself a mere six months after it had come into power, when President Sadat of Egypt undertook his peace mission to Jerusalem on 20 November 1977. Sadat's visit should have strengthened the convictions of anybody who had supported the peace movement and its insistence on withdrawal from the occupied territories. Furthermore, the visit should have created a favourable climate of opinion for withdrawal among people who had previously been undecided on this issue. Yet nothing of the kind happened.

The rise in the popularity of the Likud party and of its leader Begin was impressive. By December 1977, support of Likud had grown to 58.3 per cent from the 33.4 per cent it had received at the elections, and it was still at 50 per cent in January 1978.[7] The change of attitude towards Begin was even more dramatic, reaching a high of 78.3 per cent in December 1977 (following Sadat's visit). Though his popularity declined after the breakdown of Israeli–Egyptian negotiations in early 1978, it still registered a substantial 59.4 per cent.[8] The change in attitude towards Begin had begun long before Sadat's visit to Jerusalem. Within weeks of the new government's assumption of office, articles praised Begin where previously abuse had been his main lot. Favourable note was taken of Begin's polished style of speech 'even when one did not always agree with its contents'; Begin was admired for his skill in mobilizing support for policies which were avowedly extreme.[9]

The peace negotiations with Egypt were a crucial test for the Likud implementation of New Zionist precepts. Under strong international pressure, concessions became necessary. Sadat offered peace in return for the Sinai Peninsula, which he considered Egyptian territory, and in return for a resolution of the conflict with the Palestinians. Ironically, a pullback from the Sinai, a large uninhabited desert area which provided Israel with a real strategic buffer zone, was easily conceded, because the Sinai was not part of Erets Yisrael; the densely populated West Bank and Gaza Strip, which gave Israel no military advantage, especially if settled by Jews, could not be relinquished without loss of support from New Zionists. Regarding the latter, Begin had to find a formula which would be acceptable both to Egypt and to his New Zionist supporters. He came up with the Autonomy Plan, presented to President Sadat in February 1978.

In its platform for the 1977 elections, Likud had insisted on Israeli sovereignty in all occupied territories and had offered cultural autonomy to those Palestinians opting for Israeli citizenship. The Autonomy Plan proposed to create an autonomous civil administration by the Palestinians, for the Palestinian residents, irrespective of their choice of nationality, to replace the Israeli military one. Although the Plan reiterated Israel's claim to sovereignty over the West Bank and Gaza, it also recognized similar claims by unspecified others. To obscure this betrayal of principles, any final decision about sovereignty claims was deferred for at least five years.

Gush Emunim members were not deceived by the ruse to defer the final decision on the status of the territories and protested immediately. They staged a demonstration on the eve of Begin's departure for Ismailia, where he intended to lay out the Autonomy Plan to Sadat. Likud functionaries associated with the Land of Israel Movement also called for a new government, to be composed of Herut, the Land of Israel movement and Gush Emunim. To shore up the ostensible symbiosis with Gush Emunim, Begin made some demonstrative gesture of solidarity with Gush Emunim after each of their protests. For example, when Gush members protested in front of the Prime Minister's Office against a promised freeze of three months on settlements, Begin allegedly told Gush leaders that he had described Gush Emunim to President Carter as a miracle of revival and renewal;[10] when the Gush demonstrations over the Autonomy Plan led to 30 of its members being arrested, Begin immediately contacted the Minister of the Interior and asked for their release, so that he would not have to go to Egypt while Gush people were in jail; that same evening he also visited Rabbi Kuk Junior to obtain the Rabbi's blessing.[11]

The gestures aimed at appeasing Gush Emunim were apparently successful: its demonstrations petered out and Likud popularity did not decline dangerously (from a high of 58.3 per cent in December 1977 to 50 per cent in January 1978). However, the further concessions made at Camp David required more than mere gestures in order to shore up the Likud claim to represent Gush Emunim and to act according to New Zionist principles. The Camp David Accord, signed on 17 September 1978, provided for the abolishment of the Israeli military and civil administration in the West Bank and Gaza. In contrast to the Autonomy Plan, part of the military force would be withdrawn and the remainder assigned to specific security locations. The claim to sovereignty in the territories would be settled in negotiations between Egypt, Jordan, Israel and elected representatives of the inhabitants of the West Bank and Gaza Strip. The last provision implied Israel's willingness to relinquish its claim to some unspecified parts of Erets Yisrael. Nor did the Camp David Accord include any provision for acquiring Israeli citizenship by willing Palestinians. Indeed, the entire issue was omitted from the Accord, so that it would not raise the spectre of Israeli sovereignty.

A comparison between the Autonomy Plan and the Camp David Accord puts the Likud dilemma into sharp focus. In omitting the claim of Israeli sovereignty over all of Erets Yisrael, Likud risked forfeiting its right to represent Gush Emunim and to implement New Zionism. Indeed, protest action against the Camp David Accord was prompt. On 18 September 1978, one day after the signing of the Accord, 700 Gush Emunim members established an unauthorized settlement in Samaria, to provide 'an answer by the Land of Israel Faithful to the Camp David Accord'.[12] On the same day, Herut and Gush Emunim leaders launched a campaign against Begin and called for new elections. On 4 October 1978, the Gush organized a mass rally against the Accord in the West Bank.

The Accord was confirmed by the Israeli Cabinet on 24 September 1978, with two ministers voting against and one abstaining. In the following Knesset debate, Begin came under heavy criticism from the right wing and, more surprisingly, even from Labour. After a two-day debate, 84 out of 120 Knesset members ratified the Accord, though not its written official version. During the debate preceding the vote, Begin provided a slightly different interpretation of some of the key provisions of the Accord. He insisted that Israel had not relinquished its right to sovereignty in Judea, Samaria and Gaza. If no agreement could be reached on this basis, the autonomy and Israeli security arrangements would continue.

For fear of losing the support of his ideological vanguard, Gush Emunim, and those within his party who were committed to the principle of Greater Israel, as the settlement and incorporation in Israel of the West Bank and Gaza are generally called, Begin later qualified the Accord even further. By spring 1979, he claimed that autonomy was personal rather than territorial, meaning that Palestinians would be in charge of their civil affairs only. This interpretation became generally accepted by the public: in a poll held in May 1979, 58.4 per cent of the respondents supported the autonomy thus construed.[13] This new interpretation became the official Likud stand in its platform for the 1981 elections.

Such declarations of loyalty notwithstanding, the popularity of Likud plummeted from 50 per cent in January 1978 to 31.5 per cent in February 1979 and to a low 17.3 per cent in December 1980[14] and that of Begin from 59.4 per cent in March 1978 to 30.8 per cent in October 1979 and to 23 per cent in September 1980.[15] This was due principally to their inept management of government in general and of the economy in particular. There were irregularities in administration, misdemeanours by public figures and serious misconduct within the defence establishment. Worst of all was the handling of the economy. The initial high inflation rate of 34.6 per cent in 1977 rose to 116.8 per cent in 1981 and foreign liabilities rose from US$8,514 million in 1977 to US$13,465 million in 1981. Satisfaction with the economy was a low 37 per cent to begin with, and bottomed out at 9 per cent in January 1981.[16] Despite this, Likud received 37.1 per cent of the votes in the 1981 elections (3.7 per cent more than in 1977) and consequently remained in power.

Since Likud could hardly pride itself on its administrative performance, actual implementation of New Zionism substituted for it. The settlements which the Ministerial Committee for Settlements helped to establish in the West Bank and the Gaza Strip best demonstrate the Likud claim to represent and implement the one aspect of New Zionism most easily assimilated by a secular public, because they could be justified by security considerations, pioneering and patrimonial rights. Between 1977 and July 1982, 71 Jewish settlements were established in these areas, considered part of Erets Yisrael, compared to 12 during 1967–76.

CRYSTALLIZATION OF SETTLER IDENTITY

As Likud gained popularity, so did the ideas it espoused. To recapitulate, the Likud version of New Zionism consisted of the right of Jews to Greater Israel, inalienable because Jews had been there first, as witnessed by the Bible, and because Jews were morally superior to their adversaries. They were ethically justified in defending their ancient borders and in settling their patrimony. Israelis exercised justice by dint of their moral conduct in combat as well as in treatment of the Palestinians living within their borders. They staked their territorial claim by virtue of being Jews in the national, rather than the religious sense. This was the gist of Settler identity, a rather far cry from the original Gush Emunim doctrine, and it was identification with these values which spread.

While 34 per cent of respondents to a poll conducted in 1974 supported the first Gush Emunim settlements, 48 per cent did so in June 1979 and 58.3 per cent in November 1981.[17] This support declined over the years, but it maintained an average of 41.6 per cent until the signing of the Oslo Accords in September 1993.[18] Moreover, during this period, an average 39.2 per cent insisted that settlements were not an obstacle to peace,[19] despite international condemnation and common sense considerations. Opinions regarding withdrawal from the territories were also in line with New Zionist precepts. In September 1975, 40.3 per cent of respondents opposed territorial concessions in return for peace, rising to 51.3 per cent in November 1977, to 60 per cent in May 1980 and to a high of 62.5 per cent in April 1981.[20] Again, this intransigent attitude subsequently declined somewhat, in the period leading up to the signing of the Oslo Accords, but it still remained at an average of 47.5 per cent.[21]

Significantly, this support was given with complete disregard for the consequences, a mindset typical of the religious worldview introduced by New Zionism. It seems, though, that Israelis adopted a quasi-religious worldview instead, substituting national destiny, history and culture for God as the prescriber of present action. One could then ignore obvious warnings regarding the probable outcomes of political acts pursued, such as international condemnation and isolation and, notably, demographic predictions of a future Arab majority in Greater Israel, because the birth rate of the Arab population was over twice as high as that of the Jewish one,[22] and do so without becoming strictly religious.

Research data point to a rise in religiosity in Israel. Until 1973, about 30 per cent of respondents declared themselves orthodox or observant, growing to 56.5 per cent by 1982.[23] Such a reading of the data is deceptive, however, because the category of observant far exceeds that of orthodox and could easily comprise a large number of people who observe some religious commandments as a symbol of Jewish nationhood rather than out of real religious conviction. Since nationality and religion are so interlinked in Judaism, one may refrain from eating pork, observe the separation of meat and milk dishes, fast on the Day of Atonement and attend religious services on major holidays, yet do so because this is traditional Jewish behaviour and not because one believes in Divine Providence. A more recent study supports this premise. A research conducted in 1991 provided more categories on the religiosity–secularity scale to which respondents could assign themselves: 3.9 per cent declared themselves orthodox, 11 per cent religious and 26.7 per cent observant. What is more, 23.3 per cent of respondents declared themselves secular but observing some religious practices and only 35 per cent declared themselves completely secular or atheist.[24]

If it can be assumed that a large part of those declaring themselves observant rather than religious indeed belonged to the category of using religious observance as a symbol of Jewish nationhood, genuine religious faith has hardly grown in Israel. Instead, there has been an increased emphasis on Jewish customs – which are all religious – as a means of identifying with the nation. The 23.3 per cent of respondents who were consciously secular, yet observed some commandments, illustrate this best. Taking all the above data into consideration, it would seem that a fair part of those who supported settlement and the continued occupation of the territories beyond the pre-1967 borders did so for secular reasons, principally security and historical patrimony, and without accepting the Messianic message and the strictly religious conception of history on which Gush Emunim doctrine is based.

THE 1981 ELECTIONS

Its otherwise poor record could not account for Likud's electoral success. Three factors help to explain, at least in part, the resurgent support enjoyed by Likud: firstly, its demonstrative embrace with Gush Emunim and of the secular aspect of New Zionism, namely retention and settlement of Erets Yisrael, secondly, the concrete proof it gave of remaining true to its militancy and, thirdly, its appeal to Oriental voters.

Settlement of Erets Yisrael

As to the first factor, the large number of settlements established up to July 1982 has already been mentioned. Of these, a fair amount were set up after the 1981 elections and those were largely of a nature different from the original Gush Emunim ones. Likud launched an extensive settlement drive prior to the 1981 elections. Buses and guides were provided to familiarize Israelis with the economic and ecological advantages of moving to the West Bank. This was done because Gush Emunim proper had been unable to recruit the masses of volunteer settlers it had hoped for. Of the 71 settlements established between 1977 and July 1982, only 26 were founded by Amana, the settlement movement of Gush Emunim, while 20 were directly sponsored by the government: 10 were set up by the military and 10 by Herut, the Likud settlement movement.[25] To achieve this, land was provided at 5 per cent of its actual value and generous loans and mortgages were offered to people willing to move across the Green Line, as the pre-1967 border is called. A large part of this emigration did not go beyond 15–20 km of the Green Line.[26] The preponderance of these commuter communities notwithstanding, Likud was able to demonstrate its efforts to implement New Zionism.

Pre-emptive Militancy

Defence had been the hallmark of the Tsabar, stamping him as the upright warrior. In line with perfect justice, all belligerent actions had been conceived to be defensive ones, even when their offensive nature had been only thinly disguised, as in the 1956 Sinai Campaign. Some immediate provocation by the adversary had always served to justify a pre-emptive strike (the Sinai Campaign, the 1967 war) and to uphold the defensive stance. Likud did not totally abandon the latter and could thus preserve some continuity with the Tsabar, but neither did it renounce the avowed militancy which had distinguished the Revisionists from Labour. Pre-emptive militancy could combine both concepts – militant offensive actions were presented to be pre-empting future dangers in defence of the state.

In a sense, Jewish settlement of the occupied territories was also an instance of pre-emptive militancy since it created an obstacle to future withdrawal. If this merely implied the pursuance of such a policy, the destruction of the Iraqi nuclear reactor was an overt message that pre-emptive militancy was indeed being carried out and that Likud was faithful to the revised New Zionism which it promulgated. At the time the Iraqi reactor was still under construction and years away from the capability to produce the material required for nuclear bombs which might threaten Israel. Yet it was attacked and destroyed on 7 June 1981, just a couple of weeks prior to the elections. It is impossible to determine the separate effect of this operation on the election results because it coincided with a very vigorous campaign to mobilize ethnic resentment in favour of Likud. The combination of strategies was certainly successful. According to polls, Likud popularity rose from a low 18 per cent in February 1981 to 34 per cent in May 1981 and 37 per cent in June 1981,[27] following the attack on the reactor. Begin's popularity rose from a low 17 per cent in February 1981 to 41.7 per cent in May 1981 and remained at 40 per cent in June 1981.[28]

Appeal to Orientals

The 1981 elections in Israel were described as unprecedented, populist, an Oriental revolt, emotional, violent and a turning point in political culture. They were certainly different in style and outcome from any previous ones. For the first time in Israeli politics, Begin and other Likud campaigners addressed Oriental voters directly and unabashedly as a separate constituency which had been marginalized, disadvantaged and discriminated against by the dominant Western (of European and American origin) establishment led by Labour. In doing this, Likud tapped widespread feelings of inferiority, deprivation and resentment among the Oriental community, sentiments already mentioned and also documented in numerous studies.[29] One clear indicator of such sentiments was the five ethnic lists which ran for the elections, yet these lists also demonstrated that Orientals craved acceptance on equal terms rather than separatism. None of these lists carried ethnic names. Instead, their designations suggested social unity by social justice, by Judaism, or by both. Nor were the lists explicit about the low socio-economic status of many Orientals (estimated at about 60 per cent at the time), possibly because the heads of these lists belonged to the 40 per cent upwardly mobile Orientals and were reluctant to associate themselves with the working-class poor. This, in turn, may explain the failure of four of the ethnic lists to enter the Knesset, while the fifth, Tami, gained a mere 2.3 per cent of the votes. Likud, on the other hand, offered genuine unity in the name of the Jewish people, a unity which Labour had disrupted by emphasizing Western secular superiority and by blocking the advancement of Israeli Jews different from themselves:[30] not only had 60 per cent of Orientals failed to move up the socio-economic scale, they also constituted the vast majority of that class in Israel.

Likud emphasis on the cultural–traditional aspect of Jewishness as part of New Zionist Israeliness probably also attracted Oriental voters. As already mentioned, immigrants from Moslem countries had been largely religious. The pressure to adjust to Tsabar Israeliness had weakened religious observance, especially among the younger, Israeli-educated generation of Orientals. Yet, research indicates that even among university students of Oriental origin educated in secular schools, the percentage of those adhering to traditional religious modes of behaviour and belief was relatively large compared to students of Western origin, and only 6 per cent of the former declared themselves anti-religious compared to 11 per cent of the latter.[31]

Likud tactics in the election campaign were evidently successful, though they differed from those in previous campaigns only in intensity and not in content. The trend of Orientals to prefer Likud over Labour had begun in the 1973 elections, became pronounced among Israeli-born voters of Oriental origin in the 1977 elections and finally encompassed the older, foreign-born oriental population in the 1981 elections, when about 70 per cent of Orientals voted Likud.[32] Since Orientals constituted 55 per cent of the Jewish population by 1981, their support helped to tip the scales in favour of Likud, though by a mere 0.5 per cent (Labour gained 36.6 per cent, probably due to the dissolution of Dash and the return of many of its supporters to Labour).

Thus, the emphasis of revised New Zionism on Jewishness as a socially and culturally unifying force probably affected the Oriental vote, as did their sheer resentment of patronizing Labour. The other aspects of revised New Zionism, notably the retention of the occupied territories and their settlement, seem to have played a smaller role in initially attracting Orientals to Likud and New Zionism. Research data suggest that even among dovish Orientals, over 50 per cent supported Likud.[33] But having opted for Likud, the hawkish aspects of revised New Zionism have gradually been adopted by its Oriental supporters: by the 1990s, all polls on retention of settlements, on withdrawal from territories, on support of the peace process, etc. show Orientals to be more hawkish than Western respondents.

THE SETTLER

To some extent, Settler identity spread less due to conviction and more by default; some people seem to have seen themselves as Settlers because they supported Likud as a protest against Labour and not because they were completely convinced of the merits of revised New Zionism. That is one difference between the Settler and his predecessors, the Pioneer and the Tsabar, which leads to others.

Never had the majority of the Israeli population actually carried out all the norms and values set down by its model. Few of those who identified themselves as Pioneers engaged in agricultural labour in communities of perfect social equality and only a minority of those who identified themselves as Tsabarim dedicated their lives to the defence of their country. In the past, however, they had all conceded that those who did realize these ideals were the perfect Israelis to be emulated as far as possible. On the other hand, the Settler differed from the actual settler not merely in degree of implementation, but in substance as well. The Settler adopted revised New Zionism, rather than the original version to which Gush Emunim adhered. Even though many regarded the actual settlers as their vanguard, few adopted the Messianic message attached to settlement. Except for the ardent followers of Gush Emunim, the Settler was a quasi-religious person for whom Jewish religious practice was not necessarily an end in itself, but rather an expression of religious–cultural continuity of Jewish tradition. Tradition served as the common denominator of all Settlers, transcending country of origin, level of education, income, or degree of religiosity.

A major aspect of the Messianic message and of Jewish tradition/culture has been the ethical superiority of Judaism as a creed and the consequent imperative imposed on its believers to be a model of morality. Ethical excellence had been the one aspect of Messianism which even the Tsabar had not shed. Ironically, the quasi-religious Settler had greater difficulty than his secular predecessors in making good this claim of exercising perfect justice. Since he denied the Palestinian right to any part of Erets Yisrael and was no longer willing to share the land as a gesture of magnanimity, the only proof of ethical excellence left to him was the benevolence of the occupation. Assertions were made that, in contrast to other foreign occupiers, Israel was singularly fair to the population under its rule and had brought about an impressive rise in its living standard. The apparent acquiescence of the Palestinian population in Israeli rule was providing irrefutable evidence for this, and attempts were made to foster a Palestinian leadership willing to give its blessing to the Autonomy Plan under Israeli sovereignty as a solution to the Palestinian–Israeli conflict in order to back up this claim. Benevolent occupation had been a rather lame claim to perfect justice being exercised, and it collapsed totally with the outbreak of the Intifada, the Palestinian uprising. The latter proved that the Palestinian population did not acquiesce in the occupation; furthermore, it compelled Israel to take ever less 'benevolent' measures in order to repress the Intifada.

An even more serious flaw in Settler identity was the fact that it was based on revised New Zionism, rather than the original version. The hawkishness of the Settler was based more on Jewish closing of ranks and on security considerations, and less on God's command. That was the crux of Settler identity: it contained the same ambivalence as had that of the Pioneer. The Settler denied Palestinian rights to any part of Erets Yisrael without being able to countenance Palestinian claims to the same land because he could not, in good faith, share the belief of Gush Emunim that settlement was a commandment which would hasten the Coming of the Messiah. Since the Settler reverted to historical rights to the land as a justification for being there, bolstered by security arguments for holding on to all of it, this identity articulation again contained the inconsistency of secular claims to a land, underwritten by the Bible as title deed. The inability to solve this dilemma convincingly was probably one reason for the limited adoption of this self-image. On the other hand, the inability of those not identifying themselves as Settlers to articulate an alternative to the Settler was one reason why the dilemma remained dormant for so long, coming to public notice only with the signing of the Oslo Accords.

THE UNCONVERTED PART OF ISRAELI SOCIETY

There is a reverse side to the election and poll data quoted so far, which showed support of Likud and Settler values until Labour returned to power in 1992. Likud and the other parties claiming to represent the Settler, namely Tehia, Kah, Moledet and Tsomet[34] (all to the right of Likud) and the NRP (which included Gush Emunim leaders in its inner circle) never won more than 44.6 per cent of the votes (in 1981), receiving 40.7 per cent in 1984 and 42 per cent in 1988. That left over half of the electorate voting against what the Settler stood for, or, at least, not identifying with it. A similar picture emerges from polling data, as the following table demonstrates. Because of considerable fluctuations in responses to polls on these issues, averages were computed for the period in order to obtain a clearer picture.

TABLE 4.1 AVERAGE SUPPORT/OPPOSITION TO SETTLER-RELATED ISSUES DURING 1981–SEPTEMBER 1993 (UNTIL THE SIGNATURE OF THE OSLO ACCORDS)

Issue	% Respondents		
	Supporting	*Opposing*	*Undecided*
No territorial concessions in return for peace	47.5	47.7	5.3
Continued settlement in the territories	41.6	46.5	12.8
Settlements are not an obstacle to peace	39.2	48.3	12.5

Note: Sources are the same as those quoted in Notes 18, 19, 20, 21.

Table 4.1 above demonstrates that support for Settler-related issues declined as the issue became more specifically related to Gush Emunim doctrine proper. Opposition to these issues rose correspondingly, though less so, whereas the percentage of undecided respondents grew accordingly. It seems that some supporters of the more generally hawkish issue baulked at favouring the more mystical–religious one of actual settlement, possibly because it brought home to them the implications of their stand. This lends support to the contention that not all values held sacred by the settlers were adopted by the Settler. More to the point, though, is the outright opposition to Settler values by almost half of the respondents. This does not mean that half of all Israelis favoured a unilateral withdrawal from the occupied territories. It does mean, however, that among this half of the population, some wanted to hold on to the territories more as a bargaining chip and less as an inviolable patrimony. The general picture that emerges is an almost even split in Israeli society, in which one half regarded itself as Israelis by virtue of being Settlers, and the other half was at a loss to reach a consensus on what distinguished it as Israelis. Reactions to the Lebanon War lend support to this contention.

The Lebanon War

The PLO moved to South Lebanon when it was expelled from Jordan in September 1970. The massive influx of PLO fighters and their families into South Lebanon gradually turned this region into a virtual Palestinian mini-state, with an extensive military infrastructure, supported by a skilfully built up economic structure. Christian Maronites, who held the majority of power positions in Lebanon, objected strongly to this influx of Moslems into the country, fearing that it would finally expose their majority status as a fiction. (The demographic balance had long before tipped in favour of Moslems, but no census had been held to confirm this.) The fighting between Lebanese forces and the PLO, which broke out in April 1974 and developed into a civil war, was finally settled in 1976 when Syrian troops moved into Lebanon and allowed the PLO to retain its hold in the south. That territory became known as al-Fatah-Land and eventually attained for the PLO the status of a political entity.

The process started at the Arab Summit Meeting in Algeria in November 1973, which recognized the PLO as the sole legitimate representative of the Palestinian people and received Arafat as a head of state. This same recognition was accorded the PLO by the meeting of the Coordinating Bureau of the Unaligned Movement in Algiers held from 19–21 March 1974. The new status gave the PLO the self-assurance to moderate its line somewhat in order to change its image from that of a terrorist organization to that of a legitimate national liberation movement. The 12th PNC (Palestinian National Council) session held in Cairo on 1 June 1974 hinted at a possible PLO agreement to a Palestinian mini-state, probably meaning the West Bank and the Gaza Strip. Until then the PLO had rejected anything less than the entire territory of Mandatory Palestine as a future Palestinian state. These vague signs of moderation were convincing enough to give further impetus to the legitimation of the Palestinian claim. The Arab Heads of State Conference held on 28 October 1974 went one step further and sanctioned the right of the Palestinian people to self-determination and a state of their own. This was followed by an invitation to Arafat to address the UN General Assembly on 13 November 1974 and by a UN resolution on the Palestinian right to national independence.

The next step, in 1977, was the *de facto* recognition of the PLO by most European states by granting it the right to have offices (quasi-embassies) in European capitals. The EC declaration of June 1977 then recognized the need of the Palestinian people to have a homeland and the Vienna meeting of the Socialist International received Arafat in July 1979. Thereupon, the European media recognized the PLO as the legitimate representative of the Palestinian people, as well as the legitimacy of the Palestinian claim. That completed the process of change from terrorist organization to favoured national liberation movement with diplomatic status.

Had the PLO matched its actions with its new image, Israel might have been under considerable pressure to soften its intransigent stand regarding any possible negotiations with it. However, it did not: under the guise of cover names, the PLO continued to launch blatantly terrorist operations, such as the highjacking of the Air France airliner to Entebbe on 27 June 1976, the attack on a civilian bus near Tel-Aviv on 11 March 1978 and, finally, the attempt on the life of the Israeli ambassador to London in May 1982. Furthermore, the territorial base in South Lebanon served the PLO as a launching point for guerilla raids across the northern border of Israel. These became so intensive and caused so much loss of life in Israeli northern settlements that Israeli retaliatory operations became a common occurrence. They climaxed in the Litany Operation in July 1981, when massive Israeli forces crossed the border into South Lebanon and mopped up a large area in search of Palestinian terrorist bases. The continuing border clashes finally induced UN intervention and a cease-fire settlement between Israel and the PLO in South Lebanon, honoured by the PLO for almost a year.

Yet pre-emptive militancy prevailed. After the attempt on the life of the Israeli ambassador in London in May 1982, Israel launched another operation against the PLO in South Lebanon on 6 June 1982, ostensibly in order to clear all terrorists from a 45-kilometre security zone. On 7 June, however, Israeli forces had already penetrated 55 kilometres into Lebanon. Israel declared that it would not engage Syrian forces based in Lebanon unless it was attacked by them first. Yet sporadic fighting with the Syrians began on 10 June, the fourth day of the war. The Israeli mopping-up operation proceeded further north than at first declared. In fact, Israeli forces were outside Beirut on 11 June, the fifth day of the war. Worse still, this war necessitated clearing densely populated areas of PLO fighters and, therefore, the bombing of residential areas where the PLO had set up its offices, headquarters and arsenals. Precautions were taken to prevent civilian casualties, but these could not be avoided altogether. Furthermore, damage to Lebanese property was extensive.

The PLO was entrenched in West Beirut, using a civilian population of over half a million as cover. Israel was adamant that the PLO leave West Beirut and Lebanon. With its troops deployed around Beirut, it was quite capable of forcing the PLO out, but at the price of extensive destruction of civilian life and property. The US started a protracted process of mediation and shuttle diplomacy in order to induce the PLO to evacuate voluntarily. To Israel, the resignation of US Secretary of State, Alexander Haig, signalled a US policy change from tacit support to a bias in favour of the PLO. Public Israeli apprehension regarding an assault on West Beirut was reinforced by the declaration of the Israeli Defence Minister, Ariel Sharon, published on 26 June,[35] that one of the three aims of the war had been achieved already, namely the clearance of a 45-kilometre security zone. There were, however, still two goals remaining: all foreign forces had to be removed from Lebanon (meaning the Syrians as well as the PLO) and a new government had to be appointed in Lebanon that would be friendly to Israel. The statement belied the initially declared target of the war and undermined the credibility of the government in general, and of the Defence Minister in particular.

The coincidence of weakened US support and weakened confidence in the government set off the first wave of public protest. A committee against the war in Lebanon was formed by activists of 'Peace Now' and 'Sheli'. The committee organized a rally on 26 June, in which some 20,000 persons were reported to have participated. The speeches and posters at the rally were directed at the futility of the war: there was no military solution to the Palestinian problem and any sacrifice in human lives was purposeless. This was also the gist of a petition signed by 100 men of a reserves brigade and of a demonstration staged by mothers of soldiers fighting in Lebanon.[36] The second mass rally organized by Peace Now, carried the same message. It was held on 3 July and attracted a crowd reported to have numbered some 100,000 persons.

At another mass rally on 3 July, some demobilized reserve officers raised the more controversial issue of the justice of the war. The backlash was so severe that Peace Now dissociated itself from these dissidents and agreed to suspend protest activities for the time being. Subsequent protest actions, all undertaken by demobilized reserve officers and men who called for conscientious objection to service in Lebanon, attracted only a very small number of participants. By questioning the justice of the war they implied that an elected government lacked the right to demand service and possible self-sacrifice. This went too far beyond Israeli consensus regarding security and defence.

Only events which blatantly contravened the hallowed concept of purity of arms could again mobilize crowds numbering many thousands. Just as the first big rally had been held after reports in the media clarified the possible damage to life and property in Lebanon, so the second big rally took place on 7 August, when Israeli forces started the heavy bombardment of West Beirut in order to destroy PLO headquarters and arsenals (but at the same time endangering half a million civilians) and the third big rally occurred on 25 September, after the massacres in the two Palestinian refugee camps of Sabra and Shatila.

Public reaction to the Lebanon war was unlike anything that had happened in Israel in the past. The October 1973 war had been the only instance of a public outcry regarding a war, but it broke out well after the end of fighting and questioned the hesitancy of the government to engage in warfare which had resulted in a near-defeat. In 1982, on the other hand, protest erupted while fighting was in progress and while the IDF was reaping victories; it also questioned the purpose of the war. Because security and defence have been such integral parts of Israeli social consensus and of all versions of its identity, rally organizers felt some-what on the defensive and saw fit to point out the extraordinary nature of this war, which warranted protest against it: never before had Israel waged a war not clearly in defence of its survival; never before had Israel fought a war in order to achieve ulterior political aims; never had Israel caused suffering to civilians and disregarded its own principle of purity of arms. These points were also raised by persons at press interviews and in petitions to the government. They were summarized at a public discussion at the Jerusalem Theatre on 30 October.[37]

The first two points are refutable. Firstly, the Sinai campaign of 1956 was no more conducted in immediate self-defence than was the war in Lebanon, both were cases of pre-emptive militancy. Israel was provoked in 1956 in a manner very similar to that in 1982. At the time, Egypt encouraged and supported Palestinian guerillas to carry out terrorist attacks in Israel, which made life intolerable for the inhabitants of southern Israel. In 1982, the same had been occurring in northern Israel. Yet in neither case was there a direct military threat to Israel as a whole.

Secondly, the Sinai campaign was conducted in collaboration with Great Britain and France and the aim, agreed by all three partners, was the overthrow of the Nasserite regime in Egypt, rather than annulling the Egyptian nationalization of the Suez Canal. It thus had ulterior political aims, just as did the Lebanon war.

As to the third point raised, namely the suffering caused to civilians, that indeed seemed greater in the Lebanon war than in any previous one. It is hard to say whether this difference was real or perceived: the lack of reliable data on casualties and damage to property make it futile to compare those inflicted in Lebanon with others, such as those in Egypt along the Suez Canal during the War of Attrition. Be that as it may, never before had civilian casualties in a conflict involving Israel been the subject of such extensive and emphatic television coverage. This visual confrontation certainly had a strong impact on the Israeli public. Yet it would be an oversimplification to blame the misgivings felt by many Israelis entirely on the televised presentation of Lebanese casualties, for the first mass rally was held before any significant damage had been inflicted.

Admittedly, objection to the war was confined to a minority: support for the war amounted to 93.3 per cent of respondents to a poll in June 1982, at its outbreak, and dropped by no more than 15.6 per cent to 77.7 per cent in October, after the disastrous massacre of Palestinians in Sabra and Shatila by the Lebanese Christian militia. Israeli forces were suspected of having condoned the massacre, at least implicitly, triggering the most massive protest rally yet. Even then, only 13 per cent of respondents favoured an unconditional withdrawal from Lebanon.[38] Only after testimony before the Inquiry Commission set up to investigate Israeli complicity in the massacre had been made public by the media during October–November 1982, did support for a withdrawal from Lebanon increase to 53.5 per cent of respondents. Yet even then only some 10 per cent of the same sample condemned the Lebanon war altogether.[39]

The unprecedented aspect of the protest during the Lebanon war was not its extent, but the fact that it took place at all, namely that around 10 per cent of the adult population felt sufficiently unencumbered by Settler values, notably pre-emptive militancy, to take to the streets and condemn the security policy of the elected government. It would seem that the protesters were the hard core of the Unconverted, those who dared to contest as hallowed a principle as security and defence if exercised by a government to which they would not grant full legitimacy. The remainder of the Unconverted presumably objected to policies more specifically related to Settler values, namely the retention of Greater Israel and its settlement.

The legitimacy of a government is a function of the acceptance of the values and norms it stands for and these, in turn, constitute the core components of the identity of the society in question. The more people accept the values and norms, the more solidly founded is social identity and the greater is the legitimacy accorded to the government which represents this common identity. At the time when the Tsabar was the dominant Israeli identity and the legitimacy of Labour was unquestioned, Ben-Gurion was not publicly accused of waging a futile war in 1956, even though Israel was forced to withdraw completely to its previous border and had suffered casualties in vain. In 1974, when Tsabar identity was already impaired and Labour legitimacy questioned, public protest did break out, but merely over the conduct of the war and not over Israeli intransigence (its refusal to negotiate a withdrawal from Sinai). In 1982, the protest of a minority focused on Israeli intransigence and unwillingness to negotiate with the Palestinians rather than expel them forcibly. The remainder of the Unconverted, almost half the population, censored Likud more broadly and did not identify as Settlers. Opinion polls support this conclusion. When asked whether the Likud government represented the Israeli population, only 51.2 per cent of respondents answered in the affirmative in June 1982 (just before the war), 63.2 per cent in August, 52.7 per cent in November (after the massacre) and 48.5 per cent in July 1983.[40]

The Lebanon war was discussed at such length because the reaction to it augured things to come. Besides demonstrating the limited spread of Settler identity, including the ideology on which it was based, the themes raised by the protest were reiterated by small sectors of the Unconverted until they became salient with the onset of the Intifada on 9 December 1987. Election results give some indication of the process, as do polls. Likud lost over 5 per cent of the votes in 1984 (from 37.1 per cent in 1981 to 31.9 per cent in 1984), at least partly due to the protest over the deadlock and the continuing casualties in Lebanon. It did not lose those votes to Labour, which also declined by 1.5 per cent, but to the hawkish Tehia on the one hand and, principally, to small parties which took up the protest, namely Shinui (which promoted public rectitude); Ratz (which advocated civil liberties, first inside Israel and later in the occupied territories as well, after having been joined by some peace activists in 1981); Yahad and the Progressives (which simply opposed the policy in Lebanon).

The gains of these parties were very slight, in line with the small scope of the initial protest and with the minute change in public opinion. Opposition to further settlements grew from 34.5 per cent in 1982 to 49 per cent in 1986,[41] but the percentage of those supporting withdrawal from the occupied territories in return for peace (without specifying what people understood by peace) even declined from 42 per cent in 1982 to 37 per cent in 1986.[42] This begs the question of why the protest was so limited in scope, both as regards numbers and issues. It only broke out in anticipation of or following outrageous events. No masses could be mobilized to protest against the coercive rule over an unwilling population, nor against the continued setting up of Jewish settlements among a hostile population which claimed that territory as its own, to give but some examples. One answer seems to be the absence of a convincing alternative set of values and norms to serve as the basis for an identity which the Unconverted could have substituted for the Settler.

CHALLENGES TO THE SETTLER – A SLOW AND FEEBLE ENDEAVOUR

In contrast to religious Israelis, who tend to isolate themselves from worldviews other than their own, secular Israelis have always been influenced by the Western ideas current at the time. Just as early Zionists were influenced by nationalism and socialism, and the peace movement of the early 1970s took up New Leftist concepts of anti-imperialism and self-determination, so a nucleus of the Unconverted were attracted by modernist and some postmodernist ideas current in the 1980s. The rights of individual freedom, self-realization and self-determination promulgated by the New Left have remained focal to modernists, as has the accusation levelled at Western welfare state democracy, which is claimed to dominate the individual by making him dependent on government.[43] The New Left movement petered out, probably because its remedy was too radical to gain wide support: it recommended the elimination of the democratic state, by force if need be, and its replacement by a syndicalist anarchy. The modernist remedy of a liberal pluralistic democracy has had a wider impact because it is more viable. The freedom, self-realization and self-determination of persons and groups within society are to be guaranteed by a democracy which is as pluralistic as possible and in which consensus on norms and values is to be reached by mutual consent, rather than by being imposed by the powerful. Modernists advocate direct participatory democracy in small communities with maximum autonomy.[44]

Such an interpretation of democracy stood little chance of wide acceptance in Israel, which has regarded democracy as the absolute rule of the majority with little consideration for the rights of minorities or even individuals, as has already been noted. Nor did the insistence of some modernists that universal values and norms must replace ethnic specificity and its concomitant values and norms.[45] The Declaration of Independence, which defines Israel as a Jewish and democratic state, has created a continuing tension between the two concepts which are largely incompatible in a society that includes a large non-Jewish minority, all of it Arabic-speaking. The tension is heightened by the fact that this minority has been viewed as part of the adversary.

Minority Rights

As far as minorities are concerned (about 15 per cent of the Israeli population are rural and urban Arabs, the majority Moslems and a minority of Christians, as well as Druse and Bedouins), the Jewish component of Israel has won over the democratic one, though the most blatant legal discrimination was rescinded. The military rule over Arab-populated regions was lifted in 1966, so that Arab citizens were granted their basic civic rights, but the Law of Return has remained in place, giving absolute preference to Jewish immigrants. Arab inhabitants expelled from their villages in the wake of the 1948 war have not been permitted to return to them, despite a contrary ruling by the High Court of Justice (the Supreme Court when adjudicating cases of citizens brought against government institutions) of 1952. According to Shmuel Toledano, for many years advisor to the Prime Minister on Arab Affairs, no Israeli government or parliamentarian ever regarded Arab delegates as legitimate representatives in the legislature.[46] Arab land has been repeatedly confiscated for security reasons, the areas of Arab municipalities have hardly been extended despite population growth, and almost no new Arab townships have been authorized. The discrimination was implicitly admitted during the 1984 election campaign, when Shimon Peres, then Labour leader, promised Arab voters to abolish it. Indeed, he made good some of these promises during his shared tenure of office with the Likud leader after the 1984 elections.[47] Discrimination against minorities in government employment has been gross, again explained by security considerations, despite the fact that Druse men are conscripted to the IDF and Bedouin men serve in the IDF on a voluntary basis. For example, as late as 1998, only 1.04 per cent of senior public servants were Arab or Druse, only 0.46 per cent of senior office holders in government companies were Arabs and only 0.04 per cent of electric corporation employees were Arabs.[48]

The Jewish public seems to have been far from outraged by this state of affairs. In July 1984, only 14.9 per cent of respondents to a poll were dissatisfied with democracy as practised in Israel.[49] Moreover, until the outbreak of the Intifada, a fairly substantial number of respondents favoured further curtailment of minority rights: one third considered Israel too democratic,[50] 40.3 per cent favoured encouraging Arabs to emigrate and 25 per cent would deny Arabs the right to vote.[51] On the whole, the judiciary also toed this line, actually hardening it in the early 1970s. The High Court of Justice upheld the property rights of Arab villagers in 1952 and ruled that the cases brought in 1948 and 1949 against two Arab citizens should be dropped because their legal rights had been violated during interrogation, but it would not adjudicate in two similar cases in 1971 and 1972.[52]

Individual Rights

Regarding individual rights, notably those of Jewish citizens, a slow change has been taking place since the early 1970s. The change, introduced principally by Aharon Barak, who became President of the Supreme Court in the mid-1990s, has been very gradual and is far from complete, presumably because the new concepts he has employed contrast so sharply with the ones prevalent until then. The decided preference initially given to the collective at the expense of individual rights gave way to a cautious censure of abuse of power by the authorities.[53] The change was compatible with the replacement of the socialist orientation of the Pioneer, in which the individual is the servant of the community, by the more individualistic outlook of the Tsabar, in which service to the community is a venue for self-realization. Opposition to it has been mounting since Barak gave the change a moral–juridical underpinning and based it on universal values, ignoring the Jewish specificity of Israel. Furthermore, he did this just when the Settler was reintroducing Jewishness into Israeli identity. Barak and some of his Supreme Court colleagues gradually introduced what the New Left and modernists have been considering universal values, namely equality before the law, morality, maximum individual and civic freedoms and absolute judicial fairness. Barak holds that whenever these are not exercised *de facto* in society, or provided for by the legislature, the High Court of Justice may apply the principle of reasonableness in order to interpret existing law and bring about a change towards values held by the 'enlightened public'.[54]

Such ideas, which stressed Western universal values, could hardly be welcome by the quasi-religious Settler, who underlined his Jewish uniqueness, whereas the appeal to the 'enlightened public' aroused the ire of many because it implied that part of the public and of the legislature was not enlightened and had to be re-educated to adopt loftier principles than those it held. Even the Unconverted, to whom such values should have been less alien, have largely remained dubious and unconvinced, partly because the High Court itself has refrained from applying these principles consistently to the non-Jewish minorities and even less to the Palestinians in the occupied territories. When it did apply them in a few cases, its rulings were ignored by the authorities. Mostly, though, it condoned the violation of civic or individual rights of Palestinians, justifying this by the general good, the principle prevalent in Israel proper in the 1950s and 1960s.[55]

The inconsistency in upholding its own values has made the High Court of Justice a poor disseminator of them. If the High Court, the arbiter of justice, condoned Israeli practices in the territories, it followed that Israel was exercising perfect justice after all and that universal values could merely amend certain relationships among Israelis, not serve as the basis for an alternative identity. Thus, the Unconverted remained just that, almost half of society unable and unwilling to identify as Settlers, yet incapable of using Western liberal democracy as an alternative on which to base its own Israeli identity.

Even the peace camp, the small articulate minority among the Unconverted, found it difficult to plead convincingly for its cause. Peace Now advocated withdrawal in return for peace, initially only for security reasons.[56] Since these were easily matched by equally convincing security arguments supporting occupation, by 1985 Peace Now began to underpin its practical reasoning with an ethical one. Yet it was careful to remain within the Israeli consensus, as its leader Zeli Reshef underlined in an interview.[57] In line with the selective application of universal values by the High Court, Peace Now chose to emphasize the corruptive influence of occupation on the occupier, rather than the injustice to the occupied.[58] The repressive measures taken during the Intifada and the television coverage they received highlighted the damage to the upright warrior image and made evident the truth of this argument, so that it gradually convinced even some of the most ardent adherents of the Jewish right to the entire Land of Israel: by 1994, some Gush Emunim members admitted that the rule over an unwilling alien population might morally blemish Israelis.[59]

Yet this argument in favour of peace could not, by itself, undermine Settler identity, seeing that it was based on values included in that self-image. It merely claimed that Jewish ethical superiority was at risk and proposed withdrawal as the solution. The Settler could counter that Palestinian autonomy sufficed to avert the threat to Israeli morality. The Intifada, though, raised the more basic issue of perfect justice, which could be assumed to be exercised by Israel only so long as the Palestinians seemed to be acquiescing in the status quo. Their rebellion disproved this assumption. It started the erosion of Settler identity and strengthened the convictions of that small minority among the Unconverted who constituted the nucleus of the peace camp.

The Palestinians in the occupied territories had not really been as acquiescent as depicted by the Israeli authorities. There had been sporadic, unrelated terrorist acts committed by one or a few persons and damaging Israel at single points in space and time. The perpetrators had been members of the PLO and of factions which had split from it and they had come largely from outside the occupied territories. Though some disturbances in refugee camps had also occurred, these had been quickly suppressed. Yet dissatisfaction had been simmering, else it would not have erupted into an uprising. The objection to foreign rule as such was probably coupled with economic grievances. A rise in living standards had raised expectations which were then thwarted by the limited prospects available: an increasingly educated young generation of Palestinians could not find any employment other than the low-paid and low-status jobs offered in Israel. The Islamic movement, whose influence was spreading,[60] provided some of these young people with an ideological motivation to vent their pent-up frustration.

Al-Majma' al-Islamiya (the Muslim Council) was established as the Gaza branch of the Muslim Brothers in 1973. Initially, it followed the Egyptian Brotherhood policy of re-education to Islamic norms and of providing social services. It gradually radicalized its aims in answer to the growing frustration of its own constituency. The ideas it evolved were summarized in the Hamas Covenant, officially published shortly after the outbreak of the Intifada (shaking off (the Israeli subjugation)). Not unlike Gush Emunim doctrine, Hamas insists that Palestine is inalienable Muslim land because it is *waqf* land. In the original Quranic sense, *waqf* is land conquered in *jihad*, which has become the property of the Islamic community. Such land may never be sold and, therefore, must not be owned by anyone but the Islamic community, not even by a secular Arab body, let alone by Jews. It is a duty of the Muslim Palestinians to rise in *jihad* and re-establish Muslim ownership of this land, which Palestinians will then retain for their livelihood. Refraining from such action is a sin. It goes without saying that no Arab or Palestinian body has the right to relinquish Palestine, or parts of it, in return for a political settlement. Once liberated, Palestine must become an Islamic state: on this point, no compromise is tolerated with the secular state envisioned by the PLO.[61]

Palestinian Actions

By 1987, the simmering discontent, given a religious–national rationale, presumably needed a mere spark in order to turn into a conflagration. On

3 December 1987, an Israeli truck driver lost control of his vehicle on the road to Gaza, and collided with a car carrying labourers from Jabaliya refugee camp. Four persons were killed and seven wounded. Preachers in mosques spread the rumour that this was not an accident, but an intentional act of revenge by the driver, whose brother had been stabbed and killed in Gaza several days earlier. Following the road accident, a violent demonstration erupted on 9 December 1987. Whether provoked by the more radical splinter group Jihad Islami or by the Majma' itself, Hamas, the secret military arm of the Majma', quickly became the dominant organization in the Islamic camp in the Gaza Strip. The PLO was immediately aware of the potential competition for leadership and mobilized the Shabiba (its youth contingent) to spread the unrest to the West Bank.[62] However, the PLO immediately lost control to the local leadership, namely the UNC (Unified National Command), which represented all secular groupings in the territories.

After the initial riot, the Intifada was conducted by means of leaflets, all of them distributed in the streets, Hamas ones also in mosques and UNC ones also broadcast by the PLO radio station. The tactics employed by both Hamas and the UNC were civil disobedience, such as general strikes and the collective resignation of all Palestinian policemen, soon supplemented by low-intensity violence, notably stone-throwing by youngsters.

The rivalry for leadership of the Intifada among these three bodies, namely Hamas, the PLO and the UNC, explains the various phases of the Intifada. The complete surprise by which Israel was taken by the outbreak and its need to preserve the image of the upright warrior explain the official Israeli reaction to it. The tactics of the UNC and, later, of the PLO, explain the gradual change in attitude of some Israeli Unconverted regarding the retention of the occupied territories.

While Hamas has remained adamant regarding Palestinian rights to all of Palestine, including the territory of Israel, the UNC was willing to settle for an independent secular Palestinian state in a large part of Mandatory Palestine, obtained by a negotiated treaty with Israel. This was a clear departure from the PLO doctrine laid down in its political programme of 1974, in which any future compromise solution would be no more than an interim stage in the ultimate liberation of Palestine in its entirety.[63] Once the UNC had broken away from PLO doctrine and tactics, a struggle for leadership became inevitable. For the first two years of the Intifada, the secular camp enjoyed the support of the majority of the Palestinian population. The PLO retained nominal leadership because it provided the resources for the struggle: a constant stream of money, and possibly of arms, and the broadcasting of UNC leaflets by its radio station.

But PLO leadership was only nominal, because the initiative for each step in the struggle came from the UNC. Bassam Abu-Sharif, Arafat's assistant, declared PLO willingness to negotiate with Israel as late as mid-June 1988, six months after the outbreak; Abu Iyad (Salah Halaf, the second-in-command in the PLO leadership) admitted at the end of August 1988 that the PLO now also supported the draft declaration of Palestinian independence.[64] The document had been leaked to the press in Jerusalem on 12 August 1988. In it, the future borders of the Palestinian state were to follow the 1947 UN partition plan, thus including extensive areas within Israel. This stipulation could not possibly be acceptable to Israel and was presumably merely an initial bargaining position. The PLO promptly followed this UNC initiative. It formally declared the Palestinian state in November 1988 and on 13 December 1988 Arafat stated to the UN General Assembly in Geneva that the proposed Palestinian state was the ultimate aim of the Palestinians, not just an interim stage. At the same time, Arafat also renounced terrorism, the declared tactics of the PLO up until then, which the local leadership had replaced with low-intensity mass violence.

Under increasing international pressure and, possibly, because Israel was aware of this ongoing power struggle and wanted to foster the more moderate local leadership, it put forward a new proposal in April 1989 to hold elections in the West Bank and the Gaza Strip so that a settlement could be negotiated with the elected delegates. The PLO felt impelled to agree, as stated in the concluding communiqué of the Arab Summit in Casablanca, which ended on 27 May 1989. At the subsequent Fifth al-Fatah Conference in Tunis, which ended on 9 August 1989, it finally gave official recognition to the local leadership by incorporating its representatives in the Central Committee and the Revolutionary Council of al-Fatah.

The moderate Palestinian stance seemed to pay off more than had the former intransigence of the PLO or did the present one of Hamas. On 16 December 1988, the US had officially recognized the PLO as a negotiation partner for settling the Israeli–Arab conflict; in April 1989, Israel showed first signs of willingness to come to some compromise settlement; Israeli intellectuals and politicians of the Left had started a dialogue with Palestinian leaders and PLO representatives, of which the best-known meeting was the 'Road to Peace' conference held at Columbia University on 11–13 March 1989. These auspicious beginnings raised Palestinian expectations of rapid tangible results, and those did not materialize. Negotiations became protracted over the composition of the Palestinian delegation which was to prepare the elections. Furthermore, the wave of Jewish immigration to Israel from the USSR, which began at the end of 1989, seemed to provide a good reason for Israeli recalcitrance. Disappointment was probably a major factor in propelling previous PLO supporters and/or the unaffiliated into the camp of Hamas.

The shift in allegiance of local Palestinians was at first mainly passive: it was principally a protest against the failure of UNC strategy. Consequently, the Intifada was grinding to a relative halt when Iraqi President Saddam Hussein took up the Palestinian cause, which produced a watershed in the Intifada. The PLO quickly exploited this opportunity to regain its leadership role. The PLO and its leader Arafat chose to give their support to Saddam Hussein in return for Iraqi threats (later made good) to attack Israel unless it settled its conflict with the Palestinians. The PLO continued this support even after Iraq had invaded Kuwait, another Arab state, reiterating Iraqi claims that Kuwait was a Western pawn and that the West had no right to interfere in inter-Arab affairs.

The alliance with Iraq ostensibly produced the desired results. Palestinian support for the new PLO line increased in direct proportion to the vehemence of Iraqi threats against Israel and the linkage proposed by Iraq on 14 August 1990 between an Iraqi withdrawal from Kuwait and an Israeli withdrawal from the administered territories. The Iraqi warnings of missile attacks against Israel made on 9 August 1990 (and again on 30 August 1990) were promptly followed by massive joyous demonstrations of Palestinians in the West Bank and the Gaza Strip on 11 August 1990. However, second thoughts dampened Palestinian enthusiasm, for if they condoned the invasion of one Arab state by another, their condemnation of Israel for 'invading' their land could hardly withstand scrutiny. The dilemma is clearly reflected in responses to an opinion poll among Palestinians in the territories conducted by the al-Nadwa newspaper on 16 August 1990. It reported that 84 per cent of respondents regarded Saddam Hussein a national hero, yet only 58 per cent supported the invasion of Kuwait. A UNC leaflet issued on 17 August 1990 clarified this ambivalent position: the Palestinians opposed the invasion, but they opposed Western intervention even more and therefore supported Iraq.

Hamas, on the other hand, would not be prey to inconsistency. In a leaflet issued on 29 August 1990 it condemned the invasion of Kuwait as an infringement of Islamic fraternity and remained consistent in this stand. Its ideological firmness paid off even before the outcome of Desert Storm was to dash Palestinian hopes of an Iraqi solution to their problem. The UNC, sensing the swelling of Hamas ranks, decided to collaborate with it in order to keep all options open. On 19 September 1990, Hamas and the UNC jointly announced a cooperation agreement. The immediate result was the Temple Mount riots on 8 October 1990, at which Muslim clerics incited the crowd to violence because Jews were allegedly intending to desecrate the third most holy site of Islam. Faisal Husseini, a prominent member of the UNC, was present during the riots, allegedly taking part in the incitement. The aftermath of the Temple

Mount riots showed Hamas to have gained the upper hand. The riots were followed by a conspicuous change in Intifada tactics: a series of stabbings carried out by young men shouting the Islamic slogan '*Allahu akbar*'. Hamas influence had spread from its original stronghold in the Gaza Strip to the predominantly secular West Bank, and there, to such Leftist and Christian towns as Ramallah and Bethlehem, where it was reported to rule supreme.

The enthusiasm of Palestinians during the Iraqi scud missile attacks against Israel, which the less committed UNC was unable to staunch, discredited the PLO internationally and dampened the hopes of the Israeli peace camp of coming to terms with any Palestinian leadership. The Iraqi defeat in Desert Storm then discredited the PLO locally. The UNC was losing control to Hamas: militancy was dampened; at the elections to the Hebron Chamber of Commerce, Hamas candidates won 54.5 per cent of the seats against 36.3 per cent of pro-PLO candidates; an increasing number of attacks on Israeli border posts and settlements along the Jordanian–Israeli frontier were being committed primarily by admitted Hamas members.

In a bid to regain control, the UNC made far-reaching concessionary overtures to Israel, outbidding PLO offers. In an interview to the *Toronto Star*, Arafat conceded the retention of UN troops on the future Israeli–Palestinian border, a temporary demilitarization of the Palestinian state and territorial adjustments.[65] Local leaders were more conciliatory, as well as trying to distance themselves from the discredited PLO. Talal al-Safi proposed that Palestinians should initially confine negotiations with Israel to an interim settlement, followed by a three-year trial period. The provisional Palestinian government of 20 members should consist of 10 local representatives and only 10 representatives of the PLO abroad. Most significantly, the Palestinian National Covenant should be amended to recognize Israel's right to exist and local Palestinians should conduct most of the negotiations with Israel on their own.[66] Articles in *al-Quds*, *al-Nahar* and *al-Fajr* (all of them Arabic East Jerusalem newspapers) published in the first week of June 1991 also objected to orders being conveyed to local Palestinians by the PLO abroad, which had lost touch with its local constituents and had lost credibility.

These efforts convinced neither the United States nor the Israeli government. The Madrid Conference, convened at the end of 1991, was directed at concluding peace agreements between Israel and Arab states, rather than at settling the Palestinian issue. Furthermore, Israel accepted Palestinian representatives to the Conference only as part of the Jordanian delegation. On the other hand, the impact of these efforts on the Israeli peace camp was such that they paved the way for the Oslo Accords.

Israeli Reactions

The Israeli authorities' response to the Palestinian uprising was reactive throughout. The Intifada took Israel by complete surprise. Firstly, neither the hawkish Likud nor the more dovish Labour had regarded the local Palestinian population as a separate national entity. Labour politicians had insisted that 'Jordan is Palestine' so that any settlement regarding the West Bank should be reached with Jordan, rather than with the Palestinians.[67] Likud assumed that the land was a Jewish heritage and the Palestinian population a minority entitled only to administrative and cultural autonomy, as reflected in its Autonomy Plan. Therefore, Israel was taken aback by the national demands raised in the Intifada and was at a loss as to how to cope with them.

Secondly, Israel initially did not grasp the Islamic motivation of the uprising. It had actually fostered the Majma' as a moderating force which might divert Palestinian energies away from the belligerency of the PLO and towards quietist religious observance. It did not expect any strongly motivated discontent which would sustain the rebellion and spread. Thirdly, the stone-throwing youngsters and civil disobedience were radically different from previous instances of unrest. Consequently, Israel did not forestall any event since it could not foresee it, but merely devised new means to counter new developments.

These means became increasingly repressive and began to raise doubts within the IDF and, later, among the Israeli civilian population regarding the cost of the occupation. Naturally, the IDF was the first to feel the impact of the Intifada. The number of troops serving in the West Bank and Gaza grew tenfold and they had to perform extremely distasteful tasks, such as chasing stone-throwing boys and beating them up, as well as using rubber bullets and live ammunition against civilians. Such actions violated the 'purity of arms' principle so focal to the upright warrior image and provoked second thoughts among some soldiers. Furthermore, collective punishments, detention without trial, demolition of homes of rioters, which punished their families as much as them, and a large number of Palestinian casualties turned Israel from a benevolent occupier into a harsh one. As a result, the number of conscientious objectors to service in the territories grew and articles in the press documented the soul-searching of reserve officers regarding the continued occupation.[68]

Since many of the IDF personnel serving in the West Bank and Gaza were reservists, the change in attitude towards occupation gradually filtered through to the Israeli public at large. Peace Now's admonitions about the corrupting influence of ruling another people now found readier ears. The percentage of respondents who rejected an annexation of territories rose from 49.4 per cent in mid-1987 to an average of 66.9 per cent during mid-1988 to mid-1993 (prior to the signing of Oslo Accords);[69] Ratz, which had been joined by some Peace Now activists, gained some strength in the 1988 elections, rising from 2.4 per cent in 1984 to 4.3 per cent. Otherwise, the Intifada affected little immediate change in public attitudes. The deadlock between the two largest parties remained – Labour won 34.9 per cent in 1984 against Likud's 31.9 per cent, but could not form a coalition, then won 30 per cent in 1988 against Likud's 31.1 per cent. This resulted in a rotation of power after the 1984 elections and in a national unity government following the 1988 elections. Polls found no significant change of attitude to questions such as willingness to relinquish the territories in return for peace, the recognition of the PLO as a negotiation partner, or support for the establishment of additional Jewish settlements in the territories.

On these issues, the public remained almost equally divided, reflecting the ambiguous stand of Peace Now, the one media-skilled organization in the peace camp whose message was known to the public at large. As Zeli Reshef, the leader of Peace Now, conceded in an interview, the movement was careful not to deviate too far from what it regarded as Israeli consensual opinion. Though it recommended negotiations with the PLO and a stop to settlements, it condemned refusal to serve in the territories, would not allow pro-PLO Palestinians to take part in its demonstrations and would not support the establishment of a Palestinian state.[70] The stand of the dovish Labour party was also equivocal. Officially, it refused to negotiate with the PLO and totally rejected an independent Palestinian state.

Only two political groups admitted to recognizing the implications of the Intifada. One was the Mashov Circle of young Labour activists, founded in 1981, which advocated a Palestinian state even then. Following the outbreak of the Intifada and Arafat's assertion at the UN General Assembly that the PLO condemned terror and was willing to negotiate with Israel, Yossi Beilin, a leading member of Mashov, stated in a radio interview on 13 July 1989 that Israel should negotiate with the PLO. He was severely reprimanded by his own Labour party and even more so when he proposed a unilateral withdrawal from the Gaza Strip in December 1990.[71] The Mashov Circle remained marginal, as did Ratz which held similar views.

The turnabout occurred only at the end of 1991, following the convening of the Madrid Conference in October 1991. Only then did the Fifth Labour Conference, which opened on 19 November 1991, vote in favour of recognizing the PLO as a partner for negotiations and of freezing all settlement activity. Even then Labour rejected other Mashov proposals, such as recognizing the Palestinian right to self-determination.

By the 1992 elections, a much more substantial number of the

Unconverted had drawn conclusions from the Intifada, some in line with the proposals of Mashov and Ratz, others in line with the stand taken by Labour. Leading up to the 1992 elections, Labour elected Rabin as its leader and candidate for the premiership. Rabin, as Defence Minister in the rotation government, in place in 1987, and in the national unity government until its dissolution in March 1990, had masterminded the harsh measures employed to suppress the Intifada. However, as the uprising continued, he had realized and admitted that a political settlement was the only solution to the conflict. The Intifada also refuted the argument that the retention of the territories provided a buffer zone for Israel and thus enhanced its security, an argument which many of the Unconverted had endorsed. The relative hawkishness of Rabin reassured those Unconverted who favoured a settlement with the Palestinians in order to put an end to the bloodshed. Indeed, Labour gained 6.6 per cent in the 1992 elections, winning 36.6 per cent of the votes, while Likud lost 4.5 per cent, winning only 26.6 per cent, so that Labour formed the next government.

The Unconverted who drew the more far-reaching conclusions from the Intifada voted for Meretz, the merger of Ratz, Shinui and Mapam. The arguments which Meretz used explicitly, and which guided Mashov implicitly, were based on a selective employment of the modernist concepts of human rights, self-determination and the rule of law also promoted by the Israeli judiciary. These universal values were more radically promoted by Post-zionists still unknown to the general public at the time, but whose ideas would become more salient in the controversy following the Oslo Accords. Meretz won 10 per cent of the votes and entered a coalition with Labour.

For those holding Settler views, the Intifada strengthened their convictions, or at least did not undermine them. The Likud government did not budge from its hawkish line, allocating large sums for the establishment of additional settlements in the territories and refusing to consider any steps towards negotiations with the PLO. By offering to hold elections in the territories, in which the PLO could not run as a list, it continued its failed attempts to foster a compliant Palestinian leadership. For fear that pro-PLO candidates might still be elected under some guise, it procrastinated over procedural matters so that these elections never took place. Under strong US pressure it reluctantly agreed to take part in the Madrid Conference, then applied similar tactics at the Washington talks which followed. The government and the Settlers in general insisted that its reading of the situation had been correct all along: the Intifada had proved that the Palestinians were unwilling to reach a resolution of the conflict short of obliterating Israel; PLO behaviour during the Gulf crisis was decisive evidence of that. The settlers themselves held the same view.

Additional land was declared government property and allocated for new settlements, which were then funded generously. The settlers, in turn, regarded their own expansion as a fit response to Palestinian intransigence, as they viewed the Intifada.

The Madrid Conference was intended to pacify the Middle East, considered the last hotbed of conflict after the end of the Cold War era. Some of the Settlers and many settlers regarded the Likud government participation in that Conference as a betrayal of first principles, for it implicitly endorsed the 'land for peace' motto with which the conference was launched. In the following 1992 elections, Likud lost 4.5 per cent of its strength, while Tsomet won 6.6 per cent of the votes, gaining 4.6 per cent in comparison with its 2 per cent record in 1988. Tsomet first ran in 1988. It advocated absolute Israeli sovereignty in Greater Israel, but a more thorough application of human rights in Israel within the Green Line. Tehia, the party to the right of Likud, suffered a split between more and less extremist activists, neither faction gaining a single seat. Moledet, the most extreme rightist party which advocated a transfer (expulsion) of Israeli Arabs, gained a mere 2.5 per cent and the NRP 5 per cent. The Rightist bloc could thus muster only 40.8 per cent of the votes. The Intifada had obviously eroded the narrow Settler majority. Labour, which emerged as the single largest party by far (36.6 per cent), were able to form a coalition with Meretz (10 per cent) and Shas, an ostensibly dovish party of religious Orientals (5 per cent) and form the next government, headed by Yitzhak Rabin. Its coalition with Shas and its narrow majority (51.6 per cent), which truthfully reflected the equal split in Israeli society, were to be crucial in the events which followed.

NOTES

1. D. Ganhovski, 'Afraid to Rule', *Yedi'ot Ahronot*, 25 May 1977; G. Samet, 'No Mandate for Political Inflexibility', *Ha-arets*, 19 May 1977; Y.A. Gilboa, 'Earthquake', *Ma'ariv*, 18 May 1977; R. Kislev, 'Writing On the Wall', *Ha-arets*, 24 May 1977.
2. Y. Litani, 'Thoughts Better Left Unsaid', *Ha-arets*, 2 September 1977.
3. I. Peleg, *Begin's Foreign Policy 1977–1983: Israel's Move to the Right* (New York: Greenwood, 1987), pp.52–60.
4. *Likud Platform Paper for the 1977 Elections*, pp.2–3.
5. Begin's Address to the Knesset on 20 September 1977, on the occasion of Sadat's visit to Jerusalem.
6. *Likud Platform Paper for the 1977 Elections*, p.25.
7. *Mabat Le-kalkala Ule-hevra*, 24 March 1978; Pori Public Opinion Polls, *Ha-arets*, 2 February 1978.
8. *Mabat Le-kalkala Ule-hevra*, 26 March 1978; Pori, *Ha-arets*, 28 March 1978.
9. Y. Lapid, 'The New Style', *Ma'ariv*, 28 June 1977; Y. Yuval, 'Begin as Political Strategist', *Ha-arets*, 24 July 1977.
10. D. Eibal, 'Who Is Prime Minister, Begin or Hanan Porat?', *Ha-arets*, 14 October 1977.
11. *Ha-arets*, 26 December 1977.
12. *Jerusalem Post*, 19 September 1978.

13. Pori, *Ha-arets*, 21 May 1979.
14. Pori, *Ha-arets*, 16 February 1979; 26 December 1980.
15. Pori, *Ha-arets*, 1 November 1979; 29 September 1980.
16. *Yedi'ot Ahronot*, 20 July 1979; 22 March 1981. For a fuller discussion of Likud economic policy, see D. Weissbrod and L. Weissbrod, 'Inflation in Israel: The Economic Cost of Political Legitimation', *The Journal of Social, Political and Economic Studies*, Vol. 11, No. 2, 1986, pp.201–26.
17. B. Weiner, *et al.*, *Public Attitudes to Settlements in the Occupied Territories* (Jerusalem: Institute of Applied Social Research, 1974), p.22; *Mabat Le-kalkala Ule-hevra*, 26 June 1979; Pori, *Ha-arets*, 19 November 1981.
18. Calculated from Pori, *Ha-arets*, 8 October 1982, 5 October 1983, 3 February 1984, 22 August 1985, 9 February 1989; Smith, *Davar*, 2 October 1986; Guttman Institute of Applied Social Research, *Jerusalem Post*, 13 September 1993.
19. Calculated from Pori, *Ha-arets*, 30 March 1978, 26 February 1979, 19 November 1980; *Davar*, 10 November 1991.
20. Pori, *Ha-arets*, 7 November 1977; 20 May 1980; 1 April 1981.
21. Calculated from *Jerusalem Post*, 3 September 1982, 10 June 1983; *Mabat Le-kalkala Ule-hevra*, 18 July 1984, 22 January 1985, 29 July 1986, 11 May 1987, 16 February 1988, 19 April 1990, 9 July 1993; Smith, *Davar*, 8 September 1991.
22. A. Yariv, 'The Solution of the Problem and the Price to Israel', in A. Hareven (ed.), *Is There a Solution to the Palestinian Problem? Israeli Positions* (Jerusalem: Van Leer Institute, 1982), pp.11–24.
23. E. Etzioni-Halevi with R. Shapira, *Political Culture in Israel: Cleavage and Integration Among Israeli Jews* (New York: Praeger, 1997), p.173; Pori, *Ha-arets*, 3 August 1982, pp.40–5.
24. B. Kimmerling, 'A Return to the Family Indeed', *Politika*, No. 48, 1993.
25. I. Rabinovich and J. Reinharz, *Israel in the Middle East* (New York: Oxford University Press, 1984), pp.383, 385–6.
26. G. Shafir, 'Institutional and Spontaneous Settlement Drives: Did Gush Emunim Make a Difference?' in D. Newman (ed.), *The Impact of Gush Emunim: Politics and Settlement in the West Bank* (London: Croom Helm, 1985), pp.153–71.
27. Pori, *Ha-arets*, 13 February 1981; *Mabat Le-kalkala Ule-hevra*, 6 May 1981, 12 June 1981.
28. Pori, *Ha-arets*, 10 February 1981, 8 May 1981, 16 June 1981.
29. For a summary of these, see J. Schwarzwald and Y. Amir, 'Inter-Ethnic Relations in Israel: A Review', *Megamot*, Vol. 28, Nos .2–3, 1984, pp.207–30.
30. A. Lewis,'Ethnic Politics and the Foreign Policy Debate in Israel', *Political Anthropology*, Vol. 4, 1984, pp.25–38; H. Herzog, 'Political Ethnicity in Israel', *Megamot*, Vol. 28, Nos. 2–3, 1984, pp.332–52; D. Peretz and S. Smooha, 'Israel's Tenth Knesset Election: Ethnic Upsurgence and Decline in Ideology', *The Middle East Journal*, Vol. 35, No. 4, 1981, pp.506–26.
31. M. Bar-Lev and P. Kedem, 'Religious Observance Amongst Jewish University Students in Israel', *Megamot*, Vol. 28, Nos. 2–3, 1984, pp.265–79.
32. S. Smooha, 'Three Perspectives in the Sociology of Ethnic Relations in Israel', *Megamot*, Vol. 28, Nos. 2–3, 1984, pp.169–206.
33. Y. Peres and S. Shemer, 'The Ethnic Factor in the Elections to the Tenth Knesset', *Megamot*, Vol. 28, Nos. 2–3, 1984, pp.316–31.
34. Tehia ran in the 1981, 1984 and 1988 elections, Kah in the 1981 and 1984 elections, Moledet and Tsomet in the 1988 elections.
35. *Jerusalem Post*, 24 June 1982.
36. L. Levavi, 'Call to Demonstrate Against War in Lebanon', *Jerusalem Post*, 24 June 1982; M. Yudelman, '20,000 at Anti-War Protest', *Jerusalem Post*, 27 June 1982.
37. M. Pomerantz, 'A Question of Morality', *Jerusalem Post*, 4 November 1982.
38. Modi'in Ezrahi, *Jerusalem Post*, 19 November 1982.
39. Pori, *Ha-arets*, 27 December 1982.
40. Pori, *Ha-arets*, 14 July 1983.
41. Pori, *Ha-arets*, 8 October 1982, 2 October 1986.
42. Guttman Institute of Applied Social Research, *Jerusalem Post*, 25 March 1988.
43. J. Habermas, *Moral Consciousness and Communicative Action* (Cambridge: Polity, 1990), p.199; M. Foucault, *The History of Sexuality*, Vol. 1 (London: Allen Lane and Penguin, 1979), pp.144–55.
44. J. Habermas, *Moral Consciousness*, pp.143–48, 161, 199; F. Fukuyama, 'The End of History?', *The National Interest*, No. 16, 1989, pp.3–18; T. Luke, *Screens of Power* (Urbana: University of Illinois Press, 1989), pp.209–35.
45. Z. Bauman, 'Soil, Blood and Identity', *The Sociological Review*, Vol. 40, No. 4, 1992, pp.675–701; J. Habermas, *Moral Consciousness*, pp.53–73.

46. Y. Algazi, 'Admissible for the Struggle', *Ha-arets*, 8 October 1996.
47. I.S. Lustick, 'The Political Road to Binationalism: Arabs in Jewish Politics', in I. Peleg and O. Seliktar (eds.), *The Emergence of a Binational Israel: The Second Republic in the Making* (Boulder: Westview, 1989), pp.97–123.
48. Y. Algazi, 'Suitable for the Job, But Not in Our Organization', *Ha-arets*, 29 January 1998.
49. Institute of Democracy, *Ma'ariv*, 17 February 1988.
50. Dahaf, *Ha-arets*, 13 August 1984, 26 March 1985; Institute of Democracy, *Ma'ariv*, 17 February 1988.
51. Institute of Diaspora Relations, *Ha-arets*, 9 March 1987.
52. A. Rubinstein, 'Four Verdicts', *Ha-arets*, 21 September 1973.
53. P. Lahav, 'Power and Office: the Supreme Court in its First Decade', *Iyunei Mishpat*, Vol. 14, No. 3, 1989, pp.470–501.
54. M. Mautner, 'The Politics of Reasonableness', *Teoriya U-bikoret*, No. 5, 1994, pp.25–53.
55. A. Rubinstein, 'The Changing Status of the Territories: From a Held Trust to a Juridical Hybrid', *Diyunei Mishpat*, Vol. 11, No. 3, 1986, pp.439–56.
56. M. Bar-On, 'The Winter Years 74–77', *Politika*, No. 51, 1993, pp.38–41.
57. M. Levin, 'A Jewish Peace, a Zionist Peace', *Davar*, 19 August 1988.
58. Z. Reshef, 'The Ability to Influence', *'Al Ha-mishmar*, 20 December 1985; R. Teitelboim, 'Another Such Occupation', *Politika*, No. 2, 1985, pp.17–20.
59. Yehuda Kopel in 'Dialogue of Shdemot and Nekuda', *Shdemot*, No. 126/2, 1994, pp.7–14; A. Ariel, 'Was the Aguda Method Right?', *Nekuda*, No. 175, 1994, pp.16–19; U. Elitzur, 'On the Sin We Did Not Commit', *Nekuda*, No. 180, 1994, p.25.
60. The reversion to Islam of a largely secular Palestinian population was not noted by Israeli, Arab or foreign observers, but a careful reading of M. Shadid and R. Seltzer, 'Political Attitudes of Palestinians in the West Bank and Gaza Strip', *Middle East Journal*, Vol. 42, No. 1, 1988, pp.16–32, shows that 56.1% of Palestinian respondents to their survey supported an Islamic state in liberated Palestine.
61. *Al-A'thazam*, November 1988.
62. *Al-Qabas*, 15, 19 and 20 December 1988.
63. Y. Harkabi, *Arab Attitudes to Israel* (London: Vallentine Mitchell, 1972), pp.147–8.
64. *Al-Qabas*, 30 August 1988.
65. *Jerusalem Post*, 26 March 1991.
66. *Al-Fajr*, 13 May 1991.
67. See, for example, Rabin's position, analysed in H. Ben-Yehuda, 'Attitude Change and Policy Transformation: Yitzhak Rabin and the Palestinian Question', in E. Karsh (ed.), *From Rabin to Netanyahu: Israel's Troubled Agenda* (London: Frank Cass, 1996), pp.201–24; Y. Harkabi, *The Problem of the Palestinians* (Israel Academic Committee on the Middle East, 1974).
68. Y. Peri, 'The Impact of the Occupation on the Military: The Case of the IDF 1967–1987', in I. Peleg and O. Seliktar (eds), *The Emergence of a Binational Israel*, pp.143–68.
69. Calculated according to *Mabat Le-kalkala Ule-hevra*, 14 July 1988, 12 February 1989, 5 February 1991, 9 July 1993; *Ma'ariv*, 18 October 1988.
70. I. Milner, 'I Did Not Want to Pamper Myself', *Ha-arets*, 19 April 1996.
71. Y. Beilin, *Touching Peace* (Tel-Aviv: Miskal, 1997), pp.24, 34–49.

5. Blurry Boundaries

The Oslo Accords constituted a radical turning point in Israeli foreign policy as well as in its view of its conflict with the Palestinians. By renouncing the Israeli borders as those of Greater Israel, they also shook the self-perception of all sectors of Israeli society. Israelis had undergone numerous changes in their identity, as described above. The changes had been gradual, however, linked to core values and accompanied by well-prepared and persistent information campaigns. Adjustments of Israel's territorial boundaries had been presented as due to external forces and this had induced a re-evaluation and rearticulation of Israeliness to fit the new, coerced reality. The DOP (Declaration of Principles), on the other hand, had been negotiated secretly and was made known to a totally unprepared Israeli public. Moreover, it was not followed by a coherent attempt to explain, excuse and convince, largely because the chief Israeli actors differed on the reasons for which they signed it and put it into practice. Above all, it did not designate the future realigned borders according to which a modified Israeli identity could be articulated. Consequently, the sectors of the Israeli public have each remained perplexed, unable to come to grips with the full implications of this see-saw change in Israeli policy and helpless to adjust their self-image to the new reality. The result has been a near-crisis situation, in which the former single social split has proliferated into a multiplicity of fractures which only partially overlap. Aware of the dangers to a society devoid of any consensual core values, various groups have been in search of a common denominator in order to articulate a new Israeli identity on which all sectors can agree without forfeiting their several uniquenesses. Before discussing the repercussions of the Oslo Accords, however, a short summary of events and motives leading up to them is in order.

THE DECLARATION OF PRINCIPLES

Labour won the 1992 elections under the leadership of Rabin, who promised to put an end to the Intifada and to terrorism by reaching an autonomy agreement with a local Palestinian leadership within six to nine months of assuming office. This undertaking excluded any contacts with the PLO, considered an illegitimate organization. At the Washington talks following the Madrid Conference, the Labour government retained the stand of its Likud predecessor, insisting that the Palestinians be part of the Jordanian delegation and totally unassociated with the PLO. Intransigence on Israel's part was matched by similar intransigence on the part of the Palestinian delegation, which, in reality, received its instructions from PLO headquarters in Tunis. Consequently, no progress whatsoever was made at the talks. Recognizing that outlawing the PLO was the chief impediment to any settlement with the Palestinians, on 20 January 1993 the government abrogated the prohibition to meet PLO members.

It was then that Yossi Beilin, Deputy Foreign Minister and a leading member of Mashov, took up the Norwegian offer to host a secret negotiation track. Talks with delegates of the PLO headquarters in Tunis were initially conducted by two Israeli academics and without the knowledge of Premier Yitzhak Rabin and Foreign Minister Shimon Peres. Once Rabin and Peres had given their approval to the talks, each for his own reasons and with a different target in mind, the Director General of the Foreign Office and an Israeli lawyer were added to the Israeli team. Numerous rounds of meetings finally produced the Declaration of Principles on 19 August 1993.

Meanwhile, disturbances in the occupied territories had almost ground to a halt and were replaced by stabbing attacks within Israel proper, so that the personal safety of Israeli civilians had become a focal issue. But that point was not addressed by the DOP, ostensibly signed with the official Palestinian delegation, which was a powerless body. Concern for eradicating terror finally led to an official mutual recognition, by the PLO of Israel's right to peaceful existence and by Israel of the PLO as a representative of the Palestinians which had the power to fight terrorism against Israel. The letter of mutual recognition was signed by Rabin on 10 September 1993.[1] This was followed by the ceremony at the White House on 13 September 1993.

PRESENTATION OF THE DOP TO THE ISRAELI PUBLIC

Public Unpreparedness

The time span of negotiations over a reversal of both Palestinian and Israeli mutual perceptions and policy intentions was very short. Within seven months, both sides agreed to a compromise on a 100-year conflict which had seemed irresolvable because both sides had put forward equally defensible claims to the same territory. In their eagerness to produce results, the two sides agreed only in principle, leaving all details of the arrangement to further negotiations in stages, for which a timetable was set. The basic idea underlying the DOP was a staged withdrawal by Israel from occupied territories. The extent of any of the stages was not laid down, let alone of the final one. In return, the PLO would relinquish its claim to the territory of Israel proper and, possibly, some further areas. These areas were left undefined, since the status of the settlements, of Jerusalem and of the final borders was left totally unspecified, as was the fate of the Palestinian refugees living outside the West Bank and the Gaza Strip. Consequently, each side could interpret the implications of the DOP according to its own light and so could each sector of the Israeli public.

Worse still, the secrecy of the negotiations, which had been a definite advantage for their progress, caught the Israeli public quite unprepared for such a momentous watershed in policy. The public had a mere fortnight in which to adjust to it – details of the negotiations leaked to the press from the third week of August 1993 onward. This made it imperative to launch an intensive information campaign putting forward convincing reasons why Labour had seen fit to act contrary to the principles not only of the preceding Likud government, but also of its own previous leaders. Yet none took place.

Implications of the DOP

In 1947, Israel had once before agreed to the partition of what it considered its patrimony. At the time, Ben-Gurion had been adept at convincing his public that this step was unavoidable: the Yishuv was too small to withstand international pressure, it needed international approbation in order to obtain independence and it needed the latter in order to take in Jewish Holocaust refugees. He could invoke the Messianic message of 'ingathering of the exiles' and of exercising perfect justice by Israel's willingness to share its heritage with the Palestinians. These ethical principles were underpinned by pragmatic arguments. Agreement to partition was explained as necessity overriding the eternal right of the Jewish people to its homeland, yet not as a forfeiture of it. In reality, Israel handed over only that area of the homeland which it had not conquered during the 1948 war. As such, partition was accepted by the general public and incorporated into Israeli identity – the Pioneer turning into the Tsabar.

Such arguments could not be brought forward regarding the DOP. The Intifada had not constituted an existential threat to Israel. It had been costly, had been a moral blight, had undermined the sense of personal safety. Yet Israel had coped with it for five years and could probably continue doing so. Despite the Intifada, Israel had managed to take in a new wave of Jewish immigrants from the disintegrating USSR in 1990 (a first wave had arrived in the early 1970s). Obviously, ingathering of the exiles was not impeded and there was no need for a policy change on that count. International pressure was indeed being exerted on Israel, resulting in the Madrid Conference and the Washington talks, but the main international concern was the pacification of the region by peace agreements between Israel and its neighbouring Arab states; the conflict with the Palestinians was considered marginal, expected to be resolved within the framework of these peace treaties.

Nobody had pressured Israel into a separate agreement with the Palestinians, and certainly not with the PLO. By any measure, the DOP was a voluntary and final relinquishment of part of what the majority of Israelis regarded as their birthright. By implication, recognition of the PLO as the negotiating partner implied an Israeli admission that PLO members had not been just terrorists but freedom fighters, although they had used unacceptable methods. By further implication, Israel was recognizing the Palestinian right of self-determination, though the latter is not mentioned in the DOP, nor in any official Israeli statement. Moreover, the DOP stipulated the release of Palestinian prisoners. If the government had voluntarily agreed to this, it thereby implicitly admitted that the occupation had been none too benevolent and justice had not been overly stringently exercized.

The above ideas implicit in the DOP contravened the most basic values, not just of the Settler but of the majority of the Unconverted as well, since the latter were still holding fast to the main Tsabar values for lack of a convincing alternative. Very clear and consistent explanations, evoking core values in a new interpretation, might have brought about a gradual change in public attitudes and in Israeli identity articulation. However, nothing of the kind occurred. Instead, Post-zionist claims began to filter through to the public.

The Post-Zionist Narrative

The ideas implicit in the DOP went a step further than those propounded by the peace camp all along. They were premises developed by historians and sociologists since the mid-1980s, largely ignored at the time and propelled into prominence after the signature of the DOP, both by way of some public statements made by Meretz politicians and by an extensive debate carried out in the press. Researchers challenged the Israeli consensus that all its wars had been purely defensive,[2] that encouraging the immigration to Israel of the Jewish refugees had been motivated solely by the Messianic tenet of 'ingathering of the exiles',[3] or that the principle of justice had been satisfied by agreement to partition, exonerating Israel from any further responsibility for the Palestinian refugees.[4]

Subsequently, and particularly after the signature of the DOP, more radical views were voiced. Zionist functionaries were accused of having abandoned their communities in Eastern Europe at the outbreak of the Second World War, putting the lie to the 'ingathering of the exiles' principle.[5] Israelis were dubbed colonial settlers whose sole claim to the land was its function as a refuge from persecution or annihilation; even the October 1973 war had been provoked by Israel and had not been defensive; Israel had expropriated Palestinian property and should compensate the owners.[6] The 'original sin' of settling an area inhabited by others against their wishes could not be absolved by handouts under the slogan of exercising justice unilaterally.[7]

On a more generally ethical level, Post-zionists have been admonishing Israelis to atone for their moral self-righteousness by adopting and exercising the truly universal modernist values of human rights, the rule of laws which also protect the rights of minorities and the right of self-determination applied to Palestinians and not merely to Israelis. They have been asserting that the narrow tribalism of an ethnic/religious collective is incompatible with the pluralism and individualism of modern democracy. Because it is pluralistic, no modern society can have any common values except those which are universal. The historical rights to the territory of an ethnic group are as irrational as are religious ones. A society has a just claim to its existence in its territory only if it adheres to universal norms. Since Israel is not applying such norms to Palestinians, it must relinquish its rule over them.[8] In line with this, some have proposed changing Israel from a Jewish democratic state to a secular democracy in which ethnicity is irrelevant to citizenship, an idea which Meretz has endorsed, or even to a bi-national secular democracy.[9]

These premises challenged whatever had remained of the Israeli consensus, common to Settlers and the Unconverted. They aroused fierce opposition, especially from Unconverted intellectuals, who saw their own modernist beliefs carried to unacceptable logical conclusions. A lively debate was conducted in the daily press, so that such views became known to the public at large.

Conflicting Leadership Messages

The two chief Labour leaders made completely different appeals in support of the peace process,[10] neither of which provided a satisfactory formulation for the new Israeli identity required by such a watershed in policy. The late Prime Minister, Mr Rabin, asserted that the continued longing for their fatherland gave Jews the right to the entire land they had possessed. Yet, the Jewishness of Israel was his main concern.[11] The peace process with the Palestinians was a reluctant agreement to partition, since over 2 million Palestinian citizens would preclude a Jewish state. Instead, a complete separation between the two peoples was required, though without granting the Palestinians full sovereignty, nor the entire West Bank.[12] Israel would eventually annex areas near its pre-1967 borders which contained large blocs of Jewish settlements, as well as a strip along the River Jordan.[13] Mr Rabin reiterated these arguments in a speech to the Knesset on 5 October 1995. Clearly, his view was far removed from the moral admonitions expressed by his Meretz coalition partners, to be discussed below, nor was it guided by the principle of distributive justice. It based itself on history, ignoring Palestinian counter-claims. The ancient longing of the Jewish people to return to their homeland is a poor justification for settling a land whose inhabitants also have a long history of residence; demographic factors are a poor excuse for withdrawing from part of this land, unless democracy and the rights of minorities are a major concern. Yet they were not: instead, the safety of Israelis was his top priority, secured by separation and a somewhat mollified Palestinian population in an autonomous region.[14] This articulation of Israeli identity could convince neither Settlers, who objected to the withdrawal from parts of the Land of Israel, nor the Unconverted, who found themselves amoral occupants of an ancient heritage which they were to share with others very reluctantly.

Shimon Peres, Foreign Minister and subsequently Prime Minister of Israel, conveyed a different message. It can be summarized in the slogan 'peace for the sake of a prosperous Israel in a prosperous Middle East'. Israel was withdrawing from some occupied territories in order to reconcile the Palestinians and, thereby, the entire Arab world, to its presence in the region.[15] Israel's presence was justified by Jewish brainpower, namely the ability to help its Arab neighbours attain Western affluence and progress by creating an economically cooperating Middle Eastern bloc.[16] Since reconciliation with the Palestinians was merely a means to the end of a New Middle East, Peres envisioned a functional solution in which the Palestinian entity would have jurisdiction over civil matters (excluding water and soil resources) and would eventually join a federation with Jordan.[17] In an article published in the daily press he made no mention of his vision of the future borders of Israel, hinting that he favoured a settlement along the lines of Begin's Autonomy Plan, namely complete personal autonomy for the Palestinians within a federation with Jordan and alongside continued Israeli political and military rule over the

West Bank.[18] The Labour platform, published a few weeks later, did not endorse his view. Rather, it reiterated that of the late Prime Minister, adding the acceptance of a demilitarized Palestinian state. However, by then it was too late to change public perceptions of what the Labour candidate for the premiership stood for. This articulation of Israeli identity assumed that Israeli intellectual superiority and future service to the region justified its presence there, but it was far removed from Jewish core values. It invoked principally individual hedonism (affluence) and the wish to emulate a Western lifestyle. It could not distinguish Israelis from citizens of other Western democracies, nor would it distinguish them from their Arab neighbours once the promised New Middle East was established.

A third message was being conveyed by Meretz leaders and the young Labour politicians who had been the pioneers of the peace process with the Palestinians. Without addressing the 'right to the land' issue at all, they spoke mainly of the Israeli ethical corruption caused by rule over aliens, but also of the violation of Palestinian human rights. In contrast to the main Labour leaders, they proposed a sovereign Palestinian state, above all as a means to Israeli moral recovery and as compensation for the annexation of some territory densely populated by Jewish settlements.[19] This was by far the clearest vision of the future territorial boundaries of Israel. Though being a minority view within Labour and the platform of a small party, it fuelled public confusion even further.

Utterances of Meretz and young Labour politicians were moderate and careful compared to articles in the Meretz organ *Politika*, including those published prior to the DOP. Hamas terrorists and Jewish ultra-nationalists among the settlers were put on the same footing; demands were made to enforce the rule of law in the occupied territories.[20] After the signing of the DOP, the editor of *Politika* described the DOP as a return to normality, meaning the adoption of universal norms devoid of ethnic–religious delusions of grandeur.[21] No Meretz spokesman or functionary openly endorsed the more radical Post-zionist views. But the enthusiasm with which Meretz welcomed the DOP and its insistent promotion of a separation between State and religion allied it to Post-zionist views, even if inadvertently. Therefore, the latter have been imputed to Meretz despite denials by Meretz leaders, notably articles by Amnon Rubinstein in the daily press.

Nor did the opposition until the May 1996 elections, led by the Likud Party, offer any viable alternative formulation of Israeli identity. Benyamin Netanyahu, leader of Likud, was unable to incorporate the seemingly irreversible peace process into a reformulation of New Zionism. He simply reiterated New Zionism and proposed, at least to some extent, to preserve its relevance by reversing the peace process, at least to some extent.[22] Subsequently, this stand became ever more unrealistic, especially after the Israeli withdrawal from the major Palestinian population centres. By the end of January 1996, the party reformulated its political programme to recognize the steps taken by Israel so far as a *fait accompli*, yet it did not alter its commitment to New Zionism, which insisted on the retention of Greater Israel. That, again, was a contradiction in terms. It undermined the certainty of the Settler sector that the peace process was reversible and that its self-image could remain intact.

The Israeli public was faced with conflicting justifications of a new policy which negated many of the values on which Israeli consensus had been built. While Rabin tried to justify this policy by early Zionist slogans stripped of their moral underpinning, Peres offered affluence and technological excellence as the new parameters of Israeli identity, while Netanyahu was denying the change of the political reality. Even when coupled with the ethical compunctions of Meretz, this was hardly a satisfactory justification for shedding the ongoing Israeli identity. Affluence and technological progress do not distinguish Israelis from other modern Western countries, while the moral qualms of Meretz imply a previous state of virtue whose equivocality had meanwhile been exposed. None of these articulations of Israeli identity contained a convincing justification for Israelis living in Israel rather than elsewhere. The same holds even more true for Post-zionist arguments which reject the Jewish nature of Israel altogether.[23] Democracy and the respect for human rights are very laudable universal values. Yet deprived of any core values specific to Israelis they cannot serve as a basis for identity which, by definition, distinguishes one person/group from another.

Inconsistent Actions

The confusion of the public, due to the divergent messages of the political leaders, was exacerbated by the inconsistency of government actions relating to the peace process. The stated intention of the DOP was to end the long-standing conflict and to establish peace between Israel and the Palestinians. Peaceful relations imply an eventual reconciliation, as was overtly symbolized by the famous handshake of Prime Minister Rabin and Chairman Arafat on the White House lawn. Yet many government actions contradicted this intention and implied an unabated hostility or ambivalence with regard to the Palestinians with whom peace was to be established. A few examples of this inconsistency will illustrate the many instances, which are too numerous to list in full.

Firstly, the Jewish settlements on the West Bank constitute a major obstacle to a redrawing of final borders, the ultimate step in the peaceful resolution of the conflict. Israel undertook to stop the establishment of any further settlements, while the fate of existing ones would be agreed upon in the final stage of the negotiations. Mr Rabin frequently antagonized the settlers publicly by pointing out the obstruction which they posed to the peace process. Building in many settlements continued unhindered, though, or was even initiated by the government: during 1994–95, schools and clinics were set up for the growing population of settlers; land near Nablus and Tul Karem was confiscated, presumably to serve the expansion of nearby settlements. At the end of September 1995, the government went ahead with the second stage of the DOP, extending Palestinian self-rule to all population centres on the West Bank. However, only a month later, the government approved the appropriation of land near Ramalla from which settlers had been forcibly evicted earlier when they had staked a claim to it.

Secondly, according to the DOP, the status of Jerusalem would be determined in the final stage of negotiations. Yet building in 'Greater Jerusalem' and in East Jerusalem continued as government leaders repeatedly stated that undivided Jerusalem would remain the capital of Israel. At the same time, the Israeli government objected vehemently to the US Congress decision to move the US embassy to Jerusalem in official US recognition of this Israeli claim.

Thirdly, the light sentences passed on Israelis who committed violent acts against Palestinians implied official condonation of such acts and contrasted sharply with official protestations of reconciliation. According to a report published in 1994 by Betzelem, an Israeli human rights organization, the cases of 48 Israelis accused of causing death to Palestinians between 1988 and 1992 were still being processed in 1994. Of these, only one person was convicted of murder and given a life sentence. Another six were convicted of lesser offences: three were given prison sentences of three years, eighteen months and five months respectively, while the other three were sentenced to several months of community service. The remaining files were closed altogether.[24] The massacre of 30 Moslem worshippers in the Cave of the Patriarchs in Hebron in February 1994 was sharply condemned by Israel. Yet no steps were taken to punish supporters of the assassin, nor to expel them from Hebron.

PUBLIC REACTIONS TO THE PEACE PROCESS

On the face of it, a political solution to the conflict with the Palestinians was almost inevitable, seeing that Israel was unwilling to use excesive brutality to suppress the Intifada, that it had agreed to take part in the Madrid

Conference and that a Labour government had taken office in Israel in 1992 having declared peace with the Palestinians a major item on its agenda. The timing of the DOP and the Palestinian partner chosen (the PLO and its chairman Arafat) undoubtedly came as a surprise. Consequently, reactions to the DOP were ambivalent at best, and hostile at worst. Naturally, the more committed people had been to Greater Israel, the less realistically they had perceived events leading up to the DOP and the less prepared they were to accept all of its implications.

The Public at Large

The implications of the DOP were unclear to the public from the start, as witnessed by data from a poll published on the day of the signature ceremony on the White House lawn. In it, 62 per cent of respondents agreed to the withdrawal from the Gaza Strip and Jericho, 60 per cent of the same sample supported the DOP, but only 52 per cent supported further withdrawals from the West Bank.[25] Presumably, 10 per cent of the respondents hoped that the withdrawal from Gaza and Jericho would suffice to pacify the Palestinians and believed that the additional stages stipulated in the DOP were superfluous concessions: the DOP provided for a freeze on settlements, which only 46 per cent of the sample supported.

The diverse messages and self-contradictory actions of the government regarding the peace process following the DOP created ever greater public confusion. They produced two complementary results. Firstly, they did not temper the long-standing polarization in Israeli society. The percentage of respondents recognizing the PLO as a partner for negotiations (one of the most dramatic changes in official Israeli policy) did not rise much after the signing of the DOP, amounting to 53 per cent in 1991, to 60 per cent in 1994 and back again to 53 per cent in 1995;[26] 45 per cent of respondents supported continued expansion of settlements beyond the pre-1967 borders in 1986, 46 per cent in 1993 and 47 per cent in 1995.[27]

Secondly, and paradoxically at the same time, while the public was clearly split on some issues, some of it was also of two minds. In a survey conducted in 1995, 73 per cent of respondents supported the continuation of negotiations with the Palestinians, though 53 per cent considered Arafat a terrorist, that is, totally untrustworthy.[28] Conversely, in 1994, 41 per cent of another sample supported expanding Palestinian self-rule beyond Gaza and Jericho, though 73 per cent did not trust the PLO to honour its agreements with Israel.[29] Clearly, part of these sample populations held self-contradictory views. The unwillingness to face the consequences of the 'altruistic' support of peace is another indicator of confusion: 45.9 per cent of respondents supported the peace process, but only 22.2 per cent supported evacuation of any settlements on the West Bank.[30]

Furthermore, the percentage of undecided respondents on major issues relating to the peace process and, thus, to the future of Israel, demonstrates the failure of the leadership to convey a clear and convincing message. In the last quoted survey, 44 per cent of respondents were undecided regarding the evacuation of settlements on the West Bank; in another survey, 27.4 per cent of respondents were undecided regarding the DOP and 33 per cent could not decide whether the PLO was a partner for peace negotiations;[31] 31.5 per cent in another poll had no clear opinion regarding settlers on the West Bank.[32]

Ambivalence also prevailed regarding the very concept of peace. Between August 1994 and December 1995, support of peace in general averaged 59 per cent, but support of peace with the Palestinians averaged only 49 per cent and that with Syria 37 per cent.[33] It seems that at least for some of those 60 per cent who considered peace an attractive option, the meaning of peace in real terms was less than clear. The strong support for peace in general ostensibly indicated an acceptance of Mr Peres' vision of a regional peace in the New Middle East. Yet support of integration in that Middle East was surprisingly low: according to the Tami Steinmetz Centre, only 29 per cent of respondents wanted Israel to integrate politically in the Middle East, only 23 per cent wanted it to integrate economically and a low 14 per cent wanted cultural integration.[34] The large percentage of objectors to peace with Syria is a further indication of this lack of clarity. Mr Rabin's message was not very persuasive either if half of the respondents still rejected the PLO as a partner for negotiations. Though his desire for a Jewish state seems to have been shared by the majority – 75 per cent of respondents supported separation from the Palestinian entity – its implications were not, since only 22.2 per cent supported evacuation of any settlements,[35] without which separation is an unrealistic aim.

The Settlers

Meanwhile, changes had occurred in the organization of Gush Emunim and within the population of the settlements in the occupied territories. As already noted, the Likud-initiated campaign to settle the territories appealed to people seeking high-quality low-cost accommodation. The population in the territories changed accordingly, with non-ideological settlers becoming the majority. At the same time, Gush Emunim turned from a radical opposition force into the recognized vanguard of the political establishment and became institutionalized. The death of its spiritual leader, Rabbi Kuk Junior, in 1982, contributed to this process. Amana, the settlement movement of Gush Emunim, became the chief spokesman of the hard core of believers, while more task-oriented Gush Emunim members became the leaders of all settlers as local council heads. They formed the Council of Judea, Samaria and Gaza. Gush Emunim ceased to exist as a separate movement, though its ardent believers continued in their faith that settling Erets Yisrael was the supreme commandment which would bring about the Coming of the Messiah.

Since the political objectives were being adequately pursued by the Council, a hard core of believers were able to turn spiritually inwards. They began consulting with various rabbis on specific questions of religion pertaining to current affairs, particularly regarding relations with Palestinians. This process produced the much more orthodox and politically extremist Hardal (an acronym for orthodox nationalist) sector. Some of them, named 'the underground', committed terrorist acts against Palestinians, others tried to demolish the Al-Aqsa mosque and the Dome of the Rock on the Temple Mount in order to rebuild Salomon's Temple.[36]

The persons holding such extremist views and following the esoteric Halachic rules of rabbis remained marginal to the settlers up until the signing of the DOP. The bulk of the settlers simply went about their business of living in the territories, extending their settlements and establishing new ones. They remained oblivious to the implications of the Intifada, namely that occupation corrupted the Israeli occupier, or that some injustice done to the Palestinians had to be rectified. Nor did they take much notice of the 'land for peace' principle which underlay the Madrid Conference and which could surely affect them.

The signing of the DOP could not be ignored, however. It called into question all the principles of Gush Emunim doctrine. Settlement of the Land of Israel had not imbued Israelis with the necessary holiness required for the imminent Coming of the Messiah. Instead, a sizeable proportion of Israelis were being swayed by principles of a rival value system which might make the setting up of further settlements very unlikely and, possibly, cause the dismantling of existing ones. Gush Emunim leaders and members were acutely aware of the threat to their belief system and to their very existence as its vanguard and carriers. The DOP does not stipulate the extent of territorial concessions to the Palestinians, nor the fate of Jewish settlements in the territories to be given over to the Palestinians, deferring these decisions to the final stage of negotiations. Thus, the end of settlement and sovereignty in the entire Land of Israel was not certain, but it was so likely and so near in time as to create an existential crisis for Gush Emunim which found expression in *Nekuda*. *Nekuda* is a monthly published by the Council of Judea and Samaria, which serves as a forum of internal debate among settlers in general and Gush Emunim adherents in particular. Its authors and many of its readers are Gush Emunim activists, members and sympathizers. An analysis of views expressed in the articles published in *Nekuda* over time, both before and after the signing of the DOP, reveals the sense of crisis felt by Gush Emunim and the various ways proposed to avert the crisis or solve it. The actual steps taken by the settlers show which of these views were adopted.

By and large, Gush Emunim and other settlers refused to face political realities until the actual signing of the DOP, as can be seen from a simple count of articles in *Nekuda*. Throughout 1992, only five articles dealt with the Palestinian question. Palestinian demands were not even rebutted, they were simply ignored. Where the Intifada was addressed at all, it was seen as nothing but a Divine test of Gush Emunim steadfastness.[37] The number rose to about one third of articles in the first half of 1993, when rumours of negotiations with the Palestinians became ever more frequent. In contrast, 90 per cent of articles addressed the DOP and its repercussions from September 1993 to September 1994. Presumably, settler activists had been reluctant to face the possible outcome of the Madrid Conference and, subsequently, of the declared policies of the new Israeli government. They seem to have preferred ignoring political developments, possibly anticipating the depth of the crisis which the hard core of the faithful would experience. (For the sake of clarity and brevity, I shall continue to refer to them as Gush Emunim, though they themselves no longer use this designation.)

The dilemma facing Gush Emunim has been existential. Should the peace process outlined in the DOP proceed as laid down, it would put an end to further expansion of Jewish settlements in the West Bank and the Gaza Strip and would jeopardize the fate of the existing ones. Consequently, imminent salvation could not ensue in the manner envisioned by the radical interpretation of sacred texts on which Gush Emunim doctrine is based. Gush Emunim reactions to this clash between its faith and the political process were threefold: repudiation of its doctrine; amendment of the doctrine to accommodate the peace process in part or temporarily; and repudiation of the peace process and of the government which had entered upon it.

A minority of activists and members concluded that the predictions of their doctrine had been refuted by reality and that it was time to repent and return to the orthodox fold.[38] This was a minority view at the time, as evidenced by the absence of any large-scale manifestations of 'return to the fold', such as abandonment of settlements or a readoption of orthodox dress. However, the Hardal movement has spread, incorporating strictly orthodox youths who have adopted hawkish nationalist views.[39] At the same time, many settlers and their faithful have become highly orthodox nationalists.[40] Numerous articles in *Nekuda* discussed this phenomenon in an attempt to draw the line between the self-imposed closure and extreme exclusiveness of ultra-orthodoxy and the openess of Gush Emunim to modernity and the State of Israel.[41]

Most articles called for changing some aspect of the doctrine, without repudiating salvation by settlement as such. As Gush Emunim actions reported below indicate, this strategy was adopted by the majority. Seeing that the government had signed away part of the Land of Israel and that around half of the public supported this step, a major criticism was levelled at the assumption that secular Israelis, all of whom live in the Land of Israel, would be spontaneously converted to Judaic values. According to one view, the doctrine itself had to be reinterpreted: settlement was a necessary condition for political renaissance, but not a sufficient one for spiritual salvation. Consequently, spiritual education of the Israeli public would have to be incorporated as a second imperative of Gush Emunim action.[42] Others merely criticized the manner in which Gush Emunim had implemented its doctrine. Gush Emunim had assumed that its example was so exalted that it would be emulated automatically, bringing about settlement so massive as to be irreversible. This had obviously not occurred. Settlement had to be augmented by intensive influence on Israeli mass media and politics.[43]

According to another view, Gush Emunim doctrine had to be reformulated to accommodate those universal values of Western culture which had induced the Israeli government to sign the DOP, notably recognizing the injustice of ruling over an alien population,[44] or respecting the human rights of Palestinians.[45] This was a tacit admission that the doctrine had been overly selective in its choice of religious values, ignoring the universal ethical tenets of Judaism. The authors of this view saw this as a serious shortcoming for which they were unable to offer any immediate remedy.

The solutions suggested above are all long-term and defer salvation. Therefore, they invalidate a focal tenet of the doctrine, namely the imminence of salvation. This shortcoming can be circumvented if settlement in parts of the Land of Israel is considered sufficient for imminent salvation: the doctrine remains valid if continuous extension of settlement is not essential and can be relegated to the future. As one contributor to *Nekuda* put it, Gush Emunim had to come to terms with the idea that the Land of Israel of the twenty-first century did not extend beyond the area occupied by present settlements.[46] Proposals in this vein ranged from an independent 'Kingdom of Judea', via transfer of isolated settlements to already existing concentrations and the annexation of these blocs to Israel, to a binational state in the West Bank and the Gaza Strip modelled on Swiss cantons. Either way, this limited aim could only be achieved if the 'dovish' Israeli government could be made to accede to it, or was delegitimized and replaced by a 'hawkish' Likud government.

One can infer from Gush Emunim activities since the signing of the DOP that an initial consternation was followed by the acceptance of a modified doctrine: further expansion of settlement could be deferred to the future without relinquishing the faith in the link between settlement and salvation. Demonstrations protesting against the peace process were the first reaction, an expression of shock and outrage at what had occurred. They soon petered out as Gush Emunim activists began to face the new political reality: public willingness to make some territorial concessions to the Palestinians in return for peace had risen from 33 per cent in July 1993 to 52 per cent in September 1993 and remained at 51 per cent by August 1994.[47] Obviously, protest had swayed neither the government nor the majority of the public.

By the end of 1994, a plan of action had crystallized to preserve the status quo. As Nissan Slomiansky, a former Secretary-General of Gush Emunim and then Chief of Operations of the Judea, Samaria and Gaza Council, explained in an interview, the main thrust was to prevent the evacuation of all existing settlements by any means short of civil war. Slomiansky optimistically limited the deferment of further settlement to two years, until Labour would be defeated in the 1996 elections and the peace process would be abrogated.[48] But no reliance was put on this hope. Instead, a plan was implemented to substitute enlargement of existing settlements for territorial expansion by new settlements. Construction of housing was started on Tamar Hill in Efrat in late December 1994; in February 1995, nearly completed flats in settlements were offered for sale to diaspora Jews who could then lease them to prospective settlers at affordable rents and thus help increase the population of the settlements; in May 1995, settlers encouraged underprivileged Israelis to move into uncompleted housing in their settlements. The intention of these actions was made clear by Gush Emunim activists. Yanon Ahiman, head of the Efrat Council, stated in an interview that settlers would oppose any stoppage to the housing construction by massive demonstrations and by resistance, if need be.[49] Yehiel Leiter, spokesman of the Judea, Samaria and Gaza Council, stated that investment in the settlements involved no financial risk; Gush Emunim would see to it that settlements would not be handed over to the Palestinian Authority.[50]

In mid-1995, when the withdrawal of Israeli troops from Palestinian population centres was being negotiated, enlargement of settlements was augmented by security precautions which, at the same time, might torpedo the peace process by provoking Palestinians into renewed hostilities. In June 1995, settlers started fencing in land around their settlements vacated by Israeli forces. They also started building connecting roads between settlements in order to create blocs for self-defence. In both cases, the land used was claimed by Palestinians as previously expropriated by the Israeli authorities. In an interview, Slomiansky made the dual purpose of these actions quite clear. He stated that fencing in served to stake a claim to state land, as well as to ignite a fire that could break down negotiations.[51]

Retention of the status quo is as inconsistent a modification of the doctrine as is deferment of salvation to the future. If the status quo is regarded as a temporary freeze of the process leading to salvation, then salvation is deferred to the future and this repudiates the essence of Gush Emunim doctrine, the point on which it diverges most from orthodox Judaism. If salvation is not, or cannot be made imminent, there is no justification for asserting that settlement of the Land of Israel is the commandment transcending all others. The political action of Gush Emunim is then of no greater religious significance than observance of any other commandment and the entire purpose of Gush Emunim becomes questionable. If, on the other hand, continuous extension of settlement is no longer regarded a necessary condition for salvation, then the necessity of any settlement at all in the West Bank and the Gaza Strip becomes questionable. If settlement in parts of the Land of Israel meets the requirements for imminent salvation, the territory of Israel can suffice just as well. Gush Emunim political action becomes superfluous, as does the existence of the movement altogether. The various doctrinal changes offer no logically consistent solution to the existential crisis of Gush Emunim, which was admitted openly by those relinquishing the entire doctrine, but experienced just as deeply by those evading the issue.

Obstructing the peace process may possibly reflect the realization of this dilemma. It certainly constituted a turning point in the reactions to the DOP of the Gush Emunim majority and drew the majority much closer to the views of the minority which had repudiated all aspects of the DOP from the start. The majority of Gush Emunim activists had hesitated to take that step because it violated the Israeli conception of democracy as absolute majority rule. Gush Emunim, for whom the Jewish nation stands above individuals, naturally followed the Israeli consensual view of democracy, which had been challenged by Leftist intellectuals in recent years. Protests and steps intended to delay the implementation of the peace process until the coming elections delegitimized only specific acts of the government, while wrecking the peace process called in question the right of the government to make decisions which seriously affect the minority: it challenged the principle of obedience to majority decisions. Since the latter is such an integral part of Israeli democracy, convincing arguments were needed if its repudiation was not to alienate Gush

Emunim members from the Israeli mainstream and strip the movement of the public backing which it was enjoying.

Moreover, civil disobedience is commonly justified by Western modernist values of individualism and the rights of minorities, values that were guiding the Israeli Left in pressing for the peace process which was underway. Since Gush Emunim could obviously neither accept nor advocate values which it condemned and which were one cause of its predicament, it was facing a serious dilemma in justifying a strategy of civil disobedience. The initial proponents called for mass protests which would create public disturbances. The thousands arrested would fill up all prisons and create an atmosphere of chaos which would eventually topple the government. Civil disobedience was justified because the government did not have a Jewish majority in parliament; it ruled by a minority coalition shored up by the votes of Israeli Arab delegates and its decisions were therefore illegitimate.[52]

The above proposals were not followed while activists believed that their delaying tactics sufficed to avert what they considered a disaster. A year later, however, the Labour government was still in power and seemed intent on taking steps in the peace process which might prove to be irreversible. Moreover, there were indications that the government was also willing to withdraw from the Golan Heights in return for peace with Syria. Opposition to withdrawal from the Golan came from all sectors of Israeli society, including Labour itself. The time seemed propitious to launch a campaign against the evacuation of all settlements, including the secular Labour ones on the Golan. At first, minority rights were invoked to justify civil disobedience. Settlers were called upon to oppose evacuation by any means short of opening fire on Israeli troops, because no majority had the right to deprive a minority of its very existence. According to another view, civil disobedience was justified because truth was not determined by majority decision, nor was the ultimate national destiny.[53]

Such arguments were quickly dropped in favour of others more consonant with Gush Emunim doctrine and Israeli values. Elyakim Haetzni, spokesman of the Hebron settlers, who are most closely associated with repudiation of the peace process, was joined by a group of Gush Emunim rabbis who formulated and signed a Declaration of Principles in December 1994. It was distributed in Golan settlements and appealed to both secular and religious Israelis by declaring the evacuation of settlements a contravention of biblical commandments and of Jewish tradition, as well as a danger to Israeli security. The order to evacuate settlements was declared patently illegal so that settlers had the right and duty to resist actively, short of causing bloodshed. A second Declaration of Principles was formulated at the same time and signed by academics, senior reserve officers and Gush Emunim rabbis. Distributed in isolated

Gush Emunim settlements, it repeated the arguments of the first Declaration but added that soldiers were also prohibited from obeying the order to evacuate a settlement.[54]

At the time, the two declarations drew little public notice, firstly because their distribution was limited and, secondly, because evacuation of settlements would not be on the agenda of negotiations with the Palestinians until the final stage of the DOP was reached. Yet the radical approach of the two declarations augured later developments. They were radical in evoking Divine law to justify political action and in challenging the military duty of obedience. The first Declaration merely legitimized active opposition by civilians to a political decree carried out by armed forces, but the second one legitimized the refusal of a member of the armed forces to carry out a military order. This contravenes Israeli consensus – even Peace Now, the organization of Leftist activists, condemned the conscientious objectors who refused to serve in the occupied territories. It also violates Israeli military rules. According to the Israeli Defence Forces' code of ethics, an order may and must be refused only if it is patently illegal in contravening the most basic human rights.[55]

So far, Israelis at large, as well as Gush Emunim, had assumed legality to derive from the secular legislature and from juridical processes. (Those specific spheres to which religious law and jurisdiction apply in Israel are also laid down in secular parliamentary legislation.) Unless one claimed that the 1992 parliamentary elections had been rigged, an accusation not raised by anybody, the order to evacuate settlements was formally legal. Its legality could only be denied by contrary biblical prescriptions and/or a recourse to conscientious objection. The former put Gush Emunim on a collision course with the secular Israeli State, while the latter is based on individual rights and is, thus, incompatible with the collectivist ethics of Gush Emunim.

The high value which Gush Emunim places on military service has exacerbated the dilemma. Due to pressure from the orthodox establishment, students of Yeshivot are exempt from military service in Israel. Since the late 1950s, but particularly since the establishment and growth of Gush Emunim in the late 1960s, an increasing number of Yeshivot Hesder (arrangement) have been founded, in which students of religion combine study with military service. Since they serve part time, they mostly form separate platoons in larger combat formations. Military defence of the Land of Israel is a logical consequence of the political means chosen by Gush Emunim to achieve salvation. Its members and supporters readily volunteer and constitute the majority in the Yeshivot Hesder units. Furthermore, special pre-military religious annual programmes prepare less scholastically inclined religious young men for full military service, motivating them to volunteer for elite combat units and for command positions.

In early July 1995 it became known that an agreement had been reached to implement the second stage of the DOP, according to which the Israeli forces would withdraw from Palestinian population centres and redeploy military camps from Judea and Samaria. Settlers felt that a greatly reduced military presence in these areas would expose them to Palestinian hostile acts, a fear shared by Yeshivot Hesder and other religious soldiers and officers, regular and reserve. The still hypothetical apprehension about having to evacuate settlements suddenly became an immediate one of having to vacate military camps. In their quandary, Yeshivot Hesder soldiers applied to their rabbis for a ruling on how they should act. After deliberations, 15 rabbis issued a Halachic ruling stating that, similar to the evacuation of settlements, the uprooting of military camps contravened a biblical commandment, endangered life and jeopardized the State. It followed that an order to vacate a military camp was patently illegal and could, or should be refused, as should an order to evacuate a settlement.

This ruling was not followed. Nevertheless, it unleashed a heated controversy in Israel, as well as within Gush Emunim and its sympathizers. The secular sector regarded the ruling as an unacceptable clash between Divine law and the secular democratic order of the Israeli state.[56] Within the religious sector close to Gush Emunim, it was seen as an irresolvable clash between the sacred duty to hold on to territory in the Land of Israel and the sacred duty to defend that territory effectively, the latter becoming impaired if military discipline was breached.[57] If followed, this ruling would detach the settlers from the general consensus and offend against a major tenet of Gush Emunim doctrine which requires the consensual participation of the entire people in the process leading to salvation. This would also inadvertently promote the modernist values which were underpinning the peace process and were causing its predicament. This is so because Gush Emunim can use only two principles to justify disobedience to a military order, namely the precedence of Divine over human secular law or the right of individual dissent. The former was unlikely to convince the secular Israeli public and the latter was counter-productive.

Aware of the insoluble contradictions inherent in its inflexible doctrine, Gush Emunim activists refrained from taking a clearly declared stand on the above ruling, and so did the NRP. No acts of outright civil disobedience were committed, nor was a radical denial of government legitimacy adopted right away. Instead, the ideologically non-committed majority of settlers could be mobilized to join the protest against withdrawal. The latter did so out of anxiety for the safety and possible loss of their homes, as witnessed by the mass demonstrations which Gush Emunim organized. Furthermore, attempts to disrupt the peace process were accompanied by a drive to mobilize broad public support and participation in rallies causing public disturbances. The mayors of Israeli towns situated near towns to be handed over to Palestinian control were alerted to the potential security risks, so that they joined settler protests, as did the Third Way, a movement (which ran as a party in the 1996 elections) led by reserve generals affiliated with Labour who opposed a withdrawal from the Golan Heights.

At the same time, however, roads in Judea and Samaria were blocked by stones on 1 July 1995 and by a slow convoy on 6 July 1995. Road blocks later spread to Israel proper. Moreover, caravans were set up without a building permit in some settlements and token Yeshivot were established at the holy sites of Rachel's Tomb and Herodion, again without prior permit. These steps had some effect on the Israeli public at large, as indicated by surveys. According to one poll, 74 per cent of the public were in favour of a referendum before stage two of the DOP was implemented. The Peace Index Project of July 1995 reported that respondents favouring the evacuation of all settlements had declined from 26 per cent in May 1995 to 22.2 per cent in July of the same year.[58]

Public sympathy with the settlers was due in large part to Palestinian actions, which ostensibly corroborated the settlers' distrust of the Oslo Accords. Between 13 September 1993, the date of the signing of the DOP, and 25 February 1994, 35 Israelis were killed or kidnapped by Palestinian terrorists and hundreds more were injured. Admittedly, the terrorists were members of the opposition Hamas and Islamic Jihad intent on torpedoing the peace process, but the Palestinian Authority took no drastic steps to curb such attacks, seemingly condoning them. On 25 February 1994, Dr Baruch Goldstein, a doctor and reserve officer, decided to avenge these murders and disrupt the Oslo process in a similar manner. He shot down 29 Moslem worshippers in the Cave of the Patriarchs in Hebron. He was himself killed in the ensuing clash, as were dozens of additional Palestinians. Goldstein had been an adherent of Kach, a racist ultra-nationalist religious organization.

The Israeli public and authorities were outraged by this massacre and condemned it strongly. The government appointed a commission of enquiry, outlawed Kach, but did not remove its members from Hebron, nor any other of the Jewish settlers there. Jews constitute a small minority in this city, populated mainly by observant Moslems. Hamas and Islamic Jihad presumably interpreted the absence of any Israeli punitive action against supporters of the massacre as condonation of it. After the massacre, suicide attacks against large targets became their predominant tactics (only two such bombings had occurred prior to the massacre). Five each were carried out in 1994 and 1995 respectively and three in 1996, prior to the elections. Scores of Israelis were killed and injured in each, yet the Israeli government did not abrogate the Oslo Accords. The anxiety regarding personal safety enhanced sympathy for settler protest, resulting in mass rallies, in which the Prime Minister was depicted as a terrorist collaborator and worse. By then, Settlers were delegitimizing the government, depicting its members as traitors. The rift in Israeli society was pushed to extremes. It stigmatized supporters of the peace process as secular hedonists lacking any Jewish ethics and opponents of that process as ultra-nationalist religious fanatics lacking any values compatible with a democratic society. This was the setting for the assassination of Prime Minister Rabin.

REPERCUSSIONS OF THE OSLO PROCESS

Beilin, the initiator of the secret track and an architect of the peace process, realized the weakness inherent in the DOP long before things had come to such a head. He foresaw the difficulty in winning over the public to this total change in policy unless its targets could be clearly stated. Deferring the final status of the agreement with the Palestinians to the end was a mistake which had to be rectified.[59] With the approval of Rabin, Peres and Arafat, a new secret track was opened to skip over the stipulated stages and lay out the final plan of the treaty. These negotiations became protracted, however, and were finalized on 1 November 1995, only just before the assassination of Prime Minister Rabin on 4 November 1995. The public remained ignorant of them until much later, being presented instead with the three different versions as described above, none of them agreed upon by both parties and, therefore, mere wishful thinking. This created hesitancy, uncertainty and confusion among the public, including the Unconverted, except for a small hard core of supporters of peace at any cost. Among the Settlers, these apprehensions were reinforced by resentment at the fact that no account had been taken of their emotional attachment to the Jewish patrimony: it was being given away with little regret and without consulting at least half of the Israeli population. For the settlers, all this was compounded by their fears of losing their very homes and for the Gush Emunim settlers by the collapse of their ideational world.

A decisive blueprint of the final borders and other outstanding and highly controversial issues regarding the Oslo process might have allayed some of the suspicions and fears of the Israeli public. It could not have averted the loss of identity experienced by all but the adherents of Post-zionist and/or modernist values, but it could have made possible a well-focused search for a rearticulation of identity adapted to a new reality. Without it, people were sufficiently aware of the loss to start a search for an answer to their predicament. As will be shown, it has been no more than a tapping in the dark, so to speak, due to the absence of a clear destination. Since the peace process affected the settlers most directly, the Gush Emunim faithful were the first to perceive the ideational implications of it, though principally with regard to their own doctrine and less with regard to Israeli identity in general. Paradoxically, the self-image of the Settler sector of Israeli society was less shaken by the implications of the DOP than was that of the Unconverted. This was possibly so because Settlers paid little attention to the implications, being preoccupied with immediate events which they hoped to stall and reverse by a change of government. The Unconverted, though, who had had no ideational commitment to Greater Israel and welcomed the peace process in principle, but had accepted the Greater Israel borders as a given, were suddenly confronted with the dilemma which had haunted all articulations of Israeli identity, namely the 'right to the land' dilemma.

The voluntary relinquishment of part of the historical homeland is tantamount to an admission that a territorial claim based on ancient history may not be a valid title, as asserted, if it infringes on an equal claim made by another people and based on more recent history. If the DOP concedes the rights of Palestinians to part of Palestine, why not to all of Palestine, including the territory of Israel? Partition merely redresses the injustice of coercive rule over another people, but does not justify the Jewish return to Palestine. By conceding the Palestinian right of self-determination, secular Israelis deprive themselves of that part of their identity which provides its moral basis for being in Israel. If Israelis were intruders in 1967, they were as much intruders at the turn of the century. An unethical origin is an unacceptable constituent of identity; no group asserts distinctiveness by dint of a trait or action to which it itself ascribes a negative connotation.

At the same time, if the universal values of democracy, human rights, self-determination and individualism which have guided the peace process are accepted as the only valid ones, as their advocates demand, Israelis are also deprived of their uniqueness. Post-zionists and modernists deny any validity to group specificity, which they denigrate as tribal and obsolete. Yet universal values cannot be a substitute identity since they do not differentiate Israelis from others but, rather, underline the similarity of Israeli society with enlightened Western ones.

These issues were raised right after the DOP had been signed, at first tentatively and primarily by secular intellectuals from among the Unconverted. A new movement was founded in December 1993, calling itself Hatikva (Hope), which wanted to protect the Jewish identity of

Israelis from the onslaught of Post-zionists. At the end of 1993, the editors of *Shdemot*, a periodical of the Kibbutz, held a dialogue with the editors of *Nekuda*. The former sought to shore up their Jewish identity with arguments provided by Gush Emunim.[60] On 19 October 1994, Yad Tabenkin, a research centre of the Kibbutz movement, held a symposium on the incompatibility of democratic Post-zionist ideas with the Jewish identity of Israel. Another symposium on 'Who Is an Israeli' was held at the Journalists House in Tel-Aviv on 14 December 1994. Articles on the need for a new Israeli identity appeared, at first primarily in periodicals rather than the daily press. Titles such as 'New Israeliness', '[A Jewish state is] Not Normal', 'The New Jew as an Anomaly', or 'We Must Change Course'[61] bear witness to the recognition of the problem posed by Post-zionist assumptions and by the peace process. The authors expressed dissatisfaction with New Zionism, based on secularized Judaism, but provided no satisfactory alternative. The public was informed about the issues at stake as the debate was carried over to the daily press. Historians and writers criticized Post-zionist assumptions, either on historical–theoretical grounds, accusing them of bias or even distortion of facts,[62] or on more practical grounds: the negative self-image projected by Postzionism would break up Israeli society due to self-disgust; it was an overstatement of the 'light unto the nations' principle, demanding self-destruction in order to be ethically superior to other nations; it robbed Israelis of their Jewishness and, thus, of any distinctiveness.[63] Dialogues between the protagonists were also published.[64]

Realizing the implications of the peace process, some prominent spokes-men of the peace camp felt obliged to sustain the ethical justification of the Israeli presence in Israel. They suggested that the need of a persecuted people for a safe haven was a viable alternative to the historical claim.[65] This answer avoids the issue and is inaccurate. Zionists chose the Land of Israel as their destination long before the Holocaust, at a time when the overwhelming majority of Jews could and did emigrate to the United States. Therefore, a safe haven is merely a *post facto* excuse. Furthermore, it implies that Israel must necessarily be Jewish, which contradicts the demand of that very same peace camp for a universalist Israel.

The dilemma which the peace process uncovered was demonstrated vividly at a conference on 'Jews and Arabs in Israel in an Era of Peace', held at Tel-Aviv University on 31 October 1994. In his keynote address, Anton Shammas, an Israeli Arab poet, formulated the issue succinctly, as did two other prominent Israeli Arabs on the panel, Shaykh Abdallah Nimr Darwish, a leader of the Islamic Movement in Israel, and Dr Ahmad Tibi, special adviser to Arafat. They challenged Israel to face up to its equivocal identity and to reformulate it in light of the universal values which were guiding the peace process. The latter were incompatible with a Jewish

Israel which could not accord equal rights to its Arab minority. Israel must renounce its Jewish character and become a truly democratic state. After all, Israeli Arabs, with ancient tenure, had national rights to the country at least equal to those of Israeli Jews, who were recently arrived immigrants. All Jewish Israeli participants objected, particularly in view of the latter observation: once Israelis denied that Israel was exclusively Jewish, they automatically denied their historical entitlement to it. Since the historical argument was no longer as convincing as it had been prior to the peace process, it was not raised, but nor was any other which could provide ethical grounds for the insistence that Israel must remain a Jewish state. The principal argument was practical: Jews were the dominant majority which would never agree to such a change; the Arab demand was counter-productive and would lead to a self-defeating confrontation. Only Alouph Hareven, a director of Sikui, an association for equal rights to Arabs, tentatively admitted the inherent justice of the Arab demand. He offered a compromise solution on the symbolic level which would not replace Jewish symbols, but supplement them with joint civic ones. This suggestion, later raised in the Knesset, was condemned outright. Beilin, by then a cabinet minister, reiterated in an interview that Israel would remain a Jewish state forever. It would neither change its name nor its anthem. Any majority had the right to define itself as it wished.[66]

A temporary lull occurred in the debate, occasioned by a spate of terrorist attacks and fears/hopes that the peace process might collapse. The lull ended with the withdrawal of Israeli troops from Palestinian population centres at the end of September 1995 and, particularly, with the assassination of Prime Minister Rabin. The first event ostensibly made the peace process a *fait accompli*, so that its consequences for Israeli consensus had to be thrashed out. The second event demonstrated the deep cleft in Israeli society regarding these issues and the consequent difficulty, if not impossibility, of reaching a new consensus.

THE ASSASSINATION AND AFTER

The assassination of Prime Minister Rabin on 4 November 1995 produced a response far beyond the obvious shock that could be expected from such an outrageous event. Rabin had been harshly criticized for not reacting more strongly to Palestinian suicide bombings and for proceeding with further redeployments despite blatant Palestinian disregard for their own undertakings under the DOP. In fact, the peace rally at which he was murdered had been organized in order to refurbish his tarnished image after his popularity rating had plummeted to a low 32 per cent, as against 45 per cent for Netanyahu.[67] Neither exceedingly high regard for his leadership, nor fear that the peace process might come to a halt without him – Mr Peres was known to be at least as peace-seeking as he and was Rabin's obvious successor – can explain the anguish and prolonged mourning of the Israeli public in general and of the candle-lighting rites of teenagers in particular. The latter had so often been censored for being hedonistic and self-absorbed that their sudden show of grief was particularly astounding. It would seem that, besides the obvious sorrow over the tragic death of a leader, the shock and consternation of the public revealed the realization that social consensus had been disrupted so thoroughly as to lead to murder. A research of young people aged 15–24, conducted in 1998, illuminates this point. Seventy per cent of the respondents regarded the assassination as a severe crisis which had undermined their trust in Israeli society; 10.5 per cent of them regarded the assassination as a point of no return when 'I no longer have a state'.[68]

The Growing Social Rift

Indeed, the shock of the assassination made people perceive and admit the rift that had been present all along and which was tearing the society apart. The crisis of identity induced by the Oslo Accords had been noticed by some religious and secular intellectuals prior to the assassination. An entire issue of *Dimui* (No. 8, Summer 1994), a periodical of the Centre for Religious Zionism, dealt with this subject, as did an issue of *Meimad* (No. 3, January 1995), the organ of the Meimad movement. A.B. Yehoshua, a prominent Leftist author, feared that once the common enemy on which Israeli solidarity had been based was removed, existing repressed rifts would come to the fore and create a crisis.[69] Yet, at the time, the underlying dilemma created by the Oslo Accords was not fully understood, nor was the depth of the gulf it had produced.

After the assassination, the polarization was exacerbated by the recriminations directed by each camp at the other. This underlined the chasm in worldviews over and above the differences of political opinion. The peace camp, comprising principally secular Unconverted, accused Settlers, and specifically the religious among them, of having incited and encouraged the assassin, a Hardal youth and student of the religious Bar Ilan University. He had followed the Halachic rulings of ultra-nationalist Hardal rabbis. The mainstream religious establishment had not shared these views, but nor had it openly condemned them. In consequence, all religious Settlers were accused of collusion in the assassination. Bar Ilan University and all other religious educational institutions were charged with teaching extremist, anti-democratic values; the religious public was found guilty of hypocrisy, of secretly condoning the assassination while expressing public remorse.[70] A Labour-aligned youth organization banned joint events with religious right-wing youth groups; leaders of past mass protests were put on trial; some rabbis were interrogated by the police on suspicion of incitement; Lea Rabin, widow of the late Prime Minister, accused the entire Rightist camp of being an accomplice to the assassination; Amnon Rubinstein, the Minister of Education, similarly accused the Council of Judea and Samaria;[71] proposals were put forward to close down various religious educational institutions.

Some of the religious Settlers and Gush Emunim faithful felt genuine guilt, though not for long, while others never did. The reaction of Bar Ilan University can serve as an example. At first, it rejected any responsibility for the crime: at a mass meeting held on campus on 5 November 1995, the leaflet distributed read: 'We have not spilled this blood.' During the following days, though, meetings were held indicating regret: a public lecture was held on 6 November 1995 on the sanctity of life, the student union held a vigil on 8 November 1995 in commemoration of the late Prime Minister and a student was expelled for sending a message on the internet expressing joy at the assassination. Reactions among leaders of the religious camp affiliated to Gush Emunim were similarly ambivalent. At an assembly held on 8 November 1995, some speakers charged religious education with having deteriorated to the level of incitement to civil war and murder, while others rejected the link between legitimate political protest and assassination, which the peace camp was trying to prove.[72] Despite such self-defensive protestations, the militant settlers decided to discontinue protests and replace them by information campaigns against the peace process, while some Gush Emunim activists also called for a genuine soul-searching.[73]

But recriminations continued, bolstered by proposals to create a new secular and ethical Israeli identity, in contrast to the unethical xenophobic Settler one.[74] One article aptly summarized the growing extremism on both sides: similar to the Hardal preachers of xenophobia, Leftist modernists were turning into preachers of a new ideology of capitalist democracy, devoid of any Israeli specificity.[75] Religious Settlers counter-reacted with defiance[76] which could not be dampened by the feeble attempt of Prime Minister Peres to ameliorate the growing polarization. He appointed Rabbi Amital, leader of the dovish religious Meimad group, as Minister Without Portfolio. It was a gesture intended to symbolize reconciliation, but was seen as a cynical manoeuvre aimed at increasing support for Labour at the coming elections. Gush Emunim adherents began resenting the wholesale accusations levelled against them: two months after Rabbi Blass had advocated reconciliation and remorse, he defended the militant protest movement despite its tragic outcome; this was reiterated in an interview by a leading Gush Emunim faithful.[77]

Beginning to Recognize an Identity Crisis

By then, observers on both sides of the divide began to recognize the dangers inherent in fanaticism, when each side believes its faith to be the only truth and the whole truth. In this situation, no common ground is left for any dialogue because there is no longer any agreement on the rules governing such a dialogue, let alone on the subject matter to be discussed. A society rent apart in this way loses its common identity and collapses into chaos. To avoid such an eventuality, calls were made for some unifying principle.[78]

The Settler half of Israeli society retained its identity relatively intact, except for the Gush Emunim faithful, whose travails have already been discussed. Defiance probably played a part in that, as well as the veiled Likud platform which hinted at a possible halt to the peace process. The Unconverted, whose identity had never been properly articulated, were much more aware of the danger underlying polarization, induced as it was at least partly by the Post-zionist narrative. Except for outright protagonists of Postzionism, the Unconverted became aware of the need for consensus based on society-specific values, which could only be Jewish in the case of Israel. The subject was prominent on the public agenda. Articles proliferated with titles such as 'Ideological Bankruptcy', 'Icons of Identity', 'A Farewell to Zionism' and 'Israel Against Herself'.[79] At a conference held at Tel-Aviv University on 15 December 1995, entitled 'The Future of Israeli Society and Economy', Leftist intellectuals were agreed that, denuded of a unique identity, Israelis would opt for the lowest denominator of Westernism, namely a mindless consumerism and egoistical competitiveness. A leading Israeli Leftist author predicted that without a unique identity, which creates solidarity, conflicting interests would tear Israeli society apart. Jewish values were the only ones common to all Israelis; it was imperative to find some association between Israeli liberal democracy and its Jewish cultural heritage. The religious camp was best suited to re-imbue secular Israelis with the Jewish values abandoned under the influence of Postzionism. A Jewish state, based on a symbiosis of Jewish and universal values, would underline Israeli distinctiveness *vis-à-vis* the world and preserve the moral integrity of Israelis as returnees to their homeland.[80] This line of thought was apparently taken up by Prime Minister Peres when he coopted Rabbi Avital into the government as representative of the moderate religious camp. Similarly, Yossi Beilin attempted a dialogue with the ultra-orthodox parties.

The realization of the dilemma posed by modernist and Post-zionist assertions soon spread to the Unconverted at large, especially to young secular Israelis who were so prominent in their grief and shock following the assassination of Mr Rabin. Dialogue groups of secular and religious youngsters multiplied, initiated largely by the secular who were seeking Jewish values on which a renewed consensus could rest. Numerous Kibbutz groups met Yeshiva students; several hundred military officers and several scores of police officers attended seminars with religious young people at Elul, a religious studies centre; a group of secular secondary school pupils founded Hala, for dialogue with their religious counterparts; Gesher, an association of secular–religious rapprochement, organized scores of dialogue groups upon request.

This admission by the Unconverted that secularization and modernism had gone too far was probably one reason why Settler regret reverted to defiance. In that sense the former was counter-productive, strengthening Settlers in their certainty that their view had been the only truth all along. They demanded national reconcilition, but on their own terms: to narrow down polarization, Labour must undertake to refrain from further redeployments until elections were held;[81] at a rally held on 16 December 1995, the Prime Minister was derided for coopting Rabbi Amital of Meimad as the sole means of reconciliation. Dialogue groups did not bridge the gulf then nor later, nor has the widespread 'return to the Jewish bookcase', an attempt by secular Israelis to refamiliarize themselves with their roots by studying traditional Jewish texts.

Return of Likud to Power

There were obviously additional reasons for the Likud victory in the May 1996 elections. No social phenomenon can ever be explained by a single cause and certainly not as complex a one as election results. Three suicide bombings killed some 60 Israelis within one week between February and early March 1996, yet Peres did not abrogate the Oslo process; a faulty aim by Israeli gunners killed around 100 civilians in the Lebanese security zone, casting doubts on Peres' peaceful intentions. This self-contradictory image of Labour presumably lost them some votes. Dissatisfaction with the justifications for the peace process put forward by Labour leaders probably also played a part in bringing about this victory, as did the hope of many Settlers that the New Zionism of the Likud message would prevail over its announcement in its political programme that it would honour the Oslo Accords.

In fact, the Netanyahu platform was even more equivocal than the original Likud programme, justifying the continuation of the peace process by security and calling this policy 'a secure peace'. New Zionism had stressed the security advantage of retaining the West Bank as a strategic depth, yet New Zionist supporters were now called upon to relinquish this strategic depth. In an interview, Netanyahu clarified this point. He stated that enhanced Israeli security was a precondition for a continuing peace process. If that was so, why should Israelis support the latter if peace really constituted a danger? That question was left unanswered in the interview.[82] Despite, or possibly because of this ambivalent platform, Netanyahu won the direct elections for the Premiership by a very narrow margin and thus returned the Likud party to power.

NOTES

1. Y. Beilin, *Touching Peace* (Tel-Aviv: Miskal, 1997), pp.75–145.
2. I. Pappe, *The Making of the Arab–Israeli Conflict 1947–1951* (London: Tauris, 1992); N. Gertz, 'The Few Against the Many', *Jerusalem Quarterly*, No. 30, 1984, pp.94–104; B. Morris, *Israel's Border Wars 1949–1956* (Oxford: Clarendon, 1993).
3. E. Zartal, 'Anonymous Souls: The Illegal Immigrants and the Aliya Bet Institution in the Struggle to Set Up the State and After' *Ha-tsionut*, Vol. 14, 1989, pp.107–26.
4. B. Morris, *The Birth of the Palestinian Refugee Problem 1947–1949* (New York: Cambridge University Press, 1987); V. Shifter, 'The 1949 Israeli Offer to Repatriate 100,000 Palestinian Refugees', *Middle East Focus*, Vol. 9, No. 2, 1986, pp.13–18.
5. H. Eshkoli, 'On the Question of the Emigration of Zionist Functionaries from Europe at the Beginning of the Second World War', *Ha-tsionut*, Vol. 17, 1993, pp.191–209.
6. B. Kimmerling, 'Not Democratic and not Jewish', *Ha-arets*, 27 December 1996; Z. Sternhell, 'On Myths Which Refuse to Die', *Ha-arets*, 1 October 1997; G. Levy, 'Time to Admit the Injustice', *Ha-arets*, 28 April 1996; M. Benvenisti, 'To Break the Taboo', *Ha-arets*, 1 May 1997.
7. Interview of Ilan Pappe and Tom Segev in 'On Zionism and Postzionism', *Ha-arets*, 15 October 1995; B. Kimmerling, 'Merchants of Anxiety', *Ha-arets*, 24 June 1994; I. Pappe, 'The Refugees, An Original Sin', *Politika*, No. 51, 1993, pp.54–7.
8. I. Pappe, 'A Lesson in New History', *Ha-arets*, 24 June 1994; U. Ram, 'The Post-zionist Debate: Five Clarifications', *Davar*, 8 July 1994; Z. Sternhell, 'The Zionism of Tomorrow', *Ha-arets*, 15 September 1995.
9. U. Ram, 'The Secret of the Secular Weakness', *Ha-arets*, 14 May 1998; B. Kimmerling, 'The Palestinian Version of Brit Shalom', *Ha-arets*, 3 July 1998; G. Levy, 'The Second Way', *Ha-arets*, 2 February 1998; Z. Sternhell, 'The Israeli Cocktail', *Ha-arets*, 13 September 1996. D. Boyarin and J. Boyarin, 'The People of Israel Has No Homeland', *Teoriya U-bikoret*, No. 5, 1994, pp.79–104; A. Raz-Kratzkin, 'Exile Within Sovereignty: Towards a Critique of the "Negation of Exile" in Israeli Culture' – Part 2', *Teoriya U-bikoret*, No. 5, 1994, pp.113–32.
10. References will be mainly from TV and newspaper interviews because they reach a much wider public than the books written by political leaders.
11. D. Mankowsky, 'We Have Passed the Point of No Return', *Jerusalem Post*, 24 September 1995.
12. A. Ben, 'Separation as a Political Conception', *Ha-arets*, 14 April 1995.
13. Israel TV interview on 8 July 1995.
14. A. Ben, 'Separation as a Political Conception'.
15. B. Kimmerling, 'The Non-Peace Process', *Ha-arets*, 3 January 1996.
16. Y. Beck, 'The Other Vision', *Ha-arets*, 28 December 1995; S. Rodan, 'Peres Spars With Arab Media', *Jerusalem Post*, 31 October 1995.
17. U. Galili, 'Beilin Seeks Allies, Peres Retreats to Past Positions', *Ha-arets*, 29 November 1995.
18. S. Peres, 'We'll Settle for Less Than a Short Cut', *Ha-arets*, 3 April 1996.
19. U. Benziman, 'Where Does This Lead To?', *Ha-arets*, 1 October 1995; Israel TV interview of Yossi Sarid, who replaced Shulamit Aloni as Meretz leader, on 19 March 1995.
20. *Politika*, No. 48, March 1993.
21. R. Rosenthal, 'Return to Time', *Politika*, No. 51, November 1993, p.3.
22. *Political Programme of the Likud*, February 1995; Israel TV interview on 3 February 1995; lecture held at Bar Ilan University on 8 June 1995.
23. Alouph Hareven at a panel discussion on Jews and Arabs in an Era of Peace, held at Tel-Aviv University on 31 October 1994; Y. Barnea, 'Not Only Jews', *Ha-arets*, 12 September 1995; A. Margalit and M. Brinkner interviewed in N.T. Gross, 'Are We Still All Zionists?', *Jerusalem Post*, 29 September 1995.

24. R. Kislev, 'Our Men in the Territories', *Ha-arets*, 28 April 1995.
25. Guttman Institute of Applied Social Research, *Jerusalem Post*, 13 September 1993.
26. Guttman, *Jerusalem Post*, 5 December 1991; Jaffe Institute of Strategic Research, *Jerusalem Post*, 27 March 1995.
27. Smith, *Davar*, 2 October 1986; Guttman, *Jerusalem Post*, 13 September 1993; Dahaf, *Yedi'ot Ahronot*, 6 January 1995.
28. Survey of Haifa University, reported in *Ha-arets*, 12 September 1995.
29. Guttman, *Nativ*, July 1994, pp.29–33.
30. The Peace Index Project of the Tami Steinmetz Centre of Peace Research, *Ha-arets*, 6 August 1995.
31. BESA Institute of Strategic Studies, *Ma'ariv*, 3 January 1994.
32. Peace Index Project, *Ha-arets*, 5 December 1995.
33. Computed from the Peace Index Project published monthly in *Ha-arets*.
34. D. Leon, 'Part of the Mideast', *Jerusalem Post*, 24 March 1995.
35. Peace Index Project, *Ha-arets*, 10 May 1995, 6 August 1995.
36. For a detailed discussion of developments within Gush Emunim see G. Aran, 'Jewish Zionist Fundamentalism: The Bloc of the Faithful in Israel (Gush Emunim)', in M.E. Marty and S. Appleby (eds), *Fundamentalism Observed* (Chicago: University of Chicago Press, 1991), pp.265–344.
37. See, for example, D. Benari, 'The Likud Will Lead, But the Road Will Be Ours', *Nekuda*, No. 166, 1993, pp.18–22.
38. D. Beeri, 'The End has Come to the Common Road of Secular Zionism and the Doctrine of Rabbi Kuk', *Nekuda*, No. 181, 1994, pp.14–18.
39. By the end of 1996, the ultra-orthodox *Ha-Mahane Ha-dati* newspaper admitted that this had become a common occurrence. See S. Ilan, 'Concern Among Haredi Rabbis: Yeshiva Students Cross Over to the National-Religious Camp', *Ha-arets*, 3 November 1996.
40. C.S. Liebman, 'Attitudes Towards Democracy Among Israeli Religious Leaders', in E. Kaufman, *et al.* (eds), *Democracy, Peace and the Israeli–Palestinian Conflict* (Boulder: Lymse Rienner, 1993), pp.135–61; M. Friedman, 'Jewish Zealots: Conservative versus Innovative', in E. Sivan and M. Friedman (eds), *Religious Radicalism and Politics in the Middle East* (New York: State University of New York, 1990), pp.127–41.
41. See, for example, Rabbi M. Broyer, 'I Don't Understand the Voice of Despair Among Us', *Nekuda*, No. 184, 1995, pp.12–16; M. Karpel, 'The Paralysis in Gush Emunim, the Council and the Religious Ideological Right', *Nekuda*, No. 185, 1995, pp.60–5; Rabbi D. Shilo, 'Who Will Be the Standard Bearer of the Tora?', *Nekuda*, No. 195, 1996, pp.16–18; S. Fisher, 'Opposite the Gentiles', *Meimad*, No. 9, 1997, pp.16–19.
42. A. Ariel, 'Towards a New National Revival', *Nekuda*, No. 181, 1994, pp.30–3; Y. Hankin, 'The Defence Line Passes Through Tel-Aviv', *Nekuda*, No. 174, 1994, pp.34–5.
43. D. Beeri, 'The End Has Come'; Ben-Artzi, H., 'A New Gush Emunim', *Nekuda*, No. 180, 1994, pp.30–1.
44. Y. Kopel, in 'Dialogue Between Shdemot and Nekuda' *Shdemot*, No. 126, 1994, pp.7-14; A. Ariel, 'Was the Aguda Method Right?', *Nekuda*, No. 175, 1994.
45. U. Elitzur, 'On the Sin We Did Not Commit', *Nekuda*, No. 180, 1994.
46. T. Moses, 'To Be Magnanimous and Congratulate Rabin and Peres', *Nekuda*, No. 171, 1993, p.27.
47. Modi'in Ezrahi, *Mabat*, 9 July 1993; Guttman, *Jerusalem Post*, 13 September 1993, 17 August 1994.
48. N. Shragai, 'The Nissan Force', *Ha-arets*, 16 December 1994.
49. *Ma'ariv*, 28 December 1994.
50. *Jerusalem Post*, 14 February 1995.
51. H. Keinon and L. Collins, 'IDF Breaks Up Scuffle Over Settlers' Fencing in Land', *Jerusalem Post*, 28 June 1995.
52. E. Haetzni, 'Thousands Will Fill Up the Prisons in a Non-Violent Struggle', *Nekuda*, No. 171, 1993, pp.14–17; B. Katzover, 'To Overthrow the Rabin Government', *Nekuda*, No. 171, 1993, pp.18–19; M. Felix, 'They Don't Mind Paving the Road With Our Bodies', *Nekuda*, No. 173, 1993, pp.26–8.
53. E. Haetzni, 'Civil Disobedience Now', *Nekuda*, No. 179, 1994, pp.26–9; Y. Klein, 'Patently Immoral', *Nekuda*, No. 176, 1994, pp.64–7; Y. Etzion, 'This Is Fanaticism', *Nekuda*, No. 179, 1994, pp.26–30.
54. E. Haetzni, 'The Gate has been Opened to the Slaughter', *Nekuda*, No. 183, 1994, pp.46–9.
55. General (res.) Ehud Barak, 'Obeying Commands in a Democratic Setting', keynote address given at the international conference under that title held at Tel-Aviv University during 25–28 June 1995.

56. See, for example, U. Benziman, 'Contempt of the Temple', *Ha-arets*, 9 July 1995; R. Kislev, 'Dismantle This Palmah As Well', *Ha-arets*, 11 July 1995; Z. Segal, 'On the Threshold of the Day of Reckoning', *Ha-arets*, 10 July 1995.
57. See, for example, Rabbi T. Shimoni, 'Dialogue Instead of Annihilation', *Ha-arets*, 16 July 1995; E. Gordon quoting Rabbi Rabinovich in 'Yeshiva Head Defends Rabbis' Ruling on Disobedience in Army', *Jerusalem Post*, 18 July 1995; Rabbi J. Blass, 'Question of Conscience', *Jerusalem Post*, 14 July 1995; Rabbi M. Fruman, 'The Piercing Horn of the Dilemma', *Ha-arets*, 16 July 1995.
58. Mutagim, *Jerusalem Post*, 21 July 1995; Peace Index Project, *Ha-arets*, 6 August 1995.
59. Y. Beilin, *Touching Peace*, pp.170–1.
60. *Shdemot*, No.126/1, 1993, No.126/2, 1994.
61. U. Bar Ner, 'New Israeliness', *Shdemot*, No.126/1, 1993, pp.55–6; Y. Agassi, 'Not Normal', *Politika*, No. 49, 1993; Y. Barnea, 'The New Jew as an Immanent Contradiction', *Shdemot*, No. 126/1, pp.24–25, 1993; Y. Ariel, 'We Must Change Course', *Nekuda*, No. 174, 1994, pp.14–17.
62. Y. Landers, 'On the Sin We Committed in Establishing the State', *Davar Ha-shavu'a*, 18 March 1994; Y. Goren, 'Required: Zionist Ideological Influence on Jewish Historiography', *Davar*, 3 June 1994; Y. Porat, 'History and Wishful Thinking', *Ha-arets*, 1 July 1994; A. Rubinstein, 'Distortion of Zionism', *Ha-arets*, 12 September 1995.
63. A. Meged, 'The Jewish Suicidal Drive', *Ha-arets*, 10 June 1994; S. Aharonson, 'The New Historians and the Challenge of the Holocaust', *Ha-arets*, 24 June 1994; Y. Sheleg, 'In Favour of Non-Normality', *Ha-arets*, 10 October 1995.
64. 'On Zionism, Postzionism and Anti-Zionism', *Ha-arets*, 15 October 1995; N.C. Gross, 'Are We (Still) All Zionists?', *Jerusalem Post*, 29 September 1995.
65. Z. Sternhell, 'Farewell to Ancestral Tombs', *Ha-arets*, 25 March 1994; Interview with A.B. Yehoshua, *Davar*, 5 September 1994.
66. Y. Algasi, 'Woe to Us If We Don't Have an Arab Minister', *Ha-arets*, 13 February 1996.
67. Gallup, *Jerusalem Post*, 28 April 1995.
68. I. Keinan, 'Points of Social Solidarity: Army, Contribution to Society, Secular and Religious Attitude to the Holocaust and the Assassination of Rabin', in *Personal, Social and National Attitudes of Israeli Youth in the Jubilee* (Tel-Aviv: Israeli Institute of Economic and Social Research, 1998),pp.57–71.
69. M. Paz, 'The Second Act', *Ha-arets*, 5 September 1994.
70. D. Assaf, 'Treason in All Aspects of Our Life', *Ha-arets*, 10 November 1995; A. Ushpiz, 'The Answer: Another Star', *Ha-arets*, 10 November 1995; D. Margalit, 'The NRP on the Back of the Tiger', *Ha-arets*, 10 November 1995.
71. A. Barzilai, '10 Years Later', *Ha-arets*, 26 November 1995.
72. 'Soul-Searching Convention', *Nekuda*, No. 190, 1995, pp.58–64. Most articles in this issue rejected the blame put on the entire religious camp.
73. Y. Harel, 'The Sacrifice of Isaac', *Ha-arets*, 6 November 1995; N. Shragai, 'A Pact on the Limits of Religious Rulings', *Ha-arets*, 23 November 1995; L. Galili, 'Don't Give a Bullet to the Informer', *Ha-arets*, 6 December 1995.
74. D. Rosenblum, 'When the Cat Is Out', *Ha-arets*, 1 December 1995; B. Kimmerling, 'The Unholy Alliance', *Ha-arets*, 8 November 1995; Z. Sternhell, 'The Second Revolution', *Ha-arets*, 17 November 1995.
75. O. Almog, 'The Secular Admorim [title of Hasidic rabbis]', *Ha-arets*, 29 December 1995.
76. 'Responses', *Nekuda*, No. 191, 1996.
77. J. Blass, 'The Only Answer: Love', *Jerusalem Post*, 7 November 1995; 'Real Estate *vs.* Human Life', *Jerusalem Post*, 29 December 1995; Harel, A., 'Change to a Minimalist Programme', *Ha-arets*, 20 November 1995.
78. S. Avineri, 'Unifying Power', *Jerusalem Post*, 5 December 1995; Y. Sheleg, 'An Alliance of the Extremes', *Ha-arets*, 22 January 1996; T. Kollek with A. Kollek, 'Tip of the Iceberg', *Jerusalem Post*, 15 December 1995.
79. Y. Markus, 'Ideological Bankruptcy', *Ha-arets*, 2 February 1996; J. Shapiro, 'Icons of Identity', *Jerusalem Post*, 13 December 1995; D. Margalit, 'A Farewell to Zionism', *Ha-arets*, 2 October 1995; M. Widlansky, 'Israel Against Herself', *Jerusalem Post*, 24 September 1995.
80. A.B. Yehoshua, 'The People of Israel', *Ha-arets*, 29 December 1995.
81. Y. Harel, 'Priority to Internal Peace', *Ha-arets*, 23 November 1995.
82. A. Shavit, 'A New Middle East', *Ha-arets*, 22 November 1996.

6. Fracture

The direct election for the Prime Minister, legislated during the 1992–96 term, was first put into effect in the 1996 elections, in which Netanyahu won by a very narrow margin. Israel retained the proportional representation system and the low threshold of 1.5 per cent for parties to enter the Knesset. Since people could now choose the Prime Minister directly, they felt safe to cast their separate vote for the party they favoured most. Consequently, small parties, which had previously held a total of 30 per cent of the seats, now increased their share to 36.3 per cent and two new parties entered the Knesset, with a combined strength of 8.8 per cent. Though Labour lost almost 10 per cent of its strength, Likud made no gains and remained weaker than Labour by 1.7 per cent. Since Netanyahu needed a majority of over 50 per cent in the Knesset in order to govern, he had to form a coalition in which several other parties would constitute at least half of the cabinet (Likud had won 25.1 per cent of the votes). The obvious weakness of such a government, rent between different and often opposing interests, was exacerbated by the political inexperience of the new Prime Minister, frequent incidents of ineptitude and his equivocal programme of action. The following analysis will concentrate only on those events since the 1996 elections which are relevant to the subject at hand, namely those which have impinged on the crisis of identity which Israeli society is undergoing.

As will be shown, the latter has not been resolved by the change of government. Rather, the delaying tactics in the peace process employed by Likud left the future final borders of Israel even more uncertain than they had been previously. Since Israeli identity is so intimately linked with its territorial boundaries, no new articulation of identity could emerge during the Likud tenure. Instead, the sterile search for Jewish roots, coupled with Likud economic policies which increased the income gap, as well as the greater strength of religious parties due to the weakness of the coalition deepened the divisions within Israeli society to the point of near-fracture.

INCONSISTENT INTERPRETATIONS OF AN EQUIVOCAL MESSAGE

True to the Likud platform and the pre-election statements of Netanyahu, the new government declared itself resolved to honour the Oslo Accords. The latter had shied away from any final status outline, nor had they laid down the size of the territory to be vacated by Israel at each of the stipulated stages of redeployment. Likud did not seem to have had a clearer idea about how to proceed, but implied that it would hand over less territory than Labour would have done and that it would extract a stiffer price in return in order to ensure Israeli security.

'Peace and Security' was the slogan under which Netanyahu had campaigned during the elections and which he reiterated throughout his tenure. The interpretation of these two concepts had been left vague at the outset. They were subsequently defined variously according to circumstances, leaving the public and the media wondering what Likud's true intentions were. In negotiations for the settlement of a violent conflict, the interpretation of security depends on that of peace. Peace has many meanings, ranging from a reconciliation with the adversary based on mutual trust, to a tense truce based on total distrust of the adversary's intentions. In the former case, mutual trust would eliminate stringent Israeli security requirements, facilitate negotiations and lead towards future cooperation. In the latter case, Israeli security requirements would overshadow any quest for a settlement with the Palestinians and aim at maximum detachment from them. The Netanyahu government never opted for a reconciliation. Rather, it vacillated between various degrees of distrust, depending on which coalition partner was exerting the most pressure and on external pressures from the international community. Palestinian reactions to Israeli policy fluctuations also played their part in enhancing or allaying distrust. The following record of events will illustrate this process.

First Phase: Muted Distrust

In August 1996, shortly after assuming office, Netanyahu put forward a plan according to which Israel would make further territorial concessions on condition of strict separation between the Palestinian entity and Israel and on condition that all settlements beyond the Green Line remain in place, linked in large blocs and connected to Israel by a network of roads. A team was appointed to negotiate with the Palestinians on the basis of this plan.

Second Phase: Increased Distrust

The settlers, who had hailed Netanyahu as the saviour of their Greater Israel vision, were immediately alerted and began an intensive lobbying campaign. According to an interview with the new chairman of the Yesha (acronym for Judea and Samaria) Council in late July 1996, they demanded that Hebron, the City of the Fathers, not be vacated (it was the only West Bank city still under Israeli control), that new settlements be put up in area C (the part of the West Bank under full Israeli rule) and that existing ones be expanded.[1] The government changed course, probably in response to settler demands. The withdrawal from Hebron was delayed deliberately, ostensibly because the Palestinians were not honouring their commitments in Jerusalem.[2] Nor was the first stage of the redeployment implemented in September 1996, as stipulated previously. Furthermore, when addressing the Likud Centre in September 1996, Netanyahu added further conditions to a negotiated settlement. He visualized a non-sovereign Palestinian entity, without an army, without control over water resources and deprived of the right to determine immigration into its own territory.[3]

Declarations were then followed by an action which was as unwise as it was counter-productive. On 26 September 1996, the government gave permission to open an ancient tunnel in the Old City of Jerusalem which runs from the Temple Mount. Suspecting a tampering with their holy sites, Moslems were religiously outraged, instigating violent unrest throughout the West Bank. Armed Palestinian police opened fire and Israeli soldiers were killed.

Israeli public reactions were divided. Settlers were outraged at Palestinian violence, which contravened the Oslo Accords, and this deepened their distrust of Palestinian intentions. The Unconverted were outraged too, but as much at Palestinian violence as at government ineptitude, or deliberate provocation, which had triggered the violence. International opinion was fairly unanimous, regarding the tunnel affair as an Israeli ruse in order to justify a halt to the negotiations.

Third Phase: Lessened Distrust

The charges voiced internationally and by the Unconverted probably played a part in mitigating the government distrust of Palestinian intentions. It seemed to realize that it was partly to blame for the outbreak of unrest. Netanyahu gave in to US pressure and entered negotiations on the withdrawal from Hebron and the further redeployment stipulated in the Oslo Accords, both of which had been drawn out since the elections. Furthermore, less stringent final status proposals were put forward.

Netanyahu indicated that he accepted a separate Palestinian state, though with limited sovereignty, on the model of Puerto Rico or Andora.[4] In an interview, the policy advisor to the Prime Minister reiterated the limited sovereignty option for a future Palestinian state separate from Israel.[5]

Yet Netanyahu almost immediately qualified what might have seemed excessive trust in Palestinian intentions. The freeze on building within the settlements was lifted. Furthermore, when interviewed, Netanyahu also clarified that peace could not be equated with disarmament in the Middle East. Israel must not recognize the Palestinian right to self-determination, even in the West Bank, lest the Palestinians eventually extend this demand to Israel proper. Once Israel relinquished its claim to part of its patrimony, it lost the right to all of it. Therefore, the Palestinian entity should not be a sovereign state: Palestinians were a national minority, deserving no more than autonomy, or very limited sovereignty.[6]

Despite renewed building in settlements and the above qualification, a protocol was signed in mid-January 1997, stipulating that most of Hebron come under Palestinian control, except for the Jewish enclave in its centre. In addition, a Note for the Record reiterated the Israeli undertaking to carry out further redeployments in three stages until August 1998 (instead of September 1997, as originally laid down), the first one to take place in March 1997. No mention was made of where Israel would redeploy, nor of how far it would withdraw. In return, the Palestinians undertook to revise their charter, to fight terror and incitement and to confiscate illegal weapons. Yet in setting a final date for the phased Israeli withdrawals, the Note for the Record was a clear departure from the previous insistence of Netanyahu that reciprocity was a *conditio sine qua non* for any further Israeli redeployment.

In a newspaper article, Foreign Minister Levy expressed his satisfaction with the government commitment to the Oslo Accords. Peace with the Palestinians was the best option for Israel, even at the cost of territorial concessions.[7] The settlers, however, were less than enthusiastic. They began recruiting MKs (members of Knesset) for their cause. After having failed to avert the pullout from Hebron, they restricted their aim to preventing any redeployments, as stipulated in the Note for the Record. A permanent lobby of 17 MKs was formed in February 1997, calling itself the Land of Israel Front, which threatened to bring down the government unless it toed their line.

Fourth Phase: Rekindled Distrust

At this stage, government actions were conveying conflicting messages to the public. On the one hand, despite strong opposition from some

Ministers, on 6 March 1997 the cabinet approved a withdrawal from 9 per cent of the West Bank during the first stage of redeployment. On the other hand, probably in response to the threat from the Front and in order to appease the Council, on 24 February 1997 it gave permission for construction to start on Har Homa, a barren and very visible hilltop in the Palestinian part of Jerusalem. The Palestinians and the international community regarded the Har Homa affair as another deliberate provocation in order to halt implementation of the phased redeployments.

If that had been the intention, it certainly succeeded. The unrest following the Har Homa decision and the PA (Palestinian Authority) announcement that selling land to Jews was punishable by death (the plot on Har Homa had been sold to a Jew; ostensibly, the death sentence was to deter such sales and prevent legal Jewish building in Palestinian neighbourhoods, but it had strong racist overtones) again gave rise to Israeli mistrust. The redeployment, approved only a fortnight earlier, on 6 March 1997, was now seen as a premature forfeiture of bargaining chips. In line with this apprehension, on 20 March 1997 Netanyahu proposed skipping all interim stages and proceeding directly to final status negotiations. Events of the following day, 21 March 1997, served to confirm the government's worst suspicions: a suicide bomb in a Tel-Aviv café killed and injured civilians and riots broke out in Hebron. Thereupon, Netanyahu immediately considered breaking off talks with the PA.

In fact, that had already occurred, initiated by the PA which rejected a mere 9 per cent withdrawal and the proposed building on Har Homa (which had not yet been started in mid-1999). The PA also rejected the final status proposal put forward by Netanyahu in June 1997. This plan, named the Alon-Plus Plan, provided for Israel to retain Greater Jerusalem and the Jordan Valley, as well as a security belt east of the Green Line and around Gush Etzion.[8] That would have left 40–50 per cent of the West Bank to the Palestinians. Following another suicide attack in Jerusalem on 30 July 1997, Netanyahu restricted his previous offer further, demanding Israeli control of all border crossings of a Palestinian entity, which would have no more than full civil autonomy.[9] His insistence on reciprocity in fulfilling commitments became ever more stringent as a condition for the first stage of withdrawal and the latter was never implemented.[10]

By November 1997, US pressure to break the deadlock was mounting, because it was soliciting Arab support for a military action in Iraq. In response, Netanyahu suggested a package deal to both his cabinet and to Arafat: Israel would withdraw from 6–8 per cent of the West Bank in return for a Palestinian agreement to proceed to final status talks immediately, foregoing the last stage of redeployment. On 1 December 1997, the government approved the Israeli final status offer, which was more restrictive than any previous one. It provided for buffer zones along the Jordan Valley and the Green Line, as well as around Jerusalem and the Etzion Bloc, Israeli-controlled security strips in areas of aquifers, in strategically important regions and at sacred sites, as well as Israeli-controlled roads to the settlements, except for very isolated ones which would remain Israeli enclaves within Palestinian territory. This plan left 40–45 per cent of the West Bank to the Palestinians in disjunct enclaves. Instead of a state, Israel offered the Palestinians a functional division of authority.[11]

As the Palestinians saw it, Israel was offering increasingly less and demanding increasingly more in return. It now insisted on a further curbing of terror and the extradition of apprehended terrorists, yet also demanded that the Palestinians reduce their police force by one third. The PA rejected the Israeli proposal. Against the background of the intensifying Gulf crisis, the US increased its pressure on Israel to modify its plan so as to mollify the Arab states and to curb Palestinian support of Iraq in the crisis. In order to appease the US somewhat, Minister of Infrastructure Sharon held informal talks with Arafat's deputies in February 1998. He suggested that a final status agreement was not yet feasible because differences between the two sides were too great; instead, Israel would withdraw from 9–13 per cent of the West Bank and recognize the existence of a disarmed Palestinian state as a *fait accompli*, including a contiguous area from Nablus to Jenin.[12]

Meanwhile, the settlers had not been idle. Since any pullback whatsoever dashed their already diminished aim of retaining the territorial status quo, they would not agree to the final status plan devised by the government, let alone to the offer made by Sharon. They demonstrated in front of the Prime Minister's Office on 29 November 1997 and on 22 December 1997, while the Front threatened to support a no-confidence motion on 6 January 1998 and financed a supplement in *Ha-arets* in order to make its position known to the public. Netanyahu reacted promptly and rescinded the offer made by Sharon. In an interview he again rejected the possibility of a Palestinian state in favour of a demilitarized entity with some territorial contiguity and insisted that all settlements must remain in place.[13]

Fifth Phase: Fear for Political Survival

The impasse in the peace process, begun in March 1997, continued up to the Wye Plantation summit of 15–25 October 1998. Suicide attacks by Hamas and Islamic Jihad terrorists in July 1997 and August 1998 lent support to Israeli evaluations of Palestinian intentions and could justify Israeli intransigence and punitive actions, such as prolonged closure of crossings into Israel, as well as suspension of money transfers to the Palestinians and of any talks on redeployment or final status issues. Meanwhile, various unsavoury affairs were discrediting the Prime Minister within his own party and coalition, and his unkept assurances to foreign leaders regarding the peace process were discrediting him internationally. This contributed to his dependence on the hard-line members of his coalition.

Eventually, however, US pressure became the stronger force. President Clinton convened a summit meeting in the United States. Ten days of intensive talks in the seclusion of the Wye Plantation, with continuous prodding from the President himself and from US Middle East experts produced the intended results, or so most people believed at the time. The major articles of the Wye Memorandum stipulated a transfer of 1 per cent of area C (under full Israeli control) to area A (under full Palestinian control) and another 12 per cent of area C to area B (under Israeli security control and Palestinian administrative control), 3 per cent of the latter to be a nature reserve (no new building allowed). Furthermore, 14.2 per cent of area B was to be turned into area A. These transfers would cover the first two stages of redeployment previously stipulated, while the third stage was left open to further negotiations. Israel also undertook to expedite the opening of the Gaza industrial estate (a joint Israeli–Palestinian project) and of the Gaza airport, to arrange for safe passage of Palestinians between Gaza and the West Bank and to negotiate on the construction of a port in Gaza. In return, the Palestinians undertook to combat terror, to confiscate all illegal weapons, to legislate against incitement and to revise their charter. US intelligence personnel would supervise PA fulfilment of its obligations and President Clinton would witness the revision of the charter.

An addendum attached to the Memorandum met the reciprocity requirements of Israel: all the above commitments would proceed in stages, depending on fulfilment of a parallel commitment by the other party. Thus, the first stage of redeployment and the release of Palestinian prisoners was made conditional on a Palestinian decree against illegal weapons and against incitement, as well as the arrest of ten fugitive terrorists. The opening of Gaza airport was made conditional on a Palestinian weapon collection programme and on establishment and convening of an anti-incitement committee. After the Palestinians had amended their charter and had strictly implemented their security commitments, Israel would carry out the second stage of redeployment.

If Netanyahu's body language at the signing ceremony was any indication, he did not expect his coalition to welcome the Memorandum with any great enthusiasm. He signed it, however, in the knowledge that it would receive overwhelming Knesset support: the opposition would surely vote in favour. Furthermore, by laying down a scheduled reciprocity, the Memorandum provided Israel with greater assurances and protected Israeli security somewhat better than had the Oslo Accords. The hawkish coalition partners would surely take this into consideration and resign themselves to reality once the arrangements of the Wye Memorandum had become a *fait accompli*.

But things went awry. The press presented the Wye Memorandum as an ideological turnabout of Likud rather than as an improvement on the Oslo Accords. The Memorandum was presented as an exoneration of Labour policy and that of late Prime Minister Rabin, that is, as a Likud change towards trusting Palestinian intentions. In fact, continuing distrust had guided the insistence on a schedule of reciprocity, but that was hardly mentioned. The spate of articles which expressed glee rather than praise possibly contributed to the rejectionist stance of the settlers and of hawkish Settlers at the prospect of further Israeli pullbacks and the concomitant threat to settlements. Settlers immediately demonstrated, then warned that the Front would support a bill for early elections previously tabled by Labour.

Moreover, the schedule laid down in the Memorandum had not taken account of the Israeli requirement of prior ratification by both the cabinet and the Knesset, so that the timetable was immediately upset. This aroused Palestinian suspicions and resentment. A suicide bomb went off in Jerusalem on 6 November 1998 (for once, it caused no casualties). Thereupon, the cabinet refused to ratify the Memorandum until the PA had begun to combat terror, delaying the timetable still further. When it did ratify the Memorandum on 11 November 1998, it appeared to do so against its better judgement: only eight out of 17 Ministers voted in favour, four voted against and five abstained. The Palestinian actions which followed seemed intended to prove opponents of the Memorandum right. On 14 November 1998, Arafat announced at a rally in Nablus that the PA would unilaterally declare the establishment of a Palestinian state on 4 May 1999, the date initially set for completion of final status negotiations. On the following day he assured al-Fatah leaders that he did not rule out the use of armed force in defence of the future state.

When the Knesset finally ratified the Memorandum on 17 November 1998, the NRP, a coalition partner, and the hawkish Moledet party voted against it; the bill passed by a vote of 75:19, but only 29 coalition MKs supported it and seven cabinet Ministers absented themselves from the vote. Similarly, the cabinet decision on 20 November 1998 to implement the first stage of redeployment was reached by a vote of six Ministers in favour, five against, three abstentions and two absent. The pullback was carried out during 21–22 November 1998, as was the opening of Gaza airport, since the Palestinians had met their obligations as laid down for this stage, but the coalition was clearly falling apart.

In a last effort to shore it up, Netanyahu tried to demonstrate that signing the Wye Memorandum was no treason to Settler principles, as some settlers were maintaining. The release of Palestinian prisoners as scheduled was to prove this. Of the 250 released, only 100 were political prisoners and the rest criminal ones, including car thieves and persons who had crossed into Israel illegally. Riots and violence immediately broke out in the West Bank, interrupted briefly by the visit of President Clinton to Gaza on 14 December 1998, where he witnessed the under-taking to amend the Palestinian charter. This step was to be followed by the second part of the Israeli pullback. When the government did not implement this part on schedule, due to the ongoing violence in the West Bank, the opposition withdrew its promise of supporting the government. On 21 December 1998, it voted in favour of early elections, as did the Front. The bill passed its first reading. That let loose a veritable game of musical chairs, sparked off by the accumulated resentment felt by Likud ministers against Netanyahu and by the announcement of former Chief-of-Staff Amnon Lipkin-Shahak that he was running for the premiership at the head of a new centrist party.

The fracture within the political system became evident even before the early election bill passed its final reading on 4 January 1999, despite attempts by Netanyahu to avert this. Three Likud leaders immediately considered challenging Netanyahu for the Likud leadership; Benjamin Begin, son of the late Menahem Begin, decided to leave Likud and found Tkuma, committed to public probity and loyalty to Greater Israel principles; Minister of Defence Mordechai considered joining Labour or the new Centre party; Dan Meridor, Finance Minister under Netanyahu until he had resigned in protest against internal Likud manipulations, announced the formation of a Centre party and his intention of running for Prime Minister. This initial stage was followed by further disarray within Likud and in other political parties and bodies. A split occurred in the Yesha Council over support of Begin or Netanyahu for the premiership; the NRP became increasingly divided between moderates and hawks; some Labour MKs considered joining Shahak, or a possible joint list of Meridor and Shahak; a split threatened Israel Ba'aliya, the Russian immigrant party; a second immigrant party was formed.

Political fracture intensified after early elections had become a certainty, much of it due less to disagreement on principles and more to very narrow sectorial interests or personal ambition. Shahak and Meridor decided to run together; Meridor was known for his hawkish views and probity, while the views of Shahak remained obscure. With such an enigmatic agenda, they agreed that popularity surveys would decide the top slot on their list. On 23 January 1999, they were joined by Defence Minister Mordechai, who was put at the head of the list due to his popularity rather than to the principles he represented: he was known to favour a final agreement with the Palestinians, but the extent of his moderate stance and his stand on socio-economic issues have remained largely unknown. Moshe Arens, who had twice served as Defence Minister in the past, unseccessfully challenged Netanyahu for the Likud leadership on 25 January 1999. Thereupon, he was immediately offered the post of Defence Minister, to replace Mordechai, and accepted the offer to serve under the person he had criticized throughout his tenure. Moreover, Netanyahu, Arens and Sharon were now presented as the leading Likud trio. Fracture in other parties also continued. Two Labour MKs joined the Centre party; some members of the Shinui faction split from Meretz, to run as a middle-class free enterprise party supporting a dovish foreign policy; the Histadrut chairman announced the foundation of the 'Am Ehad workers' party whose principal membership comes from the most powerful labour unions; a plethora of narrow sectorial parties were formed, such as a party of pensioners, of casino owners, of Romanian immigrants and of a former beauty queen.

PUBLIC REACTIONS TO LIKUD MESSAGES AND ACTIONS

To sum up, the message of Likud was consistent as far as peace was concerned, in contrast to Labour, whose messages had been self-contradictory. Throughout its shortened tenure, Likud defined peace as a wary truce with the Palestinians. The basic distrust varied only in degree, not in substance. Some more moderate views were occasionally voiced by one or another minister, but little attention was paid to them since Netanyahu was seen as the sole spokesman of the Likud government and its final decision-maker. The shifts in distrust may have been due to changes in his conviction, but they also coincided with pressures exerted on his government, US pressure ostensibly reducing distrust and settler pressure increasing it. The shifts were accompanied by changes in interpretation of the second half of the slogan 'peace and security': security demands became less stringent when distrust declined and vice versa, or, conversely, security demands changed due to external pressures and were excused by a change towards greater or lesser distrust. The real views of Netanyahu have so far remained fairly obscure and can be ignored for the purpose of this study, which is concerned with the impact of leadership actions and outspoken messages on the public and its self-image, rather than with the underlying causes of the latter. Therefore, irrespective of intentions, Netanyahu never offered the Palestinians more than autonomy in an entity varying in size and viability – contiguity of territory – in accordance with his changing interpretation of Israeli security needs, with the single exception in late 1996, when he conceived of a semi-sovereign Palestinian state. Thus Likud remained consistent in its distrust, but vacillated between signed agreements with the Palestinians and partial implementations of redeployments – in Hebron in early 1997 and the first stage of the pullback in late November 1998 – and a halt to the entire peace process – the impasse during March 1997–October 1998 and after December 1998.

The General Public

Public attitudes hardly changed at all during the Likud period, compared to the previous Labour one. The deep distrust of Palestinian intentions had been a continuous ingredient of Israeli identity since the establishment of Israel, that is, of both the Tsabar and the Settler. Because of their contradictory messages and the Post-zionist motives imputed to them, the Labour leaders had failed to convince the public otherwise. Presumably, this distrust was one factor explaining the electoral victory of Netanyahu, coupled as it had been with the bloody evidence provided by Hamas violence at the time. Thus, between August 1996–January 1999, only 21.2–23 per cent of respondents rejected the statement that the Palestinians still wished to eradicate Israel, compared to an even lower 14 per cent in March 1995, during the spate of suicide attacks,[14] Similarly, 43.7 per cent of respondents believed Arafat to have remained a terrorist in December 1994 and so did 42 per cent in July 1998 (the percentage declined to 34.3 per cent in December 1995, when the assassination of Rabin produced a short spurt of increased support for his policies).[15] The average support for the Oslo process remained almost unchanged, rising from an average 49 per cent between August 1994 and December 1995 to an average 50.4 per cent between June 1996 and February 1999.[16]

In line with this distrust, unrelenting attitudes regarding the peace process continued: in June 1996, 47 per cent of respondents did not think that the Palestinians had a right to a state and nor did 49 per cent in September 1998;[17] 47 per cent of respondents supported the establishment of additional settlements in the West Bank (despite the Oslo Accords) in December 1994 and 52.6 per cent did so in June 1997.[18] Of the latter sample, around 60 per cent believed that a collapse of the peace process would lead to war, yet even among these, 47.7 per cent supported additional settlements which clearly precluded a territorial compromise.

Neither did public confusion nor its inconsistent opinions change perceptibly during the period under discussion, probably due to the unclear message conveyed by the vacillations in government actions. The gap between support for the Oslo process, for peace in general and for peace with Syria (in return for withdrawal from the Golan Heights) remained unchanged. Between August 1994 and December 1995, average support for the Oslo process had amounted to 49 per cent, for peace in general to 59 per cent and for peace with Syria to 37 per cent. The corresponding average percentages between June 1996 and February 1999 were 50.4 per cent, 60.8 per cent and 38.9 per cent.[19] It should be noted that this gap has been consistent in each monthly sample and is not a spurious outcome of calculated averages. Since the Palestinians and Syria are the only neighbours with whom Israel has not concluded peace treaties – Lebanon is a client state of Syria, incapable of conducting an independent foreign policy – the gap between support for peace in general and that with the Palestinians or Syria can only indicate confusion.

Many studies have shown the difficulty of inducing a change of opinion or attitudes over long periods of time, let alone suddenly. Therefore, the quick switches which occurred in this period probably indicate a latent uncertainty and confusion about the expected proper 'patriotic' attitude. In April 1997, 82 per cent of respondents were worried about progress in the peace process, while only a month later, in May 1997, 31 per cent regarded the government offer of 40 per cent of the West Bank as a Palestinian autonomous entity as too generous, although 69 per cent of the latter sample knew that the Palestinians would reject even this offer.[20] A month later, 60 per cent of respondents feared that a breakdown of the peace process might result in war, yet 56.4 per cent of the same sample supported a hard-line policy in that peace process.[21] Similarly, 66 per cent supported the Hebron Protocol, yet four months later, 52 per cent supported construction on Har Homa which so clearly obstructed implementation of this signed agreement.[22] Seventy per cent of respondents supported the Wye Memorandum in October 1998,[23] when in July of that year 42 per cent had regarded Arafat as an untrustworthy terrorist and 52 per cent had considered the government too lenient in its negotiations with the Palestinians.[24]

Despite the hawkish stance of the Likud government, public acceptance of the Oslo process as a *fait accompli* did not change either, though it fluctuated somewhat during the period under discussion. In December 1994 and August 1998, 66 per cent of respondents agreed that a Palestinian state was inevitable.[25] By the end of the Likud tenure, Israeli society was no longer deeply divided over the issue of territorial compromise and Palestinian independence, though the public still differed over the nature of this independence and its territorial extent. What may have been a momentary enthusiasm about the prospect of a more normal, peaceful life has become a permanent, sober acceptance of a new reality. Likud procrastinations had not effected any lasting change in this realization, though they certainly did not increase the number of those who welcomed this change. Only 39 per cent of respondents regarded Likud policies concerning the peace process as too intractable in November 1996, 37 per cent in December 1997 and 35 per cent in July 1998.[26] Yet 45 per cent of respondents believed that the Palestinians had a right to their own state in June 1996 and in September 1998.[27]

The difference between Settlers and Unconverted was largely eroded and boiled down to a question of degree, rather than substance: the size of the Palestinian state and the extent of its sovereignty. By December 1998, 63 per cent of respondents believed that any party forming the next government would sign an agreement with the Palestinians comprising withdrawals from the West Bank and recognition of a Palestinian state, though only 55 per cent of that sample welcomed such an outcome.[28]

The Settlers

The settlers had given their wholehearted support to Netanyahu, making light of his undertaking to honour the Oslo Accords and hoping that qualification of peace by security would *ipso facto* invalidate the Accord. At a protest rally of NRP supporters and settler faithfuls held in January 1996, a prominent NRP educator assured his audience that Israel would regain all of the West Bank once the Likud returned to power. This is what 26 per cent of polled settlers also believed,[29] as did the author of an article in *Nekuda*.[30] Amana, the settlement movement of Gush Emunim, planned a new settlement drive based on this expectation.[31] The victory of Netanyahu was hailed as the victory of Jewish values, seen as synonymous with loyalty to Erets Yisrael, over Post-zionist universalist ones.[32] More sober settlers did pay some attention to the peace factor in the Likud slogan. Yet even to those, the worst case scenario was the status quo, namely Palestinian autonomy in its population centres, turning into the final status: there would be no reoccupation of territory, but neither would there be any further withdrawal.[33] Greater Israel would be somewhat smaller, but the Coming of the Messiah could still be hastened.

These hopes were dashed when the negotiation team and its withdrawal maps were made public. The immediate reaction was wholesale condemnation of the proposed pullbacks,[34] but that soon gave way to resignation. Once the Hebron Protocol was being negotiated and signed, Greater Israel adherents concluded with regret that some larger Palestinian entity was inevitable.[35] Therefore, damage control was the better part of wisdom; the settlers must salvage as much of Greater Israel as possible by influencing the pullback maps.[36]

The actual withdrawal from part of the holy city of Hebron was a watershed in settler attitudes towards the peace process. For the public at large, the latter attitudes were becoming dependent more on the varying measure of distrust regarding Palestinian intentions and less on attachment to Erets Yisrael. For the Gush Emunim faithful, foregoing further settlement expansion undermined the essence of their faith. A minority of settlers still hoped that a miracle would reverse reality and that the present predicament was a Divine test, a salvation through the gutter so to speak.[37] At first, the newly elected Yesha Council even demonstrated against any withdrawals whatsoever, but the majority gradually changed course, although they were at a loss to justify this ideationally. One issue of *Nekuda* (No. 204 of April 1997), exemplifies this spiritual turmoil succinctly. It contained numerous articles on the crisis of leadership within the Greater Israel camp. At the same time, a supplement commissioned by Amana offered houses for sale in the West Bank, using the commercial inducements of any real estate agent. By implication, Amana was giving up hope of ideologically motivated new settlers. The proportion of those had shrunk over the years, reflected in the composition of the newly elected Council in which pragmatists predominated. A survey by the BESA Centre of Bar Ilan University, conducted in January 1996, sheds an interesting light on the composition of the settler population. Although it found 45 per cent of settlers to be religious and another 20 per cent to be traditional, only 34 per cent stated that they had moved to the West Bank for religious and ideological reasons.[38]

Despite a sales campaign based on a realistic assessment, Amana and the Gush Emunim hard core were not yet ready to give up the most basic tenet of their faith and still believed that pullbacks would be minimal and the greater part of the West Bank would still be available for new settlements.[39] After the Alon-Plus Plan had become public, expansion no longer seemed feasible and extension of existing settlements became the proclaimed target.[40] In the final stage, even this aim became secondary to the very safety of settler homes,[41] relevant to the majority of non-ideological settlers as much as to the Gush Emunim faithful. This explains the Council's insistence on a network of by-roads and a reinforced military presence around the existing settlements. The attachment of settlers to their homes was made clear in a poll, in which 46 per cent of settler respondents preferred to remain in their settlements even if these should come under Palestinian control.[42]

Most rank-and-file settlers and part of their leaders in the Yesha Council had become disillusioned. Gush Emunim ideology, that is the settlement of Erets Yisrael as a means of advancing the Coming of the Messiah, was a faith at worst abandoned, or at best postponed.[43] The scarcity of articles in *Nekuda* on the peace process provide evidence for this change. Only two articles on this subject appeared in *Nekuda* issues between August and December 1997, as against six on matters of religion, and none at all were published in February and March 1998. The subject again became prominent as of August 1998, when the US proposal of a 13 per cent pullback was putting the safety of settlements in jeopardy. Some of the leaders, in the Yesha Council and in the NRP, as well as a small hard core of settlers remained faithful to Gush Emunim precepts and opposed pullbacks on principle rather than pullbacks from areas too near to settlements. This created a near split in the Council on the issue of lobbying for the downfall of the government. It also created a split in the NRP when intransigent Greater Israel faithfuls were removed from realistic slots on its Knesset list.

DIVISIVE FACTORS

Controversy developed in the Yesha Council and in the NRP regarding loyalty to Erets Yisrael and pragmatists won out in both bodies. At the same time, *Nekuda* began to focus on religious matters at the expense of the peace process. Both phenomena are symptomatic of one of the several issues which are tearing Israeli society apart, as well as of those which have been largely removed from the agenda. The Palestinian issue no longer creates the principal split in Israeli society, as it had done since 1967. If Likud could not halt the peace process, let alone reverse it, then it had become a reality which two thirds of the public must recognize, albeit reluctantly. Consensus on this issue has not increased perceptibly, but the importance of the issue as a divider of Israeli society has lessened. The reluctant acceptance of reality has blurred the boundary between Settler identity and the uncertain identity of the Unconverted, a boundary defined principally by the issue of Greater Israel. The extreme adherents of Greater Israel on the one hand and of a secular Israel based on universal values on the other both became marginalized where previously they had set the tone of each camp. No longer did either Gush Emunim ideology or Post-zionist concepts of universal values fuel political controversies regarding the peace process.

Blunting of the Extreme Right and Left

The change of heart among settlers and most of their leaders has been discussed above. The same seems to have occurred among NRP voters, considered to have been the most ardent defenders of Greater Israel. When a sample of prospective NRP voters was asked what they considered to be the central problem of Israeli society, 30 per cent gave social problems top priority, 24 per cent thought that resolving the conflict between the religious and the secular deserved top priority and only 7 per cent regarded the retention of Greater Israel as the major issue. Moreover, the majority of respondents supported the Wye Memorandum.[44] It must be noted that the poll was commissioned by the NRP. The NRP list for the coming elections, chosen in February 1999, reflected this moderation in views regarding Greater Israel.

The extreme Left has undergone a similar process of attrition. Articles defending or rejecting Postzionism, which had been abundant after the signature of the DOP, almost disappeared from the daily press, which impacts most on the general public. Periodicals with a limited circulation still discussed the subject, principally refuting Post-zionist claims and insisting on the need for Judaic values to create solidarity and to justify the Jewish presence in Israel.[45] None was published during the first year of the Netanyahu tenure. In commemoration of 100 years of Zionism (since the first Zionist Congress in 1897), four articles revived the debate in June 1997. Rubinstein pointed out that Post-zionist criticism of the Israeli polity, past and present, was to blame for the Likud victory. It had delegitimized the entire Zionist enterprise, namely the just claim of Jews to their patrimony, as well as Labour, which had led the enterprise. Israelis, who refused to concede that the return to Palestine had been no better than colonial expropriation of the natives, saw the Right as their defender against such an attack. In consequence, the entire Left had become tainted.[46] Possibly realizing the truth of the above argument, namely the counter-productive effect of the Post-zionist onslaught, two of the three other articles on the subject, by authors identified with the Post-zionist camp, were largely self-defensive. Postzionism had never denied the legitimate claim to a homeland in Palestine; it had merely condemned Israeli coercive rule over another people as immoral.[47] One author remained defiant, however, restating the Post-zionist narrative.[48] The only two articles on the subject published in 1998 each reiterated the arguments of Post-zionists and Labour Zionists respectively, without adding anything new to the debate.[49] The same holds true for extracts of articles published in the winter 1999 issue of *Azure*.[50]

Post-zionist arguments were increasingly ignored rather than refuted because of the damage they had done to the fragile identity of the Unconverted. The latter were being driven towards a quest for Judaic values which could restore the ethical basis of their self-image. Thus, a call to refuse military service in the territories after the tunnel incident[51] was not even decried; it was simply ignored. More significantly, Peace Now and Meretz, the organizations most associated with universal values of equal justice for all, of self-determination and of perfect democracy, lost much of their influence because they were seen as expressing the Post-zionist condemnation of a specifically Jewish democracy. The number of participants in Peace Now rallies dwindled to a few score, compared to the hundreds the movement had been able to mobilize in the past.[52] Meretz fared even worse. For a time, it was considered disqualified from an alliance with any party because it would stigmatize the latter as anti-Jewish and, therefore, anti-Israeli.[53] In order to disassociate his party from the Leftist stigma, Barak vowed to leave all settlements in place as a symbol of his party's insistence on the Jewish right to the Holy Land, reluctantly relinquished in part. In order further to obliterate its Leftist links Labour submerged in a list comprising several other small parties and named 'One Israel'. Lipkin-Shahak refused to join Labour and opted for the new Centre party, explaining that he did not want to be seen as a Leftist.

Splintering and Realignments

Consensus did not grow, however. The debate aroused by Postzionism shifted the focus of attention from the peace process to the nature of Israeli society, the one issue which is at the heart of Israeli identity. The peace process had been debated between Left and Right, between the Settler and the Unconverted, but when the nature of Israeli society became the bone of contention, its implications revolved around the much more persistent and dormant dilemma which had plagued Zionism from the start, namely the justification of the Jewish presence in Israel. Postzionism as such became irrelevant, as did the belief in the imperative to expand Israeli rule and settlement to the entire Holy Land. Patriotic democracy had been a chief constituent of secular Tsabar identity, at the expense of the Jewish birthright, but this had applied to Israel proper, when the agreement to partition had absolved Israelis of any further obligations towards the Palestinians. To justify the occupation of the territories, Settler identity had reinfused Israeli identity with the idea of the Jewish birthright to the Land. With the Oslo process, the two concepts were at loggerheads. Moreover, modernist values cannot be wholly dismissed at the beginning of the twenty-first century, but neither can Jewish religion, tradition and culture if Israelis want to stake a morally justified claim to their ancient patrimony. Consequently, the most salient conflict regarding the nature of the society was being fought between the secular and the religious sectors, while the ongoing fissures between Orientals and Westerners, the affluent and the poor, as well as between veterans and new immigrants appeared to be of secondary importance. As will be shown, they were not. Nor are each of these groups separate. Rather, they all overlap to some extent, creating further subdivisions into smaller groups, each of which has been fighting for privileges on the one hand and for a right to determine the nature of Israeli society on the other.

In this fractured society no single value is sufficiently common to all to command loyalty, so that self-interest has often taken over. This is the most visible symptom of the identity crisis which has gripped Israeli society. The numerous splits in political parties preceding the 1999 elections and the turncoat manoeuvres of many MKs already described are one indicator of the fracture. In many cases, the latter no longer reflected the stand of an MK regarding the peace process. Most Likud and Labour members who joined the Centre party did so out of personal pique, since this party was hardly more dovish than Likud and hardly more hawkish than Labour. Only some MKs of the Rightist Likud and NRP seceded solely because they felt that their party had betrayed its commitment to Greater Israel.

Research also substantiates this diagnosis. At a symposium held at Tel-Aviv University on 23 November 1998 and entitled 'Israeli Society Between Split and Unity', all participants agreed that the former single split in Israeli society no longer prevailed. It had been replaced by a multiplicity of others. Opinions differed only on which of the fissures were the more crucially divisive. At a conference held by the Rabin Centre for Israeli Research on 12 February 1999 and entitled 'The IDF and Israeli Society', the concluding symposium discussed the IDF in a split society. Furthermore, the Rabin Centre was sponsoring a research project entitled 'Solidarity and Fissures in Israeli Society', which was to pinpoint the sectors of society at odds with each other and to gauge the depth of the various fissures.

The public has also become aware of the changing alignments in society. According to polls, respondents no longer regarded the peace process as the major problem facing Israeli society, since this issue had been largely resolved, at least in principle. On the other hand, the peace process was seen as having brought about the perceived fracture. When a sample was asked about the impact of the peace process, 54 per cent believed that it had influenced Israeli solidarity adversely, compared to 10 per cent who thought that it had improved solidarity (the remainder did not think the process had had any effect on solidarity).[54] In two separate polls, 60 per cent of respondents regarded internal conflicts as of the greatest danger to Israeli society, as against 30 per cent who considered the peace process the greatest threat. Of the internal splits, 62.6 per cent and 60 per cent of respondents respectively considered the secular–religious split as the most dangerous, as against 22 per cent and 18 per cent who rated the Left–Right split highest and only 2.6 per cent and 6 per cent who rated the ethnic rift as the most threatening to society.[55]

The Secular–Religious Rift

Observers have also diagnosed the conflict between the secular and the religious public to be the most divisive factor in Israeli society. There are several reasons for this assessment. Firstly, this rift is very visible because the religious public is easily identifiable: national religious males wear knitted skullcaps and orthodox ones wear distinctive black clothes and hats, while religious females wear long and wide skirts and a distinctive headgear.

Secondly, statistical analysis suggests an overlap between this split and the former one regarding the peace process, implying that because one has replaced the other, it is of equal preeminence. For example, the Hebron Protocol was supported by 66 per cent of respondents. Broken down by religiosity, only 17 per cent of the orthodox and 34 per cent of the religious respondents supported it, as against 64 per cent of the traditional and 76 per cent of the secular ones.[56] A poll investigating trust in Palestinian intentions revealed that only 5.2 per cent of orthodox respondents believed that peace would be achieved eventually, while around 27 per cent of religious, traditional and secular ones did. Of the orthodox 20.5 per cent supported the peace process as did 43 per cent of the religious respondents, compared to 82 per cent of the traditional and 78 per cent of the secular ones. All orthodox respondents believed that the Palestinians wished to destroy Israel, compared to 79 per cent of the religious, 68.7 per cent of the traditional and 52.5 per cent of the secular ones. Seventy-nine per cent of the orthodox, 68.5 per cent of the religious and 52 per cent of the traditional respondents believed Arafat to have remained a terrorist, compared to 31 per cent of the secular ones.[57] In another poll, 55 per cent of respondents supported an agreement in which Israel would withdraw from additional territory and recognize a Palestinian state. Broken down by religiosity, 10 per cent of the orthodox and 25 per cent of the religious respondents supported such an agreement, as against 45 per cent of the traditional and 70 per cent of the secular ones.[58]

Clearly, the degree of religiosity has a strong effect on the stand regarding peace and Greater Israel, but the overlap is only partial. As the above presentation of the data shows, not all categories along the religiosity scale move in unison along the foreign policy scale, the central ones taking up varying positions depending on the issue. No two blocs can be defined which are identical on both scales. Only the two ends on the religiosity scale, namely the orthodox and the secular, occupy corresponding positions on the foreign policy scale. Moreover, viewed from another perspective, the data provide a somewhat different picture. Seventeen per cent of the orthodox and 34 per cent of the religious did support the Hebron Protocol, which provided for withdrawal, and from the holy city of Hebron at that. Twenty-seven per cent of the religious believed in the peace process and 20.5 per cent of the orthodox and 43 per cent of the religious supported it. Even further withdrawals, the key obstacle to Greater Israel, were supported by 10 per cent of the orthodox and 25 per cent of the religious. Thus, the statistics are somewhat misleading by obscuring sharp differences within the religious camp as well as other fissures, which again overlap partly with the Left–Right and with the secular–religious rifts.

On the other hand, the secular–religious rift goes beyond foreign policy issues and represents a dispute about the nature of the Israeli polity. On the latter, opinions range from those of the orthodox, who want a society regulated by Halachic (religious) law, to those of the emphatically secular, who want a secular democracy along American lines in which citizenship, human rights and social relationships are completely divorced from religious and ethnic affiliation. Neither view accepts the official definition of Israel as a democratic Jewish state, an ambivalent concept which strikes a precarious balance between two concepts seen by these two views as mutually exclusive. As already discussed in Chapter 4 (see pp.127–9), the balance had become ever more precarious since the Supreme Court had been putting more emphasis on universal values which are not specifically Jewish. Furthermore, it has been interpreting the concept 'Jewish state' as the state of the Jewish people, with greater emphasis on ethnicity and less stress on Jewish religious law. This interpretation permits the exclusion of non-Jews from certain civil privileges (specifically, unrestricted immigration and automatic citizenship) without subjecting Israeli law to religious scrutiny.[59] The signature of the DOP and the modernist values underlying it, as well as the subsequent assassination of Rabin and the recriminations following it upset this balance. A split was created, in which the religious regarded the entire secular population as embracing non-particularistic values, seen as un-Jewish or even anti-Jewish, and in which the secular regarded the entire religious population as embracing Jewish-specific values, seen as racist and undemocratic. Thus, the secular–religious rift was diagnosed as a *Kulturkampf*.[60] In fact, and similar to the conflict over the peace process, the secular–religious one is coloured by the holders of extreme views in each camp despite their small numbers. According to one estimate, by self-definition the population consists of about 50 per cent secular persons, about 33 per cent traditional ones and about 17 per cent religious ones.[61] The ultra-orthodox and Hardal constitute at most 10 per cent of the Jewish adult population. The percentage of the avowedly secular is small, but difficult to determine. According to one poll, 52 per cent of respondents classified themselves as secular, but 77 per cent declared that they believed in God and 73 per cent fasted on the Day of Atonement.[62] A further analysis of these data suggested that 52 per cent of the secular Israelis included 21 per cent who kept some Jewish traditions, which are all religious, and only 4 per cent were atheists.[63]

Whatever the exact size of the avowedly secular population, which objects to a state defined by ethnic–religious values, it is not very large. Numbers are not the deciding factor, however. The orthodox gained considerable political clout in the Netanyahu government, while the avowedly secular are seen by the orthodox to have a highly prominent, powerful and prestigious spokesman, namely the Supreme Court. As will be shown, most of the secular public does not share the modernist universal concept of democracy attributed to the Supreme Court, but the majority of the public respects the Supreme Court as the upholder of the rule of law. In polls conducted over the years, the Supreme Court has been ranked consistently as second in public trust after the IDF, enjoying the trust of 78–84 per cent of adult respondents,[64] but not of the orthodox. According to one poll, the great majority of orthodox respondents – 78.2 per cent – stated that they did not trust the Supreme Court, compared to 19.6 per cent of religious ones, 8.5 per cent of traditional ones and 6.2 per cent of secular ones.[65]

Since orthodox males specialize in the study of Jewish law, it would seem that the rule of law is not at issue, but rather which law should rule and/or how the existing law should be interpreted. This boils down to a fundamental contest on the nature of Israeli society, a contest conducted between the holders of the two most extreme views but seen to be fought between the entire religious camp against the entire secular one. Aharon Barak, President of the Supreme Court, opened a Pandora's Box in 1992 when he insisted that everything was judicable. He then followed this up by explaining to the Knesset Law Committee in October 1996 that, when sitting as the High Court of Justice, the Court had to make value judgments and create norms whenever there was a legal vacuum. In Israel, neither democracy nor the Jewishness of the state had ever been properly defined in law, which forced the Court to step in.

Such statements aroused the ire of the orthodox community, which feared interference in those spheres which came under religious law and a curbing of its growing power. The religious parties became decisive players in politics in the Netanyahu government, firstly because of the need to form a coalition with numerous parties, as noted above, and secondly because the NRP and Shas each increased their strength from 5 per cent each in 1992 to 7.8 per cent and 8.5 per cent respectively in 1996. Of the two, both of which fully participated in government, the NRP is religious rather than ultra-orthodox. But Shas is an Oriental orthodox party, while the third religious party, Tora Judaism, is Western orthodox and joined the coalition without holding ministerial positions. For reasons of coalition, the 16.3 per cent of the NRP and Shas and the 3.2 per cent of Tora Judaism translated into five cabinet ministers, as well as several deputy ministers and chairmen of Knesset committees. The religious parties could use this power to fight for stricter enforcement of laws relating to religious matters, such as forestalling archaeological excavations at sites suspected to contain ancient Jewish graves, observance of Saturday closure laws or religious conversion procedures. They could also divert far greater financial resources to the religious sector and ward off attempts by the Reform and Conservative Movements to gain equal religious status with the orthodox establishment regarding conversion and weddings.

In fact, the High Court of Justice hardly ever implemented what its president preached. In cases pertaining to religion, it was careful not to rule against the religious litigants, but neither did it rule in their favour. Frequently, it issued temporary rulings retaining the status quo until the case could be decided by arbitration or by Knesset legislation. Thus, it referred the closing of a Jerusalem thoroughfare on Saturday to arbitration, deferred judgement and suggested arbitration or a compromise solution on the Conservative conversion of foreign-born adopted children and enjoined legislation, where none had existed, regarding the induction of orthodox men. But even such decisions were met by a vigorous campaign in the orthodox press against the Supreme Court, especially after the Netanyahu government came into power.[66] It culminated in a mass prayer rally on 14 February 1999 following the ruling that Conservative and Reform representatives be included in religious councils. Avowedly secular Israelis, led by Meretz, organized a simultaneous counter-demonstration in defence of the Supreme Court. However, the images of both camps had already been stereotyped, using the extreme ends along the religiosity scale as demarcating the entire opposite camp.[67] Prominent authors were outraged by the orthodox rally, which they regarded as an onslaught on democracy, and called for a mass joining by the secular of Reform and Conservative communities in order to spite the orthodox. Even secular modernists saw the absurdity of such a reaction, pointing out that peaceful protest was the hallmark of democracy and must not be condemned by those professing democratic values.[68]

Actually, very few of the national religious camp joined this fray: NRP leaders were conspicuous by their absence from the rally, as were wearers of knitted skullcaps. The Religious Zionists had always distinguished themselves from the orthodox by accepting modernity, religious toleration and, especially, Israeli democracy and its institutions. This is what has guided their young to serve in the IDF and volunteer for elite units, their leaders to be active partners in Israeli governments since the establishment of the state[69] and many in the rank and file to fear the growing orthodoxy of some NRP leaders and young people, as expressed in numerous articles in *Nekuda*.[70] Yet the secular public at large, and specifically its spokesmen in the press and in the arts, have portrayed this attack on what they regard as the stronghold of democracy and defender of a central value as being launched by the religious public at large, which ostensibly wants to do away with democracy altogether by a coercive imposition of religious law.[71]

Stigmas became the rule of the game. For the sake of brevity, a few instances will have to suffice. *Ha-arets* launched a series of articles (written by S. Ilan) on the iniquities of the orthodox: the number applying for deferment of military service had risen exponentially[72] and, since this deferment is conditional on full-time study in Yeshivot, these men did not work and subsisted on national insurance payments financed by the entire public.[73] Though undeniably true, these facts apply to the orthodox public and have no bearing on the religious sector at large, whose members serve in the army and take an active part in the workforce, some of them occupying leading positions in both. Conversely, the orthodox public and its leaders, including the more orthodox in the national religious camp, have been portraying the secular as lacking in values and as hedonists at best and as anti-Semites at worst.[74] The stereotypes have led to spiteful tagging and to excessive zeal. Matters were carried *ad absurdum* in May 1998. A dance troupe withdrew from the Jubilee Bells festival performance on 2 May 1998 when it was admonished to change its costumes, regarded by a religious Jerusalem Council member to constitute 'improper dress'. As if to spite such religious restrictions in the arts, Dana International, a trans-sexual, was given a hero's homecoming reception several days later for having won the Eurovision Song Contest for Israel.

The above discussion has shown that the religious camp is not monolithic. It is divided primarily into the orthodox and the religious, with Hardal members constituting sub-groups in each. The orthodox are again divided into Westerners (Ashkenasi) and the Oriental Shas. The latter group is hardest to classify because it is both an orthodox and an ethnic party. Leaders and members are largely first-generation Orientals (born in Israel to Oriental-born fathers). Its leaders have had a strictly orthodox education acquired in Western orthodox institutions, but many members apparently support it for ethnic and social reasons. According to one research, only 50 per cent of its supporters were orthodox or religious, while 40 per cent were traditional and 10 per cent were secular.[75] In Shas, the religious and ethnic rifts overlap partly, a phenomenon to be discussed at greater length when dealing with the split between Westerners and Orientals. The religious are also sub-divided into religious persons of various political persuasions and into the national religious camp, whose members are hawkish to varying degrees but which also contains a dovish group, Meimad.

The secular public is not monolithic, either, regarding the extent of its secularity, as already noted, and its socio-political orientation. Attitudes towards democracy demonstrate the latter. Firstly, democracy does not enjoy overwhelming support in Israel, with about 30 per cent of the public preferring a more autocratic regime.[76] Of those supporting democracy, some seem to be opting for a decidedly ethnic one in which Jews should enjoy privileges denied to the Arab minority. Thus, though 60 per cent of respondents supported a democratic regime, 68 per cent would deny voting rights to Israeli Arabs favouring the PLO.[77] In a survey conducted at the School of Education of the Hebrew University, a largely secular institution, 77 per cent of respondents supported a voluntary exodus of Israeli Arabs.[78] A survey by the Ministry of Education found 66 per cent of young respondents denying equal rights to Israeli Arabs.[79] Assuming that the secular constitute about 50 per cent of the population, clearly some of them must be favouring an extremely ethnic democracy, applied to Jews only and depriving Israeli Arabs of the civil rights they enjoy. One survey conducted by the Kibbutz Seminar among teacher trainees found that 46 per cent of secular respondents regarded Arab MKs a security risk, 34 per cent denied equal rights to Israeli Arabs and 29 per cent denied Israeli Arabs the right to take part in crucial political decisions.[80] Similarly, though none of the secular respondents supported a theocratic state, only 73 per cent of them supported a democracy whose policies ran counter to their own views and 28 per cent considered Israel to belong to Jews only and denied immigration rights to non-Jews.[81]

It would thus seem that the secular public is divided into those who support the modernist definition of democracy, in which citizenship is the only criterion for full and equal membership in the polity; those who define democracy as the absolute rule of the majority, so that the majority ethnic group may set down the rights and duties of citizenship differentially in its favour, and those who believe in an autocratic style in which democracy is confined to the election process, possibly limited by an ethnic criterion. The surveys examining this question are relatively few and are not fully comparable because they differ in the wording of the questions and in the age groups studied. It is therefore impossible to even approximate the sizes of these three groups. Familiarity with the Israeli scene suggests a majority of the ethnic democracy group, the two other groups constituting two minorities.

Furthermore, it is usually assumed that only completely secular Israelis support a non-ethnic democracy and only the orthodox and most of the religious support a regime democratic in name only. Yet no data are available to substantiate this claim. In one survey, over 20 per cent of religious respondents (orthodox and religious combined) believed that Israeli Arabs had equal rights to Jews;[82] in another survey, 12 per cent of the secular, 13 per cent of the traditional and 8 per cent of the religious respondents supported a non-ethnic democracy.[83] It follows that the two camps are neither monolithic, nor is there a clear-cut division between them, especially if the category of 'traditional' is taken into account, a sector which tends to be intermediary on the political and religious scales. The traditional are Israelis who observe some religious commandments, primarily because they regard them as Jewish customs; they do not fully belong to either the religious or the secular category. It would seem that a large part of them are Orientals, which leads the discussion to the ethnic rift in Israeli society.

Westerners versus Orientals

The background to this rift has been examined in Chapter 2. To sum up, in the early years of Israel, new immigrants were looked down upon because they represented the rejected diaspora and religious ones even more so because secular democracy was the hallmark of the Tsabar. Immigrants from Moslem countries had the further disadvantage of being culturally different, seen as culturally inferior. Inept absorption policies, a skewed allocation of resources and stigmatization created a society sharply stratified along ethnic (Oriental–Western) lines.

As described in Chapter 4, the ethnic gap was gradually closing in the late 1970s, with 40 per cent of Orientals having risen to middle-class status. But resentment over past deprivations and over the remaining large pockets of underprivileged Orientals in urban slums and outlying development towns was becoming increasingly outspoken. This was due in part to Likud wooing of the Oriental vote since the late 1970s by pointing out the injustice inflicted on them by Labour and, in part, by the growing number of Israeli-educated Orientals who were better equipped to articulate these grievances. Subsequently, Likud coupled the fostering of resentment with encouraging genuine Oriental participation in the political process: the party now comprises Oriental party activists, MKs and cabinet ministers. In all, there has been a very considerable political upward mobility of Orientals. In the 1996–99 Knesset, 40 per cent of Jewish MKs were Orientals, closely approaching their proportion in the Jewish population. This has created a partial overlap between the political and ethnic rifts.

Not all Orientals had ever voted for Likud – the figure was 70 per cent in the 1981 elections – and they certainly did not do so in the 1996 elections, when the vote could be split between that for Prime Minister and that for a party. Shas became a serious competitor for the Oriental vote. It grew from 5 per cent in 1992 to 8.5 per cent in 1996, due mainly to its impressive gains at the expense of Likud in development towns, the majority of whose population was Oriental.[84] But preference for Netanyahu, leader of Likud, remained steady in places of an Oriental population of low socio-economic status. According to figures published by the Central Bureau of Statistics, in 1996 Netanyahu received 39 per cent more votes than Peres in development towns, whereas he beat him by a very narrow margin countrywide; the same held true for poor urban neighbourhoods.[85]

No data are available on the voting patterns of middle and upper-class Orientals who have moved away from development towns (principally due to a lack of job opportunities for better-educated and skilled persons) and from poor neighbourhoods. These constituted about 40 per cent in the late 1970s and their percentage has probably risen since.[86] However, polls indicate a decided partiality to Netanyahu of Orientals in general. Polls preceding the 1996 elections showed an ever growing Oriental preference for Netanyahu over Peres.[87] Of Oriental respondents, 47 per cent judged Netanyahu's performance favourably in September 1996 and 62 per cent in September 1998, compared to 30 per cent and 36 per cent respectively of Western respondents.[88] They also show a correspondingly more hawkish stance of Orientals regarding the peace process. Twenty per cent of Oriental respondents considered the government too lenient in its negotiations with the Palestinians, compared to 13 per cent of Western respondents[89] and 72 per cent of Oriental respondents regarded it too lenient in negotiations with Syria, compared to 54 per cent of Western respondents.[90]

The preference for Likud as well as hawkishness are attributed to all Oriental Israelis, though the only substantiated data are an overwhelming support of Netanyahu in places where a majority of the population are Orientals of low socio-economic status, roughly 50 per cent of Israeli Orientals. As to hawkishness, one well-informed researcher attributes it to the same protest which led so many Orientals to vote for Likud, whose stance they gradually adopted.[91] Indeed, Oriental support of Netanyahu seems to be a protest against Labour rather than blind devotion to Likud and its ideology. According to a poll conducted just before the 1996 elections, the percentage of Oriental respondents believing the Likud slogan 'Secure Peace' equalled that of those disbelieving it, namely 43 per cent and 42 per cent respectively, while Western respondents believing in the Labour slogan 'A Strong Israel' exceeded the disbelievers by far, amounting to 56 per cent and 33 per cent respectively.[92] Nor do Orientals seem to be less realistic about assessing the political situation than are

Westerners. Sixty per cent of Oriental respondents feared that a war would break out in the wake of the tunnel affair, compared to 56 per cent of Western ones.[93]

Yet stigmas continue, emphasizing a political–ethnic cleavage which probably applies to only part of the Oriental population and certainly applies to only part of the Western one, a considerable proportion of whom also support the Right. Stereotyping is even more pronounced regarding the allocation of Orientals to the religious camp and of Westerners to the secular one – no data are available on the religious distribution of either group. Anecdotal and anthropological evidence suggests that the majority of first generation Israeli-born Orientals continue to be traditional rather than emphatically secular, possibly but not certainly more of them than Western ones. Anthropologists found a decline in religiosity among first generation Israeli Orientals, compared to their parents, but not in favour of complete secularity. Rather, young Orientals tended to become traditional, that is to observe fewer commandments and less strictly.[94] More recently, Oriental intellectuals have been claiming that Jews in Moslem countries never became totally secular, but neither did they turn to ultra-orthodoxy to counter the pressure of assimilation and secularization. The rank and file were religiously tolerant and moderate and have remained so in Israel.[95]

Nevertheless, the image of Shas, which gained a mere 8.5 per cent of the vote in 1996, has revived and reinforced former stereotypes of Orientals as non-modern people. They are depicted as guided by emotion rather than reason, prone to mysticism and blind obedience to their self-appointed sages and reversing the trend towards secularization and democratization in Israeli society by setting up a strictly religious educational network.[96] Uri Or, a Labour front-bencher, slipped so far as to express such sentiments in an interview, and to an Oriental journalist at that,[97] calling forth sufficient outrage to disqualify him from politics henceforth.

The stereotyping produced an Oriental backlash, reopening a cleavage which might otherwise have gradually healed. Old injuries of deprivation and perceived discrimination, which had been festering all along, burst open again. Professor Ben Ami was now revealing the insult he had felt as a boy at the deprecation of his non-Israeli diaspora culture;[98] Dr Shenhav, a sociologist at Tel-Aviv University, expressed his contrition at having felt the need, as a boy, to conceal his Oriental origin in an attempt to be accepted as an Israeli;[99] an autobiography by an Iraqi-born translator documents the need to do so in order to further her career;[100] Ben Shitrit, an Oriental film producer, testified to consistent discrimination against Oriental intellectuals.[101]

It must be noted that, although the feeling of deprivation undoubtedly existed all along, the above testimonies are recent, presumably provoked by the renewed stigmatization of Orientals. The term 'stigmatization' is used advisedly because the present deprecation of Orientals takes no account of the large proportion of upwardly mobile ones. In addition to the impressive political and economic mobility of Orientals educated in Israel, the IDF has been a significant such venue: the Chief-of-Staff and the Commander of the air force are Orientals who climbed to the very top of the military hierarchy and Orientals are well represented in all lower echelons of the military as well. To counter the renewed stereotypes, Oriental intellectuals claim that Shas is a marginal phenomenon, unrelated to the bulk of Orientals.[102] Instead, Orientals are presented as the cure to present Israeli ills, the better face of over-Westernized Israeli society. Mediterranean culture and values, of which Orientals are the natural carriers, should form a major constituent in Israeli identity: values of tolerance and mutual respect must replace the polarization in Israeli political and religious affairs, mutual aid emphasizing primary human relations must ameliorate the extreme individualism prevalent in Israel, present policies of economic Thatcherism must be rejected in favour of a more humane capitalism and pride in Jewishness must supplant the urge to imitate the West.[103]

The Mediterranean Forum was established in March 1996 with the express purpose of bridging the gap between Orientals and Westerners. It invokes the Mediterranean, which includes southern Europe, possibly in order to make Oriental culture more palatable to its Western Israeli members. But emphasis is put mainly on North Africa, Egypt, Iraq and Spain. Besides endorsing the architecture and outgoing human relations around the Mediterranean littoral, stress is placed on the glories of Jewish culture which flourished in Moslem countries.[104] The Minister of Education and Culture since 1998, himself born in Morocco, was reallocating funds to foster Oriental music and art, an Andalusian orchestra was established, a bi-weekly programme of Mediterranean music is being broadcast on Israeli television, as well as a weekly programme of Israeli music significantly named 'Friday in the Taverna'.

Another more specifically Oriental organization, established by Oriental intellectuals in early 1997, is the Oriental Democratic Arc which endeavours to improve the lot of underprivileged Orientals. It lobbied to enable long-time tenants of public housing to buy their flats at greatly subsidized prices, to set up a fund for development towns from part of the profits of Kibbutzim and Moshavim when their agricultural land is re-zoned, to change the symbols and language of the media which created an inferior image of Orientals and to recognize the hegemony of Orientals in Israeli society in line with their numerical majority.

To sum up, if objective criteria are taken into account, Orientals are no longer a single camp, neither in their voting pattern nor in their degree of religiosity. Furthermore, intermarriage with Westerners is also increasingly blurring the distinction between continents of origin. Nevertheless, the ethnic divide became more salient recently than it had been for some decades. On the one hand, the campaign for the 1999 elections was rife with ethnic allusions. The major parties were stressing the proportion of Orientals on their lists for the Knesset. Mordechai was chosen to head the Centre party because, as an Oriental, he might be better placed to mobilize the Oriental vote; he was underlining his ability to bridge the ethnic gap as his asset as future Premier. Paradoxically, Shas was hoping to gain by the conviction of its leader, Arie Deri, on a bribery and corruption charge, presenting him as a victim of the Western secular judiciary (though the presiding judge was a religious Oriental). On the other hand, two camps of Orientals have entered the struggle over the nature of Israeli society: Shas aims at an ultra-orthodox Jewish society in which Orientals will eventually predominate by gaining the electoral upper hand, while supporters of the Mediterranean Forum and of the Oriental Democratic Arc aim at an enlightened secular society whose Oriental-flavoured Judaism will be the antidote to the ills of contemporary Western culture, that is shallowness, hedonism and excessive egoism. Each of these Oriental camps depicts Israeli Westerners as representing everything they oppose and both regard them as depriving Israeliness of Jewishness, thus also creating a stereotype. In between these two camps is the silent majority of traditional Orientals whose views on the desired nature of Israeli society remain unknown. One need not add that Westerners are not a single bloc on any of the above-mentioned scales either, nor do they have a common view on preferred Israeli values. The ethnic divide thus adds to the cleavages of society, which is splintered even further by the rift between veterans and new immigrants.

Veterans versus *Newcomers*

This cleavage differs from the other divisive factors on two counts. Firstly, in this case the two camps are clearly delineated by date and visibility. A large wave of immigrants from the former Soviet Union began arriving in Israel in 1990, joining a much smaller one of the 1970s. They amounted to a total of about 1 million by 1999, roughly 20 per cent of the Jewish population. Immigrants from Ethiopia also arrived in several lots, the largest one coinciding roughly with that of the Russian-speaking ones, but comprising a total of only about 70,000. Ethiopian immigrants are easily recognized by their dark skin and ex-Soviet ones by their lifestyle.

Secondly, though noted as a cleavage, the distinction between veterans and new immigrants has not been regarded by researchers and the public as another dimension of the ongoing fracture of society, possibly because new immigrants, as a bloc, have not taken a clear stand on their preferred nature of Israeli society. Ethiopians are still too preoccupied with daily problems of employment and housing to indulge in political theorizing and mobilization. Ex-Soviets have no clear stand on either democracy or Jewishness. Having come from the disintegrated USSR, many seem to regard democracy primarily as shaking off the shackles of an oppressive regime, without a clear conception of what the opposite of the latter should be. Most seem to vacillate between a preference for almost complete individual licence (regarding police investigations and indictments by the prosecution as synonymous with police state practice) and preference for a strong and almost authoritarian government, which can conduct policies without much concern for public opinion. This is possibly one of several reasons why polls break down the respondent population by degree of religiosity, into age groups, into political preference groups, into income groups and into Westerners and Orientals, but not into new immigrants and veterans. Despite a number of anthropological and sociological studies on the two groups of new immigrants, few newspaper articles have brought the subject to the attention of the general public as an issue, compared to the religious, political or ethnic rifts. The political parties have not taken the problem seriously either, dealing with it in the time-honoured Israeli manner of coopting some ambitious new immigrants into their Knesset list for the 1999 elections as a symbolic representative of his/her group.

Presumably extrapolating from the past, politicians and researchers seem to assume that any present absorption problems will be solved with time and are unrelated to the present identity crisis. This might well have been so if there were no identity crisis splintering the society. In the past, when Israeli identity was relatively well defined, pressure could and was exerted on new immigrants to adjust to a generally accepted model of The Israeli (Pioneer, Tsabar, Settler and even Unconverted). Under present circumstances, though, society cannot provide the new immigrants with a model to be emulated. Nevertheless, the various sectors of society stigmatize the new immigrants as what they each consider to be the opposite of what is quintessentially Israeli.

One disparagement common to the two groups, despite the great differences between them, is their inadequate Jewishness. Regarding Jewishness, new immigrants have never seemed to fit the bill, for the ones in the 1950s were derided for being too Jewish altogether. The present deprecation comes from two quarters and for different reasons. Firstly, the religious sector in general and the orthodox establishment in particular, have been calling in question the religious Jewish membership of the two groups, or parts of them. Jews in Ethiopia are an ancient community, largely isolated from other Jewish communities for hundreds of years and not observing the religious strictures introduced elsewhere during that time. Consequently, the orthodox establishment at first refused to recognize their Jewishness and required them to undergo conversion. It finally relented, yet the stigma has stuck to some degree and was renewed by the recent immigration of relatives of the immigrants who are Falash Mura, that is Ethiopian Jews who converted to Christianity under pressure.

Jews in the Soviet Union lived under a very secular communist regime where inter-faith marriages were rife. Under the Law of Return, spouses, children and grandchildren of Halachically recognized Jews are also entitled to the privileges of Jewish immigrants. The 1 million immigrants from the former Soviet Union comprise a large number of persons considered non-Jews by religious standards, estimated to amount to about 30 per cent of the total. The orthodox courts have been insisting on very strict conversion procedures for them, such as a lengthy period of study during which lucrative employment is greatly restricted, as well as a written undertaking to remain strictly observant in the future. Furthermore, its institutions have been unable to cope with such large numbers of converts except by phasing them out by an even longer study period and even stricter standards. The consequent delays and difficulties have provided the Conservative and Reform movements with an opportunity to step in and gain a foothold in Israel which they had previously never had. They offer a much easier and shorter conversion process. The orthodox establishment regards this as a serious threat to its power base and rejects any such conversions as invalid (though it recognizes them when performed abroad). The problem became acute enough for a committee to be appointed, headed by the then Minister of Finance, Neeman, himself observant. The compromise it reached has not solved the problem, because the final approval of conversion remains with the orthodox Chief Rabbinate. On the other hand, the conversion issue has provided further fuel for the secular–religious controversy, especially after some ex-Soviet immigrant soldiers fell in action and were refused burial in military cemeteries because they were Halachically non-Jews.

Though secular Israelis side with the non-Jewish ex-Soviet immigrants regarding conversion, they deprecate all ex-Soviet immigrants as not being sufficiently Jewish to be turned into instant Israelis. Indeed, having lived in an atheistic society, these immigrants are largely unfamiliar with Jewish customs and traditions which are an integral part of public and private life in Israel. What veterans really resent, however, is the Russian lifestyle which the immigrants insist on retaining. As already mentioned, new immigrants had been looked down upon since the 1950s as needing re-education and 'civilization' in order to fit into the 'superior' and 'advanced' Israeli society. The Ethiopian immigrants could be treated in this manner without much protest on their part, because a large proportion of them came from a pre-modern village society. Moreover, coming from Africa, the incidence of HIV carriers among them is higher than among the general Israeli population, projecting onto them an image of unhygienic backwardness.

But ex-Soviet immigrants do not fit this bill at all. Forty-four per cent of them had a post-secondary education upon arrival, 60 per cent of those previously employed were professionals, including 3 per cent doctors and dentists, 3 per cent artists, 17 per cent engineers, over 4 per cent nurses and 2 per cent scientists.[105] To maintain their superiority, Israelis have been tagging ex-Soviet immigrants as Mafiosos (a few cases were discovered of some Jews involved with Russian organized crime who used Israel as a base for laundering money) and the women as prostitutes (Russian criminals, some of them Jews, smuggled non-Jewish Russian women into Israel to work as prostitutes). In response to this offence and possessing the necessary skills, ex-Soviet immigrants have been nurturing their Russian culture, refusing to adopt what they consider the inferior Levantine Israeli one. A large number of Russian-language newspapers cater to these immigrants, who watch Russian television, attend concerts by immigrant musicians, founded a theatre company of international renown, have opened classes and held competitions of ballroom dancing, attend performances of their 'bards' (political–philosophical poets) in Russian and jazz sessions of immigrant performers. Poets and authors continue to write in Russian. Above all, they have established their own supplementary education system, insisting that the Israeli one is inadequate, especially regarding the teaching of mathematics, exact sciences and English. These afternoon classes are taught in Russian. One such enterprise developed into an acclaimed regular school to which some Israeli pupils are also admitted. To clinch their separate group identity, they established their own party in 1996, which won 5.7 per cent of the votes, joined the coalition and held two portfolios in the Netanyahu government.

The Soviet experience made ex-Soviet immigrants wary of anything smacking of socialism and Russian imperialism instilled in them a high regard for territory. Many regarded Labour as far too socialist and dovish and preferred the hawkish camp. According to one poll, 52.3 per cent intended to vote for Netanyahu as Premier in the 1999 elections and only 20 per cent for Barak (the rest were undecided).[106] A research found 30 per cent of them favouring extreme parties and, among those, 66 per cent favoured hawkish extreme parties.[107] The 1999 election results refuted these predictions, though.

Thus, the Orthodox and religious decry the new immigrants for being non-Jewish or of doubtful Jewishness, while the secular sector decries them for being un-Jewish in looking African and carrying a reprehensible disease (Ethiopians), or by preferring Russian food (including pork) and culture to the Jewish–Israeli one. Ethiopian immigrants are too few and insufficiently skilled to confront their stigmatization effectively. Their contribution to the veteran–new immigrant rift is therefore small compared to that of the ex-Soviets, who have founded a counter-culture in order to fend off Israeli derogation. The latter is reinforced further by the resentment felt by lower socio-economic status Orientals of the quick economic and political success of the ex-Soviets. Less than 30 per cent of ex-Soviets settled in the major three cities. The remainder constitute 30–50 per cent of smaller town and development town residents, whose population was largely Oriental before their arrival.[108] The proximity of still underprivileged Orientals and the successful newcomers, who also brandish their European cultural superiority, has created tensions which culminated in several cases of murder. To sum up, the veteran–newcomer rift is superimposed on the political, religious and ethnic rifts, splintering Israeli society even further.

SYMPTOMS OF THE SOCIAL FRACTURE

The fracture in Israeli society is evident in the political arena, in the partial erosion of the most consensual and previously hallowed value of defence and in the widespread search for a renewed consensus and solidarity.

The Political Arena

The unprecedented splintering of parties, of opportunistic camp-swapping by politicians and of the multitude of new, narrowly sectorial parties founded towards the 1999 elections has already been described. Paradoxically, the agreement in principle between Left and Right regarding the peace process with the Palestinians has turned a single split into multiple fissures, rather than producing a greater measure of solidarity. Probably realizing that the values which they had represented had broken down – Greater Israel on the one hand and a return to perfect justice by a genuine reconciliation with the Palestinians on the other – Likud and Labour have both moved to what they call the centre. The Centre party placed itself there from the start.

In their election campaigns, all three major parties were speaking of peace and security. All are distrustful of Palestinian intentions, differing only in the degree of distrust and, therefore, in what they regard as essential Israeli security requirements. All three promised to retain parts of the West Bank, to leave all settlements in the West Bank in place and to solve the South Lebanon impasse by renewing negotiations with Syria. Given that the aims were identical, the parties differed only on the price Israel was to pay for attaining them, but none of the parties was specific on that score. Instead, each was claiming that its leader was better qualified to negotiate and, above all, better qualified to mobilize consensus for his policies by reunifying the fragmented Israeli society. The election campaign was fought as a personal duel between the contenders for premiership, as the first television debate between Netanyahu and Mordechai on 13 April 1999 vividly demonstrated. In fact, Lipkin-Shahak launched the Centre party by declaring that Netanyahu was a menace and his removal the primary aim of the party.

The stress on the ability to unify implies the realization that fracture is prevalent. Mordechai, leader of the Centre party, was stressing his ability to bridge the ethnic divide by his own Oriental origin and the religious–secular divide by paying symbolic deference to the spiritual leader of Shas, former Sephardic (Oriental) Chief Rabbi Yosef. He also helped the religious parties to pass the first reading of a bill by casting his decisive vote for it. Barak, leader of Labour, formed a new bloc significantly named 'One Israel', in which he incorporated Gesher, a secular Oriental party which had split from Likud, and Meimad, a moderate and liberal religious party claiming to represent original NRP values. He was also flaunting the Oriental origin of his wife. Netanyahu, on the other hand, was reiterating Likud achievements in incorporating Orientals and stressing his government's close cooperation and coalition with the religious parties. At the same time, he chastised Labour for having failed to do so. Rather than creating unity, these efforts exacerbated the ethnic and religious splits by drawing attention to them, as noted by numerous commentators.[109]

Discredit of the IDF

As already discussed, the IDF had been the incarnation of the upright warrior image, the core of Tsabar identity. It had lost this focal role in Settler identity, yet military service was still regarded an essential task in conquering and holding the Holy Land. This is why settlers had faced such a dilemma when some of their rabbis pronounced their own interpretation of Scriptures to supersede military commands, should the latter require the withdrawal from any settlements. In addition to its military role, the IDF was also seen as a primary tool for forging Israeli identity. It was perceived as the institution in which all differences between the various social groups were smoothed out. It integrated young new immigrants into Israeli society, it was a democratic venue of mobility since it promoted people upon merit and could thus bridge economic and ethnic gaps. In it, secular and religious Israelis were comrades-at-arms and lived together in harmony, in contrast to their mutual segregation in civilian life.

The October 1973 war had dented the image of IDF invincibility and the Intifada that of the upright warrior image. When the Oslo process and the peace treaty with Jordan began to call into question the preeminence which defence and security had been accorded in Israel, the IDF could no longer maintain its role as a major focus of Israeli identity. As one observer put it, the IDF was the last common glue to be dissolved.[110]

A long series of polls indicates that the IDF still is the most highly trusted Israeli institution, receiving the highest rating compared to the courts, the Knesset and the government. Yet the decline in IDF prestige was noted by the former Chief-of-Staff, Lipkin-Shahak, at a Rabin Commemoration ceremony in late November 1996, by leaders of the Kibbutz movement,[111] by a social scientist specializing in military–civil relations,[112] by journalists[113] and by IDF officers. In a survey conducted by the IDF among middle-rank officers, the great majority of respondents considered the IDF image greatly tarnished; only 42 per cent considered unit morale high, 18 per cent did not believe in the combat ability of the IDF and 26 per cent did not trust the decisions of the higher command.[114]

Lower prestige has been accompanied by a decline in willingness to serve altogether, to do reserve duty, to serve in combat units or as officers. One survey among 12th-graders found that willingness to serve had declined among secular respondents from 93 per cent in 1986 to 75 per cent in 1995 and among religious ones (excluding the orthodox) from 94 per cent to 86 per cent respectively.[115] General Shefer, head of IDF manpower, confirmed an earlier statement by the Chief-of-Staff to the Knesset, noting that there was a steady increase in shirkers, who got exempted on fake medical or psychological grounds.[116] Service dodging had always existed, possibly to a lesser extent than after the signing of the DOP, but brazen dodging was novel enough to elicit comment. Four youngsters interviewed by the press described their successful service dodging as an exercise in smartness.[117] The number of reservists actually shirking service has also been on the increase, as noted in the State Comptroller's Report for 1995 and by General Shefer.[118] The Forum of Reserve Battalion Commanders reported to the Knesset that only about 75 per cent of reservists fit for combat actually served.[119] In an IDF survey among officers up to the rank of captain, 50 per cent of respondents admitted that they would refuse to do reserve duty if they could.[120]

Shirking apart, willingness to perform tough and/or dangerous military jobs has been declining somewhat in general, and among secular Westerners in particular. Selection for service in combat units is based on fitness only. But when even dodging military service altogether is seen as less reprehensible than in the past, shirking combat service in favour of desk jobs has become more widespread and a semi-legitimate practice. Never had all conscripts wished to risk their lives, but surveys by the IDF Manpower Department noted a decline in such readiness of 20 per cent, from 64 per cent of surveyed 12th-graders in 1989 to 44 per cent in 1994.[121] This has worried the IDF sufficiently to raise the pay and discharge grant of combat troops incrementally for every year of front-line duty. The decline in motivation, as the IDF has termed it, applies principally to secular Western conscripts, as numerous surveys have shown. According to a study by the Ministry of Education, 52 per cent of respondents declared their willingness to do combat duty. When broken down by religiosity, that percentage rose to 68 per cent among Yeshiva high school pupils, to 85 per cent among high schoolers in settlements and to 89 per cent among high schoolers in religious Kibbutzim.[122] A survey by a Bar Ilan University researcher showed that willingness to do combat duty was decreasing faster among secular 12th-graders – from 48 per cent of respondents in 1986 to 34 per cent in 1995 – than among religious ones – from 55 per cent to 49 per cent respectively.[123] General Shefer summed up the situation by stating that the number of religious officers was rising, while that of secular ones, and especially those coming from Kibbutzim, was decreasing, reinforcing the trend towards legitimizing army dodging among the secular.[124] In sharp contrast to other sectors of young people, the willingness to serve in combat units has risen among 12th-graders from outlying Moshavim, whose population is largely Oriental. Among respondents from those, it rose from 44 per cent in 1988 to 67 per cent in 1994, while it declined from 73 per cent to 59 per cent respectively among respondents from secular Kibbutzim and from 72 per cent to 48 per cent among those from urban secular schools.[125]

The gradual shift from secular Westerners to the religious and/or Orientals in combat command positions, noted by the Chief-of-Staff in a television interview on 12 May 1996, has caused dismay in some quarters. Some secular senior reserve officers feared a deliberate attempt by the religious camp to take over the IDF in order to ensure continuation of its Greater Israel agenda. Religious soldiers and officers might follow the dictates of their rabbis and refuse to obey military orders, undermining the absolute authority on which any military organization is based.[126] To avert this danger, one Labour MK and former senior officer proposed dissolving the Yeshivot Hesder units and a former head of intelligence research proposed replacing knitted skullcaps (the symbol of the national religious camp) by IDF issue ones in order to prevent mutual recognition and concerted action among religious troops.[127] The prospect of Orientals taking over command and combat positions has also elicited negative comment. They might obstruct the peace process, it was claimed, because, being less well-educated than Westerners and barred from social mobility in civilian life, they were motivated by career considerations rather than patriotism. Their vested interest in a strong IDF might influence policy makers.[128]

These are extreme views, not validated by any data. Yet they were sufficiently credited to trigger counter-measures by the secular camp. A secular pre-military programme was set up in mid-1997, ironically in a West Bank settlement because of funding problems, and the Kibbutz movement opened a pre-military programme in September 1998, both to raise motivation for combat and officer duty. The Kibbutz movement also applied for an arrangement similar to that of Hesder Yeshivot, whereby Kibbutz recruits could serve and study alternately, but this request was turned down. Another programme was launched in early 1997, in which reserve officers would each work with a group of secular youngsters and raise their motivation. Such programmes are hardly likely to tip the scale in favour of secular Westerners in command positions, because the latter are less keen to serve in an IDF whose prestige has declined. Many of them no longer regard the IDF as a desirable career option. The decrease in voluntarism for top elite units is reputed to have been less pronounced, probably since these roles still carry high prestige. Even in these, though, the religious and Orientals have increased their share, as the 1997 pilot graduation class showed.[129]

It goes without saying that comments on the excessive proportion of religious and Oriental commanders in combat and elite units are one more expression of the religious and ethnic divides and have fomented them further. At the same time, these comments have contributed to the decline in IDF prestige. Firstly, the penetration of a profession by marginal groups always lowers its prestige rating; these comments underlined a phenomenon which might otherwise have remained less noticed. Secondly, they bear witness to the divisive forces within the IDF, thus denuding it of the integrative role it allegedly played and which had been one constituent of its focal place in Israeli identity. The suspicions raised against religious troops have triggered a counter-reaction: in addition to their demand to serve in separate units whenever possible, religious troops have begun to request separate entertainment with a religious content and even a different swearing-in ceremony. Incidentally, new immigrants have also been said to be clustering in one infantry division, calling into question the melting pot role attributed to the IDF.

The increasing criticism levelled at IDF performance is an outcome of its loss of prestige and also contributes to the latter. Bereaved families no longer accept the inevitability of their loss and demand punishment for officer negligence or ineptitude; human rights activists demand indictment of troops suspected of brutality against Palestinians; the public demands transparent investigations of IDF accidents and operational fiascos, such as the helicopter crash in which 72 troops were killed, an accident in which 6 men died in a bush fire and a naval commando operation in which 12 men were killed, all of them occurring in 1997. Such criticism, openly voiced by many, was unheard of when the IDF still served as a focus of identity. Then it signified a hallowed value common to most. Any derogation of it was considered to damage the self-image of each member of society and was therefore ruled out. But once the justice of the Israeli presence in Israel had been called into question, so that Israeli identity was no longer intact, the IDF ceased to enjoy immunity from scrutiny as the symbol of a revered value. The exposure of its failings has further undermined its focal role as a social glue.

The Search for Unity

The search for unity underway in Israel is the most decisive evidence of the fragmentation in Israeli society, while the emphasis placed on Judaism as an integrative factor bears witness to the recognized need to find a new moral justification for the Israeli presence in Israel. The realization has become widespread that Post-zionist contentions had undermined the certainty of Israelis in the justice of their cause, that is, in their ethical right to live in the country of their forefathers despite the counter-claim of Palestinians. Post-zionist arguments had succeeded in this because the secular camp was increasingly equating Judaism with orthodox religious doctrine and its representatives. The political power recently attained by the orthodox parties raised the spectre of a future theocracy. To avert this at all costs, a part of the secular camp shook off not just Jewish religion as interpreted by the orthodox, but Judaism altogether. In its attempt to replace Judaism with universal values it was losing its unique identity and its right to its patrimony. Even an outspoken critic of Judaism, who had asserted that it represented obsolete tribalism, was now admitting as much.[130] Secular and religious intellectuals have both pointed out that a return to Judaic values which incorporate democracy has become imperative.[131]

In addition to the 'return to the Jewish bookcase' movement described above, which has proliferated since, a multitude of secular and non-orthodox religious organizations and groups have been founded with the aim of imbuing secular Israelis with Judaic values. For the sake of brevity, only a few are listed here. The Ef'al Seminar of the United Kibbutz Movement opened Bina, the Centre for Jewish Identity and Israeli Culture. Between November 1996 and June 1997, it held courses on modern Jewish identity and, in 1997, a programme for preparing boys and girls for Bar Mitzva and Bat Mitzva ceremonies; it held a Judaism festival in Kibbutz Kfar Blum in June 1997 and a Jewish–Israeli happening named 'Gather' in October 1998. Tsav Piyus (Imperative of Reconciliation) was founded in 1996 to find a link between democracy and Jewish tradition. It organized Hakhel in conjunction with the Ef'al Seminar in October 1997 and October 1998, an event of Jewish text readings with a modern interpretation. In its pamphlet of September 1997 it listed its activities as holding dialogues between religious and secular students and opening a college in Yeruham, a development town, for dialogues between secular and religious pupils. Shaharit is a group of intellectuals studying Jewish texts. The Jewish leadership movement was founded on 7 April 1997 to bridge the secular–religious split. Congresses and symposia on this subject included a symposium entitled 'The Jewish Character of Israeli Society' organized by Meimad in Jerusalem on 19 May 1996 and a symposium entitled 'The State of Israel, the State of the Jews Or a Jewish State', held at Bar Ilan University on 6 October 1997. Bar Ilan University also conducts regular dialogue classes of religious and secular students. The Institute of Democracy has been formulating a 'secular manifesto' which is to stress the need to incorporate the Jewish cultural heritage (which consists largely of religious texts) in Israeli secular culture; no final version had been completed by early 1999. Similarly, a group of academics established Basha'ar in January 1999 with the purpose of educating Israelis to a rational discourse, instead of the ongoing emotional one. The discourse is to lead to an incorporation of the Jewish heritage in a democratic and enlightened Israel.

Neither of these last two efforts has yet come up with concrete ideas on how this is to be accomplished. Nor has any of the above groups, organizations or symposia come up with a convincing body of ideas able to integrate Judaism and liberal democracy in a manner which is in phase with contemporary Israeli reality. To redefine themselves successfully, secular Israelis will have to extract from the reservoir of Judaism Jewish values which meet two requirements. Firstly, in order to offset the challenge of modernism, these values must be sufficiently universal to satisfy modern ethical imperatives, that is, they must not run counter to the fundamentals of liberal democracy. Secondly, they must also be sufficiently specific to make Jewish Israelis distinct from others and morally entitled to their part of what once was the 'Land of Israel', or 'The Holy Land'. That is no easy feat. Furthermore, all these attempts at redefining Israeli identity ignore the other fissures in society enumerated above, probably on the reasonable assumption that Judaism can bridge all of them, since it is the one factor which all sectors have in common.

A more modest approach is trying to find a *modus vivendi* between the religious and the secular camps, hoping that the final redefinition of identity can be worked out peaceably once the heat of battle has cooled down. Meimad leaders and Yossi Beilin formulated a social covenant in 1998 which would legalize a reasonable accommodation of live and let live and make legal allowances for the large number of Halachically non-Jewish new immigrants. Similarly, Bar Ilan University held a conference on Jewish approaches to conflict resolution on 25–26 April 1999 in an attempt to suggest ways for managing the secular–religious conflict.

NOTES

1. N. Shragai, 'Wallerstein Will Take Care of the Baby', *Ha-arets*, 9 August 1996.
2. Y. Markus, 'Even If It Takes Six Months', *Ha-arets*, 27 August 1996.
3. U. Heitner, 'Is This a State?', *Ha-arets*, 24 September 1996.
4. A. Ben, 'The PM's Office Examines Various Models of Palestinian Sovereignty for a Permanent Settlement', *Ha-arets*, 10 November 1996.
5. D. Makowsky, 'Eye on the Government', *Jerusalem Post*, 20 December 1996.
6. A. Shavit, 'A New Middle East?', *Ha-arets*, 22 November 1996.
7. D. Levy, 'The Years Ahead', *Ha-arets*, 12 February 1997.
8. J. Bushinsky, 'PM Unveils Final Status Proposal', *Jerusalem Post*, 5 June 1997.
9. D. Makowsky, 'Terror Is Like Organized Crime', *Ha-arets*, 1 August 1997.
10. J. Bushinsky, 'Arafat Must Make a Choice', *Jerusalem Post*, 5 September 1997.
11. R. Kislev, 'The Second Rubicon', *Ha-arets*, 18 December 1997; J. Bushinsky, 'Cabinet Defines Essential Security Areas', *Jerusalem Post*, 15 January 1998.
12. D. Margalit, 'Sharon 98 Following Dayan 72', *Ha-arets*, 2 March 1998.
13. H. Keinon and S. Singer, 'We Are Not Freiers [Suckers]', *Jerusalem Post*, 29 April 1998.
14. Peace Index Project, *Ha-arets*, 4 September 1997, 5 March 1998, 5 February 1999.
15. Peace Index Project, *Ha-arets*, 5 February 1996, 3 August 1998.
16. Computed from the Peace Index Project published monthly in *Ha-arets*.
17. Peace Index Project, *Ha-arets*, 1 October 1998.
18. Dahaf, *Yedi'ot Ahronot*, 6 January 1995, Peace Index Project, *Ha-arets*, 6 July 1997.
19. Computed from the Peace Index Project.
20. Peace Index Project, *Ha-arets*, 6 May 1997, 3 June 1997.
21. Peace Index Project, *Ha-arets*, 7 July 1997.
22. Peace Index Project, *Ha-arets*, 5 February 1997; Smith, *Ha-arets*, 1 May 1997.
23. Peace Index Project, *Ha-arets*. 1 November 1998.
24. Peace Index Project, *Ha-arets*, 3 August 1998.
25. Peace Index Project, *Ha-arets*, 2 September 1998. The percentage declined to 53% in June 1996 and to 57% in September 1998, according to the Peace Index Project, *Ha-arets*, 1 October 1998.
26. Peace Index Project, *Ha-arets*, 8 December 1996, 5 January 1998, 3 August 1998.
27. Peace Index Project, *Ha-arets*, 1 October 1998.
28. Peace Index Project, *Ha-arets*, 4 January 1999.
29. H. Keinon, 'New 'Exile' Heralds New Prayer: Next Year in Ramallah', *Jerusalem Post*, 26 January 1996.
30. M. Merhavia, 'Settlement Will Win Over Oslo', Nekuda, No.195, May 1996, pp.32–3.
31. 'Amana Programme to Renew Settlement Drive After Elections', *Nekuda*, No.193, March 1996.
32. D. Shalit, 'The Story of a Cantor' *Nekuda*, No. 196, June 1996, pp.26–30; M. Felix, 'Another Spirit', *Nekuda*, No.196, June 1996, pp.14–17.
33. R. Sini, 'Ideology was Poured into Pragmatic Vessels in the West Bank', *Ha-arets*, 25 June 1996.
34. Y. Harel, 'Road to Deception', *Ha-arets*, 30 August 1996.

35. Y. Sheleg, 'Courage for Change', *Ha-arets*, 22 December 1996.
36. 'The Yesha Council After Hebron'; U. Elitzur, 'Go Into Details, Draw Maps', *Nekuda*, No. 202, February 1997, pp.20–1; 'The Gewirtzman Plan', *Nekuda*, No. 203, March 1997.
37. M. Bleicher, 'We Don't Fight Over Hebron, But Over the State of Israel and Its Soul', *Nekuda*, No. 202, February 1997, pp.16–19.
38. H. Keinon, 'Principles versus Practicality', *Jerusalem Post*, 9 February 1996.
39. See, for example, U. Elitzur, 'Very Near the Line', *Nekuda*, No. 204, April 1997, p.3; Y. Mor-Yosef, 'What Was Promised, What Was Kept', *Nekuda*, No. 206, July 1997, pp.16–21.
40. Y. Harel, 'One Must Not Criticize, Though One Should', *Nekuda*, No. 209, November 1997, pp.24–6; B. Katzover, 'Don't Crown and Don't Overthrow', *Nekuda*, No. 209, November 1997.
41. M. Mor-Yosef, 'Arik, Oslo and the Settlers', *Nekuda*, No. 216, July 1998, pp.18–20.
42. Israel Radio Poll, *Jerusalem Post*, 30 January 1998.
43. H. Keinon, 'More Than an Agreement – A Sea Change', *Jerusalem Post*, 11 September 1998.
44. N. Shragai, 'The NRP to Your Right, the Centre to Your Left', *Ha-arets*, 21 February 1999.
45. See, for example, the entire issue of *Mifne*, No. 14, 1996; Y. Liebman, 'Secular Judaism and Its Prospects', *Alpayim*, No. 14, 1997, pp.97–116.
46. A. Rubinstein, 'The Revolution has Failed, Zionism has Succeeded', *Ha-arets*, 10 June 1997.
47. B. Kimmerling, 'Everything Goes in Zionism', *Ha-arets*, 13 June 1997; B. Morris, 'I Committed a Zionist Act', *Ha-arets*, 16 June 1997.
48. I. Pappe, 'The Academic Is Also Political', *Ha-arets*, 16 June 1997.
49. Y. Barnea, 'The Wrong Path', *Ha-arets*, 6 May 1998; D. Margalit, 'Justice Needs No Apology', *Ha-arets*, 16 March 1998.
50. 'The State of the Jewish State', *Jerusalem Post*, 25 December 1998.
51. Z. Sternhell, 'Peace in the Shadow of Tanks', *Ha-arets*, 4 October 1996.
52. D. Newman, 'Peace Inactivity', *Jerusalem Post*, 28 September 1997.
53. G. Samet, 'Not Because of a Breakdown of Order', *Ha-arets*, 30 March 1998; D. Zucker, 'The Politics of Recognition', *Jerusalem Post*, 29 January 1999.
54. Peace Index Project, *Ha-arets*, 2 February 1999.
55. Peace Index Project, *Ha-arets*, 2 February 1998, 3 February 1999.
56. Peace Index Project, *Ha-arets*, 5 February 1997.
57. Peace Index Project, *Ha-arets*, 4 September 1997.
58. Peace Index Project, *Ha-arets*, 4 January 1999.
59. A. Rubinstein, *From Herzl to Rabin: 100 Years of Zionism* (Tel-Aviv: Schocken, 1997), pp.302–4.
60. B. Kimmerling, 'Kulturkampf', *Ha-arets*, 7 June 1996; M. Benvenisti, 'Beyond the Melting Pot', *Ha-arets*, 13 June 1996; Y. Oron, 'The Opposite of the Jewish Experience', *Ha-arets*, 21 June 1996.
61. E. Yaar, 'Survey Data', lecture delivered at the symposium entitled 'The Academic Community, Rationalism and Public Discourse in Israel', held at Tel-Aviv University on 12 January 1999. The symposium inaugurated Basha'ar, a group attempting to bridge the religious–secular divide.
62. Reported in T. Segev, 'Who Is Secular?', *Ha-arets*, 25 September 1996.
63. B. Kimmerling, 'The Year 2004', *Ha-arets*, 7 October 1996.
64. Institute of Israel–Diaspora Relations, *Ha-arets*, 9 March 1984; Na'amat Poll, *Ha-arets*, 10 November 1991; Peace Index Project, *Ha-arets*, 5 February 1997.
65. Peace Index Project, *Ha-arets*, 5 February 1997.
66. E. Gordon, 'The Haredi Attack on Barak', *Jerusalem Post*, 27 August 1996; Y. Harel, 'The Battle Cry of the Admor of Vizhnitz', *Ha-arets*, 29 November 1996.
67. G.M. Steinberg, 'The Dangers of Negative Stereotypes, Simplistic Images', *Jerusalem Post*, 18 September 1998.
68. D. Margalit, 'Three Secular Mistakes', *Ha-arets*, 15 February 1999; A. Tal, 'Freedom by the Creeping Method', *Ha-arets*, 15 February 1999.
69. See Y. Sheleg, 'Israelis versus Jews', *Ha-arets*, 31 October 1997, for a thoughtful discussion of this point. Sheleg is himself a member of the national religious camp.
70. See, for example, E. Aviner, 'Renewal, Not Revolution', *Nekuda*, No. 217, 1998, pp.28–31; Y. Shorek, 'Is God Religious', *Nekuda*, No. 206, 1997, pp.34–8; many articles in *Nekuda*, Nos. 208, 1997 and 213, 1998; A. Pepper, 'They Already Recognize the State', *Nekuda*, No. 220, 1998, pp.20–4.
71. See, for example, M. Aridor, 'Judaism for Ulterior Purposes', *Ha-arets*, 8 October 1996; Y. Dan, 'Why This Fierce Self-Mutilation?', *Jerusalem Post*, 16 May 1997.
72. *Ha-arets*, 24 November 1996.
73. *Ha-arets*, 2 March 1998, 17 March 1998, 2 June 1998.
74. A series of articles in *Yated Neeman*, the organ of the Degel Ha-tora party, published during

November 1996; a comment made in public by Rabbi Ovadya Yosef, the spiritual leader of Shas, in early July 1997; a comment made in public by General Amridor in May 1998.

75. Data presented at the seminar '50 Years of Surveys in Israel' held at the Hebrew University on 6 January 1998.

76. See, for example,   Dahaf, *Ha-arets*, 18 March 1984, 26 March 1985; Institute for Israel–Diaspora Relations, *Ha-arets*, 9 March 1987 and *Jerusalem Post*, 24 January 1990; *Personal, Social and National Attitudes of Israeli Youth in the Jubilee* (Tel-Aviv: Institute of Economic and Social Rersearch, 1998), p.64.

77. Institute of Israel–Diaspora Relations, *Ha-arets*, 9 March 1987.

78. T. Trabelsky, 'Survey: Youth Against Peace', *Yedi'ot Ahronot*, 5 October 1994.

79. H. Keinon, 'Survey Reveals 37% of Jewish Israeli Youth Hate Arabs', *Jerusalem Post*, 26 November 1996.

80. *Davar Rishon*, 19 November 1995.

81. The Israeli Institute of Democracy, quoted in S. Ilan, 'Not Champions of Democracy', *Ha-arets*, 2 June 1998.

82. *Davar Rishon*, 19 November 1995.

83. *Personal, Social and National Attitudes*, p.33.

84. Election analysis in *Ha-arets*, 7 June 1996.

85. Bureau of Statistics figures quoted in U. Heilman, 'Voter Turnout in Last Elections Up 13 Percent', *Jerusalem Post*, 12 February 1997. Urban figures quoted in U. Shohat, 'Fed Up With Your Haughty Bearing', *Ha-arets*, 20 September 1996.

86. Available data are equivocal. Table No. 11.3 of the *Statistical Yearbook 1998*, on money income distribution of urban households, does not break down Israeli-born household heads into first and second generation ones, nor into their father's continent of origin. According to Table 2.23 of that *Yearbook*, 60% of first generation Israelis are of Oriental origin, while they constitute only a small percentage of second generation ones. The latter comprise 41% of all Israeli born. Very roughly, Orientals comprise about 40% of all Israeli-born household heads. Calculating from Table 11.3, Orientals take up a fairly proportional share in all income deciles. Actually, they are somewhat overrepresented in the top four deciles and somewhat underrepresented in the lower six. Not unexpectedly, the situation is reversed for foreign-born Oriental household heads, indicating economic upward mobility of Israeli-educated Orientals.

87. Smith, *Globs*, 16 February 1996, 15 March 1996, 18 April 1996, 17 May 1996.

88. Smith, *Globs*, 3 September 1996, 20 September 1998.

89. Smith, *Globs*, 20 September 1996.

90. Smith, *Globs*, 2 February 1996.

91. S. Smooha, 'The Oriental Parting Off', *Politika*, No. 51, 1993, pp.42–5.

92. Smith, *Globs*, 10 May 1996.

93. Smith, *Globs*, 27 December 1996.

94. M. Shoked, 'Commandments versus Tradition: Trends in Religiosity of Orientals', *Megamot*, Vol. 28, Nos. 2-3, 1984, pp.250–64.

95. See, for example, D. Hamo, 'Remove Judaism from Control of the Ultra-Orthodox and Religious', *Globs*, 16 August 1996; interviews with Professor Ben Ami, who holds the second slot on the Labour list for the 1999 Knesset, in A. Shavit, 'The Last European', *Ha-arets*, 23 May 1997, and in A. Melamed, 'Invitation to a Cocktail Party', *Ha'ir*, 5 March 1999.

96. See, for example, U. Benziman, 'Who Runs the State?', *Ha-arets*, 20 July 1997; G. Gornberg, 'The Lesson which Has Not Been Learnt', *Ha-arets*, 19 May 1997; D. Weinberg, 'Shutting Shas Out', *Jerusalem Post*, 6 September 1998.

97. D. Ben-Simon, 'Apology for What, What Apology?', *Ha-arets*, 29 July 1998.

98. A. Melamed, 'Invitation to a Cocktail Party'.

99. At a lecture at a conference entitled 'War, Revolution and Generational Identity', held at Tel-Aviv University on 7–8 March 1999.

100. A. Marcado, *In the Shadow of Discrimination* (Ramat Gan: Bar Ilan University, 1998).

101. L. Galili, 'His Own Canton', *Ha-arets*, 2 August 1998.

102. M. Karif, 'In Life as in Sports', *Ha-arets*, 10 May 1998.

103. D. Hamo, 'Westerners Deprived Us of the Naivete of Simple Human Relations', *Globs*, 7 June 1996; D. Hamo, 'Remove Judaism from Control of Ultra-Orthodox and Religious', *Globs*, 16 August 1996; A. Shavit, 'The Last European', *Ha-arets*, 23 May 1997.

104. See, for example, A. Alcalay, *After Jews and Arabs* (Minneapolis: University of Minnesota Press, 1993).

105. Data of the Central Bureau of Statistics, quoted in A. Luri, '100 Things You Have to Know About 1 Million Immigrants from the CIS in Israel', *Ha-arets*, 12 March 1999; M. Sikron and

E. Leshem (eds), *Portrait of an Immigrant Group – Absorption Processes of Ex-Soviet Immigrants* (Jerusalem: Magnes, 1998).

106. *Ha-arets*, 11 September 1998.
107. M. Mualam, 'New Immigrants for Moledet', *Ha-arets*, 14 March 1999.
108. A. Luri, '100 Things You Have to Know'.
109. See, for example, Y. Olmert, 'Say Something Different', *Jerusalem Post*, 18 January 1999; D. Weinberg, 'The End of Ideology', *Jerusalem Post*, 3 January 1999; U. Benziman, 'A Counterfeit Conciliation Order', *Ha-arets*, 10 January 1999.
110. D. Newman, 'The State of Change', *Jerusalem Post*, 13 January 1999.
111. A. Barzilai, 'The Battle Over Motivation', *Ha-arets*, 13 August 1996.
112. Lecture by S. Cohen at a conference entitled 'National Identity in New States', held at Tel-Aviv University on 2–4 March 1998.
113. See, for example, A. Golan, 'The New Soldiers', *Ha-arets*, 20 September 1998.
114. A. Oren, 'Why He does not Rejoice', *Ha-arets*, 28 November 1997.
115. A. O'Sullivan, 'Youth Less Willing to Serve in IDF', *Jerusalem Post*, 7 June 1996.
116. A. Ben, 'To Build the IDF Anew', *Ha-arets*, 4 April 1995; E. Rabin, 'Proportion of Recruits to Combat Units Down', *Ha-arets*, 24 October 1996.
117. A. Tal, 'Accelerated Exercise in Complacency', *Ha-arets*, 29 August 1996.
118. E. Rabin, 'Proportion of Recruits Down'.
119. L. Collins, 'Reserve Dodgers Could Affect Combat Readiness', *Jerusalem Post*, 26 November 1996.
120. R. Sini, 'Motivation Begins at Home', *Ha-arets*, 12 September 1996.
121. A. Barzilai, 'The Devotees, the Shirkers and Those In Between', *Ha-arets*, 19 January 1997.
122. H. Keinon, '37 per cent of Youth Hate Arabs'.
123. R. Sini, 'Motivation Begins at Home'.
124. 'Orthodox Who Do Not Enlist Amount to 7% of Potential Conscripts', *Ha-arets*, 17 November 1996.
125. A. Golan, 'As in the Kibbutz of Yesteryear', *Ha-arets*, 7 November 1996.
126. L. Galili, 'The Target After the Conquest of the Recce Unit', *Ha-arets*, 21 August 1996; I. Miller, 'God's Hosts', *Ha-arets*, 21 January 1997; A. O'Sullivan, 'A Gun and a Prayer', *Jerusalem Post*, 31 January 1997.
127. D. Rosenblum, 'Let's Part as Friends', *Ha-arets*, 31 January 1997; comment made by Shlomo Gazit at the conference 'National Identity in New States', held at Tel-Aviv University.
128. A. Golan, 'The New Soldiers'.
129. Y. Limor, 'Small History in the IDF: This Is the Pilot Course Completed Today', *Ma'ariv*, 3 July 1997.
130. B. Kimmerling, 'Between Hegemony and Dormant Kulturkampf in Israel', *Israel Affairs*, Vol. 4, Nos. 3–4, 1998, pp.49–72.
131. See, for example, M. Shamir, *Searchlight in Depth: Our Jewish Identity – Heritage and Challenge* (Tel-Aviv: Dvir, 1996); A. Yadlin, 'He Saw and Renewed', *Ha-arets*, 26 December 1996; Y. Harel, 'A Secular Message', *Ha-arets*, 26 September 1996; J. Dan, 'Why This Fierce Self-Mutilation?', *Jerusalem Post*, 16 May 1997; an interview with A.B. Yehoshua in A. Rabinovich, 'The Alef-Bet of Zionism', *Jerusalem Post*, 29 August 1997; Y. Sheleg, 'Beyond the Jewish Bookcase', *Ha-arets*, 15 October 1997; G.M. Steinberg, 'The Pluralist Jewish Renaissance', *Jerusalem Post*, 27 November 1998.

7. Concluding Remarks

I have traced the changes in Israeli identity from the inception of Zionism, the body of ideas which gave it its initial impetus, to the present in an attempt to understand and explain the crisis it is currently undergoing. The several changes in Israeli identity from the time of the first Zionist immigrants show a link between them and crucial decisions made by Israel regarding its boundaries. Each such decision was taken in connection with an external event, though I do not argue for a deterministic causal chain. Events can be viewed as historical junctions, at which one path must be chosen among several alternatives. But once chosen, it leads to the next junction and so forth. To understand the reason why one alternative was chosen, rather than another, one must look back to the previous junction. The short history of Zionism and Israel made it possible to trace the entire process back to its beginnings.

The Israeli case seems worth exploring on several counts. Firstly, on the face of it, it seems ironic that Jews, who could maintain their identity intact during 2,000 years of exile and dispersion among numerous nations, should lose sight of it just when they have finally returned to their original homeland and set up an independent polity. Secondly, most theories of national identity posit a strong link between it and the territory within which people identify themselves as members of a separate entity.[1] Jewish history refutes this postulate, while the changes in Israeli identity articulation lend some support to it: Jews maintained a firm identity without a territory, while Israelis changed theirs as their territory contracted or expanded. Thirdly, the Israeli case lends support to recent citizenship theory and the communitarianist thesis. The latter argue that, since democracies depend more on consent and less on coercion than other forms of government, compliance with laws and norms depends more on a consensus regarding the core values from which the laws and norms are derived. In contrast to views, according to which collective identities are being obliterated in postmodern societies, the above theories reassert the need in democratic societies for a basic consensus of citizens regarding their distinct identity.[2] Just because Western democracies are pluralistic, they would easily disintegrate unless some basic common values overrode the different views and values held by their multiple groups. As Smith[3] has noted, such values cannot be freely invented. Rather, they must rely on the culture of the society, that is, they are a reinterpretation of its past values and symbols to fit present circumstances and needs. To be more specific, any society, and a pluralistic one in particular, can be visualized as consisting of numerous concentric circles, each of them surrounding a decreasing number of groups. A circle represents the common denominator, those norms and values which members of the groups encompassed share and which distinguish them from groups outside the circle. The more complex the society, the greater the number of circles and the more basic is the common denominator which delineates the boundaries of the entire society *vis-à-vis* other ones. It follows that when consensus on the core values and norms breaks down, the society splinters into its various constituent groups and these, again, may disintegrate into yet smaller ones. This is precisely the process which Israel has begun to undergo in the past five years.

Going back to the roots of the Zionist idea was necessary in order to solve the ostensible riddle of Jews searching for their identity just when conditions for a firm one are more propitious than they had been for the past two millennia. Rather than being a paradox, this turned out to be an almost necessary result of Zionism on the one hand and of circumstances in the retrieved homeland on the other.

The Messianic idea of an eventual return to Zion had been a central ingredient of Judaism since the exile, a core value common to all Jews. But orthodox Judaism interdicted a mass return to the fatherland until the Coming of the Messiah. Zionists, who wanted to defy this prohibition, had to secularize the Messianic message, yet had to retain it in its secular version in order to mobilize broad support. That is so because only core values, common to all of society, can recruit groups of various opinions and interests. In shedding Jewish religion, however, Zionists had to find a substitute justification for their claim to their patrimony, a claim which had been based on the Bible which is undeniably a Jewish religious text. To overcome this problem, the Bible was reinterpreted as a historical text.

Besides being contested by scholars on historical–archaeological grounds and by the Jewish religious establishment as being sacrilegious, the exclusively historical interpretation of the Bible posed a more practical legal problem. Palestine was already inhabited by Arabs who staked an equal historical claim to the land. At a time when colonialism was still a morally acceptable practice, this dilemma need not have been acute had Zionists not invoked a secularized version of the Messianic idea as their *raison d'être.* But they had, and that idea also contained the injunction to exercise perfect justice, both as a community and as individuals. Perfect justice and any injury to the native population could not go hand in hand. This dilemma was solved first by asserting that Jewish reclamation of a badly underdeveloped and neglected land was evidence of their greater devotion and superior claim to it. Later, the Balfour Declaration, reaffirmed by the League of Nations, provided international legitimation for the Jewish claim to exclusive political rights, which were indirectly reinforced by the pan-Islamic and pan-Arab arguments put forward by Palestinian Arabs. The Zionist immigrants could contend that the latter had the entire Fertile Crescent as their homeland and were thus merely residents in Palestine, without political rights to it.

The solution was not altogether satisfactory. To prove their devotion to the land, Zionist immigrants first had to appropriate it. Similarly, the Balfour Declaration and the League of Nations affirmation of Jewish rights were *post facto* legitimations of an appropriation already under way. And Palestinian Arabs other than those supporting pan-Islam or pan-Arabism raised objections to Jewish immigration on Palestinian national grounds. The Pioneer identity which crystallized in the Yishuv period stood on shaky ground. National resurrection and ethical perfection could not be completely reconciled and neither could a secular historical claim to the land whose title deed was the Bible. Pioneer identity remained firm all the same as long as Pioneers could believe that they exercised perfect justice within the Yishuv society by their exaltation of egalitarianism, asceticism and physical toil and by offering to grant the Arab residents all civic rights, short of recognizing their political right to the land, demarcated as Mandatory Palestine. Moreover, Pioneer identity persisted despite the fact that only a small fraction of the Yishuv population were practising pioneers, that is, despite the growing disparity between the ideal and reality. Skilful and persistent messages by the Labour leaders, which justified the Zionist cause in terms of secularized Messianism, were able to override the doubts which such a disparity possibly raised.

Pioneer identity could no longer prevail, however, once the boundaries of the homeland contracted with the establishment of the State of Israel. Living within the new boundaries, which involved relinquishing part of the patrimony and expropriating part of the Arabs who had resided there, had to be justified anew. This amounted to a redefinition of Israeli identity. The Pioneer was replaced by the Tsabar. Yishuv consent to the UN Partition Plan, given very reluctantly and under duress, was also presented as magnanimity in line with the principle of perfect justice. Furthermore, if the boundaries of Israel extended beyond those laid down by the UN Plan, this was due to Arab intransigence and aggression. Israeli militancy was defensive only, guaranteed by the 'purity of arms' principle. The Tsabar was the upright warrior.

Again, the solution was far from perfect: Israelis did relinquish part of their heritage and the justice they accorded the Arab population, both during the 1948 war and in the following retaliatory operations, was not perfect. Despite this ambivalence, Tsabar identity remained firm, not least because it performed important functions of social identity articulation: it still based itself on one Jewish core value, namely the perfect justice aspect of the Messianic message, though somewhat equivocally, and it distinguished Israelis within their 1949 borders from other groups. Firstly, the upright warrior was ethically superior to the offensive, intractable Arab neighbours and, therefore, distinct from them. Secondly, in order to shake off Israeli dependence on the Zionist Organization, the native-born Israeli Tsabar was no longer seen as the vanguard of the Jews by dint of living in Palestine, but as the only Jew living in his sovereign State of Israel. He was clearly distinct from those Jews who preferred exile and he was superior to them. This was imprinted in Tsabar identity as a superiority of Israeliness over Jewishness, but finally as a derogation of Jewish ethnicity and religion, both of which were seen as smacking of the inferior diaspora.

This contradiction between the Tsabar as founder of the Jewish state, defined in the Declaration of Independence, and the Tsabar as disdainer of Jewishness did not detract from the identification of most Israelis with this self-image until the boundaries of Israel changed once more. In its extended borders after the 1967 war, the previous protestations of exercising perfect justice by having magnanimously given up part of their patrimony no longer held water. Nor did the Tsabar distinction between Israeliness and Jewishness. The occupied territories had not been part of Israel, to which Tsabar identity had confined itself. In the later 1960s, it was generally judged unethical to retain areas conquered in war unless this could be regarded as a liberation of the rest of the Holy Land given to the people of Israel by God, as stated in the Bible. The ensuing crisis of identity was soon resolved by adopting New Zionism, a less utopian–religious version of Gush Emunim doctrine.

The Settler replaced the Tsabar as the Israeli self-image. Using Gush Emunim as its vanguard, the Settler reintroduced the Messianic message and Jewish virtues into Israeli identity, both in a quasi-religious sense only. Assertion of proprietorship over Greater Israel was the secular aspect of Messianic national resurrection, augmented by secular strategic arguments. The Jewish virtues of mutual responsibility, tenacity and defiance of world opinion because of Jewish ethical superiority could demarcate Israelis *vis-à-vis* others. Israelis also exercised perfect justice by offering the Palestinians cultural and administrative autonomy in

Greater Israel, the latter seen as the inalienable property of the Jewish people.

Being only quasi-religious, Settler identity could and did appeal to secular Israelis as well, yet for two principal reasons was only adopted by roughly half of the population. Firstly, Settler identity was as flawed as had been Pioneer identity by dint of secularization. Again, the claim to all of Erets Yisrael was historical rather than religious, yet based on the Bible as title deed. Furthermore, underwritten by history alone, Israeli rights were hardly more legally justified than were Palestinian ones. Secondly, the protestations of exercising perfect justice towards the Palestinians were being refuted by reality. Autonomy was never implemented and the claim of a benevolent occupation, called into question throughout, was refuted by the outbreak of the Intifada and the repressive measures taken in its wake. These logical inconsistencies, quasi-religiosity and self-deceptive claims deterred half of the public, largely secular Israelis, from adopting Settler identity, leaving them somewhat exposed to the modernist values of liberal democracy which had been prevailing in the West since the 1970s.

Yet the counter-pressure of Settler identity remained strong enough and no identity crisis ensued until the Labour government signed the DOP. By entering negotiations with the Palestinians towards a final settlement of the conflict with them, the Israeli government eroded all of the values underlying Settler identity, but provided no convincing substitute. It was willing to relinquish part of Greater Israel voluntarily, thus ostensibly denying the Jewish right of proprietorship over the Holy Land. In doing so, it did not exercise tenacity, defiance of world opinion, or even responsibility towards the settlers across the Green Line. Because the Oslo track had been secret, no prior information campaign had been possible to prepare the public for this turnabout in Israeli policy. Worse still, nor was any consistent explanation offered after the event either. Labour leaders used mutually contradictory arguments. Rabin stressed the need to safeguard the Jewishness of Israel by a separation from the Palestinians through withdrawal from Palestinian-populated areas. In contrast, Peres hoped for a peaceful coexistence within a single polity which would mollify hostile Arab countries and create a prosperous region under the superior technological guidance of Israel.

Each stressed the material benefits accruing to Israel from the peace process, the one related to security and ethnic purity, the other to affluence. Neither of these benefits was regarded by settlers in general, and by the Settlers in particular, as sufficient to justify the voluntary relinquishment of part of the patrimony. Contrary to the Israeli response to the UN Partition Plan in 1947, Israel did not enter the Oslo process under duress, nor did it claim to do so as an act of magnanimity demonstrating its ethical superiority in line with the Messianic message. If any ethical considerations were guiding the peace process, they were the modernist values of liberal democracy voiced by Post-zionists. Yet the latter also castigated Israel for its past sins, principally that of ignoring the Palestinian right to self-determination. In judging acts performed in the 1950s by the values prevalent in the 1990s, the peace process became an act of repentance and restitution. As such, it re-evoked the original dilemma of reconciling perfect justice with settling a country already inhabited by others. If Israel repented of the occupation in 1967, provoked by an Arab attack on it, why should it not repent of the territorial gains made in 1948, provoked by a similar attack, or even of the Jewish settlement in Palestine despite Arab protests? To put it another way, if these were the values guiding the Oslo process, they denied Israel any justification for being what it was and where it was, that is, they completely undermined Israeli identity.

The public refused to draw this conclusion which would have been tantamount to collective suicide. The settlers in particular, and Settlers in general, rejected the entire Post-zionist argument as incompatible with the Jewish heritage, with the Jewish historical right to the land. No sin had been committed and no restitution was necessary. The Oslo process was an act of betrayal which had to be reversed. One fanatic assassinated Prime Minister Rabin, while the remainder returned the hawkish Likud to power in the hope of reversing the entire peace process, or, at least, of halting any further withdrawals from Greater Israel. The Unconverted half of the population also recoiled from the modernist values propounded by Post-zionists once it had realized the implications. The Unconverted endorse the peace process, but have not been provided with any convincing justification for it, nor with one for their guiltless presence in Israel. Certain that only Jewish values could supply an answer to their dilemma, they have instituted an extensive search to reconcile the democratic values of their secular worldview with selected Jewish ones, to constitute a rearticulated Israeli identity. So far, this search has been futile.

Contrary to Settler expectations, the Likud government merely stalled the peace process, but did not rescind it. Whenever the process threatened to collapse, the government revived it with some small step forward which signalled its intention of bringing negotiations to a conclusion. Settler identity, which was firmly rooted in the retention of Greater Israel, became increasingly eroded with each step towards an accommodation with the Palestinians, no matter how small. The dilemma for Settlers was the reverse of that which beset the Unconverted: once they consented to the relinquishment of part of the Holy Land, there was no moral or religious justification for making no further territorial concessions for the sake of peace. Resistance to additional withdrawals appeared as pure selfishness on the part of the settlers, an indifference to possible human sacrifices just so they could remain in their homes. The non-religious among the Settlers were clinging to security arguments in order to bolster their historical one, but these have become increasingly anachronistic: the IDF has officially redefined the order of perceived security threats. According to press reports of May 1999, the major defence effort has been shifted to counter long-distance weapons of mass destruction launched from hostile countries not neighbouring on Israel. The occupied territories cannot serve as a buffer zone for these. Consequently, Settler identity has been deprived of its ethical and practical underpinning and is being eroded, without any substitute to fall back upon.

The result has been an acute identity crisis which is ripping Israeli society apart. The previous split into Settlers and Unconverted has turned into a fracture in which previous divisions and subdivisions overlap only in part and in which no underlying values common to all provide any focus of cohesion. The Palestinian issue and Greater Israel have become secondary to a struggle among a multiplicity of groups, each of which wants to redefine the nature of Israeli society, that is, to reconstruct Israeli identity according to is own light. At present, the primary focus is on a struggle between protagonists of a Jewish religious society and those of a Jewish secular one. It is not the rule of law which is being called into question, as many observers assert. Rather, it is a struggle over which law is to prevail. The struggle over predominance of Jewish versions of Christian Western values as against Moslem Mediterranean ones is partly linked to the former and will also have its imprint on the future nature of Israeli society. The 1999 election results lend support to my contention. The national hawkish camp was shattered. It declined from 42.5 per cent of its Knesset representation to 26.6 per cent, principally because Likud, its main constituent and leader, lost almost half of its strength, declining from 25.1 per cent to less than 16 per cent. Instead, Shas, as champion of the hegemony of religious law and of a Jewish Oriental society, rose from 8.3 per cent to almost 14.1 per cent. At the same time, Shinui gained 5 per cent of the votes. Shinui was founded just six weeks before the elections and advocates an anti-religious secular Westernism. It is thus the exact opposite of Shas. Together with Meretz, which represents similar views, though it is less extremely anti-religious, the emphatically secular Western democratic camp is almost equal in strength to Shas (13.3 per cent compared to the 14.1 per cent of Shas). Time will tell whether the new government can incorporate such opposing views in the broad coalition it wants to set up. If it can do so, it will have found a formula common to both which might form the nucleus of a new identity articulation. Otherwise, the rift is likely to deepen.

The nature of society is what social identity is all about. The latter must distinguish the society from others in a manner which is consonant with its core values. In the Israeli case, it must also justify the presence of Israelis in a land inhabited by others and it must do so by ethical arguments because the Messianic message, which prophesies the Jewish return to its fatherland, also posits an ethically immaculate society which returns in order to be a light unto the nations. Israelis must necessarily define themselves as Jews, in the religious or the ethnic sense, in order to stake a morally justified claim to their patrimony. Because the Labour leaders conveyed confusing and self-contradictory justifications for the Oslo process, the default one, based on universal modernist values rather than Jewish ones, was seen to guide Labour policy. The Oslo process contained a major additional flaw: it did not demarcate the future borders of Israel. Without these, no new articulation of identity is possible. All these factors have resulted in the present identity crisis.

This study has tried to show the intricate link between the boundary formation of Israeli identity and the territorial borders within which Israelis live. Israelis repeatedly adjusted their self-image to the then current political reality so that it could include an ethical justification of the latter. It follows that their present crisis of identity is also due to the uncertainty regarding their future frontiers. Unless and until the conflict with the Palestinians is resolved and the Israeli borders are clearly delineated, at least for the foreseeable future, there is little chance of a resolution of the identity crisis.

Even when this finally comes about, it would be foolhardy to predict the form which Israeli identity will take. Although worst-case scenarios are very unlikely, in principle the future borders can range from Greater Israel, if the peace process collapses and Israel reoccupies all territories ceded to the Palestinians during the protracted negotiations, to the pre-1967 borders or even those laid down in the 1947 UN Partition Plan, if an agreement with the Palestinians is reached. Whichever they will be, they can be justified by various sets of arguments of roughly equal validity. But the above analysis of Israeli identity along its history leads to one conclusion: whatever the future self-image, it must be based on Jewishness, which is the only denominator common to all groups.

Democratic values cannot be ignored, either, if Israeli identity is to be attuned to the twenty-first century and if the secular sector of society is to adopt it. Democracy is universal only as a generic term, though. In practice, each Western society interprets democracy in the light of what it regards as its specific virtues. Whereas American democracy is guided by the principle of human equality, equal opportunity and civil rights, such as freedom of speech and religion, the English one is guided by that of fair opportunity to the excellent and social rights, such as public education and health, and the German one by that of formalistic equality before the law and bureaucratically regulated social welfare. Moreover, as Smith[4] has noted, such virtues cannot be freely invented. Rather, they must rely on the culture of the society, that is, on its core values. In Israel, democracy is already conceptualized as Jewish–ethnic, so that it is specific to Israel. Except for radical Post-zionists, Israelis insist that the Jewish majority determine the boundaries which set their society apart. As Tamir[5] argues, this may be undesirable from a liberal democratic standpoint, but is a necessity in many cases, of which Israel has been shown to be a particularly pertinent example. According to Tamir, such necessity can be turned into a virtue if discrimination against the ethnic minority is decreased to the minimum required in order to delineate the separate identity of the majority. Israelis must know that they are ethically justified in practising an ethnic democracy and that the latter is compatible with the principle of justice. Some Jewish values will have to be selected from the vast reservoir available to form a focus of cohesion around which identity can coagulate.

Another conclusion which may be drawn from this study is the urgent need to resolve the conflict with the Palestinians sooner rather than later in order to prevent an irreversible rift in Israeli society. In Israel, confrontation with an outside adversary is no longer creating internal solidarity, as was the case in Israel in the past and as it so often is in general. Internal differences in Israel can be resolved, or, at least palliated, only after a formula is found with whose most basic values the large majority can identify, values which can also underpin the ethical right to the presence of Israelis within a clearly delineated territory. At present, the Israeli identity formulation is analogous to a negative feedback process. The fragmentation, intricately linked to the identity crisis, is an obstacle to the final settlement with the Palestinians, while the latter is one condition for a healing of the fracture and a redefinition of identity. Beilin, the architect of the Oslo Accords, admitted that, if Labour wished to return to power, it would have to spell out the advantages of peace much more pointedly than it had done in the past.[6] Labour did not do so in the 1999 election campaign. It was returned to power, but largely by default because Netanyahu had governed so badly. It remains to be seen whether Labour will follow Beilin's advice, thus promoting a reformulation of the Israeli self-image within its new borders when these have been finalized.

NOTES

1.   See, for example, E. Gellner, *Nations and Nationalism* (Oxford: Basil Blackwell, 1982), pp.1–5; B. Anderson, *Imagined Communities: Reflections on the Origins and Spread of Nationalism* (London: Verso. 1983), pp.15–16; A.D. Smith, *National Identity* (Harmondsworth: Penguin, 1991), pp.8–18.

2. For a discussion of citizenship theorists and references, see W. Kymlicka and W. Norman, 'Return of the Citizen: A Survey of Recent Work on Citizenship Theory', *Ethics*, Vol. 104, No. 2, 1994, pp.352–81. A prominent exposition of the thesis on the postmodern levelling of societal variety is F. Fukuyama, 'The End of History?', *The National Interest*, No. 16, 1989, pp.3–19. For the communitarian view, see A. Etzioni, 'The Responsive Community: A Communitarian Perspective', *American Sociological Review*, Vol. 61, No. 1, 1996, pp.1–11.
3. A.D. Smith, *National Identity*, p.11
4. A.D. Smith, *National Identity*, p.11
5. Y. Tamir, *Liberal Nationalism* (Princeton: Princeton University Press, 1993).
6. H. Keinon, 'More Than an Agreement – a Sea Change', *Jerusalem Post*, 11 September 1998.

Epilogue

The period between the completion of the original manuscript and its final publication has been long and very eventful, influencing Israeli identity to the extent that an epilogue to the book is in order. On the face of it, fracture within Israeli society has been greatly reduced, replaced by increased consensus. This is in line with the move towards the centre of the political map already noted when discussing the 1999 election campaign. The trend of the two large parties to drift towards the centre has intensified and given rise to the national unity government headed by Ariel Sharon of Likud. In it, the more Rightist views of Likud and the more Leftist views of Labour have been largely neutralized. One symbol of this phenomenon is the changed nature of the annual commemorative ceremonies for assassinated Premier Yitzhak Rabin. While they were highly political in their condemnation of the Right at first, the one in November 2001 was an artistic event in which no political speeches were permitted.

The move towards the centre, then observed among politicians, can now be seen to be spreading among the public as many Israelis try to identify themselves anew, drawing on components from both the Tsabar and the Settler regarding foreign and security affairs, as well as putting greater stress on the Jewish component of Israeliness. In this emergent reformulation of identity, the tenets of peace and justice are still at loggerheads with those of security and the inalienable right to the Holy Land. The predominance of either is changing with the fortunes of the Israeli–Palestinian conflict. Rifts have not disappeared, but their outspoken expression is confined largely to the fringes on either side of the centre. It seems that the security situation has been overriding all other issues and, as common wisdom has it, a common danger produces solidarity. And the danger has grown recently, as the armed struggle with the Palestinians is becoming ever more violent. Their attempted illegal import of more sophisticated weapons is seen as an indicator of their determination to continue the conflict rather than return to peaceful negotiations. However, I shall argue that the greater cohesiveness of Israeli society is as yet just a thin veneer and is not necessarily as permanent a feature as it was in the early years of the State. Having the benefit of hindsight and for the sake of some brevity, I shall confine the discussion to those events since the 17 May 1999 elections which have had an impact on the situation in 2002.

When Ehud Barak, the former Chief-of-Staff, won the elections for Prime Minister as leader of Labour, expectations of a peaceful solution to the conflict with the Palestinians were high. People had forgotten his initial opposition to the Oslo Accords, but they were soon reminded of it. In interviews to the press before and immediately after the elections, Barak committed himself to negotiating peace with the Palestinians and with Syria and to a complete withdrawal from southern Lebanon within one year.[1] The election of a government declaring such intentions immediately improved Israel's battered foreign relations, including those with Egypt and Jordan, as well as raising the hopes of the Palestinians regarding Israeli concessions towards a negotiated solution of the conflict. Little attention was paid to the conditions which Barak stipulated even then for concluding these peace agreements: no full withdrawal from the Golan Heights, no return to the 1967 borders, no foreign army west of the River Jordan (meaning a demobilized Palestinian state) and the annexation of settlement blocks to Israel.[2] These conditions, and his reluctance to implement the terms of the Wye Memorandum because the Palestinians had not fulfilled their part of it, became the primary bones of contention as negotiations with the Palestinians set in. The tight schedule set for the renewed negotiations (February 2000 for completing an interim agreement and September 2000 for the final one) were an additional obstacle.

Furthermore, neither of the two prime negotiators encouraged the trust of the other, as Barak's inconsistency was matched by Arafat's lack of integrity. The Palestinian Authority had failed to honour many of its commitments, such as the collection and destruction of illegal arms, the reduction of its military personnel, or the cessation of incitement. Whenever pressured by the United States or Israel, Arafat would undertake to arrest proven terrorists, or to curb incitement, announcing such measures in English to the foreign press, then refrain from doing so and reassure his own constituency when addressing it in Arabic. Barak, on the other hand, changed tactics with great frequency, each change overturning his previously announced policy. Thus he delayed implementing the second stage of the Wye Memorandum, then rescinded on the third stage and linked it to the final status stage. In October 1999, he raised the idea of a unilateral economic separation from the Palestinians, then rescinded that in November 1999, instead offering to establish the Palestinian capital in one of the villages bordering on

Jerusalem. He never handed over these villages to Palestinian control. By March 2000, Barak had given up on his previously stipulated schedule and considered an interim agreement by September 2000 on a demobilized but contiguous interim Palestinian state on 50 per cent of the area, a proposal which the Palestinians rejected outright. An Israeli withdrawal from 6.1 per cent of the area was carried out on 21 March 2000, yet building in the settlements continued uninterrupted.

Negotiations with the Syrians fared no better. Talks started in Washington in mid-December 1999, then continued in Shepherdstown from 3–10 January 2000, but broke down over a land strip around the Sea of Galilee which Israel refused to give up. Israel then withdrew unilaterally and rather hastily from southern Lebanon on 24 May 2000, leaving Hizbullah triumphant and probably a model for emulation by the Palestinians. The latter began resorting to violence on 12 May 2000, as preparations for the withdrawal from Lebanon were underway.

In April 2000, an impasse had been reached in Israeli–Palestinian negotiations. Arafat refused to accede to the annexation of settlement blocks by Israel and to the removal of the Palestinian capital from East Jerusalem to Abu Dis, while Israel published tenders for new homes to be built in settlements. Palestinian violence comprised suicide attacks in Israeli towns, as well as fire opened on Israeli military and civilian targets. When it broke out, it confirmed Israeli mistrust, while Israeli building plans in the settlements which it wished to annex fuelled Palestinian mistrust. In backchannel talks in Stockholm during May and June 2000, Israel offered a Palestinian state on 92 per cent of the territory, 10 per cent of which it would lease for 99 years, but the Palestinians remained adamant in their demand for 100 per cent of the territory, of the right of Palestinian refugees to return to Israel proper and of East Jerusalem becoming their capital. Thereupon, Barak changed tactics once more, proposing a temporary agreement on a sovereign Palestinian state on 50 per cent of the area for a period of 1–2 years until a framework agreement could be reached (the final one to be deferred to an unspecified date). Palestinian distrust seemed further justified by the weakness of the Israeli government, which was rent by internal strife between coalition partners and which was unbalanced by an almost general strike.

As shooting incidents and suicide attacks continued, Barak concluded in press interviews that the conflict was probably insoluble for the time being. Yet he also stated that the Palestinian state would have to be contiguous (meaning that many small settlements would have to be evacuated) and that Palestinian religious sensibilities in Jerusalem would have to be respected.[3] The inconsistency of these statements continued when, just a month later, Barak pressed for a summit at which all problems would be solved and the conflict would come to a final solution.

The failure of the Camp David Summit, held from 11–24 July 2000, is hardly surprising. The talks were preceded by a statement made by Barak in which he doubted the fitness of Arafat to be a partner for peace and by a press conference held by Barak at which he again made public his red lines. These were surely unwise steps to take prior to negotiations. Furthermore, the Israeli coalition collapsed just prior to the scheduled summit and because of opposition to it, leaving a minority government. In view of the latter, Arafat was probably sceptical about Barak's ability to carry out any promises made.

Since they were never made public, numerous Israeli, Palestinian and American participants' versions exist regarding the Israeli promises made. According to Israeli sources, Israel had offered the Palestinians over 90 per cent of the territory, had agreed to territorial exchange for the annexation of settlement blocks, to some partition of Jerusalem and to a sharing of sovereignty on the Temple Mount, as well as to the return of some Palestinian refugees on humanitarian grounds. Palestinian intellectuals countered that the 90 per cent of territory and the part of eastern Jerusalem offered were not to have been contiguous, the exchange of territory was to have been at a ratio of 1:9 in Israel's favour both in size and quality of land and that Israel had continued to shirk its responsibility for the Palestinian refugee problem. An American journalist and a former aide to President Clinton claimed that both sides were equally to blame for the failure. Others asserted that Barak had gambled on Palestinian recalcitrance in making these generous proposals. By 'showing up their true face', as he put it in television appearances, he could appeal to the Right in the impending elections and by his substantial concessions he could appeal to the Left. If that was his intention, the ruse did not succeed.

All these reasons for the breakdown of the Camp David Summit seem plausible, but fail to explain why Arafat resorted to such violence as a consequence, instead of just turning down the Israeli proposals or, better still, making some counter-proposals. The consistent refusal of the Palestinians to amend their Covenant was ignored in these analyses and may serve as an additional, if not crucial explanation for the Intifada al-Aqsa.

The Palestinian National Covenant of 1968 is a documented declaration of Palestinian identity and ideology.[4] Article 1 states the separateness of the Palestinian people within the Arab nation, namely its distinct identity, while Article 2 declares all Mandatory Palestine to be the Palestinian homeland; Articles 3, 7, 8 and 10 state its ideology, namely its ultimate aims and the means of attaining them, which are the retrieval of Palestine by armed struggle with Israel. An ostensible modification of the aims took place in 1988, when the declaration of the Palestinian state was leaked to the press, but it was never officially acknowledged. In the declaration, the Palestinians accepted the UN Partition Plan boundaries of 1947, which left large parts of Israel within the borders of the future Palestinian state. This concession was reiterated by Arafat in a statement to the UN General Assembly on 13 December 1988.

Subsequently, Palestinian ostensible relenting went one step further. In Chairman Arafat's letter to Prime Minister Rabin, dated 9 September 1993 and which formed part of the Oslo Accords, Arafat accepted UN Resolution 242, which confines the future Palestinian state to the territory outside the 1967 boundaries of Israel. In the same document, Arafat also undertook to replace violent struggle with peaceful negotiations and to submit to the PNC (Palestinian National Council) for approval the necessary changes in the Palestinian National Covenant, which would annul those articles inconsistent with the Oslo Accords. The latter Arafat meanwhile declared inoperative and no longer valid.

The PNC twice reiterated the invalidity of these articles, but the Covenant was never changed accordingly, despite Israel's repeated admonitions. On 24 April 1996, the PNC overwhelmingly voted in favour of annulling the call for the destruction of Israel, with the PNC legislative committee assigned the drafting of a new covenant to be submitted for approval within six months. The undertaking to redraft the Covenant was repeated in the Note for the Record attached to the Protocol signed in January 1997, after the Tunnel fiasco, then in an addendum to the Wye Memorandum of 25 October 1998 and finally in the presence of President Clinton in Gaza on 14 December 1998. But the actual redrafting never took place.

This procrastination may have been the result of intentional deception, or of a precautionary delay due to mistrust. In the latter case, increasing mutual distrust would have made any changes ever more difficult to effect. Even if one assumes that the Palestinian leadership had genuinely wished to make as dramatic a change in its strategy as to relinquish armed struggle and part of its declared homeland, it never took any steps to carry out such a policy while retaining its legitimacy. A leadership is accorded legitimacy by dint of being seen to implement the tenets of the ideology of its society and, thus, being the ultimate carrier of the society's identity. If circumstances demand a radical change in strategy, ideology and identity have to be adjusted so as to be in line with the new policy pursued. A change in ideological tenets, or core values, can come about in two ways. Firstly, it occurs as a total change, which is tantamount to a revolution, with an accompanying replacement of the leadership. Secondly, the extant leadership can retain its position by a reshuffle in the precedence of the core values, as Ben-Gurion had done so well.

Israel had at least made some attempts in this direction after the signing of the Oslo Accords, though hardly very successful ones. The Palestinians had made none. The omission to amend the Covenant is hardly as trivial and technical as was suggested by Palestinian spokespersons, Israeli peace supporters and outside observers, for a change in the Covenant is tantamount to a change in ideology. This would indeed have been difficult, given that Articles 16–18, 24 and 27–33 are the only ones which do not mention Israel as the enemy to be expelled from the region. Even these Articles are fairly martial in tone, but Articles 16–18 mention security, peace and human dignity. Security and peace could have been given top priority, Israel redefined from enemy to adversary and the final aim of a Palestinian state in the territory of Mandatory Palestine deferred to the distant unspecified future. That would have been one way to re-articulate Palestinian aims and identity without a loss of legitimacy by the leadership. Either intentionally, or out of ignorance on how to proceed, no attempt was made to do that. Rather, legitimacy was retained by the unchanged messages conveyed to the Palestinian people and by the unchanged Covenant. This would appear to be one reason why Arafat not merely rejected the Israeli proposals at Camp David, but also immediately called for an outbreak of violence. The Israeli concessions were made conditional on a final Palestinian waiving of all further demands, tantamount to a change of Palestinian aims (the size of their homeland) and the means to attain these (armed struggle). Arafat had been able to justify his negotiations with Israel as a change in tactics, but presumably felt that he could not afford to make a change in strategy incompatible with the ideas he stood for and which underpinned his leadership. Since the precedence of values had not been changed, the original tenets had to be implemented if his government was to retain its legitimacy.

Whatever the real causes of Palestinian recalcitrance and renewed violence, the Israeli public became fairly unanimous in its judgement that Arafat was not interested in peace and that his public would follow suit, whatever line he took. Support for the Oslo process dropped from an average of 50 per cent between the 17 May 1999 elections and the outbreak of violence on 12 May 2000 to 43.5 per cent at the end of May 2000, rose to 46.5 per cent just prior to the Camp David Summit and again dropped to 44.3 per cent after it.[5] Even prior to the outbreak of violence, the public had been ambivalent regarding the peace process. At a poll taken in early March 2000, only 32.1 per cent of the sample believed that the peace process would lead to peace with the Palestinians, yet 46.4 per cent supported the Oslo process.[6] Prior to the Camp David Summit, 49 per cent of respondents believed that the Palestinian leadership genuinely wanted peace, yet only 40 per cent of the same sample believed that an agreement would lead to a final solution of the conflict.[7] Subsequently, ambivalence was greatly reduced. After the Camp David Summit, the percentage of believers in the peaceful intentions of the Palestinians had dropped to 25 per cent, with 71 per cent regarding Arafat as a terrorist.[8] Sixty-one per cent of respondents had supported negotiations with the Palestinians prior to Camp David, dropping to 20 per cent some months later.[9] The majority of respondents (65 per cent) blamed the Palestinians for the failure of the Summit, and only 35 per cent of the same sample approved of the alleged concessions made by Barak.[10] Attitudes were obviously hardening as hope was disappearing. The past 50:50 split in Israeli society was being replaced by greater consensus on Rightist attitudes. The outcome of the elections on 6 February 2001 is the best indicator of that.

The failure of the Camp David Summit exacerbated Barak's shaky position as head of a minority government. The Right protested against his excessive concessions to the Palestinians. The Left suspected him of deceptively stopping short of the last necessary concessions, so that Israel would have its cake and eat it too: it would exhibit its genuine commitment to peace, yet need not concede anything because the Palestinians were the rejectionists. The above-mentioned polls indicate that the latter message was accepted by the Israeli public, but not so Barak's leadership. In order to regain the support of the Left, Barak announced a 'secular revolution' in August 2000, including the conscription of orthodox men, the introduction of public transport and commerce on Saturday and civil marriage. Nobody was deceived by this, since the minority government was unable to pass such laws. In turn, he appealed to the Right, hinting in a press interview that the accusations of the Left regarding his deceptive intentions had been well founded.[11] None of these measures helped.

In early October, the opposition tabled a bill for early elections, while the sporadic fighting accelerated to a low-intensity Holy War. In late September 2000, Ariel Sharon, the former general and leader of Likud, known for his belligerency, paid an official visit to the Temple Mount, surrounded by a large entourage. The Moslem religious establishment of both Palestinian and Israeli Arabs immediately branded this event as a threat to the mosques on the Mount. Riots broke out on the following day, significantly named 'Intifada al-Aqsa' (uprising of the al-Aqsa mosque). The religious aspect of the uprising could and did mobilize a much wider public to much greater frenzy. The police shot dead 13 Israeli Arab rioters, a measure as unacceptable in a democratic society as it was unwise. It further alienated Israeli Arabs, some of whom have since joined the Palestinian Intifada, including one suicide bomber. Palestinian attacks increased in scale, with suicide bombings inside Israel, attacks on settlements and fire on Gilo, a neighbourhood in southern Jerusalem.

Barak then tried to shore up his position by calling for a national unity government, but neither One Israel nor Likud would join it. Instead, the

Knesset dispersal law received its first reading on 27 October 2000. Meanwhile, Israeli retaliatory measures intensified. In November 2000, it began pinpointed killings of Palestinian terrorists, then retaliated against the attack on a school bus by an air raid on Palestinian installations in the Gaza Strip. Thereupon, Egypt recalled its ambassador and Jordan refrained from replacing its ambassador, who had completed his assignment in September 2000.

Under attack from all sides, Barak made a last attempt to stay in power. On 9 December 2000 he announced on television his personal resignation and new prime ministerial elections within 60 days. Since only serving MKs could run in prime ministerial elections, it seems that Barak had chosen this step in order to exclude Netanyahu from the contest, considering him a much more formidable adversary than the ageing Sharon. Popularity ratings indicated as much, though even Sharon became an increasingly preferred candidate. The slight score difference of 41:38 in favour of Netanyahu against Barak after the Camp David Summit had grown to 46:29, while the difference of 43:31 in favour of Barak against Sharon had only just reversed to 35:37.[12]

By that time, Barak's own constituency was losing faith in him and preferring Shimon Peres, the Nobel Peace Prize laureate. Peres had not topped Netanyahu in popularity ratings, but once the latter had been neutralized, the 45:41 preference of Peres over Sharon seemed impressive, compared to the 46:28 preference of Sharon over Barak.[13] Yet Barak would not step down and Peres could not put forward his candidacy unless ten MKs endorsed it, and that was prevented. In a last attempt to retain, or rather regain, his position, Barak initiated further meetings with the Palestinian leadership. A summit meeting with Arafat and President Mubarak of Egypt, held in Sharm a-Sheikh on 28 December 2000, produced no agreement. Neither did the marathon talks held in Taba from 21–24 January 2001. Days prior to the elections, Barak still tried to hold another summit meeting with Arafat in the hope of a turnabout in public opinion, but neither occurred. In fact, he was losing not only support, but also legitimacy by offering concessions to the Palestinians while leading an interim minority government. Sharon won the prime ministerial elections, held on 6 February 2001, gaining 62.4 per cent of the votes, as against 37.6 per cent for Barak.

The boycott of the elections by Israeli Arabs contributed to the defeat of Barak, as did the intensifying war with the Palestinians and what seemed like frantic attempts by Barak to appease them. Sharon won, despite his advanced age and blemished record in the Lebanon war of 1982, because he promised to restore security and bring about an eventual peace at a time when Barak had failed to provide either. Known for his forceful military actions in the past, the public voted for Sharon. His messages prior to the elections had appealed to both hard-liners and the moderate centre. He would accede to a Palestinian state, but in 42 per cent of the territory only and within the framework of a long-term interim plan; meanwhile, he would leave all settlements in place, including remote, small ones.[14] Negotiations could resume and his plan discussed only after Palestinian violence had ceased completely. He noted further that, since the Palestinians had never reconciled themselves to the existence of Israel, whose Jewish heritage was the basis of its legitimate presence in its historic homeland, military operations would probably be necessary to enforce the end of violence. Terror could be eradicated by targeting terrorists.[15]

Sharon won partly by default because Barak's peace efforts had failed so miserably. Yet, this cannot be the only explanation for a mandate granted by 62.4 per cent of the largely Jewish electorate (most Israeli Arabs boycotted the elections), when Barak had won 56.8 per cent, including Israeli Arabs (over 15 per cent of the electorate, most of whom had voted for the candidate promising peace). During the campaign, Sharon had managed to obliterate his former image of an extremist warmonger and unconditional patron of the settlers and their aims. His messages did not appeal to hard-liners, for they contained the possibility of a future Palestinian state, though under fairly restrictive conditions. Rather, they appealed to the centre, which had probably been swollen by Leftists disillusioned with the peace process. Compared to his former image, Sharon now seemed moderate. Moreover, he conducted a gentlemanly campaign, careful to avoid unnecessary offence to either his domestic adversaries of the Left or to the Palestinians, with whom he was willing to negotiate conditionally. These tactics commanded respect, belatedly even of the Leftist and Centrist press.[16]

Sharon's new image was further enhanced by his acts after the elections, which remained consistent with his previous messages. This contrasted favourably with the inconstancy of Barak, who stepped down as party leader and MK on 6 February 2001, retracted on 11 February 2001 and wished to join the Sharon government as Minister of Defence. The outrage of his party finally induced him to resign on 20 February 2001. Meanwhile, Sharon offered to form a wall-to-wall national unity government, to which Labour acceded. The coalition also included Shas, the Rightist Ha-ihud Ha-leumi–Yisrael Beiteinu, the religious Torah Judaism, Yisrael Ba'aliya and another two small parties. Shimon Peres was appointed Foreign Minister and Benyamin Ben-Eliezer of Labour was appointed Minister of Defence. One guideline of the new government was a complete freeze on new settlements, but not on the extension of existing ones.

Subsequently, some balance was struck between US admonitions to contain the violence by renewed negotiations and intensified retaliatory operations against Palestinian attacks. The US-sponsored Mitchell Report, made public at the end of May 2001, recommended a complete cease-fire, followed by a freeze on all building in settlements and renewed negotiations thereafter. Sharon rejected the second phase, yet announced a unilateral cease-fire on condition that Israel was not provoked any further. Arafat agreed to the cease-fire only after a particularly vicious Palestinian suicide attack on 1 June 2001. During the relative calm that ensued, George Tennet, head of the CIA, drafted a cease-fire plan which Israel accepted, the Palestinians rejected at first, then signed. Israel lifted its closure on Palestinian towns, but Palestinian sporadic attacks and fire continued. In response, Israel renewed its targeting of Palestinians it held responsible for organizing these attacks. It also renewed its siege on Palestinian towns and disrupted Palestinian traffic in order to stop infiltration of suicide bombers, foiling three such attempts but failing to do so in Jerusalem on 9 August 2001, when 17 persons died and 130 were injured. In response to the latter, Israel also closed down Orient House, the symbol of the Palestinian political presence in East Jerusalem. Violence continued unabated, each side vindicating itself: Israel claimed to exercise restraint by abstaining from air raids and from prolonged actions inside Palestinian territory, while the Palestinians justified any action against Israel as the legitimate right of a people opposing foreign occupation. The terrorist attack on the World Trade Centre on 11 September 2001 produced only a temporary lull in Palestinian terrorist attacks on Israeli civilians.

For Israeli identity, the failure of the Camp David summit constituted a watershed. Its ramifications became obvious after the 2001 elections, with polls indicating an unprecedented support for Likud at the expense of almost all Centrist, all Jewish Leftist and all extreme Rightist and religious parties. If elections had been held in May 2001, 39.2 per cent of respondents would have opted for Likud, compared to 15.8 per cent in the 1999 elections. In July of that year, the same pollsters found a support of 36 per cent for Likud[17] despite the absence of security and peace which Sharon had promised to supply. In fact, the fire and suicide attacks intensified during his tenure and Israelis were well aware of this. If 33 per cent of respondents had hoped for an improvement in security in late March 2001, that percentage dropped to 10 per cent in August; the 14 per cent expecting a deterioration in security in March rose to 52 per cent in August; the 43 per cent expecting no change dropped to 35 per cent.[18] Yet, Sharon's support did not waver and actually increased for a time, from 44 per cent in late March 2001 to 62 per cent in early June, dropping again to 49 per cent in mid-August. Moreover, the support for Sharon among Centrist party voters (in the 1999 elections) was equal to that of Rightist party voters and sometimes even exceeded it.[19] Equally, Sharon enjoyed extensive support for his policies regarding the Palestinians, even though, or just because they alternated between hard-line militancy and restraint. Seventy-nine per cent of respondents supported the policy of no negotiations under fire in April 2001[20] and 58 per cent in August.[21] Although 51 per cent of respondents supported Sharon's policy of restraint, 51 per cent considered measures against the Palestinians to be too soft, and 76 per cent supported the pinpointed targeting of terrorists.[22] Sixty-one per cent of respondents shared the assessment of Sharon that negotiations with the Palestinians would not lead to peace, yet 60 per cent supported his decision to permit cease-fire discussions between Foreign Minister Peres and Arafat.[23]

The differential support for Sharon provides interesting insights into the public mood. According to polls, the public was initially as dissatisfied with government handling of economic and social issues as with the security tactics of Sharon, though not with his political handling of the situation, but that changed over time, with his security tactics enjoying increasing support.[24] Furthermore, support for Sharon among Leftist party voters increased from 31 per cent in May 2001 to 43 per cent in August.[25] This does not necessarily mean that the Israeli public has moved to the extreme Right regarding the Israeli–Palestinian conflict. The doubling support for Likud in July 2001, mentioned above, was at the expense of all parties, including the extreme Rightist ones. Indeed, the extreme Rightist Ha-ihud Ha-leumi–Yisrael Beiteinu party threatened to resign from the coalition in protest against government restraint.

Presumably, Likud has become identified with the more balanced policy pursued by Sharon, although it has not enjoyed a blank endorsement. Sixty per cent of respondents still supported a unilateral separation from the Palestinians in 2001, compared to 66 per cent in 1998,[26] though Sharon and Likud have rejected this option since it would mean evacuation of settlements. Moreover, once government moderation was called into question, support for its action dropped, again revealing a split, though not the old one between Left and Right but rather between moderates and extremists. Israel took very strong measures after the assassination by Palestinians of Rehavam Zeevi, the Minister of Tourism, on 17 October 2001. It entered and encircled six Palestinian towns and arrested members of terrorist organizations. Palestinians were killed and wounded in the ensuing fire. Subsequently, Israeli forces entered Ramallah, where Arafat was staying temporarily, and placed tanks at a short range from his headquarters. Israel has been preventing him from going abroad or from going back to his residence in Gaza until he apprehends the murderers of Minister Zeevi. Rumours have spread that Sharon was intending to topple the Palestinian authority and exile Arafat. Yet a poll conducted while the above measures were underway showed only 39 per cent of respondents supporting an all-out war, then perceived to be government policy, while 42 per cent supported accelerated peace efforts and 12 per cent supported a continuation of the status quo.[27]

The greater support given Sharon by voters of Left and Centre parties seems to corroborate other data which demonstrate public disillusion with the peace process rather than broader support for militancy. As already noted, support for the Oslo process, which held an average of 43.6 per cent while various summits and talks were still going on, has dropped to an average of 34 per cent since the Camp David Summit.[28] The percentage of respondents believing the Palestinians to be a partner for peace dropped from 61.5 per cent in March 1999 to 27 per cent in March 2001.[29] The percentage of respondents regarding Arafat as a terrorist rather than a statesman rose from 42 per cent in 1998 to 71 per cent in 2001.[30] The Israeli public had never been naive about Palestinian intentions, despite its initial support of the Oslo Accords. But distrust has certainly increased, especially since the failure of Camp David. In 1997, 62.2 per cent of respondents did not believe the Palestinians to have reconciled themselves to the existence of Israel; a figure which rose to 75 per cent in 2001.[31] Nevertheless, in 1999 61.2 per cent of respondents believed the Palestinians to be genuinely interested in peace with Israel and 49 per cent still believed so prior to Camp David, but that has dropped to 25 per cent in 2001.[32]

As already noted, the increased cohesiveness of Israeli society extends beyond solidarity *vis-à-vis* a threatening enemy. A marked dulling can be observed in the fracture which had been so prominent. The groups contending for a renewed articulation of Israeliness have not disappeared, but at least some of them seem to be seeking a compromise rather than a decisive victory. This holds particularly true for the religious–secular rift.

When the idea of the 'secular revolution' was raised, 14 per cent of self-declared secular respondents opposed the operation of buses on Saturday and 20 per cent opposed the operation of shopping malls on Saturday. Given the liberal image which secular Israelis project, such tolerance among them is not nearly as surprising as is that of the religious respondents. Of the latter, 47 per cent supported opening shopping malls on Saturday and 52 per cent supported the running of buses on Saturday.[33] On the assumption that they themselves would not use these facilities on Saturday, this indicates an impressive amount of tolerance, something religious persons in Israel had not been noted for in the past.

Similarly, public confrontations between the religious and secular sectors have subsided. As noted, the High Court of Justice refused to rule on the conscription of orthodox Yeshiva students, ordering the Knesset to legislate on the matter within one year. The latter has evaded legislation, postponing it several times, and prefers an agreed solution. Subsequently, a contingent of orthodox youths volunteered for full military service and a second contingent has followed suit, without much protest from the orthodox establishment. Nor have there been any vociferous attacks on the Supreme Court by the orthodox, especially since May 2001 when its president, Aharon Barak, retracted his controversial statement that everything was judicable.

Prominent members of the young generation in the national religious camp, whose leadership had turned to stricter orthodoxy (Hardal), have more recently become the bridgehead for renewed accommodation with secular Israelis through attempts to introduce modern liberal values into their worldview. At the Lavi conferences they have been holding, rabbis have spoken of re-incorporating the universal values of the Prophets in modern religious practice, such as equality of women and making Jewish law relevant to present circumstances.[34] Furthermore, a group of young national religious rabbis, calling themselves 'Rabanei Tsoar', have been holding wedding ceremonies and proper religious services in community centres rather than in synagogues in order to render them more user-friendly to the secular.[35]

The hard core of the settlers, the Gush Emunim faithful, are a marker of the rift between secular and religious Israelis, as well as between hawks and doves. Developments among them also point in the same direction. On the one hand, the settlers enjoy increased public sympathy because of their greater exposure to Palestinian attacks. The initiative of some of their younger generation to set up illegal extensions of settlements at strategic points has not been as censored by the peace camp and by the government as in the past. On the other hand, some of the second-generation settlers have decided to abandon militancy and are volunteering for educational projects in the periphery in order to demonstrate their involvement in Israeli society, rather than their single-mindedness.[36] This may be a tactical, temporary step to garner sympathy and political support, or a genuine attempt at closing the rift. Time will tell.

At the same time, the search of secular Israelis for Jewish values has become more focused. Some of them have turned to the Reform movement, which offers a highly modernized version of Jewish religious practice. Others have established communities of secular persons studying Jewish religious texts. They want to re-identify with religious tradition by adapting it to modernity.[37]

The most significant attempt at accommodation is the 'Foundation for a New Social Charter Between Observant Jews and Freethinkers in Israel', compiled by Ruth Gabison, a professor of law at the Hebrew University, and Yaakov Medan, a Hardal rabbi.[38] Firstly, it must be noted that Rabbi Medan belongs to that sector of the national religious camp which is strictly observant of religious laws, while Professor Gabison is a completely secular person. As the two state in the introduction, they undertook this project because of their apprehension that the growing rift on religious grounds might lead to alienation of secular Israelis from Judaism and eventually undermine the Jewish nature of the state. Professor Gabison emphasized that such a development would rob Israel of its justification to exist, thus depriving Israelis of any social identity. Therefore, the Charter attempts to accommodate both sides, not so much by compromise as by avoiding coercion being exercised by either side.

Secondly, each paragraph of the Charter was finalized after extensive consultations with various teams representing all sectors of Israeli society, except for the ultra-orthodox and the Reform and Conservative movements (the latter two are unacceptable to the Israeli religious community and the former is totally uncompromising; followers of the three comprise a small minority only). The Charter deals mainly with those religious laws which most distinguish Jews *vis-à-vis* others. Thus, it proposes changes in the Law of Return, the law of naturalization and of marriage, to allow for a distinction between citizenship and membership in the Jewish religious community. It also underwrites observance of the *Shabat* in the market-place and by public institutions, but does not extend it to all private enterprises. The Charter also deals with other controversial issues in the same spirit, such as secular burial, religious councils, prayer at the Western Wall, etc.

Even if never adopted as a basis for legislation, the very compilation of the Charter formalizes the search for identity based on Jewishness discussed above. These initiatives strive for greater cohesiveness, not merely between the religious and the secular, but also between the veteran society and the immigrants, mainly those from the former Soviet Union. That rift has been closing too, as tragic circumstances underlined. One suicide attack occurred at a discotheque frequented by immigrant youths; a Russian passenger aircraft carrying immigrant vacationers to Siberia was shot down accidentally by a Ukrainian missile. The sympathy and help extended by veteran Israelis expressed unquestioning solidarity, also felt and admitted by the bereaved immigrants. Furthermore, the orthodox establishment is reported to have reached out to Soviet immigrants, where it had previously dubbed them apostates. An orthodox educational system, named 'Shuvu' (return), includes sciences and mathematics in its curriculum in addition to the usual religious studies. Most of its science and mathematics teachers are themselves Soviet immigrants, as are a substantial number of its pupils.[39]

The rift between Orientals and Westerners has not closed, but its manifestations are much more muted, with an attempt to translate it into socio-economic terms. Shas strategy is an important indicator of this trend because this party claims to represent the protest of Orientals. Shas is taking steps to change its image of a sectoral orthodox–Oriental party to one representing the interests of the poor and of the entire society. In an interview published in two Arabic newspapers,[40] its spiritual leader Rabbi Ovadia Yosef voiced moderate views on the Israeli–Palestinian conflict and was said to plan a meeting with Moslem and Christian clerics in that spirit.[41] In the present economic crisis in Israel, its political leader Eli Yishai, who serves as Minister of Interior, is not just using his clout to increase funding for the Shas school system. He is also appealing to the working class in general by trying to curb the growing unemployment; he is exerting pressure to increase the budget deficit and to protect the poor by fighting against cuts in education and in health and social benefits.

Such encouraging signs of growing solidarity notwithstanding, the feeling of unity seems to be confined to matters of security, though cracks are seeming to appear even there. A group of reserve officers publicized a letter sent to the Chief-of-Staff in which they announced their refusal to serve in the occupied territories on ethical grounds. Similarly, the Speaker of the Knesset has made public his intention to address the Palestinian parliament as a gesture of reconciliation while the government is accusing the Palestinian Authority of direct responsibility for the recent suicide attacks in Jerusalem, Tel-Aviv and elsewhere.

In other spheres, fracture has erupted again. The Prime Minister, though enjoying continuous impressive support in polls, has been unable to get the state budget passed in the Knesset. Israel is undergoing a very serious economic crisis. In 2001, the GDP growth was –0.5 per cent, exports dropped by 13.1 per cent and private consumption by over 3 per cent, the current account deficit increased to 4.1 per cent of GNP and unemployment rose to 9.9 per cent. Under such circumstances, and with growing security expenses, a tightening of the belt by politicians and by the public seems in order. Instead, rather than foregoing financial privileges and using political clout for increased funding and power, the various political parties have been vying for greater slices of the dwindling economic cake. Strikes for increased salaries or benefits have multiplied. Parties have been threatening to resign from the coalition unless their demands are met, making any tightening of the budget virtually impossible, to the short- or long-term detriment of the population at large. Furthermore, public trust in the government has dropped to an all-time low, from 63 per cent of respondents in 1996 to 37 per cent in January 2002; trust in the Knesset dropped from 62 per cent to 25 per cent respectively and trust in the political parties from 36 per cent to 16 per cent respectively.[42]

Some intellectuals and public figures have not been deceived by the apparent cohesiveness, which seems to be a result of apprehension and defiance rather than a unity due to common values.[43] The 'Kineret Charter' is an attempt to extract the values from former Israeli identities on which consensus can still be reached by formulating a constitutional statement. Incidentally, Professor Gabison and Rabbi Medan have taken part in this initiative. Regional councils held public discussions on the various contentious issues with local populations in order to obtain the necessary feedback for their proposals submitted to a public council of 100 members. These comprise all sectors of Jewish–Israeli society, including the orthodox, and include academics, politicians and public figures.

The 'Kineret Charter' asserts that the Jewish people have a moral and historical right to their own state in Israel; that Israel is a Jewish-democratic state and that there is no contradiction between these two concepts, so that it respects the rights of its Arab minority; that Israel strives for peace; that it must revive its original emphasis on social justice and respect the variety of its population.[44] The need to formulate such a charter underlines the realization that the social fracture is serious indeed. Professor Yuli Tamir, a former minister in the Barak government and an initiator of the charter, made this quite clear. She stated that the government had become inept in remedying the ongoing crisis which might break Israeli society apart, so that responsible citizens had had to take this initiative.[45]

The efforts made to recreate Israeli identity ignore one major factor in the present crisis, namely the continued absence of clearly demarcated borders. Sharon and his government concede to a future Palestinian state, but refuse to outline its nature and extent. In fact, Sharon vehemently rejects the widely supported proposal of a unilateral separation from the Palestinians because any fence would prejudge the future borders of Israel. And as long as Israelis do not know where the territory ends in which they are by right, they are unable to know who they are. As far as Israeli identity is concerned, even an interim solution, such as a cease-fire, which delineates temporary borders, seems preferable to the present blurring which each contending sector of society can interpret according to its own values, by now almost diametrically opposed to those of all others. Some accommodation with the Palestinians and resort to the charters mentioned above, or future ones formulated in the same vein, will hopefully become the focus for a re-articulated Israeli identity, which must surely incorporate Jewish values and some democratic ones, however vaguely defined. This is likely to be a temporary identity once more, but that would merely continue a phenomenon with which Israelis have become familiarized.

NOTES

1. D. Harman and J. Barak, 'Netanyahu is Living the Truman Show', *Jerusalem Post*, 11 May 1999; H. Kim, 'One Need Not Place a Teacher of Citizenship into Shas Classes', *Ha-arets*, 18 June 1999.
2. D. Harman and J. Barak, 'Netanyahu is Living the Truman show'; H. Kim, 'One Need Not Place a Teacher'.
3. A. Shavit, 'The Question of the PM', *Ha-arets*, 19 May 2000; D. Landau, 'The Whole Truth', *Ha-arets*, 30 June 2000.
4. See Y. Harkabi, 'The Position of the Palestinians in the Israeli–Arab Conflict and Their National Covenant (1968), *New York University Journal of International Law and Politics*, Vol. 3, No. 1, 1970, pp.209–44.
5. Computed from the Peace Index Project published monthly in *Ha-arets*.
6. Peace Index Project, *Ha-arets*, 6 March 2000.
7. Peace Index Project, *Ha-arets*, 5 July 2000.
8. Peace Index Project, *Ha-arets*, 6 November 2000.
9. Peace Index Project, *Ha-arets*, 5 July 2000, 6 November 2000.
10. Peace Index Project, *Ha-arets*, 7 August 2000.
11. H. Keinon and J. Barak, 'If There's an Agreement, It Will Be Very Painful', *Jerusalem Post*, 29 September 1900.
12. Gallup Polls, *Ma'ariv*, 8 September 1900, 1 December 2000.
13. Gallup, *Ma'ariv*, 22 December 1900.
14. R. Man, 'A Virtual Plan', *Ma'ariv*, 19 January 2001.
15. A. Shavit,'A Choice Between Two Worlds', *Ha-arets*, 2 February 2001.
16. See, for example, G. Samet, 'The Big Question', *Ha-arets*, 7 March 2001; Miberg, R., 'The Man Without a Tick', *Ma'ariv*, 2 March 2001.
17. Gallup, *Ma'ariv*, 25 May 2001, 20 July 2001.
18. Gallup, *Ma'ariv*, 30 March 2001, 10 August 2001.
19. Gallup, *Ma'ariv*, 30 March 2001, 8 June 2001, 17 August 2001.
20. Peace Index Project, *Ha-arets*, 4 April 2001. Gallup, in *Ma'ariv* of 27 April 2001, found 72 per cent supporting this policy.
21. Gallup, *Ma'ariv*, 10 August 2001.
22. Gallup, *Ma'ariv*, 5 June 2001, 17 August 2001, 10 August 2001 respectively.
23. Gallup, *Ma'ariv*, 8 August 2001, 17 August 2001.
24. In March 2001, 44% of respondents approved of him generally and of his politics and only 34% of his security policy and 31% of his socio-economic policy. In July, the support amounted to 58%, 42% and 29% respectively. See Gallup, *Ma'ariv*, 30 March 2001, 6 July 2001.
25. Gallup, *Ma'ariv*, 25 May 2001, 10 August 2001.
26. Peace Project Index, *Ha-arets*, 2 December 1998, 4 July 2001.
27. Gallup, *Ma'ariv*, 7 December 2001.
28. Computed from the Peace Index Project published monthly in *Ha-arets*.
29. Peace Index Project, *Ha-arets*, 17 March 1999; Gallup, *Ma'ariv*, 30 March 2001.
30. Peace Index Project, *Ha-arets*, 3 August 1998, 5 March 2001.
31. Peace Index Project, *Ha-arets*, 4 September 1997, 4 April 2001.
32. Poll of the Tami Steinmetz Centre and Jerusalem Media and Communication reported in B. Lynfield, 'Most Israelis See a PA as Genuine Peace Partner', *Jerusalem Post*, 17 March 1999; Peace Index Project, *Ha-arets*, 5 July 2000, 4 April 2001.
33. Smith, *Globs*, 13 September 2000, 17 September 2000.
34. H. Shapiro, 'Stretching Halacha to the Limit', *Jerusalem Post*, 6 October 1999; D. Weinberg, 'Searching for Spirituality', *Jerusalem Post*, 10 October 1999; M. Kave, 'To Incorporate and Draw Near', *Ha-arets*, 17 May 2001.
35. Y. Sheleg, 'Kol Nidrei and Asrei and One Understands the Text', *Ha-arets*, 5 October 2000; Y. Sheleg, *The New Religious Jews: Recent Developments Among Observant Jews in Israel* (Jerusalem: Keter, 2000) pp.54–93.
36. N. Shragai, 'From Settlement on Hillsides to Settlement in the Hearts', *Ha-arets*, 2 December 2001.
37. T. Rotem, 'Everyone Will Choose His Preference from Judaism', *Ha-arets*, 13 October 2000.
38. The project was sponsored by the Yitzhak Rabin Center and the Shalom Hartman Institute. The Charter is not yet published. A draft of it is dated June 2001.
39. A. Isakova, 'Not All of Them Eat Pork', *Ma'ariv*, 13 November 2001.

40. Interview published in *Al-Shark al-Awsat* and in *Al-Watan*, quoted in J. Hugi, 'I Am Willing to Meet Any Religious Leader in Order to Stop the Bloodshed', *Ma'ariv*, 23 October 2001.
41. M. Rabat, 'Rabbi Ovadia Will Act Against Terrorism with Christian and Moslem Clerics', *Ma'ariv*, 26 October 2001.
42. Peace Index Project, *Ha-arets*, 7 January 2002.
43. This assessment is substantiated by polling data. In September 2001, 70% of respondents expressed anxiety about the future of the State due to the deteriorating security situation, yet 70% also believed that Israeli society was steadfast nevertheless. See Gallup, *Ma'ariv*, 14 September 2001.
44. The 'Kineret Charter' was distributed as an attachment to the daily press in January 2002.
45. Y. Tamir, 'In Lieu of the Government and the Knesset', *Ha-arets*, 1 January 2002.

Bibliography

A Handbook of Youth Leaders: The Month of Elul (Jerusalem: Youth & Hehalutz Department of the Zionist Organization, 1955).

Adar, A. and H. Adler, 'Teaching Values at Immigrant Children Schools', in S.N. Eisenstadt *et al.* (eds), *Education and Society in Israel* (Jerusalem: Akademon, 1968), pp.57–86 [Hebrew].

Aderet, A., 'Trends and Struggles Within Israeli Youth', *Niv-Ha-Kvutsa*, Vol. 4, No. 4 (1955), pp.714–29 [Hebrew].

Adler, H., 'Secondary School As a Socially and Educationally Selective Factor' (Hebrew), in S.N. Eisenstadt *et al.* (eds), *Education and Society in Israel*, (Jerusalem: Akademon, 1968), pp.215–25.

Agassi, Y., 'Not Normal', *Politika*, No. 49 (1993) [Hebrew].

Ahad Haam, 'Flesh and Spirit', in his, *At the Crossroads* (Berlin: Juedischer Verlag, 1921), pp.222–32 [Hebrew].

—— , 'The Time Has Come', in L. Simon (ed.), *Essays on Zionism and Judaism* (London: Routledge, 1922), pp.91–113.

—— , 'A Spiritual Centre', in L. Simon (ed.), *Essays on Zionism and Judaism* (London: Routledge, 1922), pp.120–9.

Alcalay, A., *After Jews and Arabs* (Minneapolis: University of Minnesota Press, 1993).

Allon, Y., 'The West Bank and Gaza Within the Framework of a Middle East Peace Settlement', *Middle East Review*, Vol. 12, No. 2 (1979/80), pp.15–18.

Amishai, H.M., 'Talk of Oldsters', *Shdemot*, No. 38 (1970), pp.5–11 [Hebrew].

Anderson, B., *Imagined Communities: Reflections on the Origins and Spread of Nationalism* (London: Verso, 1983).

Aran G., 'Jewish Zionist Fundamentalism: The Bloc of the Faithful in Israel (Gush Emunim)', in M.E. Marty and S. Appleby (eds), *Fundamentalism Observed* (Chicago: University of Chicago Press, 1991), pp.265–344.

Arian, A., *The Choosing People: Voting Behavior in Israel* (Cleveland: Case Western Reserve University Press, 1973).

Ariel, Y., 'We Must Change Course', *Nekuda*, No. 174 (1994), pp.14–17 [Hebrew].

—— , 'Was the Aguda Method Right?', *Nekuda*, No. 175 (1994), pp.16–19 [Hebrew].

—— , 'Towards a New National Revival', *Nekuda*, No. 181 (1994), pp.30–3 [Hebrew].

Arieli, J., 'Drift or Mastery', *New Outlook* (October 1969), pp.14–16. [Hebrew]

Aspects of the Palestinian Problem, Information Briefing 29 (Jerusalem: Israel Information Centre, 1974).

Avi-Hai, A., *Ben-Gurion: State Builder* (Jerusalem: Academic Press, 1974).

Aviner, R. 'Renewal, Not Revolution', *Nekuda*, No. 217 (1998), pp.28–31 [Hebrew].

Ayali, M., 'Where is Sincerity, Whence Wholeness?', *Shdemot*, No. 32 (1969), pp.128–9.

B.H., 'Zionism is Alive', *Ba-ma'ale*, Nos 6–7, (1949), p.122.

Bacciocco, E.J., *The New Left in America: Reform and Revolution 1956 to 1970* (Stamford: Hoover Institution, 1974).

Bar-Lev, M. and P. Kedem, 'Religious Observance Amongst Jewish University Students in Israel', *Megamot*, Vol. 28, Nos 2–3 (1984), pp.265–79 [Hebrew].

Barnea, Y., 'The New Jew as an Immanent Contradiction', *Shdemot*, No. 126/1 (1993), pp. 24–5 [Hebrew].

Bar-Ner, U., 'New Israeliness', *Shdemot*, No. 126/1 (1993), pp.55–6.

Bar-On, M., 'The Winter Years 74–77', *Politika*, No. 51 (1993), pp.38–41 [Hebrew].

——, *Personal Signature: Moshe Dayan in the Six Day War and After* (Tel-Aviv: Yedi'ot Ahronot, 1997) [Hebrew].

Barzel, A., 'Ways of the Youth Movement in Israel', *Niv Ha-Kvutsa*, Vol. 1, No. 4 (1952), pp.91–4 [Hebrew].

Bar-Zohar, M., *Ben-Gurion* (Tel-Aviv: Am Oved, 1978) [Hebrew].

Bauman, Z., 'Soil, Blood and Identity', *The Sociological Review*, Vol. 40, No. 4 (1992), pp.675–701.

Beeri, D., 'The End Has Come to the Common Road of Secular Zionism and the Doctrine of Rabbi Kuk', *Nekuda*, No. 181 (1994), pp.14–18 [Hebrew].

Begin, M., 'Concepts and Problems in Foreign Policy', *Ha-uma*, Vol. 16 (1966), pp.461–87 [Hebrew].

Beilin, Y., *Touching Peace* (Tel-Aviv: Miskal, 1997) [Hebrew].

Benari, D. 'The Likud Will Lead, But the Road Will Be Ours', *Nekuda*, No. 166 (1993), pp.18–22 [Hebrew].

Ben-Artzi, H. 'A New Gush Emunim', *Nekuda*, No. 180 (1994), pp.30–1 [Hebrew].

Ben-David, Y., 'Membership in Youth Movements and Social Status', in S.N. Eisenstadt *et al.* (eds), *The Social Structure of Israel* (Jerusalem: Akademon, 1966), pp.457–81 [Hebrew].

Ben-Gurion, D., 'Rights of Jews and Others in Palestine', *Der Yidisher Kempfer*, No. 4 (1918), pp.68–73 [Yiddish].

——, *Vision and Way* (Tel-Aviv: Mapai Publication, 1951–57) [Hebrew].

——, 'Affinity to the Glory of Israel', *Vision and Way* (Tel-Aviv: Mapai Publications, 1951–57), p.63 [Hebrew].

——, *In Battle* (Tel-Aviv: Am Oved, 1957) [Hebrew].

——, *When Israel Fought* (Tel-Aviv: Am Oved 1957) [Hebrew].

——, 'Investigating an Issue', *Hazut*, Vol. 3 (1957), p.29 [Hebrew].

——, *Letters to Paula and the Children* (Tel-Aviv: Am Oved, 1968) [Hebrew].

——, *Uniqueness and Vocation* (Tel-Aviv: Ma'arahot, 1971) [Hebrew].

——, *War Diary* (Tel-Aviv: Ministry of Defence, 1982) [Hebrew].

Ben-Yehuda, B., *Foundations and Ways* (Jerusalem: Jewish National Fund, 1952) [Hebrew].

Ben-Yehuda, H., 'Attitude Change and Policy Transformation: Yitzhak Rabin and the Palestinian Question', in E. Karsh (ed.), *From Rabin to Nenatyahu: Israel's Troubled Agenda* (London: Frank Cass, 1996), pp.201–24.

Berdichewsky, M.J., *Collected Essays* (Tel-Aviv: Am Oved, 1952) [Hebrew].

Bleicher, M. 'We Don't Fight Over Hebron, But Over the State of Israel and Its Soul', *Nekuda*, No. 202 (February 1997), pp.16–19.

Bloch, M.H.A. (ed.), *A Book to Make the Sleeping Speak: Opinions of Torah Scholars Opposed to Zionism* (New York: Tiferet, 1959) [Hebrew].

Blue-White Papers (London: The World Union of Zionist Revisionists, 1935).

Borochov, B., 'Class Conflict and the National Question', in B. Borochov, *Collected Essays* (Tel-Aviv: Marx-Engels Publications, 1934), pp.13–48 [Hebrew].

——, 'Bases of Proletarian Zionism (Our Platform)', in B. Borochov, *Collected Essays* (Tel-Aviv: Marx-Engels Publications, 1934), pp.51–199 [Hebrew].

——, *Collected Writings* (Tel-Aviv: Ha-kibuts Ha-meuhad/Sifriyat Ha-po'alim, 1955) [Hebrew].

Boyarin, D. and J. Boyarin, 'The People of Israel Has No Homeland', *Teoriya U-bikoret*, No. 5 (1994), pp.79–104 [Hebrew].

Brecher, M., 'Eban and Israeli Foreign Policy: Diplomacy, War and Disengagement', in B. Frankel (ed.), *A Restless Mind: Essays in Honour of Amos Perlmutter* (London: Frank Cass, 1996), pp.104–43.

Brenner, Y.H., *Collected Writings*, Vol. 7 (Tel-Aviv: Am Oved, 1946) [Hebrew].

Broyer, Rabbi M. 'I Don't Understand the Voice of Despair Among Us', *Nekuda*, No. 184 (1995), pp.12–16 [Hebrew].

Buber, M., 'Policy and Ethics', *Ba'ayot* (April 1945), pp.110–13 [Hebrew].

——, *Israel und Palaestina: zur Geschichte einer Idee* (Zurich: Artemis, 1950).

Chertoff, M.S. (ed.), *Zionism* (New York: Herzl Press, 1975).

Cohen, E. *et al.*, *Summary Report: Research on Immigrant Absorption in a Development Town* (Jerusalem: Hebrew University, 1962) [Hebrew].

Cohen, R., 'The Security of Israel and Her Borders', *Siah* (November 1969), pp.15–18 [Hebrew].

Conversi, D., 'Reassessing Current Theories of Nationalism as Boundary Maintenance and Creation', *Nationalism and Ethnic Politics*, Vol. 1, No. 1, (1995), pp.73–85.

Darin-Drabkin, H., *The Other Society: Kibbutz in the Test of Economy and Society* (Tel-Aviv: Ha-kibuts Ha-artsi, 1961) [Hebrew].

Derber, M., 'Israel's Wage Differentials: A Persisting Problem', in S.N. Eisenstadt *et al.* (eds), *Integration and Development in Israel* (Jerusalem: Israel University Press, 1970), pp.185–201.

Deshen, S., 'Image of a Village', *Ha-uma*, Vol. 9, No. 4, 1972, pp.442–7 [Hebrew].

Don-Yihya, E., 'Etatism and Judaism in Ben-Gurion's Discourse and Policy', *Ha-tsionut*, Vol. 14 (1989), pp.51–88 [Hebrew].

Eban, A., 'Top Priority', *Petah*, (January 1968), pp.61–79 [Hebrew].

Eisenstadt, S.N., *Immigrant Absorption* (Jerusalem: Jewish Agency and Hebrew University, 1952) [Hebrew].

——, *Israeli Society* (Jerusalem: Magnes Press, 1967) [Hebrew].

Eliav, A.L., *Glory in the Land of the Living* (Tel-Aviv: Am Oved), 1972 [Hebrew].

Elitzur, U. 'On the Sin We Did Not Commit', *Nekuda*, No. 180 (1994), p.25 [Hebrew].

——, 'Go Into Details, Draw Maps', *Nekuda*, No. 202 (February 1997), p.3 [Hebrew].

——, 'Very Near the Line', *Nekuda*, No. 204 (April 1997), pp. 20–1 [Hebrew].

Epstein, Y. 'An Unasked Question', *Ha-shiloah*, No. 17 (1907/8), p. 3 [Hebrew].

Eshkoli, H., 'On the Question of the Emigration of Zionist Functionaries from Europe at the Beginning of the Second World War', *Ha-tsionut*, Vol. 17 (1993), pp.191–209 [Hebrew].

Etzion, Y., 'This is Fanaticism', *Nekuda*, No. 179 (1994), pp.26–30 [Hebrew].

Etzioni, A., 'The Responsive Community: A Communitarian Perspective', *American Sociological Review*, Vol. 61, No. 1 (1996), pp.1–11.

Etzioni-Halevi, E. with R. Shapira, *Political Culture in Israel: Cleavage and Integration Among Israeli Jews* (New York: Praeger, 1977).

Felix, M., 'They Don't Mind Paving the Road With Our Bodies', *Nekuda*, No. 173 (1993), pp.26–8 [Hebrew].

——, 'Another Spirit', *Nekuda*, No. 196 (June 1996), pp.14–17 [Hebrew].

Fisher, S., 'Opposite the Gentiles', *Meimad*, No. 9 (1997), pp.16–19 [Hebrew].

Fishmann, Rabbi Y.L.H., *Azkara: A Religious–Scientific Collection* (Jerusalem: Rav Kuk Institute, 1937/38) [Hebrew].

Foucault, M., *The History of Sexuality* (London: Allen Lane and Penguin, 1979).

Frankel, J., 'Assimilation and Survival Among European Jews in the Nineteenth Century: Towards a New Historiography?', in J. Reinharz *et al.* (eds), *Jewish Nationalism and Politics: New Perspectives* (Jerusalem: Zalman Shazar Centre, 1996), pp. 23–56 [Hebrew].

Frankenstein, C., *Between Past and Future* (Jerusalem: Henrietta Szold Foundation, 1953).

Friedman, M., *Society and Religion: The Non-Zionist Orthodoxy in Erets Yisrael 1918–1936* (Jerusalem: Yad Ben Zvi, 1978) [Hebrew].

—— , 'Jewish Zealots: Conservative versus Innovative', in E. Sivan and M. Friedman (eds), *Religious Radicalism and Politics in the Middle East* (New York: State University of New York, 1990), pp.127–41.

Fukuyama, F., 'The End of History?', *The National Interest*, No. 16 (1989), pp.3–19.

Gellner, E., *Nations and Nationalism* (Oxford: Basil Blackwell, 1982).

Gertz, N., 'The Few Against the Many', *Jerusalem Quarterly*, No. 30 (1984), pp.94–104.

—— , 'The War of Liberation: Contest Between Models in Israeli Culture', *Ha-tsionut*, Vol. 14 (1989), pp.9–50 [Hebrew].

Giladi, D. (ed.), *Immigrant Moshavim* (Tel-Aviv: Tnu'at Ha-moshavim, 1972) [Hebrew].

Goldmann, A., 'Simplified Messianism', *Be-tfutsot Ha-gola*, Vol. 18, Nos 79–80 (1977), pp.112–13 [Hebrew].

Goldstone, J.A., 'Ideology, Cultural Frameworks and the Process of Revolution', *Theory and Society*, Vol. 20, No. 4 (1991), pp.405–53.

Gordon, A.D., *Selected Essays* (New York: League for Labour Palestine, 1938).

—— , 'Letters from the Galilee', in A. Yaari (ed.), *Letters from Palestine* (Tel-Aviv: Zionist Federation and Gazit, 1943), pp.508–18 [Hebrew].

—— , *Nation and Labour* (Jerusalem: Zionist Federation, 1952) [Hebrew].

Gorni, Y., *Selected Essays From the Period of the Second Wave of Immigrants* (Tel-Aviv: Tel-Aviv University, 1966) [Hebrew].

——, 'The Roots of Acknowledging the Jewish–Arab Confrontation and Its Reflection in the Hebrew Press During 1900–1918', *Ha-tsionut*, Vol. 4 (1975), pp.72–113 [Hebrew].

——, *Collaboration and Strife: Haim Weizmann and the Palestine Workers' Movement* (Tel-Aviv: Ha-kibuts Ha-meuhad, 1976) [Hebrew].

——, *The Arab Question and the Jewish Problem* (Tel-Aviv: Am Oved, 1985) [Hebrew].

Gurdis, R., 'Israel and the Diaspora' , *Gesher*, Vol. 22, No. 3 (68) (1976), pp.37–52 [Hebrew].

Habermas, J., *Moral Consciousness and Communicative Action* (Cambridge: Polity, 1990).

Haetzni, E., 'Thousands Will Fill Up the Prisons in a Non-Violent Struggle', *Nekuda*, No. 171 (1993), pp.14–17 [Hebrew].

——, 'Civil Disobedience Now', *Nekuda*, No. 179 (1994), pp.26–9 [Hebrew].

——, 'The Gate Has Been Opened to the Slaughter', *Nekuda*, No. 183 (1994), pp.46–9 [Hebrew].

Haft, A., 'Abundant Harvest', *Niv Ha-Kvutsa*, Vol. 4, No. 6 (1954), pp.25–8 [Hebrew].

Hankin, Y., 'The Defence Line Passes Through Tel-Aviv', *Nekuda*, No. 174 (1994), pp.34–5 [Hebrew].

Harel, Y. 'One Must Not Criticize, Though One Should', *Nekuda*, No. 209 (November 1997), pp.24–6 [Hebrew].

Harkabi, Y., 'The Position of the Palestinians in the Israeli–Arab Conflict and Their National Covenant (1968)', *New York University Journal of International Law and Politics*, Vol. 3, No. 1 (1970), pp.209–44.

——, *Arab Attitudes to Israel* (London: Vallentine Mitchell, 1972).

——, *The Problem of the Palestinians* (Israel Academic Committee on the Middle East, 1974).

Hatagli, T., 'The Jewish National Fund is Forty-Seven Years Old', *Ba-ma'ale*, No. 1 (1949), pp.4–5 [Hebrew].

Hen, M., 'Class Composition and Oriental Pupil Attitudes Towards Israeli Society', *Megamot*, Vol. 19, No. 2 (1973), pp.117–26 [Hebrew].

Herman, S.N., *Israelis and Jews: The Continuity of an Identity* (New York: Random House, 1970).

Herzl, T., 'Tagebuecher', in T. Herzl, *Gesammelte zionistische Schriften*, Vol. 1 (Berlin: Juedischer Verlag, 1905).

——, 'Judenstaat' in T. Herzl, *Gesammelte zionistische Schriften*, Vol. 1 (Berlin: Juedischer Verlag, 1905).

Herzog, H., 'Political Ethnicity in Israel', *Megamot*, Vol. 28, Nos 2–3 (1984), pp.332–52 [Hebrew].

Ilam, Y., 'Crisis of Zionism: Crisis of Judaism', *Be-tfutsot Ha-gola*, Vol. 17, No. 75/76 (1975), pp.52–8 [Hebrew].

Isaac, R.J., 'The Land of Israel Movement: A Study in Political Deinstitutionalization', Ph.D. Thesis, City University of New York, 1971.

Israel Government Yearbook 1952 (Tel-Aviv: The Government Press, 1952) [Hebrew].

Jabotinsky, V., *Was wollen die Zionisten-Revisionisten* (Paris: Imprimie polyglotte, 1926).

—— , *Die Idee des Betar* (Lyck: Kaulbars, 1935).

Jaffe, J., *Love of Zion and Jerusalem* (Jerusalem: Wallenstein, 1947), first published in Manchester 1890 [Hebrew].

Kalisher, Rabbi Ts. H., *The Call of Zion* (Jerusalem, 1925) [Hebrew].

Karpel, M., 'The Paralysis in Gush Emunim, the Council and the Religious Ideological Right', *Nekuda*, No. 185 (1995), pp.60–5 [Hebrew].

Karsh, E., 'Benny Morris and the Reign of Error', *Middle East Quarterly*, Vol. 6, No. 1 (1999), pp.15–28.

Katz, S., *The Jewish Presence in Palestine* (Jerusalem: Israel Academic Committee on the Middle East, n.d.).

Katzenelson, B., *Essays*, Vol. 11 (Tel-Aviv: Mapai Publication, 1948) [Hebrew].

Katzover, B., 'To Overthrow the Rabin Government', *Nekuda*, No. 171 (1993), pp.18–19 [Hebrew].

—— , 'Don't Crown and Don't Overthrow', *Nekuda*, No. 203 (1997) p.28 [Hebrew]

Keikh, H., 'The Six Day War and Jewish Identity', *Shdemot*, No. 32 (1969), pp.18–26 [Hebrew].

Keinan, I., 'Points of Social Solidarity: Army, Contribution to Society, Secular and Religious, Attitude to the Holocaust and the Assassination of Rabin', in *Personal, Social and National Attitudes of Israeli Youth in the Jubilee* (Tel-Aviv: Israeli Institute of Economic and Social Research, 1998), pp.57–71 [Hebrew].

Kimmerling, B., 'Status Conceptions of Security Occupations in Israel', *Medina U-mimshal*, Vol. 1, No. 1 (1971/72), pp.141–9 [Hebrew].

—— , 'A Return to the Family Indeed', *Politika*, No. 48 (1993), pp.40–5 [Hebrew].

—— , 'Between Hegemony and Dormant Kulturkamp in Israel', *Israel Affairs*, Vol. 4, Nos 3–4 (1998), pp.49–72.

Kissinger, H., *Years of Upheaval* (London: Weidenfeld & Nicolson and Michael Joseph, 1982).

Klein. Y., 'Patently Immoral', *Nekuda*, No. 176 (1994), pp.64–7 [Hebrew].

Klinov, R. and N. Halevi, *The Economic Development of Israel* (Jerusalem: Academic Press, 1968) [Hebrew].

Knesset Reports 1950 (Jerusalem: The Knesset press, 1950) [Hebrew].

Kuk, Rabbi A.Y.H., *Epistles of R.A.Y.H.* (Jerusalem: Jerusalem Publications, 1923) [Hebrew].

—— , *Orot Ha-kodesh* (Jerusalem: Rabbi Y.A.H. Kuk Publication, 1938) [Hebrew].

—— , *Orot* (Jerusalem: Rabbi Y.A.H. Kuk Publication, 1950) [Hebrew].

—— , *Epistles of R.A.Y.H.* (Jerusalem: Rav Kuk Institute, 1963/65) [Hebrew].

—— , *Adar Ha-yakar Ve-'ikvey Ha-tson* (Jerusalem: Rav Kuk Institute, 1967) [Hebrew].

Kymlicka, W. and W. Norman, 'Return of the Citizen: A Survey of Recent Work on Citizenship Theory', *Ethics*, Vol. 104, No. 2 (1994), pp.352–81.

Lahav, P., 'Power and Office: the Supreme Court in Its First Decade', *'Iyunei Mishpat*, Vol. 14, No. 3 (1989), pp.470–501 [Hebrew].

Lamm, Z., 'Traditional Patterns and Processes of Modernization in Judaism', *Betfutsot Ha-gola*, Vol. 17, Nos 73–4 (1974), pp.62–72 [Hebrew].

Laquer, W., *A History of Zionism* (Tel-Aviv: Schocken, 1974) [Hebrew].

Levin, S., 'Address', *The Zionist Council: In Preparation for the Zionist General Council Meeting* (Jerusalem: 1975), pp.15–21.

Levy, Y. and E.L. Guttman, *Values and Attitudes of Pupils in Israel* (Jerusalem: Institute of Applied Social Research, 1976) [Hebrew].

Lewis, A., 'Ethnic Politics and the Foreign Policy Debate in Israel', *Political Anthropology*, Vol. 4 (1984), pp.25–38.

Liebman, C.S., 'Attitudes Towards Democracy Among Israeli Religious Leaders', in E. Kaufman *et al.* (eds), *Democracy, Peace and the Israeli–Palestinian Conflict* (Boulder: Lymse Rienner, 1993), pp.135–61.

Liebman, Y. 'Secular Judaism and Its Prospects', *Alpayim*, No. 14 (1997), pp.97–116 [Hebrew].

Likud Platform Paper for the 1977 Elections [Hebrew].

Lissak, M., 'Stratification Patterns and Mobility Aspirations: Sources of Mobility Motivation', *Megamot*, Vol. 15, No. 1 (1967), pp.66–82 [Hebrew].

—— , 'Society and Class Images in the Yishuv and in Israeli Society' in S.N. Eisenstadt *et al.* (eds), *Integration and Development in Israel* (Jerusalem: Israel University Press, 1970), pp.141–61.

Lissak, M. and D. Horowitz, *From Yishuv to State* (Jerusalem: Hebrew University, 1972) [Hebrew].

Livne, E., *On the Road to Alon More: Zionism Through 'Emunim'* (Jerusalem: Gush Emunim Publication, 1976) [Hebrew].

Livne, M., 'Our Israel: The Rise and Fall of a Protest Movement', M.A. Thesis, (Tel-Aviv University, 1977) [Hebrew].

Locker, B., *In the Throes of Survival and Revival* (Jerusalem: Bialik Institute, 1963) [Hebrew].

Luke, T., *Screens of Power* (Urbana: University of Illinois Press, 1989).

Lustick, I.S., 'The Political Road to Binationalism: Arabs in Jewish Politics', in I. Peleg and O. Seliktar (eds), *The Emergence of a Binational Israel: The Second Republic in the Making* (Boulder: Westview, 1989), pp.97–123.

Luz, K., 'The Union and Its Task', *Niv Ha-Kvutsa*, Vol. 1, No. 1 (1952), pp.20–6 [Hebrew].

Mandel, M., 'Gnawing at the Roots', *Niv Ha-Kvutsa*, Vol. 1, No. 4 (1952), pp.45–59 [Hebrew].

Mansfield, P., *The Middle East: A Political and Economic Survey*, 4th edn (London: Oxford University Press, 1973).

Marcado, A., *In the Shadow of Discrimination* (Ramat Gan: Bar Ilan University, 1998) [Hebrew].

Marcuse, H., *One-Dimensional Man* (London: Routledge & Kegan Paul, 1964).

Mautner, M., 'The Politics of Reasonableness', *Teoriya U-bikoret*, No. 5 (1994), pp.25–53 [Hebrew].

Mayer, T., 'Egypt and the General Islamic Conference of Jerusalem in 1931', *Middle Eastern Studies*, Vol. 18, No. 3 (1982), pp.311–22.

Meir, G., *My Life* (Tel-Aviv: Ma'ariv, 1975) [Hebrew].

Merhavia, M., 'Settlement Will Win Over Oslo', *Nekuda*, No. 195 (May 1996), pp.32–3 [Hebrew].

Mills, C.W., *The Marxists* (Hamondsworth: Penguin, 1963).

Morris, B., *The Birth of the Palestinian Refugee Problem, 1947–1949* (New York: Cambridge University Press, 1987).

—— , *Israel's Border Wars 1949–1956* (Oxford: Clarendon, 1993).

—— , 'Falsifying the Record: A Fresh Look at Zionist Documentation of 1948',

Journal of Palestine Studies, Vol. 24, No. 3 (1995), pp.44–62.

Mor-Yosef, Y., 'What Was Promised, What Was Kept', *Nekuda*, No. 206 (July 1997), pp.16–21 [Hebrew].

——, 'Arik, Oso and the Settlers', *Nekuda*, No. 216 (July 1998), pp.18–20 [Hebrew].

Moses, T. 'To Be Magnanimous and Congratulate Rabin and Peres', *Nekuda*, No. 171 (1993), p.27 [Hebrew].

Myths and Facts: A Concise Record of the Arab–Israeli Conflict (Washington: Near East Report, 1976).

Nedava, Y. (ed.), *The Israel–Arab Conflict* (Ramat-Gan: Revivim, 1983) [Hebrew].

O'Dea, J., 'Gush Emunim: Roots and Ambiguities; the Perspective of the Sociology of Religion', *Forum*, Vol. 2, No. 26 (1976), pp.39–50.

Ofir, A., 'The Anvil', *Niv Ha-Kvutsa*, Vol. 4, No. 1 (1954), p.3–4 [Hebrew].

Ormian, H. (ed.), *Education in Israel* (Jerusalem: Ministry of Education and Culture, 1973) [Hebrew].

Our Aims (Jerusalem: Brit Shalom Publication, 1927/28) [Hebrew].

Pappe, I., *The Making of the Arab–Israeli Conflict 1947–1951* (London: Tauris, 1992).

——, 'The Refugees, An Original Sin', *Politika*, No. 51 (1993), pp.54–7 [Hebrew].

Peled, Z., *Attitudes of the Israeli Public to the Interim Agreement* (Jerusalem: Institute of Applied Social Research, 1975) [Hebrew].

Peleg, I., *Begin's Foreign Policy 1977–1983: Israel's Move to the Right* (New York: Greenwood, 1987).

Pepper, A., 'They Already Recognize the State', *Nekuda*, No. 220 (1998), pp.20–4 [Hebrew].

Peres, Y. and S. Shemer, 'The Ethnic Factor in the Elections to the Tenth Knesset', *Megamot*, Vol. 28, Nos 2–3 (1984), pp.316–31 [Hebrew].

Peres, Y. *et al.*, 'Predicting and Explaining Voters' Behavior in Israel' in A. Arian (ed.), *The Elections in Israel 1973* (Jerusalem: Academic Press, 1975), pp.189–202.

Peretz, D. and S. Smooha, 'Israel's Tenth Knesset Elections: Ethnic Upsurgence and Decline of Ideology', *The Middle East Journal*, Vol. 35, No. 4 (1981), pp.506–26.

Peri, Y., 'The Impact of Occupation on the Military: The Case of the IDF, 1967–1987', in I. Peleg and O. Seliktar (eds), *The Emergence of a Binational Israel: The Second Republic in the Making* (Boulder: Westview, 1989), pp.143–68.

Personal, Social and National Attitudes of Israeli Youth in the Jubilee (Tel-Aviv: Institute of Economic and Social Research, 1998) [Hebrew].

Pinsker, L., *Autoemanzipation*, 2nd edn (Berlin: Yuedischer Verlag, 1919).

Political Programme of the Likud, February 1995 [Hebrew].

Problems of the Zionist Organization Upon the Establishment of the State (Jerusalem: Zionist Executive, 1950).

Rabinovich, I. and J. Reinharz (eds), *Israel in the Middle East* (New York: Oxford University Press, 1984).

Raz-Kratzkin, A., 'Exile Within Sovereignty: Towards a Critique of the 'Negation of Exile' in Israeli Culture' – Part 2, *Teoriya U-bikoret*, No. 5 (1994), pp.113–32 [Hebrew].

Reines, Y.Y., *New Light on Zion* (Vylna: Rom, 1901) [Hebrew].

Reinharz, J., 'The Transition From Yishuv to Sovereign State: Social and Ideological Changes', *Ha-tsionut*, Vol. 14 (1989), pp.253–62 [Hebrew].

'Responses', *Nekuda*, No. 191 (1996), pp.36–9 [Hebrew].

Riger, A., *Hebrew Education in Palestine* (Tel-Aviv: Dvir, 1940) [Hebrew].

Rosenthal, R. 'Return to Time', *Politika*, No. 51 (November 1993), p.3 [Hebrew].

Rubinstein, A., *The Constitutional Law of Israel* (Jerusalem: Schocken, 1969) [Hebrew].

——, *To Be A Free People* (Tel-Aviv: Schocken, 1977) [Hebrew].

——, 'The Changing Status of the Territories: From a Held Trust to a Juridical Hybrid', *Diyunei Mishpat*, Vol. 11, No. 3 (1986), pp.439–56 [Hebrew].

——, *From Herzl to Rabin: 100 Years of Zionism* (Tel-Aviv: Schocken, 1997) [Hebrew].

Sachar, H.M., *A History of Israel From the Rise of Zionism to Our Time* (Jerusalem: Steinmatzky, 1976).

El-Sadat, A., *In Search of Identity: An Autobiography* (Glasgow: Collins, 1978).

Schwarzwald, J. and Y. Amir, 'Inter-Ethnic Relations in Israel: A Review', *Megamot*, Vol. 28, Nos 2–3 (1984), pp.207–30 [Hebrew].

Session of the Zionist Executive Committee in Jerusalem, 5–15 May 1949 (Jerusalem, 1949) [Hebrew].

Session of the Zionist Executive Committee in Jerusalem, 19–28 April 1950 (Jerusalem, 1950) [Hebrew].

Shadid, M. and R. Seltzer, 'Political Attitudes of Palestinians in the West Bank and Gaza Strip', *Middle East Journal*, Vol. 42, No. 1 (1988), pp.16–32.

Shafir, G., 'Institutional and Spontaneous Settlement Drives: Did Gush Emunim Make a Difference?', in D. Newman (ed.), *The Impact of Gush Emunim: Politics and Settlement in the West Bank* (London: Croom Helm, 1985), pp.153–71.

Shalit, D. 'The Story of a Cantor', *Nekuda*, No. 196 (June 1996), pp.26–30 [Hebrew].

Shalom, 'With the Return of Herzl', *Ba-ma'ale*, No. 15 (1949), pp.306–7 [Hebrew].

Shalom, B., 'Wither Jewish Youth?', *Focus*, Vol. 2, No. 1 (1958), pp.79–88.

Shamir, M., *Searchlight in Depth: Our Jewish Identity: Heritage and Challenge* (Tel-Aviv: Dvir, 1996) [Hebrew].

Shapira, A., 'The Balfour Declaration: A Backward Look' (Hebrew), in S. Stempler (ed.), *The History of the Yishuv: Landmarks Before Statehood* (Jerusalem: Ministry of Defence, 1983), pp.217–30.

——, *Land and Power* (Tel-Aviv: Am Oved, 1992) [Hebrew].

Shapira, O. (ed.), *Immigrant Moshavim in Israel* (Jerusalem: Jewish Agency, 1972) [Hebrew].

Shapiro, Y., *Leadership of the American Zionist Organization* (Urbana: University of Illinois Press, 1971).

——, *The Formative Years of the Israeli Labour Party* (London: Sage, 1976).

——, *Democracy in Israel* (Ramat Gan: Massada, 1977) [Hebrew].

Shefer, Z., 'Values and Ways', *Niv Ha-Kvutsa*, Vol. 1, No. 3 (1952), pp. 9–15 [Hebrew].

Sheleg, Y., *The New Religious Jews: Recent Developments Among Observant Jews in Israel* (Jerusalem: Keter, 2000) [Hebrew].

Shifter, V., 'The 1949 Israeli Offer to Repatriate 100,000 Palestinian Refugees', *Middle East Focus*, Vol. 9, No. 2 (1986), pp.13–18.

Shilo, Rabbi D., 'Who Will Be the Standard Bearer of the Tora?', *Nekuda*, No. 195 (1996), pp.16–18 [Hebrew].

Shinui, Social and Political Renewal Movement, Platform Proposal (Tel-Aviv, 16 July 1974) [Hebrew].

Shoked, M., 'Commandments versus Tradition: Trends in Religiosity of Orientals', *Megamot*, Vol. 28, Nos 2–3 (1984), pp.250–64 [Hebrew].

Shorek, Y., 'Is God Religious?', *Nekuda*, No. 206 (1997), pp.34–8 [Hebrew].

Sikron, M. and E. Leshem, *Portrait of an Immigrant Group: Absorption Processes of Ex-Soviet Immigrants* (Jerusalem: Magnes, 1998) [Hebrew].

Silver, A.H., 'The Case of Zionism', *Reader's Digest* (1949), pp.28–32.

Smilansky, M., 'Coping of the Educational System with Problems of Special-Care Pupils', in H. Ormian (ed.), *Education in Israel* (Jerusalem: Ministry of Education, 1973), pp.121–40 [Hebrew].

Smith, A.D., *National Identity* (Harmondsworth: Penguin, 1991).

Smooha, S., 'Three Perspectives in the Sociology of Ethnic Relations in Israel', *Megamot*, Vol. 28, Nos 2–3 (1984), pp.169–206 [Hebrew].

——, 'The Oriental Parting Off', *Politika*, No. 51 (1993), pp.42–5 [Hebrew].

Smooha, S. and Y. Peres, 'Ethnic Disparity in Israel', *Megamot*, Vol. 20, No. 1 (1974), pp.5–28 [Hebrew].

'Soul Searching Convention', *Nekuda*, No. 190 (1995), pp.58–64 [Hebrew].

Sprinzak, A., *Budding Politics of De-Legitimacy in Israel 1967–1972* (Jerusalem: Levi Eshkol Institute, 1973) [Hebrew].

Stanover, M., 'Following the 30th Council', *Ba-ma'ale*, No. 10 (1949), p.202 [Hebrew].

Summaries (Histadrut Statistics and Information Department, 1929) [Hebrew].

Sussmann, Z., *Differentials and Egalitarianism in the Histadrut* (Ramat Gan: Massada, 1974) [Hebrew].

Syrkin, N., *Essays* (Tel-Aviv: Davar, 1939) [Hebrew].

Talks In the Kibbutz Among Young People (Tel-Aviv: Am Oved, 1969) [Hebrew].

Talks of Warriors (Tel-Aviv: Group of Young Kibbutz Members Publication, 1967) [Hebrew].

Talmon-Garber, Y., 'The Position of the Communal Settlement Movement in Israeli Society', in S. Shor (ed.), *The Kibbutz and Israeli Society* (Tel-Aviv: Ha-Kibuts Ha-artsi, 1972), pp.49–52 [Hebrew].

Tamir, Y., *Liberal Nationalism* (Princeton: Princeton University Press, 1993).

Tanhum, 'From the First Days', *Niv Ha-Kvutsa*, Vol. 4, No. 1 (1954), pp.5–9 [Hebrew].

Al-Tawil, M., *The Recent Disturbances in Erets Yisrael* (Jerusalem: Abiksos, 1930) [Hebrew].

Teitelboim, R., 'Another Such Occupation', *Politika*, No. 2 (1985), pp.17–20.

'The Democratic State', Symposium of Leaders of Several Fidayun Organizations, *Al-Anwar* (8 March 1970) [Arabic].

The Palestinian National Covenant 1968, reproduced in Y. Harkabi, 'The Position of the Palestinians in the Israeli–Arab Conflict and Their National Covenant (1968)', *New York University Journal of International Law & Politics*, Vol. 3, No. 1 (1970), pp.209–44.

Tsur, M., *Doing It the Hard Way* (Tel-Aviv: Am Oved, 1976) [Hebrew].

Viteles, H., *A History of the Cooperative Movement in Israel* (London: Vallentine Mitchell, 1968).

Weiner, B. *et al.*, *Public Attitudes to Settlements in the Occupied Territories* (Jerusalem: Institute of Applied Social Research, 1974) {Hebrew].

Weinrieb, D., 'The Second Generation in Palestine and Its Occupational Choice', *Metsuda*, Vol. 7 (1954), pp.245–330 [Hebrew].

Weissbrod, D. and L. Weissbrod, 'Inflation in Israel: The Economic Cost of Political Legitimation', *The Journal of Social, Political and Economic Studies*, Vol. 11, No. 2 (1986), pp.201–26.

Weissbrod, L., 'Economic Factors and Political Strategies: The Defeat of the Revisionists in Mandatory Palestine', *Middle Eastern Studies*, Vol. 19, No. 3 (1983), pp.326–44.

—— , 'The Rise and Fall of the Revisionist Party, 1928–1935', *The Jerusalem Quarterly*, No. 30 (1984), pp.80–93.

—— , 'Protest and Dissidence in Israel', *Political Anthropology*, Vol. 4 (1984), pp.51–68.

—— , *Arab Relations With Jewish Immigrants and Israel 1891–1991: The Hundred Years Conflict* (Lewiston: Edwin Mellen, 1992).

—— , 'Gush Emunim and the Israeli–Palestinian Peace Process: Modern Religious Fundamentalism in Crisis', *Israel Affairs*, Vol. 3, No. 1 (1996), pp.86–103.

—— ,'Israeli Identity in Transition', *Israel Affairs*, Vol. 3, Nos 3 and 4 (1997), pp.47–65.

Werblowsky, R.J.Z., *Zionism, Israel and the Palestinians* (Jerusalem: Israel University Study Group for Middle Eastern Affairs, 1975).

Werfel, Y., *Writings of Rabbi Yehuda Alkalai* (Jerusalem: Rav Kuk Institute, 1960) [Hebrew].

Winer, G., *The Founding Fathers of Israel* (New York: Bloch, 1971).

Yariv, A., 'The Solution to the Problem and the Price to Israel' in A. Hareven (ed.), *Is There a Solution to the Palestinian Problem? Israeli Positions* (Jerusalem: Van Leer Institute, 1982), pp.11–24 [Hebrew].

Yaron, Z., *The Philosophy of Rabbi Kuk* (Jerusalem: World Zionist Organization, 1974) [Hebrew].

Yoske, M., 'Organization of Education Action', *Ba-ma'ale*, Nos 17–18, p.1 [Hebrew].

Zartal, E., 'Anonymous Souls: The Illegal Immigrants and the Aliya Bet Institution in the Struggle to Set Up the State and After', *Ha-tsionut*, Vol. 14 (1989), pp.107–26 [Hebrew].

Zionist Thought at Present (Jerusalem: Executive of the World Zionist Organization, 1962) [Hebrew].

Zur, M., 'Secular, Messianism', *Shdemot*, No. 27 (1968), pp.14–15 [Hebrew].

ZIONIST CONGRESSES

Protokoll des 1. Zionisten-Kongresses in Basel vom 29 bis 31 August 1897, 2nd edn (Prague: Barissa, 1911).

Stenographisches Protokoll der Verhandlungen des V. Zionisten-Kongresses in Basel,
   26, 27, 28, 29 und 30 Dezember 1901 (Vienna: Verlag des Vereines Erez Israel,
   1901).
Stenographisches Protokoll der Verhandlungen des VI. Zionisten-Kongresses in Basel,
   23, 24, 25, 26, 27 und 28 August 1903 (Vienna: Verlag des Vereines Eretz Israel,
   1903).
Stenographisches Protokoll der Verhandlungen des XVII. Zionisten-Kongresses und der
   zweiten Tagung des Council der Jewish Agency fuer Palaestina, Basel, 30. Juni bis 17.
   Juli 1931 (London: Zentralbuero der zionistischen Organisation, 1931).
The 20th Zionist Congress and 5th Session of the Jewish Agency Council, Zurich 3–21
   August 1937 (Jerusalem: Zionist Federation and Jewish Agency, no date)
   [Hebrew].
The 22nd Zionist Congress, Basle, 9–24 December 1946 (Jerusalem: Executive of the
   Zionist Organization, 1946) [Hebrew].
The 23rd Zionist Congress, Jerusalem, 13–30 August 1951 (Jerusalem: Executive of
   the Zionist Organization, 1951) [Hebrew].
The 26th Zionist Congress, Jerusalem, 30 December 1964–10 January 1965
   (Jerusalem: World Zionist Executive, 1966) [Hebrew].
The 28th Zionist Congress, Jerusalem, 18–27 January 1972 (Jerusalem: World Zionist
   Organization, 1974) [Hebrew].

NEWSPAPERS (IN ENGLISH)

Jerusalem Post

ARABIC DAILIES, WEEKLIES AND MONTHLIES

Ad-Difa'a
Akhbar al-Yom
Al-A'thazam
Al-Fajr
Al-Qabas

HEBREW DAILIES, WEEKLIES AND MONTHLIES*

Al Ha-mishmar   *Ha-sha'ar*
Davar   *Ma'ariv*
Davar Ha-shavu'a   *Mabat Le-kalkala Ule-hevra*
Globs   *Nativ*
Gush Emunim   *Nekuda*
Ha-arets   *Yedi'ot Ahronot*
Ha'ir   *Zot Ha-arets*
Ha-po'el Ha-tsa'ir

*Titles translated from Hebrew.

Index